Pier Luca Lanzi   Wolfgang Stolzmann
Stewart W. Wilson (Eds.)

Learning
Classifier Systems

5th International Workshop, IWLCS 2002
Granada, Spain, September 7-8, 2002
Revised Papers

Springer

Series Editors

Jaime G. Carbonell, Carnegie Mellon University, Pittsburgh, PA, USA
Jörg Siekmann, University of Saarland, Saarbrücken, Germany

Volume Editors

Pier Luca Lanzi
Politecnico di Milano
Dipartimento di Elettronica e Informazione
Artificial Intelligence and Robotics Laboratory
Piazza Leonardo da Vinci 32, 20133 Milano, Italy
E-mail: lanzi@elet.polimi.it

Wolfgang Stolzmann
Universität Würzburg
Institut für Psychologie III
Röntgenring 11, 97070 Würzburg, Germany
E-mail: stolzmann@psychologie.uni-wuerzburg.de

Stewart W. Wilson
Prediction Dynamics, Concord MA 01742,USA
and
The University of Illinois
Department of General Engineering
Urbana-Champaign IL 61801, USA
E-mail: wilson@prediction-dynamics.com

Cataloging-in-Publication Data applied for

A catalog record for this book is available from the Library of Congress.

Bibliographic information published by Die Deutsche Bibliothek
Die Deutsche Bibliothek lists this publication in the Deutsche Nationalbibliografie;
detailed bibliographic data is available in the Internet at <http://dnb.ddb.de>.

CR Subject Classification (1998): I.2, F.4.1, F.1.1, H.2.8

ISSN 0302-9743
ISBN 3-540-20544-6 Springer-Verlag Berlin Heidelberg New York

Springer-Verlag is a part of Springer Science+Business Media

springeronline.com

© Springer-Verlag Berlin Heidelberg 2003
Printed in Germany

Typesetting: Camera-ready by author, data conversion by Olgun Computergrafik
Printed on acid-free paper   SPIN: 10969229   06/3142   5 4 3 2 1 0

Preface

The 5th International Workshop on Learning Classifier Systems (IWLCS 2002) was held September 7–8, 2002, in Granada, Spain, during the 7th International Conference on Parallel Problem Solving from Nature (PPSN VII). We have included in this volume revised and extended versions of the papers presented at the workshop.

In the first paper, Browne introduces a new model of learning classifier system, iLCS, and tests it on the Wisconsin Breast Cancer classification problem. Dixon et al. present an algorithm for reducing the solutions evolved by the classifier system XCS, so as to produce a small set of readily understandable rules. Enee and Barbaroux take a close look at Pittsburgh-style classifier systems, focusing on the multi-agent problem known as *El-farol*. Holmes and Bilker investigate the effect that various types of missing data have on the classification performance of learning classifier systems. The two papers by Kovacs deal with an important theoretical issue in learning classifier systems: the use of accuracy-based fitness as opposed to the more traditional strength-based fitness. In the first paper, Kovacs introduces a strength-based version of XCS, called SB-XCS. The original XCS and the new SB-XCS are compared in the second paper, where Kovacs discusses the different classes of solutions that XCS and SB-XCS tend to evolve. Landau et al. compare two approaches aimed at solving non-Markov problems, i.e., the new ATNoSFERES and the extension of XCS with internal memory, XCSM. Llorà et al. introduce a novel model of Pittsburgh-style classifier system in which multiobjective optimization is used to develop solutions that are both accurate and compact. Metivier and Lattaud apply an Anticipatory Classifier System (ACS) enriched with behavioral sequences to tackle non-Markov problems. Vargas et al. discuss the similarities and the differences of Artificial Immune Systems and Learning Classifier Systems, and they show how a mapping between these two approaches can be defined. The volume ends with a complete bibliography of papers related to learning classifier system research, based on Kovacs' on-line bibliography.

This book is the ideal continuation of the three volumes from the previous workshops, published by Springer-Verlag as LNAI 1813, LNAI 1996, and LNAI 2321. We hope it will be a useful support for researchers interested in learning classifier systems and will provide insights into the most relevant topics and the most interesting open issues.

June 2003

Pier Luca Lanzi
Wolfgang Stolzmann
Stewart W. Wilson

Organization

The 5th International Workshop on Learning Classifier Systems (IWLCS 2002) was held September 7–8, 2002 in Granada, Spain, during the 7th International Conference on Parallel Problem Solving from Nature (PPSN VII).

Organizing Committee

Pier Luca Lanzi   Politecnico di Milano, Italy
Wolfgang Stolzmann   DaimlerChrysler AG, Germany
Stewart W. Wilson   University of Illinois at Urbana-Champaign, USA
     Prediction Dynamics, USA

Program Committee

Alwyn Barry   University of Bath, UK
Erik Baum   NEC Research Institute, USA
Larry Bull   University of the West of England, UK
Lashon B. Booker   MITRE Corporation, USA
Martin V. Butz   University of Würzburg, Germany
Lawrence Davis   NuTech Solutions, USA
Terry Fogarty   Southbank University, UK
John H. Holmes   University of Pennsylvania, USA
Tim Kovacs   University of Birmingham, UK
Pier Luca Lanzi   Politecnico di Milano, Italy
Rick L. Riolo   University of Michigan, USA
Sonia Schulenburg   Napier University, UK
Olivier Sigaud   AnimatLab-LIP6, France
Robert E. Smith   University of The West of England, UK
Wolfgang Stolzmann   DaimlerChrysler AG, Germany
Keiki Takadama   ATR International, Japan
Stewart W. Wilson   University of Illinois at Urbana-Champaign, USA
     Prediction Dynamics, USA

Table of Contents

Balancing Specificity and Generality
in a Panmictic-Based Rule-Discovery
Learning Classifier System

William N.L. Browne

Department of Cybernetics, University of Reading, Whiteknights, Reading,
Berkshire, RG6 6AY, UK
w.browne@cyber.reading.ac.uk

Abstract. A Learning Classifier System has been developed based on industrial
experience. Termed iLCS, the methods were designed and selected to function
with common data properties found in industry. Interestingly, it considers a different strategy to XCS type systems, with the rule discovery being based pan-
mictically. In order to show the worth of the iLCS approach, the benchmark
data-mining application of the Wisconsin Breast Cancer dataset was investigated. A competitive level of 95.3% performance was achieved; mainly due to
the introduction of a generalisation pressure through a fitness to mate (termed
fertility) that was decoupled from a fitness to effect (termed effectiveness). Despite no subsumption deletion being employed the real-valued rule-base was
simple to understand, discovering similar patterns in the data to XCS. Much
further testing of iLCS is required to confirm robustness and performance. Currently, the iLCS approach represents a flexible alternative to niche-based LCSs,
which should further the advancement of the LCS field for industrial application.

1 Introduction

The Learning Classifier System (LCS) technique has recently been applied to data-
mining applications [1-4]. An LCS had been designed to work with industrial data
from the steel industry [5]. This industrial LCS, termed iLCS, employs many methods
motivated by the industrial problem features. This paper seeks to describe iLCS
through its application to a benchmark data-mining problem in order to highlight
novel features in the iLCS approach and motivate its application to further datasets.

The LCS concept, of a learning system in which a set of condition-action rules
compete and co-operate for system control, was developed originally by Holland [6].
The rules plus the associated statistics, such as fitness measure, specificity and number of evaluations, are termed 'classifiers'. A classifier within the population will gain
credit based on the system's performance in some environment when it is active. The
cumulative credit is used to determine the probability of the classifier winning such
system control competitions. If a LCS performs well under the control of some rule,
that rule has an improved chance of winning further competitions for system control
and therefore improving the likelihood of the overall system performing well. This

P.L. Lanzi et al. (Eds.): IWLCS 2002, LNAI 2661, pp. 1–19, 2003.

'fitness' also determines the influence of a particular classifier in an evolutionary process of rule discovery that seeks to improve the system's overall performance, replacing weak rules with plausibly better variations.

Plant condition monitoring domains include a highly sparse environment, multi-modal solutions, a degree of epistasis (unknown a priori) and a mixture of integer and real-numbered discrete or continuous variables. A main feature is that important fault conditions occupy a small environmental niche with few training examples. If sufficiently large datasets exists, a small frequency of examples is not a problem as the database can be rationalised to give equal examples of each action. However in many real-world data-mining type applications this is not possible.

A panmictic based rule discovery has the flexibility to be directed towards small niches so was chosen for this application. However, a Panmictic approach has a number of serious problems that must be overcome [7], with the most serious being a lack of generalisation pressure. It is worth noting that XCS type systems create a generalisation pressure through niche-based rule discovery and utilise an advanced rule deletion operator to protect small niches [8]. Alternative designs are worth considering in order to understand the LCS concept, provide flexibility when selecting an LCS for application and as a basis for future development.

Early examples of Learning Classifier Systems (LCS) used panmictic based rule discovery [9] that could search the entire rule base for mating pairs. Since the introduction of ZCS [10] and XCS [7] the rule discovery is commonly based in a subpopulation. Namely, the set of classifiers that match a given environmental message or the set that effect their action. The basis for the change was to create a generalisation pressure in the system, i.e., the more general classifiers occur in more of these sets so are more likely to mate (and hence propagate their genes) than the more specific classifiers, even if equal accuracy.

"Small" niches are formed in three main ways. Firstly, they represent a small area of search space compared with the alternative actions. Secondly, there exist a relatively small number of examples in the training set. Often both causes occur together, e.g., detecting fault conditions in plant condition monitoring. Thirdly, in some alphabets, such as binary code, a single classifier cannot represent the whole niche, so requires a complementary classifier representing a small part of the niche [5]. This often occurs when the discriminant-surface is oblique [11].

Therefore, the aim of this work is to investigate whether a panmictic based rule discovery could be used to identify and encourage small niches. The generalisation pressure, which in set-based classifier systems assists in rule hierarchy formation, is to be introduced. In order to create this generalisation pressure it was necessary to identify the properties that general rules possess when compared with specific rules.

Smith and Goldberg [12] demonstrate that rules of low specificity do not necessarily occupy the lowest ranks (priority) of the default hierarchy. Therefore, a count of specificity could be misleading in some domains. Throughout this paper a hierarchy is considered to have formed when classifiers with different actions overlap. A better differentiating factor for classifier generality is the ratio of action to match sets for an individual classifier. This ratio should be much higher for a specific rule.

One further differentiating factor may be accuracy[1]. It could be thought that specific rules have a much higher accuracy than general rules, but this is not always the case. In stable hierarchies the general rules are protected by the specific rules so have similar accuracies. The situation is more complex as the hierarchy is forming from complete rules; where the specific rules are less accurate than the general rules as they must be incorrectly selected in order to find their place in the hierarchy. The final case is when the rules themselves are forming; where half-formed specific rules may be more accurate than a fully formed general rule. Therefore, using accuracy as a basis for fitness on its own has problems, especially if no generalisation pressure exists.

This paper describes a method by which effectiveness, generality and accuracy may be combined into a classifier's fitness measure that allows a panmictic rule discovery. The other supporting methods, which are required, are again motivated from the industrial environment. To determine whether these features are useful in the development of the LCS technique in general, a common testbed was employed. The Wisconsin Breast Cancer (WBC) dataset was chosen, as it is readily available and results from the XCS classifier applied to this problem are known [13].

The iLCS system involves fundamentally different methods to XCS. The comparison with XCS is made as a reference in order to understand the new methods developed and to show that there is worth in developing them further. XCS has been tested across a wide range of problem domains [1-4, 14], so is superior in terms of robustness and performance. Therefore, the comparison is made not in competition, but in cooperation to show an alternative approach, which may be suitable in certain domains.

The paper begins with the background to the work, including comparison with alternative approaches to the main methods in iLCS. Next, the novel fitness measures are detailed together with an analysis of how these create a generalisation pressure within the panmictic structure. Considering the remaining parts of the developed LCS is necessary as the fitness of classifier is used throughout the system from effecting to mating to deletion. The data and results from applying iLCS to the Wisconsin Breast Cancer dataset are presented next. The discussion is on whether it is possible to balance the specificity and generality requirements within an LCS with a panmictic rule discovery. Conclusions are drawn on the worth of the iLCS approach.

2   Development of iLCS

The main focus of this paper is the development of a panmictic based LCS with split fitness measure for industrial use. Sufficient detail of the supporting methods is provided to allow the work to be duplicated, but they are not described in detailed, e.g. the real-valued alphabet rule discovery operators are not described (see Browne [5] for comprehensive details).

---

[1] Accuracy is considered here as lack of error, as opposed to accuracy of prediction [8]. In this domain, both measures will be similar as it is single-step with equal reward for correct prediction of action.

The iLCS was developed as a whole concept, see Fig. 1. Therefore, care must be taken if adopting individual developments, as they may not function as described without the other supporting methods.

The first industrial consideration is that iLCS must be easy to use. The internal parameters of the LCS should be kept simple, flexible and robust to reduce the time-consuming effort of setting evolutionary computation parameters [15]. A Michigan style LCS was adopted due to its flexibility to adjust to unknown structures in environments. A transparent rule-base was considered important, so a real-alphabet was designed [16].

Exploration of a sparse domain must consider the effect of individual parameters, parameter combinations and rule combinations representing a vast search space. Exploitation must avoid local optima, assign correct fitness values to rule hierarchies and determine the best action for a given message. The balance needed between exploring and exploiting (E/E) information is due to both the domain and changes that occur as training progresses. Too much exploration results in the global optimum never being reached, whilst too much exploitation traps the system in local optima.

Considering that the desirable E/E balance changes depending on the stage of training and the environment, an LCS that has a static balance, which is hard to adjust, may not be suited to the complex domains found in industry. Simulated Annealing type schemes, which reduce the amount of exploration as training progresses, have been tested [17], but these are hard to control. Investigating the stages of training in simple domains showed three main phases: exploring for information, combining exploring and exploiting to develop useful rules and then stabilising the rules into exploitable hierarchies. Therefore, the rule-base was split into three distinct phases, linked by a stepping-stone approach to transfer rules from search to combine to stable phases. Long surviving rules could also be fed back to the search population to guide search into areas of interest.

A real-alphabet is proposed, as it is easier to decode then ternary alphabets and simpler to implement than fuzzy or S-type alphabets [11]. Upper and lower bounds define the range of an attribute, coupled with resolution to govern the precision of the range during mutation operation, shown below. During mutation, bound inversion occurs as necessary to ensure that the upper bound is greater than the lower bound. The resolution can be reduced in value in successive phases and as training reaches high levels of performance. Initially, ten percent of the maximum attribute range is used, reducing to one percent once ninety-five percent performance has been reached. Note that the first condition is 'wild' as the upper and lower bound are at maximum and minimum values respectively.

Up	Lo	R	Up	Lo	R	Up	Lo	...	R	Up	Lo	R	Up	Lo	Class
10	0	1	10	1	1	10	0	...	1	10	3	1	10	3	[1]

Partial match can be implemented as follows:

```
DO MATCH (Classifier (cl), Message (σ)):
1 for each attribute x in Ccl
2     if (x_lower bound < σ_(x) < x_upper bound)
3         match score += 0
```

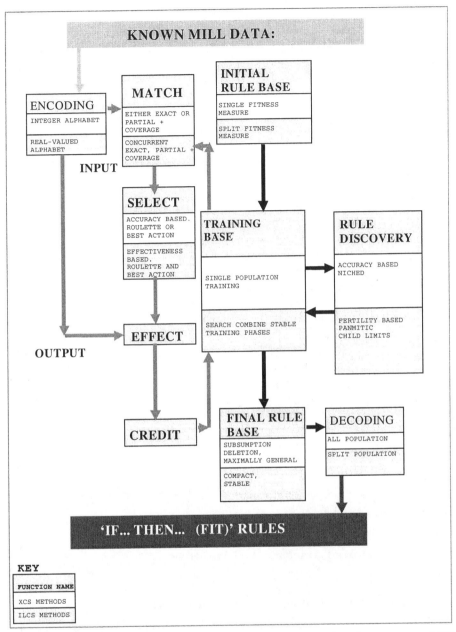

Fig. 1. The concept of iLCS (grey shading) compared with niche-based systems, e.g., XCS (white)

```
4    else
5        match score += integer (abs(σ_(x) - x_closest bound) / x_resolution)
6 return match score
```

Where $\sigma_{(x)}$ is the condition at position x of message σ.

If match score equals zero, the exact match criterion has been met, which is necessary in the stable phase.

An observation in industrial domains is the increased complexity over standard test problems, which increases the time needed to search the solution space. To facilitate graceful learning, life limits are used (evaluation limits have been utilised before in rule discovery [18] to prevent incorrect information being duplicated). This concept is extended so that new classifiers do not share rewards (or punishments) within their action sets, which could contain rules that would not otherwise have been effected, thus distorting the original hierarchy. Old rules can cause problems as their genetic information can stagnate the population, if they produce too many offspring. The *child limit* is introduced to limit duplication of information and trigger a copy of the rule to the next training phase.

In a stable hierarchy the fitness measure for selecting the classifier to effect into action must be lower in the general rules to allow the specific rule to be chosen ahead of them when both match. Care must be taken when rewarding general rules in a stable hierarchy to prevent their strength eventually becoming the same as specific rules and causing a catastrophic collapse of the hierarchy. Additional problems that are not applicable here, arise in domains where different correct actions lead to different rewards and in domains that are multi-step [19].

The fitness of a classifier is split into two measures: *Fertility* controls selection in rule discovery and *Effectiveness* controls selection in the auction. Fertility exerts a generalisation pressure as it combines a measure of a classifier's generality with its accuracy. Effectiveness is the expected environmental pay-off, but could easily be changed to other measures.

```
UPDATE FITNESS EFFECTIVENESS ([A]):
1 for each classifier cl in [A]
2    UPDATE STATISTICS on [A]
3       if (experience < 1/β)
4          p ← (p * (experience - 1) + P) / experience
5       else
6             if (cl = winner) discount = 1,
7             else discount = phase discount
8                p ← p + β* (P * discount - p)
```

Where pay-off is P, effectiveness is p and learning rate is β.

Phase discount may be employed to differentiate individual classifiers by increasing the separation of effectiveness between similar classifiers. However, if the discount is not equal to one, then the effectiveness does not give a true reflection of expected payoff for most of the classifiers. Equal reward (discount equals one) is useful in the search phase to encourage all plausible rules. Rewarding only the winner (discount equals zero) could be used in the stable population to encourage optimum rules at the risk of the population becoming trapped in local optima. Phase discount

(discount between zero and one) is mostly useful in the combine stage, where both encouragement and differentiation of rules are necessary.

Rule deletion in the stable phase is simply the lowest fertile rule that has had sufficient life. In the search and combine phases a roulette wheel selection is used, with care taken to replace classifiers of similar action. Subsumption deletion could be introduced to compact the rule base, but for this experiment it was insightful to determine the generalisation pressure without this method present.

The belief is that generalisation pressure should reside in the selection for mating, i.e. preferably select general rules ahead of specific rules for the same accuracy/utility. Thus, the fertility measure should incorporate a generality component and an accuracy component. Rather than a genotypic measure (such as specificity), which may be misleading, a phenotypic measure (such as the normalised number of match sets since last rule discovery) is proposed. In the studied domain, the correct action is known, so a direct measure *'usefulness'* is used, but other measures could be used in reinforcement domains, where only the reward is known.

```
UPDATE FITNESS FERTILITY ([A], [M], [RD])

1 for each classifier cl in [A]

2    error = (actions_since_rule_discovery -

3                 rewards_since_rule_discovery) /

4                 actions_since_rule_discovery

5    expected error (e) ← e + β * (error - e)

6    expected accuracy (a) = 1 - e

7 for each classifier cl in [RD]

8    Usefulness (U) =

9        (environmental_actions_since_rule_discovery

10        number of occurrences in [M]) /

11        environmental_actions_since_rule_discovery

12   Fertility = a^k * U

13 for each classifier cl in [M]

14   Fertility_normalised (Fn) ← Fn + β * (

15                     (F / sum of all F in [M]) - Fn)
```

Where [A] is the action set, [M] is the match set and [RD] are the parent classifiers in rule discovery.

3 Testing Methods

The main experiments on iLCS were conducted on the WBC dataset because the database and associated benchmark results are readily available. The standard testing method of a stratified tenfold cross-validation procedure was used. However, the folds are highly unlikely to be the same as those used by Wilson, but this paper only intends to show that although iLCS is significantly different to XCS type systems it has similar performance in this domain and is worth investigating in other domains. It is noted that industry would prefer first time, repeatable results without significant parameter tuning or optimisation.

Generating simulated data with known properties is beneficial when developing an LCS to handle these properties, especially as the optimum results are known. However, the simulated data would not be a widely recognised benchmark. The system performance is also likely to be different on real data due to the difficulties in obtaining and mimicking the properties of real data.

3.1 Wisconsin Breast Cancer Data

A survey of LCS literature showed the Wisconsin Breast Cancer dataset [13] (available at http://www.ics.uci.edu/~mlearn/MLRepository.html) had industry type data-properties and benchmark performance by known systems. This allows the iLCS system's methods and the experiments described here to be repeated and validated.

The WBC dataset consists of nine condition attributes (Clump Thickness, Uniformity of Cell Size, Uniformity of Cell Shape, Marginal Adhesion, Single Epithelial Cell Size, Bare Nuclei, Bland Chromatin, Normal Nucleoli and Mitosis) linked to one action attribute (Malignancy). The output value of 0 is used to represent the benign state (458 instances, 65.5%) and 1 to represent the malignant state (241 instances, 34.5%). Examples of the raw data are shown below:

3	3	6	4	5	8	4	4	1	|1
4	4	2	1	2	5	2	1	2	|0
1	1	1	1	2	1	3	1	1	|0
3	4	5	3	7	3	4	6	1	|0
2	3	1	1	3	1	1	1	1	|0
2	5	3	3	6	7	7	5	1	|1
4	7	8	3	4	10	9	1	1	|1
1	1	1	1	2	1	1	1	1	|0

4 Results

iLCS was applied to the WBC dataset using a stratified tenfold cross-validation procedure similar to that employed by Wilson when testing XCS on the same dataset [11]. An important feature of this procedure is that the system learns on the majority of the dataset and is tested on the unseen remainder, which highlights overfitting if it occurs.

To create the ten subsets, the dataset was separated into different actions: 0 for normal and 1 for malignant. Stratification requires that an action has the same likelihood of occurring in a fold as it does in the main dataset. Therefore, a separate tenth of each action was recombined and randomly sorted to form a fold. Each trial consisted of using a different fold for the test set and learning on the remaining nine folds.

The combined population size, N, is equivalent to other LCSs and is 1600 for each phase. Similarly, the learning rate (0.1), tolerance (0), reward (100) and rule discovery usage (400 iterations), are all standard across the training phases to reduce setup time. The reward discount for the stable phase is 0 (winner only), combine phase is 0.71 (a differentiating shared reward) and search phase is 1 (share reward equally).

The selection of rule discovery operators is shown in table 1, but many combinations of values, including 0 to remove an operator, could be used. A decrease in the proportion of mutation used as the phase became more stable was found to be useful. Extensive parameter optimisation was not performed, although the values in table 1 performed well in the range of +/-0.05 change in the rule discovery operator proportion. Morphigh and Morphlow are crossover type operators developed for a real-valued alphabet to account for similarities and differences within parents (for further details see Browne [5]). The fertility balance, k, is set to 20 in order to reduce the importance of accuracy relative to generality, but values from 2 to 50 are envisaged. The life limits are set depending on the domain, with the evaluation limit set at 8, 9 and 10 evaluations in successive phases for the standard test data. Similarly, the child limit is set at 40, 30 and 20 offspring in successive phases to encourage diversity in genetic information when the exploring domain.

Table 1. Rule discovery operators for the stable, combine and search phases

	Stable	Combine	Search
Mutation	0.25	0.35	0.35
Crossover	0.15	0.15	0.15
Circular	0.25	0.20	0.20
Morphigh	0.15	0.10	0.10
Morphlow	0.20	0.20	0.20

Table 2. Results of stratified cross-validation test on the WBC dataset. Last line is the mean score for the ten tests

Correct	Incorrect	Not matched	Fraction Correct
64	6	0	0.9143
68	2	0	0.9714
67	3	0	0.9571
66	4	0	0.9429
65	5	0	0.9286
70	0	0	1.0000
67	3	0	0.9571
65	5	0	0.9286
66	3	0	0.9565
68	2	0	0.9714
		Mean	0.9528

The mean performance of iLCS was 95.3% (Stable phase), table 2, which on this initial investigation on this problem suggests iLCS is competitive with the best alternative approaches, including alternative LCS designs. Much further testing on this and other datasets is required to determine the true performance and robustness of iLCS.

The performance of the stable phase reached 100%, see Fig. 2, but could not maintain this level. This was due to iLCS not having a mechanism to fix the performance of a correct hierarchy. In a correct hierarchy, the general rules gain accuracy until they match the accuracy of the specific rules resulting in a collapse of the hierarchy. Although this allows alternative hierarchies to be evaluated, this is not desired. The collapse stage happens rarely and the hierarchy soon re-establishes, so the overall effect on mean performance is negligible, but further work to remove this problem is necessary (see Sect. 7).

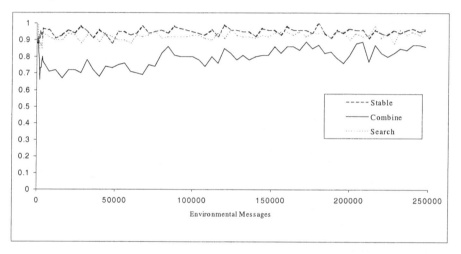

Fig. 2. The performance of iLCS, showing the interaction of the three phases

The exploit nature of the stable phase is shown by slow initial training, although this is more noticeable in other domains, but ultimately the best performance. The explore nature of the search phase enables good rules to be discovered quickly and continues throughout the training period as the roulette wheel selection does not enable maximum performance. However, the performance of the combine phase is significantly lower than the other phases, this is due to the heavily random nature of the effecting auction used to encourage all levels of the hierarchy to form.

The generalisation pressure may be seen in the specificity trends during training, shown in fig. 3. The stable phase trend shows an interesting ability of iLCS, in that specificity can increase when needed to form specific rules to give building blocks of useful information (noting the much reduced use of coverage in iLCS). This is partly explained by the initial rule population containing less rules than the maximum limit. If 100% performance was reached quickly, then the rule base size would decrease, otherwise expansion occurs. Once these are combined into useful rules, around

60,000 iterations, hierarchies may form that allow general rules to survive. The generality continued to increase in the population after the maximum performance had been reached at 200,000 iterations.

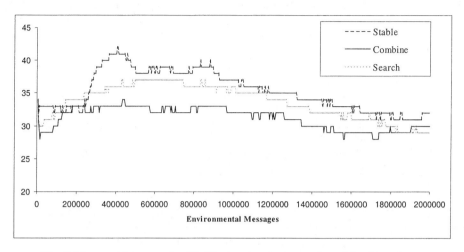

Fig. 3. The specificity trends of iLCS, showing the interaction of the three phases

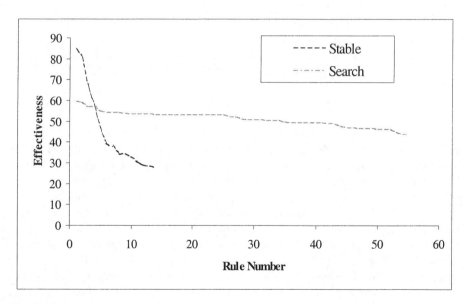

Fig. 4. The effectiveness distribution within iLCS, showing the stable and search phases, for rules used on the test set

A clear difference between the functioning of the phases is shown during the performance on the test fold. The classifiers used during the test phase (i.e. those that effected their action) were tagged and their effectiveness plotted in rank order as shown in fig 4. Hierarchy formation is also shown in the effectiveness distribution for classifiers in a population, fig. 4. The search phase has all classifiers at a similar effectiveness, whilst the stable phase is more distributed throughout the range, with clusters showing hierarchy formation. This is supported by examining the specificity distribution, which is wider in the stable phase. The performance differences can be seen in Table 3, again with the combine phase being the worst.

Table 3. Results of stratified cross-validation test on the WBC dataset. Last line is the mean score for the ten tests

Stable (Delete Worst)		Combine		Search		Stable (Delete Stochastic)	
Not Matched	Fraction Correct	Not Matched	Fraction Correct	Not Matched	Fraction Correct	Not Matched	Fraction Correct
0	0.9143	0	0.7429	0	0.8857	0	0.9286
0	0.9714	0	0.9000	0	0.9143	0	0.9286
0	0.9571	0	0.8000	0	0.9571	0	0.9429
0	0.9429	0	0.7714	0	0.9714	0	0.9286
0	0.9286	0	0.8000	0	0.8714	0	0.9286
0	1.0000	0	0.7714	0	0.9571	0	0.9714
0	0.9571	0	0.8000	0	0.9571	0	0.9429
0	0.9286	0	0.7857	0	0.8286	0	0.9286
0	0.9565	0	0.8551	0	0.9565	0	0.9420
0	0.9714	0	0.8000	0	0.8571	0	0.9571
Mean	0.9528	Mean	0.8027	Mean	0.9157	Mean	0.9399

The generality of iLCS is shown by the fact that all the unseen test instances were matched.

To demonstrate the flexibility of iLCS a second stable population was inserted with the roulette wheel deletion instead of the worst fertility classifier. This achieved a similar mean performance to the original, but with slightly less variance in results. The introduction of phases resulted in the running time of iLCS being longer than an XCS type implementation, but this was mainly due to inefficient programming.

The rules used in the test phase of the stable and search phase is a shown in Tables 4 and 5 respectively. Due to the deterministic auction versus the stochastic auction selection methods, the stable phase utilises 14 rules compared with 66 rules for the search phase. The last three stable rules are newly formed, so are in the process of being evaluated to determine the correct hierarchy priority. Comparing the evaluations since rule discovery (evals since ga) with the number of times a classifier has won an auction (wins since ga), indicates the hierarchy priority.

In order to determine the generality of the rules produced, examination of the stable phase rules shows long experiences, high accuracy and a range of specificity values, which suggests high generality. The large number of offspring would have tested increases in generality and replaced their parents if possible. Subsumption deletion is not used, which may result in some rules not being maximally general, but these would have lower fertility measures and hence greater likelihood of deletion. To fully test if the rules were maximally general, it would be necessary to halt the training near the end (say with 10,000 iterations left), manually expand an individual rule and then restart training to determine if its accuracy decreased.

Table 4. Statistics from generated rules from the stratified cross-validation test on the WBC dataset

Stable	Effective	Accuracy	Fertility	Classifier	Specificity	Evals. since ga	Wins since ga	Evaluated	Children.
1	84.45	0.19	0	[0]	37	1	1	12	1
2	80.35	0.27	0	[1]	26	1	1	12	0
3	66	0.57	0	[1]	18	1	1	18	0
4	56.96	0.27	0	[1]	12	3	1	18	0
5	46.67	0.61	0	[1]	23	2	1	22	0
6	39.32	0.93	0.02	[1]	17	14	12	42110	46
7	38.18	0.97	0.03	[0]	22	42	41	168809	41
8	34.65	0.81	0	[1]	17	2	1	25717	20
9	34.46	0.9	0	[1]	14	4	2	23885	41
10	33.22	0.98	0.04	[0]	18	43	2	166292	41
11	30.7	1	0.02	[1]	19	4	1	13026	39
12	29.1	1	0.01	[1]	17	2	1	6435	4
13	28.49	1	0.01	[1]	15	3	1	7047	11
14	27.44	0.93	0.01	[1]	12	13	1	39247	46

Search	Effective	Accuracy	Fertility	Classifier	Specificity	Evals. since ga	Wins since ga	Evaluated	Children.
1	59.57	0.98	0.01	[0]	35	21	1	73594	21
2	59.15	1	0	[1]	44	1	1	98	0
3	57.21	0.93	0.01	[1]	21	14	2	39443	21
4	57.08	0.97	0.01	[0]	25	29	3	112304	21
5	55.11	0.96	0.01	[0]	25	28	1	95347	21
6	54.33	0.97	0	[0]	38	7	1	23097	21
7	54.32	0.98	0.02	[0]	27	42	2	134407	21
8	54.31	0.97	0.01	[0]	30	22	1	90805	21
9	54.08	0.98	0.02	[0]	39	44	2	149898	21
10	53.63	0.96	0.01	[0]	20	46	1	160493	21
11	53.62	0.96	0.02	[0]	19	46	5	160274	21
12	53.59	0.97	0.03	[0]	21	45	1	160610	23
13	53.57	0.96	0.01	[0]	24	30	1	101363	21
14	53.52	0.95	0.01	[0]	24	27	1	105667	21

Table 5. Rules generated by the stratified cross-validation test on the WBC dataset

	Up	Lo	Up	Lo	Up	Lo	Up	Lo	Up	Lo	Up	Lo	Up	Lo	Up	Lo	Up	Lo	Class
	Stable																		
1	9	1	6	0	3	0	8	0	8	0	2	0	8	2	9	1	9	0	[0]
2	10	1	9	1	9	6	9	1	9	2	9	1	10	0	10	0	10	2	[1]
3	10	0	10	1	10	0	10	2	10	0	7	0	8	0	10	3	10	3	[1]
4	10	1	10	0	9	0	10	0	10	0	10	0	10	1	10	0	10	3	[1]
5	10	4	10	1	10	1	10	2	10	0	7	0	8	2	10	0	10	4	[1]
6	10	2	9	1	9	1	10	1	10	0	10	3	9	1	10	0	10	0	[1]
7	9	0	6	0	5	0	8	0	10	0	10	0	8	0	9	0	9	0	[0]
8	10	0	8	0	10	1	9	1	10	0	8	1	7	0	10	0	10	0	[1]
9	10	2	10	0	10	1	10	1	9	1	9	3	10	0	10	0	9	0	[1]
10	9	0	8	0	6	0	9	0	10	0	6	0	9	0	9	0	9	0	[0]
11	10	3	10	0	10	3	9	1	10	0	10	1	9	0	10	2	9	1	[1]
12	10	1	10	2	10	2	10	2	10	0	9	2	10	0	10	1	10	2	[1]
13	10	2	10	0	10	3	9	1	10	0	10	0	10	0	10	1	10	3	[1]
14	10	0	9	2	10	1	9	1	10	1	10	3	10	0	10	0	10	0	[1]
	Search																		
1	7	3	5	0	8	0	7	0	3	0	10	0	4	0	9	0	9	0	[0]
2	8	3	8	3	9	4	8	2	9	3	10	4	9	2	10	3	8	2	[1]
3	9	3	10	1	10	2	10	0	10	1	10	3	10	1	10	0	7	0	[1]
4	9	1	7	0	8	0	7	0	10	0	5	0	5	0	9	0	10	0	[0]
5	10	1	8	0	6	0	7	0	9	1	6	0	8	0	9	0	9	0	[0]
6	8	1	6	0	3	0	8	0	9	1	3	0	8	2	8	0	10	0	[0]
7	10	0	5	0	6	0	6	0	9	1	10	0	3	0	10	0	9	0	[0]
8	7	3	5	0	7	0	7	0	10	0	9	0	5	0	9	0	9	0	[0]
9	9	0	6	0	6	0	7	0	6	0	4	0	7	0	9	0	2	0	[0]
10	10	0	6	0	7	0	7	0	10	0	8	0	8	0	9	0	10	0	[0]
11	10	0	7	0	6	0	8	0	10	0	8	0	8	0	9	0	10	0	[0]
12	9	0	7	0	5	0	9	0	10	0	6	0	9	0	9	0	9	0	[0]
13	10	0	5	0	8	0	5	0	10	0	9	0	5	1	9	0	9	0	[0]
14	10	1	6	0	7	0	5	0	10	1	7	0	8	0	9	0	10	0	[0]

Interpretation of the rules allows hypothesis to be drawn on the problem domain - these are limited by the original low sampling size of the dataset in the breast cancer domain. A hierarchy is shown by the stable classifiers 6 and 7 in Tables 4 and 5, where rule 6 protects rule 7 (note specificity does not correspond to hierarchy position). This hierarchy suggests that high values of all attributes (except 5,6) indicate malignancy. Medium to high values of uniformity of cell size and uniformity of cell shape (attributes 2,3) also indicate malignancy, except where bare nuclei are low (attributes 6). This hierarchy is further extended: if bare nuclei are low, then uniformity of cell size and shape have to be high for malignancy (rules 10, 11).

The rule-based did show similarities with that found by Wilson [11], e.g. rule 3 from XCS, also identifies medium to high uniformity of cell size as a sign of malignancy, but strongly links this to high clump thickness, which is only a weak link in iLCS. The rule-bases formed are not identical due to different hierarchy structures, the stochastic nature of the process and differences in performance.

5 Discussion

iLCS performance on the WBC dataset was at a competitive level to alternative algorithms, suggesting that the panmictic based rule discovery, split fitness measure and the resultant generalisation pressure is viable. It further supports the assertion that the

LCS's boxy approximation of the oblique discriminant surface does not cause overfitting and can be applied successfully to data-mining applications. A real-valued representation may not be optimum for oblique data, but it is a functional. Lisp like expressions have been proposed [20], but these could introduce problems associated with genetic programming, such as bloat [21]. An alternative to evolving higher-order classifiers is suggested by the iLCS approach. The search phase would remain the same, but an abstraction algorithm would produce higher-order classifiers for the stable phase based on the similarities between searching rules.

The fundamentally different design of iLCS, including separate populations, shows the flexibility of the LCS concept to be adapted to varying industrial domains. Further testing on different problem types is required to determine the robustness of the iLCS technique itself.

In this static, single-step data-mining application, the only objection to a generalisation pressure formed by a niche-based rule discovery is aesthetic. In order to balance resources in infrequently visited niches a rule replacement policy that accounts for the action-set size is used in niche based systems. It does not seem obvious to use rule replacement as a mechanism to balance frequency of input messages - the mating fitness mechanism seems more intuitive. It is also noted that coverage is much more important to niche-based systems in order to balance the resources during the initial rule-base formation. The stable population matched every test message, which was not the case in a niche-based trial [1]. This was probably due to the initial rule-base created in iLCS being more general than a rule-base mainly created by coverage.

Lethals are cited as a major problem with panmictic operation, but these can be avoided in the stable phase by restricting mating to similar actions. However, in industry different actions are often related, such as different severities of steel strip pinching have similar causes, so sharing of information between actions/niches is important, which can be achieved in the search and combine phases. The other cited problem with panmictic operation is that there is no inherent generalisation pressure, which is overcome in iLCS through the fertility fitness measure.

The fertility fitness measure is dedicated to rule discovery, so can directly measure the benefit of mating a classifier. Alternative schemes utilise the same measure (e.g. accuracy, prediction of payoff or accuracy of prediction) in selection for effecting as well as selection for mating. Fertility functions by estimating a classifier's usefulness compared to its neighboring classifiers. Inaccurate classifiers have low fertility, unless there are few similar classifiers. Similarly, accurate classifiers have low fertility if they occur in less match sets than similar classifiers of equal accuracy. The effectiveness measure could use any standard fitness measure. In this domain the predicted payoff of the classifier is used, as reward is the same for all actions, so using accuracy of predicted payoff provides no additional information, but would be worth investigating in more complex domains.

The three phases allows parallel explore and exploit to occur in this domain. In domains were only one action is permitted, e.g. in autonomous learning for mobile robots, the stable phase output would be effected. If correct, the phases advocating the same action would be rewarded; whilst if incorrect, winning classifiers from phases advocating alternative actions would be reinforced.

A final advantage of the three phases is reducing the amount of decoding necessary to one third of a standard population. However, subsumption deletion has not been introduced, so the population was not as compact as possible. A simple method of contracting the rule base is to produce a representative testset in order to identify the classifiers used during the test. Wilson [19] proposes a Compact Ruleset Algorithm, which deterministically identifies the useful classifiers and is applicable to iLCS.

The classifiers are crisp in nature due to the winner-takes-all auction in the stable population. This is advantageous compared with multiple classifiers combining to win a single auction, as each combining classifier must be taken into account to determine the knowledge learned, which may cause problems to engineers in large-scale domains. In small domains were multiple runs are possible, the best discovered rule base can be utilised. However, if time constraints were important then robust performance would be required.

Splitting the population into three phases allows iLCS to discover general and specific building blocks of information in the search phase. Combining the small blocks of information into complete rules becomes increasingly difficult as the size of the domain increases, with the dedicated combine phase in iLCS facilitating this task. Whereas in a simple LCS, by the time general rules have been formed, the building blocks of information needed for specific rules have already been removed from the population. The different types of rules within the combine phase test alternative hierarchy structures, which is required if sub-optimum hierarchies, such as homomorphic or "flat", are not to form. Once good rules survive, proving their long-term use, they can be transferred to the stable population, where the information can be exploited through exact matching and best classifier selection.

The insertion of an additional stable phase, which utilises a stochastic deletion method instead of a deterministic method, enabled iLCS to evaluate different set-ups without multiple tests. This did result in a small performance decrease, although with slightly less variance in the stochastic method. The stochastic removal of good rules prevents an LCS being stuck in local optima, but could lead to sub-optimum performance if a good rule is deleted just prior to testing. The iLCS approach is useful as multiple tests are not required to determine which set-up is best suited to a particular domain.

Life limits are essential for introducing new (including transferred) rules into a stable population or hierarchy, as their appropriate level can be determined without interrupting the existing structures. Similarly, the evaluation limit prevents the rule discovery from mating untested rules. Evaluation limits are now common [22], but the child limit is rare. Subsumption deletion and Numerosity counts [14] assist in removing redundant information from the rule-base, whilst protecting good information [22]. However, as the number of attributes in a classifier increases, the likelihood of subsumption and numerosity occurring decreases, and the computational time required for these methods increases. The child limit prevents the stable population stagnating with similar information, whilst encouraging the search population to contain a variety of information.

Real-alphabets are essential for transparency in industry, but they also improve boundary definition in continuous domains. Fine tuning rule boundaries can occur through mutation and resolution tuning, but is often achieved through the result of appropriate crossovers, where upper and lower attribute bounds are swapped. Adjusting the upper/lower bounds allows a single rule to describe a range, whereas ternary-alphabet may require more than one rule to complete the range.

The XCS approach does scale-up to large problem domains [23], but scalability is still an important issue. The iLCS approach needs further testing, but offers flexibility to choose alternative methods suited to particular domain features with less need to set-up for individual problems.

6 Future Work

A major question in the design of the iLCS system is the choice of fitness measure used to decide the effecting classifier. Implementing an accuracy of prediction measure is not expected to stabilise hierarchies on its own. A 'train and test' cycle could be used with the test cycle essential to stabilise a classifier's place in the hierarchy. However, the concept of relying upon a classifier to make errors on environmental messages appears contradictory to the industrial focus of the design. Therefore, a slight variation is considered: a 'train and review' cycle is proposed, where a small memory is used to store examples of common, rare and difficult environmental messages. The messages would be replayed during the review part of the cycle to establish correct hierarchy separation. The operation should be faster than the train and test cycle due to the fewer messages used, but at the expense of program complexity and higher memory requirements.

Once the current rule-base training in iLCS is capable of maintaining 100% performance in applicable domains, whilst avoiding overfitting, the robustness across different domain types requires investigating. Multi-step problems have not yet been attempted, although there are no fundamental design reasons to prevent iLCS from operating in such domains. The panmictic rule discovery can be biased in favour of scene-setting classifiers by increasing the fertility of early chain classifiers, which are traditionally the most difficult to maintain [24]. Dimensionality of test problems should also be increased, but with domains exceeding 20 variables, ease of interpretation of discovered knowledge needs to be managed.

7 Conclusion

An LCS developed for large-scale industrial data-mining applications, iLCS, has been presented. A generalisation pressure has been successfully introduced into a panmictic based rule discovery. This was facilitated by decoupling a classifier's fitness for effecting from its fitness to mate. The results on the Wisconsin Breast Cancer dataset achieved a competitive level despite the choice of the fitness for effecting measure being considered poor. No subsumption type method was employed; but assisted by the real-valued alphabet, the rule-base could easily be understood. The iLCS approach represents a flexible alternative to niche-based LCSs, which will help in the advancement of the LCS field for industrial application.

References

1. Wilson, S.W.: State of XCS Classifier System Research. In: Lanzi, P.L., Stolzmann, W., Wilson, S.W. (eds.): Learning Classifier Systems: From Foundations to Applications. Lecture Notes in Artificial Intelligence, Vol. 1813. Springer-Verlag, Berlin Heidelberg New York (2000) 63-82

2. Bernadó, E., Llorà, X., Garrell, J. M.: XCS and GALE: a Comparative Study of Two Learning Classifier Systems on Data Mining. In: Lanzi, P.L., Stolzmann, W., Wilson, S.W. (eds.): Advances in Learning Classifier Systems. Lecture Notes in Artificial Intelligence Vol. 2321, Springer-Verlag, Berlin Heidelberg New York (2001) 115-133.

3. Dixon, P. W., Corne, D. W., Oates, M. J.: A Preliminary Investigation of Modified XCS as a Generic Data Mining Tool. In: Lanzi, P.L., Stolzmann, W., Wilson, S.W. (eds.): Advances in Learning Classifier Systems. Lecture Notes in Artificial Intelligence Vol. 2321, Springer-Verlag, Berlin Heidelberg New York (2001) 133-151.

4. Llorà, X., Garrell, J. M.: Co-evolving Different Knowledge Representations with Fine-grained Parallel Learning Classifier Systems. In: Proceeding of the Genetic and Evolutionary Computation Conference (GECCO2002). Morgan Kaufmann, (2002) 934-941.

5. Browne, W. N. L.: The Development of an Industrial Learning Classifier System for Application to a Steel Hot Strip Mill, Doctoral Thesis, University of Wales, Cardiff (1999)

6. Holland, J. H.: Adaptation in Natural and Artificial Systems, University of Michigan Press, Ann Arbor, MI. (1975)

7. Wilson, S. W.: Classifier Fitness Based on Accuracy. Evolutionary Computation, Vol 3 **2** (1995) 149-175

8. Kovacs, T.: Deletion Schemes for Classifier Systems. In: Wolfgang, B., Daida, J., Eiben, A.E., Garzon, M.H., Honavar,V., Jakiela, M., Smith, R.E., (eds.): Proceedings of the Genetic and Evolutionary Computation Conference (GECCO-99). Morgan Kaufmann, (1999) 329-336

9. Horn, J., Goldberg, D.E., Deb, K.: Implicit Niching in a Learning Classifier System: Nature's Way.", Evolutionary Computation, MIT press, Vol 2 **1** (1994) 37-66

10. Wilson, S. W.: ZCS: A Zeroth Level Classifier System. Evolutionary Computation. Vol 2 **1** (1994) 1-18

11. Wilson, S. W.: Mining Oblique Data with XCS. In: Lanzi, P.L., Stolzmann, W., Wilson, S.W. (eds.): Advances in Learning Classifier Systems, Vol 1996 of LNAI, Springer-Verlag, Berlin (2001)

12. Smith, R.E., Goldberg, D.E.: Reinforcement Learning with Classifier Systems: Adaptive Default Hierarchy Formation. Applied Artificial Intelligence, Hemisphere Publishing Corporation, Vol 6 **1** (1992) 79-102

13. Blake, C., Merz, C.: UCI repository of machine learning databases. Available at: Http://www.ics.uci.edu/~mlearn/MLRepository.html (1998)

14. Lanzi, P.L.: A Study of the Generalization Capabilities of XCS. Proc. 7th Int. Conf. on Genetic Algorithms, Morgan Kaufmann, USA, (1997) 418-425

15. Michalewicz, Z., Fogel, D. B.: How to Solve It: Modern Heuristics. Springer, (2000)

16. Fairley, A., Yates, D.F.: Inductive operators and rule repair in a Hybrid Genetic Learning System: Some Initial Results. In: Evolutionary Computation, Lecture Notes in Computer Science, AISB Workshop, Leeds 94, Springer-Verlag, (1994) 166-179

17. Venturini, G.: Adaptation in Dynamic Environments through a Minimal Probability of Exploration. In Cliff, D., Husbands, P., Meyer, J.A., Wilson, S.W. (eds) From Animals to Animats 3: Proceedings of the Third International Conference on Simulation of Adaptive Behaviour, MIT Press Cambridge Massachusetts (1994) 371-379

18. Frey, P.W., Slate D.J.: Letter Recognition Using Holland-Style Adaptive Classifiers. Machine Learning, Kluwer Academic Publishers, Boston, Vol 6 (1991) 161-182

19. Holmes, J. H., Lanzi, P.L., Stolzmann, W., Wilson, S.W.: Learning Classifier Systems: New Models, Successful Applications. Information Processing Letters, to appear. Available at http://world.std.com/~sw/pubs.html (2002)

20. Wilson, S. W.: Get Real! XCS with Continuous-Valued Inputs. In Booker, L., Forrest, S., Mitchell, M., Riolo, R. L., eds.: Festschrift In Honor of John H. Holland, Centre for the Study of Complex Systems (1999) 11-121

21. Koza, J. R.: Genetic Programming: on the Programming of Computers by Means of Natural Selection (Complex Adaptive Systems). MIT Press (1992)

22. Kovacs, T.: Strength or accuracy? A comparison of two approaches to fitness calculation in learning classifier systems. In Wu, A.S. (ed.): Proceedings of the 1999 Genetic and Evolutionary Computation Conference Workshop Program, (1999) 258-265

23. Butz, M.V., Wilson, S.W.: An Algorithmic Description of XCS, Technical Report 2000017, Illinois Genetic Algorithms Laboratory, Illinois. Http://prediction-dynamics.com/. (2000)

24. Carse, B., Pipe, A.G.: Involving Temporal Rules with the Delayed Action Classifier System - Analysis and New Results. In Parmee, I.C. (ed.): Adaptive Computing in Design and Manufacture V, Springer-Verlag, London (2002) to 31-242

A Ruleset Reduction Algorithm
for the XCS Learning Classifier System

Phillip William Dixon, Dawid Wolfe Corne, and Martin John Oates

Department of Computer Science, University of Reading, Reading, RG6 6AY, UK
{pwdixon,d.w.corne}@reading.ac.uk, moates@btinternet.com

Abstract. XCS is a learning classifier system based on the original work by Stewart Wilson in 1995. It has recently been found competitive with other state of the art machine learning techniques on benchmark data mining problems. For more general utility in this vein, however, issues are associated with the large numbers of classifiers produced by XCS; these issues concern both readability of the combined set of rules produced, and the overall processing time. The aim of this work is twofold, to produce reduced classifier sets which can more readily be understandable as rules, and to speedup processing via reduction of classifier set size during operation of XCS. A number of algorithmic modifications are presented, both in the operation of XCS itself and in the post-processing of the final set of classifiers. We describe a technique of qualifying classifiers for inclusion in action sets, which enables classifier sets to be generated prior to passing to a reduction algorithm, allowing reliable reductions to be performed with no performance penalty. The concepts of 'spoilers' and 'uncertainty' are introduced, which help to characterise some of the peculiarities of XCS in terms of operation and performance. A new reduction algorithm is described which we show to be similarly effective to Wilson's recent technique, but with considerably more favourable time complexity, and we therefore suggest that it may be preferable to Wilson's algorithm in many cases with particular requirements concerning the speed/performance tradeoff.

1 Introduction

XCS is a learning classifier system based on the original work by Stewart Wilson (1995). The important new feature of XCS was that it was based on accuracy and not strength of classifiers and that genetic algorithms were applied to subsets of the classifier population generating a highly directed learning process developing accurate and general rules covering the input space.

One application area for LCSs is that of data mining, where the environment to be modeled is a (typically) large and complex dataset, and the LCS is asked to map data instances to known categories. Wilson's XCS classifier system has recently been modified and extended in ways which enable it to be applied to real-world benchmark data mining problems. Problems are associated with the large numbers of classifiers produced within XCS. The consequent lack of 'readability' of the ruleset becomes an issue where applications involve the discovery and use of the underlying knowledge held in the database, especially perhaps in a non-computer based system where the rules generated are used offline as a knowledgebase. In applications which are computer based the number of rules is of little importance until processing time becomes

P.L. Lanzi et al. (Eds.): IWLCS 2002, LNAI 2661, pp. 20–29, 2003.

an issue. In 'first generation' classifier system applications the processing time will not be an issue as the vast majority of the processing time is taken up with training the system and this will tend to be an offline operation. However, as processors (and in particular mobile processors) become more powerful, we can expect the commercial application of XCS to a wide range of data mining problems. In these 'second generation' systems it will be required for the system to regularly take newly acquired inputs and regenerate the classifier set based on operator classification of the new data, in this case processing time will become a major issue to usability.

The aim of this work is twofold, towards the production of reduced classifier sets which can more readily be understandable as rules, and (longer term) towards the speedup of XCS processing via the reduction of classifier set size during operation of XCS. Of course, this research aims to investigate ways of achieving these objectives with minimal impact on XCS performance in the data mining application.

The rest of the paper is set out like this: In section 2 we describe Wilson's algorithm for ruleset reduction (Wilson, 2002) we will designate this algorithm as 'CRA' (Classifier Reduction Algorithm). Section 2 describes CRA, in a way which indicates its time complexity, and then provides some implementation notes which supplement those in the original paper. Section 3 presents the design of an alternative ruleset reduction algorithm later referred to as CRA2. Section 4 outlines a modified XCS which we call XCSQ, in which the modifications are inspired by the concepts involved in CRA2, and which consequently produces more compact rulesets than XCS. Section 5 then describes three salient concepts related to classifiers, rulesets and the associated algorithms within XCS – namely 'spoilers', 'uncertainty' and 'qualified' classifiers. Section 6 presents results which compare CRA and CRA2 and some initial results obtained from XCSQ, we then have a concluding discussion in Section 7.

2   Wilson's Reduction Algorithm (CRA)

Wilson's paper 'Compact Rulesets from XCSI' (Wilson, 2002) on classifier reduction and the formation of reduced rulesets is the basis for this work. In Wilson's case the reduced classifier set was produced purely to make the interpretation of the rules easier and more understandable. The reduction process is run after completion of the XCS test run.

Wilson's ruleset reduction algorithm, which we call CRA, is a three stage process. After first ordering the classifiers based on a selected property, say numerosity or experience. Stage 1 involves finding the smallest subset of classifiers which achieve 100% performance. Stage 2 is the elimination of classifiers which, added to the subset, do not advance performance. Finally, in stage 3 classifiers are ordered by the number of inputs matched and processed until all inputs have been matched at which point the remaining unmatched classifiers are discarded.

Full details of CRA are in Wilson (2002); we now consider its time complexity in terms of the number of classifiers in the original set offered for reduction, calling this number c, the final reduced set size is r, and the amount of time to evaluate a single classifier against all data examples, which we call a. So, stage 1 requires a process which adds each classifier in turn and tests all inputs until 100% performance is achieved, and it therefore takes up to the number of classifiers times a single pass of testing on all input data set entries. In practice as the classifiers have been suitably ordered to place the reduced classifiers at the beginning then the time taken here is actually related to the number of reduced classifiers. Stage 1 therefore has a time complexity of :

$$O(a + 2a + 3a....ra) = O(\frac{r(r+1)a}{2}) \approx O(\frac{r^2a}{2})$$

CRA stage 2 could be based on the series of performance figures produced in stage 1, where classifiers not increasing performance are deleted, but this has been found in our experience to sometimes have an adverse effect on performance. A better option, which maintains performance at 100%, is to retest after each classifier deletion and replace (addback) the classifier if performance is found to be degraded. (Table 2 later on illustrates better performance with the addback method when using CRA).

The time taken for stage 2 under CRA is very short as it is a simple matter of removing classifiers as indicated in the performance figures obtained in phase 1. For CRA with add-back however stage 2 can potentially double processing time as each classifier removal is retested.

CRA stage 3 is the equivalent of a single pass test on all input data set entries, and hence has little impact on complexity. The actual time taken will depend on the generality of the classifier population; low generality will produce the longest processing periods as in this case more classifiers are required to map the entire input data set.

The Wisconsin Breast Cancer (WBC) problem is a standard database which has previously been used to demonstrate the efficacy of XCS (Dixon et al, 2002; Wilson, 2000a). As WBC was chosen by Wilson to demonstrate his reduction system for direct comparison purposes this has also been used here. We now describe some experience of using CRA on the WBC dataset, which motivated our design of CRA2.

Examination of the classifier set for WBC produced by CRA suggested that it was most likely that classifiers which had non-zero errors associated with them were being included in the reduced set and were influencing the results. Tests were carried out to produce classifier sets with 100% performance (prior to reduction techniques being applied), but which also had no classifiers with non-zero errors. This was achieved by modifying the test routines in XCS to only include classifiers from the overall population which were both sufficiently experienced and had zero errors. In this case XCS ran completely normally creating and removing classifiers within the population as usual but the decision to terminate the run was based on data tested only on selected qualifying classifiers. The final classifier population was then initially reduced by elimination of the classifiers not included in the testing process.

The zero error classifier sets were then reduced using CRA with less than perfect results, always failing to achieve 100% performance at stage 2 of the process. In reality it is not possible to fail to achieve 100% performance on stage 1 of the process as by requirement the original classifier set had 100% performance and stage 1 was defined to ensure 100% performance.

Best results in terms of performance were obtained when the classifier set being operated upon had low generality though of course in these cases the final population size was obviously higher.

By modifying XCS to include in the test routines only classifiers with payoff predictions equal to the positive reward it was found that it was possible for CRA (and also for CRA2, which we describe later) to reliably achieve 100% performance. The use of a subset of the total population of classifiers is not a completely new approach as the use of experience limits, by definition, segregates classifiers for different processing streams within XCS as part of normal operations. Stewart Wilson was kind enough to provide the author with the classifier set he used to produce the ruleset reduction results in Wilson (2002). This classifier set did produce very similar results when processed using this implementation of CRA so it may be assumed, (though not guaranteed), that the code does not include any unwanted 'features'. To enable direct comparison of results the same coding of database input was used in all tests, for description of coding see Wilson (2000a).

3   An Alternative Reduction Algorithm (CRA2)

In the initial phase of operation (which follows the same sequential process as Wilson's), CRA2 is run on the final classifier set produced by XCS (or XCSQ, see later) once the non-qualified classifiers have been removed.

The implementation of CRA2 involves testing every input case on the classifier set, and as each matchset is formed and the action is selected then selected classifiers are marked as 'useful'. Once all input data has been processed then any non-marked classifiers are removed and the reduced classifier set remains. Pseudocode is given below.

```
For each input situation
    Create MatchSet
    Select Action
    Create ActionSet
    Find ActionSet member with highest payoff prediction
        numerosity product
    Mark classifier with highest payoff prediction
        numerosity product as USEFUL
End For
Remove all classifiers not marked as USEFUL
```

Using this algorithm within XCS simply involves allowing the useful classifiers to be marked during training, and periodically removing the non-useful classifiers. The periodic removal serves to refocus the classifier set and is set to happen only occasionally, so as to allow the classifier population time to develop before the removal process takes place. In many respects this is equivalent to restarting the XCS application with a constantly revised and hopefully improved initial classifier set.

The reasoning behind CRA2 is that in each matchset the dominant classifier is the only important classifier to be retained; as long as the dominant classifier is not lost from any of the matchsets then every matchset will produce the correct result. This algorithm only works correctly, providing 100% performance, if there are no classifiers with errors greater than zero or with payoffs less than the positive reward value. If classifiers are present that do not match these criteria then spoilers may be required to balance a matchset with the dominant classifier requiring their support. This effect can be seen in classifier sets not matching the criteria, which only produce 100% performance when spoilers are included in CRA2.

In addition variants of CRA2 include:

- keeping all classifiers in the matchset with the selected action.
- overpower secondary actions in matchset, if the highest payoff classifier does not overcome the effect of the combined efforts of any other action's prediction, then flag as USEFUL more selected action classifiers.
- keep the best of the non-selected action classifiers.
- use spoilers; this is similar to overpowering secondary actions but classifiers which do not have the selected action are retained.

The basic implementation requires a single pass of tests on the input data set, and hence has a complexity of $O(ca)$, so CRA2 is $O(\frac{r^2}{2c})$ times faster than CRA.

4 Processing with Qualified Classifiers (XCSQ)

We have modified our XCS implementation to use only qualified classifiers in the calculations that lead to outcome predictions. The implementation changes required are to the GENERATE PREDICTION ARRAY and GENERATE ACTION SET code (as so named in Butz and Wilson [2000]). To follow a naming tradition, though with some hesitation, we refer to XCS thus modified as XCSQ. In our case, prior to adding classifier fitness to the prediction array, the classifier concerned is first checked for qualification – i.e. we check that it has zero error, sufficient experience, and payoff prediction equal to the positive reward. Non-qualifying classifiers are not processed and are not added to the prediction array. In GENERATE ACTION SET, first the matchset classifiers are checked for inclusion in the actionset (if they match the selected action); if no classifiers qualify for inclusion, then classifiers are passed through to the actionset as per the non-modified XCS. This enables very immature populations to produce an actionset even though the population is not yet experienced enough to have sufficient numbers of qualified classifiers. As the use of qualified classifiers means that the non-qualified classifiers are not used in the production of the test results, then at the end of the run, non-qualified classifiers can be eliminated from the classifier set with no impact on performance.

5 Additional Concepts

During the development of CRA2 a number of interesting points were raised; these are now presented and may be the basis of further work in the future.

5.1 Notes Concerning Generality

The algorithms discussed partially work with the concept of classifier generality. It will be instructive to step back a moment and revisit the basics of generality in XCS (and similar systems), to help clarify and put into context the later descriptions.

Generality is defined as the number of #'s (don't care symbols) divided by the total number of symbols in the classifier condition, this definition has been extended to cover the population as a whole by the use of an average over all classifiers.

If XCS was constrained to never generalise, then its results would essentially be a lookup table; this is a one-to-one mapping and results in one 'rule' per data input and would not be useful at all in classifying previously unseen cases. In this case any aliasing would cause problems for the system in outcome resolution. Aliasing can be the result of either incomplete data or insufficient data where a significant variable has not been recorded which would have directly affected the outcome in the aliased situation. The problem with a lookup table is that previously unseen inputs cannot be resolved. By having generality in the classifiers, this allows for the possibility of unseen inputs (with combinations of features not apparent in the training data) to be given a classification.

Turning generalisation on reduces the number of 'rules' produced as many different input cases may trigger a single rule, but this now leads to potential overlap (and conflict) between the responses of different classifiers to the same input case. Generality thus leads to classifier sets where resolution of multiple and conflicting outcomes must be resolved. Currently this resolution is achieved by the combination of weighted payoff predictions.

5.2 Uncertainty

In the original papers on XCS, results were given in terms of three possible outcomes – an input case was either classified correctly, classified incorrectly, or 'non-matched' – that is, the system could not arrive at a classification of such an input case, since no rules covered the condition part. These numbers were the basis of a straightforward 'fraction correct' figure used for comparison of results. For our purposes we describe and use an additional outcome, which we term 'uncertain'. The system response to an input is 'uncertain' in cases when it is certainly covered by more than one classifier, but the weighted evidence does not favour any single outcome as 'best'. Essentially, adding up the votes for conflicting predictions results in a tie. Notice that the collection of equally supported predictions in such a case may not include the correct prediction at all. Arguably, such an input could be happily classed as incorrect, but we have not adopted that route here. It is not completely clear to us how other XCS researchers generally handle 'uncertain' outcomes. They may, for example, use a randomly assigned prediction (since they are fairly uncommon anyway, and this doesn't seem too harmful), or perhaps take the classification to be the lexicographically first of the equally predicted ones, or perhaps something else. We note here that we treat them as 'incorrect' for the purposes of general XCS operation, and also for the purposes of ruleset reduction. On balance we feel that classifying uncertain results as 'incorrect' is the most reliable mode of operation compared to the various alternatives.

Comparison of test runs has shown that (in our XCS implementation anyway) uncertain cases can persist in the population throughout the run and may not be completely eliminated prior to termination; this may also be a source of conflict in the reduction algorithm and may be the reason that reduction algorithms can fail to maintain 100% performance.

5.3 Spoilers

A single classifier can dominate a matchset by having a payoff prediction and numerosity product which is larger than any other combination of classifiers with a differing action. Matchsets which include a dominant classifier whose predicted action is incorrect, can nevertheless produce a correct prediction of action if additional classifiers with the same incorrect action are included. This is a feature of the mathematics involved in the combination of classifiers. We use the term 'spoilers' for these additional classifiers, whose presence reduces the influence of the dominant classifier.

Table 1. Example classifier set.

Classifier	Outcome (Action)	Numerosity	Fitness	Payoff Prediction
C1	O1	1	0.5	1.0
C2	O1	1	0.4	0.1
C3	O2	1	0.3	0.9

Imagine that a set of three classifiers have conditions which match the presented input with values of numerosity, payoff prediction, fitness and outcome as in table 1. Calculating the fitness-weighted prediction for the two yields 0.6 for O1 and 0.9 for O2, thus predicting outcome O2. C1 seems like the dominant classifier, in terms of fitness and payoff, however its prediction is outvoted. If, however, the classifier C2 is omitted from the calculation, then the fitness weighted prediction for O1 is 1.0 and outcome O1 is predicted. It can be seen therefore that the addition of C2 acts as a spoiler on the outcome which would have been dominated by C1 otherwise, despite the fact that it predicts the same outcome as O1.

In a case where the matchset includes classifiers advocating different actions it may be necessary to allow 'spoiler' classifiers which dilute the power of the incorrectly advocating action classifiers, these 'spoiler' classifiers may be required in perhaps only a few or a single input case and may not have a very high numerosity. CRA (Wilson, 2002) may remove such low numerosity classifiers, hence removing 'necessary' spoilers, and upset the delicate balance required to achieve 100% performance. Spoilers can be selected by single or combinations of, classifier order of presentation, lowest or highest prediction factor where the prediction factor comprises the product of fitness, payoff and numerosity or any combination.

It has been found by the authors that spoilers operating within a less than 100% performance classifier set when removed can actually improve the overall performance achieved, this has been seen in practice as a result of classifier reduction. This may in future be found to be a very desirable feature especially if the reduction is applied periodically to XCS as it may lead to higher performances being achieved at faster processing times.

6 Experiments and Results

Classifier reduction was carried out on data supplied both by Wilson and from our own implementation of XCS, comparing CRA and CRA2. Table 2 shows the results. The first row refers to experiments using a classifier set supplied by Wilson, which was the end result of running his XCS implementation on the WBC dataset, achieving

100% performance. The resulting ruleset containing 1155 classifiers. The addition of the 'Add-Back' feature to CRA yielded a compact ruleset with just 23 classifiers, still achieving 100% performance. It can be seen that CRA2 applied to this data also maintains 100% performance but with considerable speedup, CRA2 yields a result similar to the first of the two CRA variants at 24 rules.

Table 2. Comparison of CRA (with and without Add-Back) and CRA2, on rulesets emerging from both a long duration run (2 million presentations) and running XCS to the point of 100% performance on the Wisconsin Breast Cancer Dataset. CRA+A indicates CRA with Add-Back, APG indicates average population generality, and ONC indicates original number of classifiers.

APG	ONC	Number of iterations	Reduced no. of classifiers			Reduction time (seconds) based on PentiumIII 350MHz		
			CRA	CRA+A	CRA2	CRA	CRA+A	CRA2
0.5601^a	1155	2,000,000	$25 / 26^c$	23	24	11.4 / 27.5	22.2	2.6
0.1387	887	553,608	292^d	291	294	177.1	363.3	1.3
0.1162^b	319	553,608	292	291	294	82.3	147.1	0.6
0.2238	792	1,338,585	261	262	261	137.9	279.6	1.0
0.1978^b	291	1,338,585	261	262	261	67.6	123.9	0.6

[a] Original ruleset supplied by Wilson
[b] Classifier set pre-processed to remove non-qualified entries
[c] CRA using numerosity / experience
[d] Average Fraction Correct (AFC) = 0.9986 (loss in performance)

CRA2 readily finds a reduced set of a size close to that achieved by CRA, but considerably faster. In one case CRA did not emerge with a 100% performance compacted ruleset, but CRA2 did. The loss of performance is due to the immature nature of the classifiers as evidenced by the large number of classifiers resulting in the reduced sets. Immature classifier sets are a feature of shorter test runs where the classifier set has not had sufficient time to eliminate unnecessary classifiers or strengthen the most valuable members.

To end this section we mention some supplemental notes of importance for readers intending to replicate or further this work. First, it is important to note that the Wilson data includes classifiers with payoff prediction less than the positive reward value, and classifiers with prediction errors greater than zero.

Second, analysis of the supplied classifier set (re. row 1) revealed that the 1155 classifiers included 156 with prediction error greater than zero. After applying stage 1 of CRA, the remaining classifier set contained no such classifiers. After applying stage 2, no classifiers with payoff prediction different from the positive reward value were present. Notice of these facts, and some further thought, led directly to the formulation for the implementation of XCSQ (described earlier), which promises to directly produce compact classifier sets without the need for further processing. Preliminary results for XCSQ are looking good Table 3 below demonstrates some initial results where a range of classifier populations have been developed up to the point where 100% performance has been achieved.

It can be seen from these results that both CRA and CRA2 produce similar results in terms of numbers of reduced classifiers but that CRA2 is between 5 and 100 times faster. It may be expected however that for more mature classifier populations the processing time advantage may be eroded while this is borne out by the complexity analysis this has yet to be determined by experimental results.

Table 3. Comparison of reduction algorithm performance using XCSQ derived classifier populations. CRA+A indicates CRA with Add-Back, APG indicates average population generality, ONC indicates original number of classifiers, and NQC indicates number of qualified classifiers.

APG	ONC	NQC	Number of iterations	Reduced no. of classifiers			Reduction time (seconds) based on PentiumIII 350MHz		
				CRA	CRA+A	CRA2	CRA	CRA +A	CRA2
0.0888	610	344	245349	342	342	342	106.9	183.2	0.9
0.1655	517	294	99258	292	292	292	81.3	135.6	1.0
0.2394	513	247	159372	245	245	245	60.8	102.2	0.9
0.3071	720	214	166362	214	214	214	51.8	86.3	1.2
0.3739	948	157	428487	157	157	157	37.7	54.9	1.5
0.4223	1262	140	397731	134	134	135	26.9	45.0	1.8
0.4658	1205	107	106947	105	105	106	19.4	30.5	2.1
0.5143	1711	79	185235	77	77	77	14.9	20.8	3.2
0.5606	1691	75	102054	70	67	70	14.1	20.3	3.0
0.5624	1227	66	137004	65	65	66	11.1	17.1	2.1

7   Concluding Discussion

Via the characterisation of certain concepts related to classifiers in rulesets – namely 'spoilers', 'uncertainty', and the consequent notion of 'qualified' classifiers, we have described a ruleset reduction algorithm which, we then find, produces results similar to Wilson's ruleset reduction method, but in much more reasonable time. We have also discussed a modified version of XCS called XCSQ which makes more use of these concepts (the 'Q' stands for 'Qualified classifiers') and is capable of directly producing compact classifier sets without the need for post-processing with a reduction algorithm, and does so with no unacceptable increase in processing time.

The main focus of our further work on this is in tuning XCSQ towards a system which is both speedy in operation and compact in result. This requires research on both reduction algorithms themselves and details of their incorporation (e.g. periodic use in some form) into the XCS operating cycle.

As noted above, results shown here indicate that the new reduction algorithm is almost as effective at classifier reduction as Wilson's algorithm but that it is many times faster in operation. Actually, the speed of such an algorithm may not seem a major issue if one only cares about finding a maximally reduced 100% accurate ruleset, however long it takes, however we think our earlier comments about 'second generation' classifier systems still apply, while the speed issue is of course much more important when it comes to future work on including the reduction algorithm somehow within the training stage.

Acknowledgements

The authors wish to thank BT Exact Plc for ongoing support for this research, and we also thank Stewart Wilson for invaluable assistance. Finally, we would like to thank Evosolve (UK registered charity no. 1086384) for additional support of this work.

References

Butz, M.V. and Wilson, S.W. (2000), 'An Algorithmic Description of XCS', Technical Report 2000017, Illinois Genetic Algorithms Laboratory, IL, USA.

Dixon, Corne, Oates (2002), 'A Preliminary Investigation of Modified XCS as a Generic Data Mining Tool', in Lanzi, Stolzmann, Wilson (eds), Proceedings of the 4th International Workshop on Learning Classifier Systems, to appear.

Pier Luca Lanzi 'A Study of the Generalization Capabilities of XCS',

Wilson, S.W. (1995) 'Classifier fitness based on accuracy', Evolutionary Computation, 3(2):149–175.

Wilson, S.W. (2000a) 'Mining Oblique Data with XCS', Technical Report 2000028, University of Illinois at Urbana-Champaign, MI, USA.

Wilson, S.W. (2000b) 'Get Real! XCS with Continuous-Valued Inputs', in Lanzi, P.L., Stolzmann, W. and Wilson, S.W. (eds.), Learning Classifier Systems: From Foundations to Applications, Springer Lecture Notes in Computer Science 1813, pp. 209–219.

Wilson, S.W. (2002) 'Compact Rulesets from XCSI', www.world.std/~sw/pubs.html, Presented at the Fourth International Workshop on Learning Classifier Systems (IWLCS-2001).

Wilson, S.W. (1998) 'Generalization in the XCS Classifier System', Genetic Programming 1998: Proceedings of the Third Annual Conference, pp. 665-674.

Adapted Pittsburgh-Style Classifier-System: Case-Study

Gilles Enée[1] and Pierre Barbaroux[2]

[1] Laboratory I3S, Les Algorithmes / Bât. Euclide B, 2000 Route des Lucioles – BP 121,
06903 Sophia-Antipolis Cedex, France
enee@i3s.unice.fr
[2] Laboratory IDEFI-LATAPSES, IDEFI-LATAPSES, 250 Avenue Albert Einstein,
06560 Valbonne, France
barbaroux@idefi.cnrs.fr

Abstract. The aim of this paper is to study why we should have a closer look
to Pittsburgh-style Classifier-Systems (Pitt-CS). This kind of classifier-systems
were introduced by Smith during the early 80's and was nearly forgotten during 20 years. We revisit those kind of classifiers adapting them. We choose as
background of our study the 'El Farol' bar problem introduced by Arthur. This
multi-agents system problem leads us to test several abilities as memory, problem response and uniformity of population, using GA-independent parameters.
Results have shown that adapted Pitt-CS have useful abilities.

Keywords: Adapted Pittsburgh-style Classifier Systems, Spontaneous Coordination, Memory.

1   Introduction

Classifier systems were introduced by [Holland, 1992]. The original framework of Holland was to create tools having the ability to solve problems learning potential solutions
from simulation using a payoff function. The first classifier system was the Michigan
style classifier systems (Michigan-CS) [Holland, 1985] which was breaking the long
chain solution due to the genetic algorithm evolution mechanism. Other solutions exist
that use a Q-based learning algorithm [Watkins, 1989] instead of a bucket-brigade algorithm to make the classifier system learn. We are talking about ACS [Stolzmann, 1998]
Anticipatory Classifier System and XCS [Wilson, 1995]. Those classifier systems are
able to solve Markovian problems. As [Kovacs and Kerber, 2001] note, if differentiation bits are added to solve a non-Markovian problem, the problem becomes Markovian.
In the early 80's, Smith [Smith, 1980] proposed a fully genetic algorithm based classifier system: the Pittsburgh style classifier system (Pitt-CS). Pitt-CS, named GALE
[Bernadó, Llorà and Garell, 2001], scales XCS when talking about data-mining. Pitt-
CS behaves as well as XCS to solve a minimal model of communication problem
[Enée and Escazut, 2001a] [Enée and Escazut, 2001b]. But those classifier systems dynamic was never fully studied. We propose, in this paper to first review the Pitt-CS and
its adapted version we used. Second we propose a spontaneous coordination problem,
the bar problem, as background for studying the adapted Pitt-CS dynamic. We will then
conclude on the interest of such a classifier system.

P.L. Lanzi et al. (Eds.): IWLCS 2002, LNAI 2661, pp. 30–45, 2003.
© Springer-Verlag Berlin Heidelberg 2003

2   Pitt-CS: Technical Review

Pittsburgh classifier systems are different of other kinds of classifier systems on many points. We will see in the next sub-sections how differ structure, evaluation and evolution mechanism from original framework.

2.1   Structure

Pittsburgh style classifier-systems are filled with production rules also called classifiers. Those classifiers are split into a condition part that reads the environment signal and an action part that acts on the environment. Usually, the condition part is defined upon a ternary alphabet $\{0, 1, \#\}$, where $\#$ replaces 0 and 1, it is also called *wildcard*. The action part contains only bits. Classifiers are melt together to form an individual i.e. an individual is a set of classifiers also called *knowledge structure* or *knowledge base*. Finally, a population of Pitt-CS is filled with several individuals (see fig. 1).

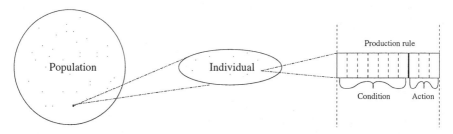

Fig. 1. Pitt-CS Population.

We will not describe here the internal language proposed by [Smith, 1984] to instantiate variables within condition part. So a population is initially created using four parameters:

- A fixed number of individuals in population.
- A varying number of classifiers per individual.
- A fixed bit size for all classifiers.
- An allelic probability of having a wildcard in the condition part.

A population is first filled with random classifiers. We will focus now on how this population is evaluated.

2.2   Evaluation Mechanism

Individuals interact with the environment through captors and effectors and are rewarded thanks to a multi-objectives fitness function. Thus, individuals have a strength that globally reflects the mean strength of the classifiers filling it. The specific structure of Pitt-CS implies a specific evaluation mechanism. Individuals are evaluated at once i.e. with parallel firing rules. This is due to the fact that individuals are potential solutions to the problem so they are not linked to each others as in the Michigan-CS.

Individuals are composed of classifiers, so to ensure that all classifiers had a chance to be tested before evolution occurs, individuals must have been tested a number k of *trials*. Evolution algorithm, here the genetic algorithm, is applied when all individuals had been evaluated that k number of trials. So reward can be continuous, using a Q-Learning method for fitness / strength update, or reward can be reset at each generation and based only upon the last generation trials.

When an individual is evaluated, many classifiers can match the environment signal. Smith proposed to give a relative weight to each action of matching classifiers. Those weights are used as a probability of choosing a particular action. This mechanism can be found in XCS with a more sophisticated evaluation of action weights.

Let's have a look to the evolution mechanism.

2.3   Evolution Mechanism: The Genetic Algorithm

Genetic Algorithm is essential to Pitt-CS: it is the learning and evolution mechanism. Genetic algorithm applies its four main operators among individuals of the population using their fitness. It first **selects** parents that will eventually reproduce using **crossover** and **mutation** operators to create new offsprings that can also be **inverted**.

The selection mechanism use the roulette wheel or the tournament method to select parents that will be present in next generation.

The crossover operator chooses randomly n, i and n', i where i is the bit position where crossover will occur within classifier numbered n from first parent and within classifier numbered n' from second selected parent. The crossover is thus one point and manipulates individuals with different size. Smith has proved that the crossover operator described here will mainly accentuate the difference of length between the two offsprings. The added length of the two offspring is the same has the added length of the two parents. The selection mechanism will progressively erase short individuals that won't be able to answer problems because they do not have enough classifiers. Thus, the bigger individuals will be selected and the individual size tends to grow through generations.

Mutation operator is allelic. Crossover and mutation and inversion are probabilities.

The inversion operator can be used with Pitt-CS because each classifier is member of an unordered knowledge structure: an individual. So inversion of classifiers within an individual allows classifiers to be better exchanged when crossover occurs.

Best genetic algorithm parameters usually taken by Smith are (except for the selection mechanism):

– Selection mechanism: roulette wheel.
– Crossover probability: 50-100%.
– Allelic mutation probability: 0,01-0,5%.
– Inversion probability: 50%.

2.4   Adapted Pitt-CS

The main difference between Pitt-CS and Adapted Pitt-CS is that the number of rules per individual is fixed. This first permits the use of a standard genetic algorithm that manipulates fixed length individuals. Second, it allows to study the role of such parameter in the classifier system behavior. Smith notes that his system was creating too heavy individuals with useless and noisy rules. The results he obtained were quite good but not as good as expected. When he tried to fix the max number of rules per individual with a specific mechanism, the system was also creating some noise while converging to solution. The Adapted Pitt-CS does not use the inversion operator to allow system to make a supra-individual to emerge within population.

The several matching rules selection problem can be solved for example:

- Taking randomly one rule among the matching ones.
- Taking the most specific rule i.e. with the least number of #.
- Taking the most generic rule i.e. with the most number of #.

For the last two methods, if several rules still match, the first mechanism of selection is used among the selected more or less specific rules.

The simulator of the environment that is used to make the population learn, can be used in two ways. It can be reset at each generation or set to its previous status using a learning algorithm. The last method is not within the original framework of Smith where system is GA dependent only for learning. Parallelism can be easily simulated through the simulator that keep track of its status with each individual at the end of previous evaluation. If the simulator is reset, parallelism can be easily translated in sequential evaluation of individuals also.

To have a clear and complete view of the evaluation mechanism, see algorithm 1.

The ending criteria can be a number of generation or when the k trials are successful for an individual. So to evaluate a Pitt-CS, you need those parameters:

- Simulator / Environment reset mode: To zero / To previous status.
- A number of trials.
- A selection rule mechanism: random / specific / generic as example.
- A number of generations.

Crossover operator can be n-point with n ranging from 1 to $l - 1$ where l is the length of individual. Because crossover is applied between two individuals, it can, whether or not, break classifiers. The inversion mechanism was not implemented in the version we present.

We have made a quick technical tour of Pitt-CS and its adapted version, let's see now how it behaves with the 'El-Farol' problem.

3 'El-Farol' Problem

The 'El-Farol' problem was introduced by [Arthur, 1994]. The problem consists in a population of students that wants to spend a nice moment in the famous 'El-Farol' bar of the Santa-Fae institute. The difficulty is that there is an upper bound of attendance after which all students that came feel bad. A student that didn't come to the bar while there is room for him is also disappointed. The only information students have to make their decision is the attendance of the week before. If we represent students as agents in a multi-agents system, we can consider them as physically homogeneous

---

Algorithm 1 of Adapted Pittsburgh style classifier system.

Begin
  Fill(P); { *Random initialization of P.* }
  Generation = 1;
  Repeat
   For (All I_k of P) **Do**
    Reset_Environment(k); { *Reset environment to individual I_k last status or reset it to zero.* }
    Reward = 0;
    For (A number of Trials NbT) **Do**
     Fill(Mesg-List); { *with message from environment.* }
     Fill(Match-List); { *Create Match-Set from I_k classifiers that match signal.* }
     If (IsEmpty(Match-List)) **Then**
      Reward = Reward + 0; { *Was unable to decide what to do with that signal.* }
     Else
      If (Size(Match-List)> 1) **Then**
       C =BestChoice(Match-List); { *Choose classifier in Match-List.* }
      Else
       $C = First(Match - List)$;
      Endif
      Reward = Reward+ActionReward(C)/NbT; { *ActionReward acts upon environment using action from C and then returns action's reward.* }
     Endif
    EndFor
    ChangeStrength(I_k,*Reward*); { *Change individual I_k strength using Reward.* }
   EndFor
   ApplyGA(P);
   Generation = Generation + 1;
  Until (Ending Criteria encountered);
End

---

agents [Enée and Escazut, 1999] with same task to deal with and with same input and output to make their choice. But each agent are autonomous from each other in the way they do not have any information from other agents to make their decision i.e. they are agents of a coordinating multi-agents system. Hence, each student is a Adapted Pittsburgh style classifier system with previous attendance to the bar as input and with Go or Stay as action to take. After all agents have taken a decision, we obtain a new attendance that will be both used for reward and for input in next trial.

3.1   Measures

To fully measure dynamics of Adapted Pitt-CS, we added a little difficulty to the problem, changing it into a dynamic changing environment. This change occurs on ideal attendance (equilibrium) to attain after different static numbers of generations. We measured:

- The influence of the frequency of equilibrium changes.
- The influence of changing the number of individuals per classifier system.

- The influence of changing the number of classifiers per individuals.
- The uniformity of population.
- The memorization abilities.
- The non-deterministicness.

The equilibrium changes occur each 50, 100, 150 and 250 generations. The equilibrium changes cyclically and sequentially between 32, 48, 64 and 80 students. The number of individuals was set to 6 then 12 and finally to 18 as the number of rules was. The uniformity of population is a mean measure of the resemblance of individuals in each classifier systems. Resemblance is measured comparing sequentially rules of each individuals with ones of any other individuals within the same agent. This measure is possible thanks to the fact that the inversion operator is not implemented: The rule order within an individual is not changed after crossover. When a wildcard replace a bit value, the rule is counted as similar to the compared one. The memorization reflects the ability of an agent to come back to its previous behavior for the same previous equilibrium to attain. The memorization shows the main behavior of an agent on a defined ideal attendance to the bar. Finally, the non-deterministicness indicates what percentage of the available input values from the environment leads to a non-deterministic choice for the agents i.e. it can both, for a determined signal, go and stay to the bar thanks to its available classifiers.

Results will be presented as the distance gain (%) to the ideal attendance to the bar (Eq) from a reference value ($V_{Reference}$) to the current value ($V_{Current}$):

$$Gain = \frac{(V_{Current} - V_{Reference})}{(Eq - V_{Reference})} * 100$$

The $Gain$ measures the effort that furnished the system to reach Eq from a reference point.

3.2   Experimentation

Our experimentation was made using 127 agents trying to adapt to a changing equilibrium. 127 students lead to 128 different possible values of attendance to the bar detected through classifiers having a 7 ternary bit long condition part. The action part is coded with a simple bit that indicates whether (1) or not (0) the student (agents) goes to the bar. We did not use the original framework of Smith upon variables mechanism[1] because we are working on a fully distributed artificial intelligence architecture where agents have only to rule one single part of the complex problem. Thus agents are simple reactive mechanisms. We aim to make "simple" agents able to act with each other autonomously, homogeneously [Enée and Escazut, 1999] and heterogeneously [Enée and Escazut, 2001a].

---

[1] See [De Jong and Spears, 1991] for more details.

These are the parameters we used for our experimentations:

Parameter	Setting	Parameter	Setting
AgentsNumber	127	$P_\#$	33%
IndividualNumber	6,12,18	$P_{CrossOver}$	70%
RuleNumber	6,12,18	$P_{Mutation}$	0,5%
Trials	$\frac{RuleNumber}{2}$	Selection	Roulette Wheel
Rule Selection	Random	Crossover	One point
Experimentations	30	Elitism	Always keep 2
EquilibriumChange (EC)	50,100,150,250	Generations	$100 \times EC$

The number of generations is "Equilibrium Change dependent" to always have 100 changes to plot results. All GA parameters were set to as standard as possible values seen in the GA theoretical literature. The aim of those settings was to observe Adapted Pitt-CS dynamic, it was not to get the best results. Fitness function is:

$$\begin{cases} At > Eq \begin{cases} Agent\ goes \Rightarrow \frac{AgentsNumber - At}{AgentsNumber - Eq} \\ Agent\ stays \Rightarrow 1.0 \end{cases} \\ At \leq Eq \begin{cases} Agent\ goes \Rightarrow 1.0 \\ Agent\ stays \Rightarrow \frac{At}{Eq} \end{cases} \end{cases}$$

where At is the attendance in the bar at the end of a trial and where Eq is the current ideal number of students to attain.

Figure 2 shows an example of the fitness function with equilibrium set to 48.

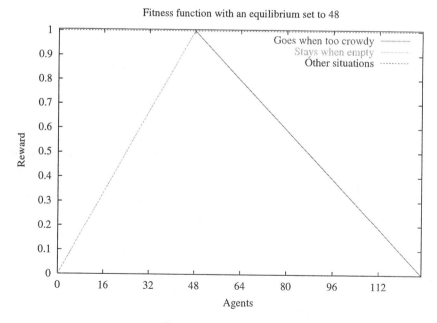

Fig. 2. Fitness function.

3.3   Results

We made 36 different experimentations to test all configuration available. First we present in figure 3 the result we obtained with 18 individuals of 18 rules and changing equilibrium each 250 generations. There are two plots, one presents the ideal attendance to the bar and the other presents the averaged attendance measured in agents number (y-axis) through generations (x-axis). We can see that agents need only about 20 generations in the worst case to adapt to each change.

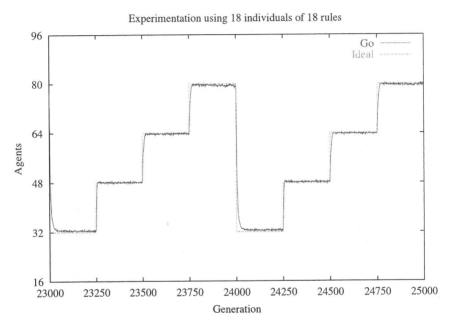

Fig. 3. Best result.

To better understand why this result is as good as it is, we will first study the effect of the changing equilibrium frequency upon results. We present results obtained with agents composed of 6 individuals of 6 rules. Results of figure 4 show the way attendance evolves when the number of generations, between two equilibrium changes, increases from 50 to 100 then to 150 and finally to 250. We see that the more time agents have to learn, the more they are able to attain the desired equilibrium. The gain measured to attain equilibrium globally reaches 69, 29% with the four equilibriums when frequency increases from 50 to 250. The mean number of agents missing in the bar for each equilibrium is about 2,7 for equilibrium changes frequency of 250. The number of individuals and the number of rules seem too small to allow agents to perfectly answer the problem. Indeed, the results are quite good when time permits.

We present in figure 5 the evolution of the number of students that decided to stay at home (y-axis). Thus, the corresponding equilibrium ideals to 32, 48, 64 and 80 are respectively 95 (127 agents - 32 agents that should come), 79, 63 and 47. We expect

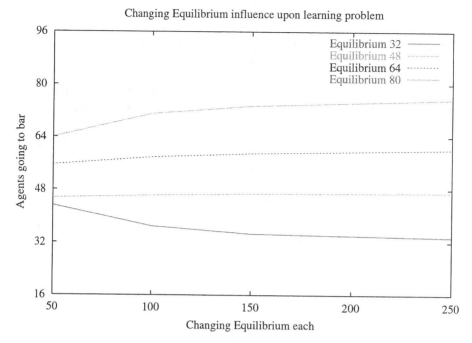

Fig. 4. Frequency of equilibrium changes: Attendance evolution.

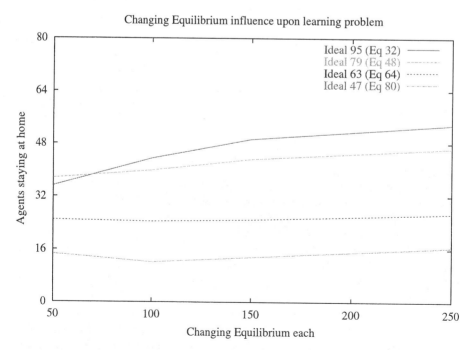

Fig. 5. Frequency of equilibrium changes: Agents staying at home evolution.

to find the missing agents we found in the previous results. It is obvious that many agents that should have stayed at home did not. This number of missing agents is about 35,2 when equilibrium is changed each 250 generations. Even if time allows system to gain 15,75% to reach expected equilibrium, there is still missing 50,4 agents when we sum "missing" staying agents and "missing" going agents. Those agents are called undecided agents because they did not take any decision.

The next results presented in figure 6 show the evolution of the number of undecided agents inside the multi-agent system. Those agents appeared to be a third choice for the possible actions, even if no reward is their fate. Results show that when time between two equilibrium changes increases, the number of undecided agents (y-axis) decreases slightly with a gain of 20,87% toward the ideal of 0 undecided agents. These results clearly demonstrate that when agents have too small abilities due to the number of individuals and rules that compose them, many of them are unable to answer the problem. We now have a look to memorization measure.

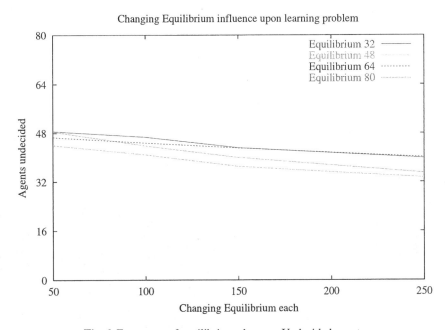

Fig. 6. Frequency of equilibrium changes: Undecided agents.

When changing equilibrium from 50 to 250 generations, the memorization rate slightly decreases from 50,58% to 44,43%. This counter-intuitive result can be explained by the agent structure. When time between two equilibrium changes increases, agent has more time to adapt its individuals to the problem; but agent is unable to keep strategic choices for the next same equilibrium phase due to its small abilities for that experimentation. Complementary explanation is that undecided agents are taken into account with the memorization measure i.e. if an agent is always undecided for a specific phase, it is considered as having memorized a behavior for that phase. And we have seen that the number of undecided agents decreases when number of generation between changes increases. What is obvious after those experimentations is that an equilibrium change each 250 generations is the best way to answer the bar problem with an agent having a restricted capacity. This leads us to present next results with an equilibrium change set to 250 generations.

Next results presents the influence of changing the number of individuals from 6 to 18 with a number of rules set to 6. Figure 7 shows evolution of the number of agents going to the bar (y-axis) for each equilibrium phase while number of individuals increases on the x-axis. The more there are individuals, the better the problem is answered. The gain from 12 individuals to 18 is lower than from 6 to 12. We expect that increasing individuals tends slowly to reach the ideal expected number of attendees in the bar on the average.

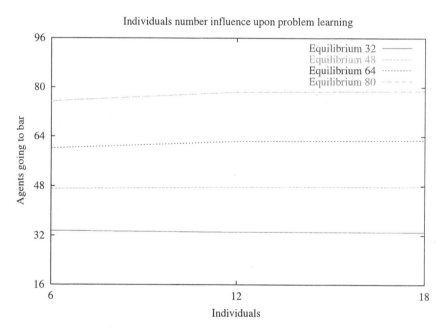

Fig. 7. Increasing individual number: Attendance evolution.

Next figure 8 displays how undecided agents (y-axis) evolves when individual number increases (x-axis). The number of agents left undecided is approximatively divided by 2 while individual number grows from 6 to 18. The more the agents has individuals composing it, the less agents stay undecided. The gain is more significant when individual number increases from 6 to 12. It seems that the gain when changing number of individuals from 12 to 18 is not worth the complexity cost when comparing it to the gain from 6 to 12.

The memorization rate evolves positively that time, increasing from 44,43% to 55,74%. It seems that individuals influences the memory abilities of agent but not that

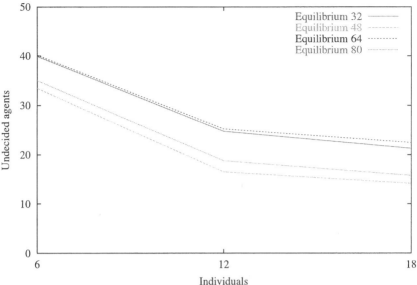

Fig. 8. Increasing individual number: Undecided agents.

much. Regarding the classifier system architecture, we may think that the rule number will be the clue to increase memorization abilities of agents.

The two next figures will show changing rule number influence with an individual number set to 6. First figure 9 presents evolution of the number of agents going to bar (y-axis) when increasing the number of rules per individual (x-axis). Gain is not as good as gain obtained when the number of individuals per agent was increased.

The rule number influence upon undecided agents is shown in figure 10. The number of undecided agents (y-axis) is divided by more than 3. As expected, the number of rules per individual directly enhances the answering abilities of agents allowing them to answer to a wider range of input. The gain is significant for both rule number increase.

Hence, memorization evolves from 44,43% to 62,70%. Number of rules directly permits agents to have a behavior strategy for each available equilibrium. We now have explanations of the good results of the experimentation using Equilibrium Change each 250 generations, 18 individuals and 18 rules per individual. For that experimentation, memorization reaches 65,82% and the average number of undecided agents is 8.48. Those results are encouraging and they lead us to measure how uniform is the agents population within this ideal framework.

Figure 11 shows how population quickly stabilizes around 84% of uniformity in agents. Thus around 16% of differences between individuals composing each agent partially explain the 65,82% memorization rate: A different strategy can occur in 16% of the classifiers of each individual.

When several rules match the signal, the rule that will be activated is chosen randomly accordingly to our experimentation settings. This choice can lead to non-deter-

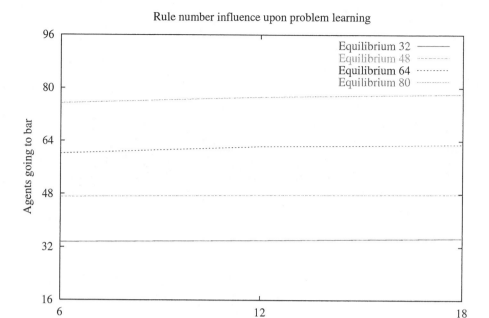

Fig. 9. Increasing classifier number: Attendance evolution.

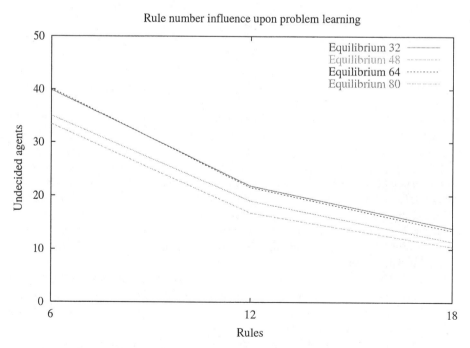

Fig. 10. Increasing classifier number: Undecided agents.

Population Uniforimity : 18 individuals of 18 rules

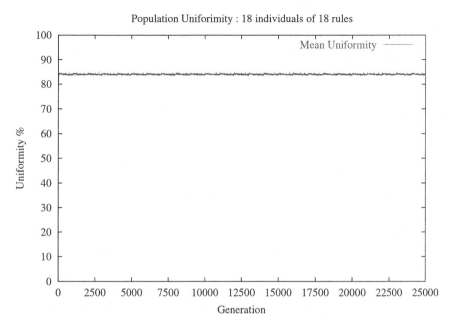

Fig. 11. Population uniformity.

ministic choice for a specific value or range of values. We measure the average non-determinisiticness of agents and we obtained a rate of 30,73% of non-determinisiticness. Thus about one third of the available input signal leads to a behavior change of our agents. This result is interesting because on one hand $\frac{2}{3}$ of the agents are able to have a strategy to answer the problem and on the other hand they can change their mind nearly $\frac{1}{3}$ of the time. Agents number 16 study (see fig. 12) shows this particular ability linked to the Pitt-CS. This figures presents the average agent (y-axis) behavior (Go / Stay) in percentage for each possible equilibrium.

Agent 16 clearly choose to go to the bar when equilibrium is 32; then its behavior changes. Decision for other equilibrium is not clear-cut. We have an agent that globally goes to the bar when equilibrium is 32 or 48. The agent stays most of the time when equilibrium is above 48. Those observed rates confirm the non-determinisiticness of agents and explain the fact that only $\frac{2}{3}$ of them are able to keep a strategy between two identical equilibrium phases. While agents are non-deterministic upon their choices, they are able to coordinate as figure 3 has shown.

4   Conclusion

We made experimentation on Pitt-CS without modifying the Genetic Algorithm parameters and we pointed out the following properties:

– The number of individuals increase allows first a better answer to the problem, second less undecided signals and last a better strategy regarding dynamic problems.

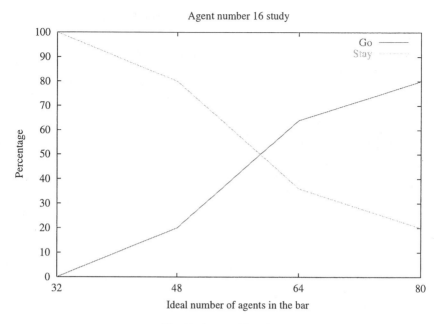

Fig. 12. Agents 16 study.

– The number of rules increase lets both less undecided signals and a better strategy.
– Population tends to become uniform.
– Non-deterministicness is nicely ruled by Adapted Pitt-CS.

The Adapted Pittsburgh style classifier system has shown a remarkable behavior in a simple dynamic coordinating multi-agent problem. This work needs to be extended. Fixing the number of classifiers per individual allows agent to be non-deterministic if that number is greater than needed to solve problem, so we need to bound more precisely this phenomenon. Further work need to be done implementing the inversion GA operator.

References

[Arthur, 1994] Arthur, W.B. (1994). *Inductive reasoning and Bounded Rationality.* In American Economic Review P.P., 1994, pp. 406-411.
[Bernadó, Llorà and Garell, 2001] Bernadó, E., Llorà, X. and Garrell, J. M. (2001). *XCS and GALE: a Comparative Study of Two Learning Classifier Systems with Six Other Learning Algorithms on Classification Tasks.* In the Workshop Proceedings of GECCO 2001 (San Francisco), Fourth International Workshop on Learning Classifier Systems (IWLCS 2001) pages 337-341.
[De Jong and Spears, 1991] De Jong, K. A. and Spears, W. M. (1991). *Learning Concept Classification Rules Using Genetic Algorithms.* In the Proceedings of the International Joint Conference on Artificial Intelligence (IJCAI 91), pages 651-656. Sydney, Australia.

[Enée and Escazut, 1999] Enée, G. and Escazut, C. (1999). *Classifier Systems: Evolving Multi-Agent System with Distributed Elitism.* In the Proceedings of the Congress on Evolutionary Computation 1999, pages 1740-1746.

[Enée and Escazut, 2001a] Enée, G. and Escazut C. (2001). *A Minimal Model of Communication for Multi-Agent Systems.* In Proccedings of ETFA 2001.

[Enée and Escazut, 2001b] Enée, G. and Escazut, C. (2001). *A Minimal Model of Communication for a Multi-Agent Classifier System.* Fourth International Workshop on Learning Classifier Systems (IWLCS 2001). In 2001 Genetic and Evolutionary Computation Conference Workshop Program (GECCO 2001) Proceedings p 351-356.

[Holland, 1985] Holland, J.H. (1985) *Properties of the bucket brigade algorithm.* In Proceedings of the First International Conference on Genetic Algorithms and their Applications, pages 1-7, Hillsdale, New Jersey: Lawrence Erlbaum Associates.

[Holland, 1992] Holland, J.H. (1992). *Adaptation in Natural and Artificial Systems.* A Bradford Book, The MIT Press, Cambridge, Massachusetts, London, England, reprint.

[Kovacs and Kerber, 2001] Kovacs, T. and Kerber, M. (2001). *What Makes a Problem Hard for XCS?* In Lanzi, Pier Luca, Stolzmann, Wolfgang, and Wilson, Stewart W. (eds.), Advances in Learning Classifier Systems. Springer-Verlag.

[Smith, 1980] Smith, S. (1980). *A learning system based on genetic algorithms.* Ph.D. thesis, University of Pittsburgh.

[Smith, 1984] Smith, S.F. (1984). *"Adaptive Learning Systems".* In Expert Systems: Principles and Case Studies, (ed.) R. Forsyth, Associated Book Publishers Ltd, October, 1984.

[Stolzmann, 1998] Stolzmann, W. (1998): Anticipatory Classifier Systems. In Koza, John R., Banzhaf, Wolfgang, Chellapilla, Kumar, Deb, Kalyanmoym Dorigo, Marco, Fogel, David B., Garzon, Max H., Goldberg, David E., Iba, Hitoshi, and Riolo, Rick. (editors). Genetic Programming 1998: Proceedings of the Third Annual Conference, July 22-25, 1998, University of Wisconsin, Madison, Wisconsin, 658-664. San Francisco, CA: Morgan Kaufmann.

[Watkins, 1989] Watkins, C.J.C.H. (1989). *Learning from Delayed Rewards.* Ph.D. thesis, King's College, Cambridge University, 1989.

[Wilson, 1995] Wilson, S.W.. (1995). *Classifier fitness based on accuracy.* Evolutionary Computation, 3(2), pp 149-175.

The Effect of Missing Data
on Learning Classifier System Learning Rate
and Classification Performance

John H. Holmes and Warren B. Bilker

Center for Clinical Epidemiology and Biostatistics
University of Pennsylvania School of Medicine
Philadelphia, PA 19104 USA
jholmes@cceb.med.upenn.edu
wbilker@cceb.upenn.edu

Abstract. Missing data pose a potential threat to learning and classification in that they may compromise the ability of a system to develop robust, generalized models of the environment in which they operate. This investigation reports on the effects of the various types of missing data, present in varying densities in a group of simulated datasets, on learning classifier system performance. It was found that missing data have an adverse effect on learning classifier system (LCS) learning and classification performance, the latter of which is not seen in See5, a robust decision tree inducer. Specific adverse effects include decreased learning rate, decreased accuracy of classification of novel data on testing, increased proportions of testing cases that cannot be classified, and increased variability in these metrics. In addition, the effects are correlated with the density of missing values in a dataset, as well as the type of missing data, whether it is random and ignorable, or systematically missing and therefore non-ignorable.

1 Introduction

Learning Classifier Systems (LCS) are used for a number of functions, including agent control and data mining. All of the environments in which LCS operate are potentially plagued by the problem of incomplete, or *missing*, data. Missing data arise from a number of different scenarios. In databases, fields may have values that are missing because they weren't collected, or they were lost or corrupted in some way during processing. In real-time autonomous agent environments, data may be missing due to the malfunctioning of a sensor. In any case, missing data can cause substantial inaccuracies due to their frequency, their distribution, or their association with features that are important to learning and classification. As a result, missing data has attracted substantial attention in the data mining and machine learning communities [1, 12, 13, 21, 24].

Several well-known algorithms for knowledge discovery have been designed or augmented to deal with missing data. For example, naïve Bayes is known to deal well with missing data, [11]. The EM algorithm has been refined to create accurate parameter estimations in the face of missing data, and inductive logic programming, which has been notoriously poor in handling missing values has been augmented using a rough set approach [5]. Neural networks, another notoriously poor performer

P.L. Lanzi et al. (Eds.): IWLCS 2002, LNAI 2661, pp. 46–60, 2003.

in the face of missing data, have been targeted for improvement using a distance-based metric [16, 26]. The problem of missing data has also been investigated in the context of clustering [17] and evolutionary algorithms to learn Bayesian networks under incomplete data [20].

Although one study [14] has investigated the use of a genetic algorithm in analyzing clinical data with missing values, and one other [10] has investigated their use in spectral estimation, the effects of missing data on LCS learning and classification performance have not yet been described.

This paper reports on an investigation into the effects of missing data on the learning and classification performance of a stimulus-response LCS when it is applied to a simulated database with controllable numbers of missing values. As a result, this investigation focuses on the use of LCS in a simulated data mining task, rather than one in agent-based environments. However, the results of this investigation are applicable to a variety of settings wherever missing data are present in the environment.

1.1 Types of Missing Data

The values of fields in a database can be considered as "responses" to a query, such that for a field such as gender, the value for any given record (or row) in the database reflects a response to the question "What is the gender of [what or whom is represented by the record]?" within the response domain {MALE, FEMALE}. Responses can be *actual*, that is, valid responses within the domain, or they can be *missing*, such that a response value does not exist for that field in the database. Note the important distinction between missing data and erroneous data: missing data are not responsive, while erroneous data are responsive, but not within the response domain.

Missing responses, or more generally, missing data, are typically categorized into one of three types, depending on the pattern of the response [5] on a given field, x, and the other fields, y, in the database. The first type of missing data is characterized by responses to x that are statistically independent of responses to x or y. That is, the probability of a missing value for x is independent of the value of x, as well as of the values of the variables y. This type of missing data is referred to as *missing completely at random* (MCAR). An example of MCAR data would be where the value for gender is randomly missing for some cases, but the "missingness" of gender for any particular case is unrelated to the value of y, as well as the true, but unknown, value of x itself.

A second type of missing data occurs when the probability of a response to x is dependent on the response to y (or, more simply, the value of y). Data such as these are *missing at random* (MAR). An example of MAR data would be where the value for gender is missing when the value of y is at a certain value, or more specifically, if the probability of a missing value for gender is highest when another field, such as race, is equal to Asian. In this case, the missing values for gender are MAR. While the probability of a missing value for gender is essentially random, there is an implicit dependency on race which lessens the degree of randomness of response to the gender field. Thus, it can be seen that MAR data are qualitatively less desirable, and potentially more problematic than MCAR, in analyses and possibly classification.

The last type of missing data is *not missing at random* (NMAR), and these pose the greatest threat to data analysis. NMAR data are found where the probability of a response to x is dependent on the value of x or a set of data which have not been measured. An example of NMAR data would be where the probability of a missing value for gender is highest when gender is male. NMAR data are not ignorable in a statistical analysis, due to the possibility of extreme bias that may be introduced by them.

In traditional statistical analyses, MCAR and MAR data may be ignorable, depending on the type of analysis to be performed. NMAR data, however, are not ignorable, and must be dealt with using a variety of procedures loosely grouped under the rubric of *imputation*, which calls for the replacement of missing data with statistically plausible values created by means of one of numerous algorithmic approaches. This is the only viable option when there is a large fraction of missing data. However, for cases where the fraction of missing data is small, it may be reasonable to omit cases with missing data only for MCAR. For MAR or NMAR, omitting these cases will result in uncorrected bias. The problem of missing data has also been investigated in machine learning systems [2, 11]. This investigation focuses on the effects, rather than the treatment, of missing data on learning and classification performance in a LCS. Thus, discussions of imputation are deferred to a later report.

2 Methods

2.1 Data

Generation of the Baseline Dataset. This investigation used datasets that were created with the DataGen [19] simulation dataset generator. This software facilitates the creation of datasets for use in testing data mining algorithms and is freely available on the Web. The datasets were created in sequential fashion, all starting from the same baseline dataset. The baseline dataset contained 1,000 records consisting of 20 dichotomously coded predictor features and one dichotomously coded class feature. A future investigation will look at more complicated cases where the features could be ordinal or real-valued.

The baseline data were created in such a way as to incorporate noise at a rate of 20%; thus, over the 20,000 feature-record pairs, there were 4,000 features that conflicted or contradicted a putative association with the class feature. This was done to ensure that the dataset was sufficiently difficult in terms of learning and classification. No missing values were incorporated into the baseline dataset. In addition to incorporating noise, the user of DataGen has the capability of specifying the number of expected conjuncts per rule; the higher the number, the more complex the relationships between the predictor features and the class. For this investigation, the maximum number of conjuncts per rule was set at six. After examining the resulting conjuncts, two of the 20 predictor features were found to be prevalent in most, or all, of the rules. These two features were used as candidates for missing values, and thus correspond to x and y that are discussed in Section 1.1. No other features were set to missing.

Generation of Datasets with Missing Values. From the baseline dataset, separate versions were created to simulate five increasing proportions, or *densities*, of missing data: 5%, 10%, 15%, 20%, and 25%. The density of missing data was determined as a proportion of the possible feature-record pairs that result from multiplying the number of possible candidate features by the number of records (1,000). For the MCAR and NMAR protocols, there was only one feature that was a candidate to be replaced with a missing value. However, under the MAR protocol, both x and y were candidates, with equal probability of alteration. Thus, a total of either 1,000 or 2,000 features (1,000 x, or 1,000 x and 1,000 y) could be candidates for a missing value. The actual number of feature values that were changed depended on the missing value density. For example, at the 5% density under the MCAR protocol, there were a total of 50 missing values, all in feature x. Under MAR, however, there were 100 missing values, equally distributed between x and y. The protocol for setting a value to missing under MCAR is as follows:

```
Do while not eof()
    Repeat
        If value of x is not missing
            If rand(0,1)<=0.05  /* sampling fraction of 5% */
            Replace value with missing value
    Until number of required number of features updated
```

The sampling fraction was set to 0.05, as the datasets were created at 5% intervals in missing value density. Note that under MCAR, only feature x was a candidate to be replaced with a missing value. Variations were made to this protocol to create MAR, and NMAR datasets.

Under MAR, both x and y were candidates for replacement with missing values, where the probability of setting the value of feature x value to missing was determined by the value of feature y. Specifically, x was set to missing, with a probability of 0.05, if the value of y in the same record was 1. Under NMAR, the value of x was set to missing, with a probability of 0.05, if its value was 1.

Each of the protocols were applied to the baseline dataset to derive the dataset at 5% density; then it was applied to the 5% dataset to derive the 10%, and so on, in succession, such that the missing values that were present in lower density datasets remained in datasets at higher densities. This was done to ensure comparability between the datasets at successively increasing densities within the same missing value type.

In summary, separate datasets were created at five missing value densities for each of the three missing data types, for a total of 15 datasets, in addition to the baseline dataset. These datasets were labeled as shown in the table below.

Table 1. Layout of datasets created for this study. All datasets at 5% density were derived from a single baseline dataset, which contained no missing data. Datasets at successive densities were created from the immediately preceding datasets.

Missing Value Density	5%	10%	15%	20%	25%
MCAR data	MCAR5	MCAR10	MCAR15	MCAR20	MCAR25
MAR data	MAR5	MAR10	MAR15	MAR20	MAR25
NMAR data	NMAR5	NMAR10	NMAR15	NMAR20	NMAR25

Creation of Training and Testing Sets. Once created, the datasets were partitioned into training and testing sets by randomly selecting records without replacement at a sampling fraction of 0.50. Thus, each training and testing set contaned 500 mutually exclusive records. Care was taken to sample the records so as to preserve the original class distribution, which was 52.8% positive and 47.2% negative cases.

2.2 EpiCS

System Description. EpiCS [8] is a stimulus-response LCS employing the NEW-BOOLE model [3]. It was developed to meet the unique demands of classification and knowledge discovery in epidemiologic data. The distinctive features of EpiCS include algorithms for controlling under- and over-generalization of data, a methodology for determining risk as a measure of classification, and the ability to use differential negative reinforcement of false positive and false negative errors in classification during training. EpiCS was further modified to accommodate prevalence-based bootstrapping [7] and to use predictive values as a means for driving the performance and reinforcement components [9].

Developed to work in clinical data environments for explanatory and predictive rule discovery, EpiCS includes a variety of features such as risk assessment and metrics for system performance that derive from those used commonly in clinical decision making.

Classifier Representation and Handling of Missing Values in EpiCS. Classifiers were represented as 20-bit strings (taxon) with each bit coded as 0 or 1, with missing values represented as "*" characters. A single bit represented the action, coded as 0 or 1; thus, the action was never missing. The "*" was also used internally in EpiCS to represent the "don't care" or wild card value for a given feature in the macroclassifier representation. Other characters could easily be used for this purpose, as well, as long as the system is informed as to the type of missing value character, so that match sets can be created correctly. Match sets were created in the traditional way; that is, the taxon of an incoming training or testing case was compared to all members of the macroclassifier population. The comparison was performed on a bit-by-bit basis, where 0s (or "*"s) on a classifier had to match 0s on the input taxon and 1s (or "*"s) had to match 1s. However, if a bit on the input taxon was a "*" then this was considered a match at that locus on the classifier, regardless of its value. Population members with taxa completely matching the input taxon were added to the match set.

2.3 Metrics and Analytic Issues

Several metrics were used to evaluate the learning and classification performance of EpiCS in this investigation. First, the *area under the receiver operating characteristic curve* (AUC) was used to evaluate evolving classification accuracy during learning and accuracy on classifying novel data. The AUC is preferable to the traditional accuracy metric (usually expressed as percent correct), as it is not sensitive to imbalanced class distributions such as is found in the simulation data used in this investigation [6]. In addition, the AUC represents, as a single metric, the true positive and false positive rate, thereby taking into account the different types of error that can be measured in a two-choice decision problem.

Second, *learning rate* was evaluated by means of a metric, λ, created specifically for this purpose. This metric was calculated as follows:

$$\lambda = \left(\frac{\text{AUC}_{Shoulder}}{\text{Shoulder}} \right) 1000 \qquad (1)$$

Shoulder is the iteration at which 95% of the maximum AUC obtained during training is first attained, and $\text{AUC}_{Shoulder}$ is the AUC obtained at the shoulder. Thus, the higher the value of λ, the faster is the learning rate. As the first AUC is not measured until the 100th iteration, and the maximum AUC measurable is 1.0, the maximum value of λ is 10.0. The minimum λ is 0.0.

Third, the ability of the trained EpiCS system to classify previously unseen cases of similar genre to the training cases was assessed. This was done by comparing the AUCs obtained at testing across the range of missing value densities. In addition to classification accuracy, as measured by the AUC, it is important to assess the extent to which novel data is unclassifiable, and therefore doesn't factor in to the calculation of the AUC. A metric designed for this purpose, the *Indeterminant Rate* (IR), was used to quantify the proportion of testing cases that could not be classified on testing:

$$\text{Indeterminant Rate} = \frac{\text{Number of testing cases not classifiable}}{\text{Total number of testing cases}} \qquad (2)$$

These metrics were used in a variety of statistical analyses. To evaluate the effects of missing data on learning performance, the λs were correlated by Spearman's rho (ρ) the nonparametric equivalent of Pearson's *r*. The nonparametric test was chosen because the independent variable in the correlation analyses, missing value density, is ordinal. The λs were compared, using the baseline dataset as the reference, across the range of missing value densities separately for each of the three types of missing data, MCAR, MAR, and NMAR. Finally, the variability of the observed values for AUC and λ is of considerable interest in this investigation, and this is reported as the coefficient of variation (CV). The CV provides a simple metric that captures the mean and standard deviation in a single value. The CVs for λ obtained for each type of missing data were correlated with the missing value densities.

To evaluate the effects of missing data on classification performance, the AUCs obtained separately by EpiCS and See5 on testing with novel data first were compared for significant differences using Wilcoxon's nonparametric technique [18]. This was done to identify any significant differences in classification accuracy between EpiCS and See5, a well-known benchmark decision tree inducer. Second, the AUCs, IRs and their respective CVs, obtained on testing data from the two systems for the five missing value densities, were correlated separately for each of the three missing value types.

2.4   Experimental Procedure

Training. EpiCS was trained over 10,000 iterations, comprising a *training epoch*. At each iteration, the system was presented with a single training case. As training cases were drawn randomly from the training set with replacement, it could be assumed that the system would be exposed to all such cases with equal probability over the course of the 10,000 iterations of the training epoch. At the 0th and every 100th iteration thereafter, the learning ability of EpiCS was evaluated by presenting the taxon of every case in the training set, in sequence, to the system for classification. As these iterations constituted a test of the training set, the reinforcement component and the genetic algorithm were disabled on these occasions. The decision advocated by Ep-iCS for a given training case was compared to the known classification of the training case. The decision type was classified in one of four categories: true positive, true negative, false positive, and false negative, and tallied for each classifier. From the four decision classifications, the AUC and IR were calculated and written to a file for analysis.

Testing. After the completion of the designated number of iterations of the training epoch, EpiCS entered the testing epoch, in which the final learning state of the system was evaluated using every case in the testing set, each presented only once in sequence. As in the interim evaluation phase, the reinforcement component and the genetic algorithm, were disabled during the testing phase. At the completion of the testing phase, the AUC and IR were calculated and written to a file for analysis, as was done during the interim evaluations. The entire cycle of training and testing comprised a single *trial*; a total of 20 trials were performed for this investigation for each of the 16 datasets.

Parameterization. The major EpiCS parameters used in this investigation were: crossover probability, 0.50; mutation probability, 0.001; invocations of the genetic algorithm at each iteration, 4; penalty factor, 0.95. The population sizes were fixed at 2,000. All parameter settings were determined empirically to be the optimal settings for these data.

Comparison Method. See5 [23], a decision tree inducer based on the C4.5 algorithm [22] was used as the comparison method for evaluating the classification performance of EpiCS. The same training and testing sets as used for the EpiCS trials were used for the See5 runs. To maintain comparability with EpiCS, no boosting or cross-validation was used; in fact, empirical investigation proved these to be detrimental to classification performance using See5. The See5 system was parameterized to produce rule sets, and the AUC was calculated from the classification matrix produced by the software on the testing set.

3   Results

3.1 Effects of Missing Data on Learning Performance

MCAR Data. The effects of MCAR data on learning are demonstrated in Figure 1, which compares the learning rate (λ) obtained at each of the missing value densities. A statistically significant inverse linear trend is evident between λ and the density of missing values (ρ=-1.0, p<0.0001). Generally, the variance in λ, expressed as CV, decreases with increasing density, but this is not statistically significant.

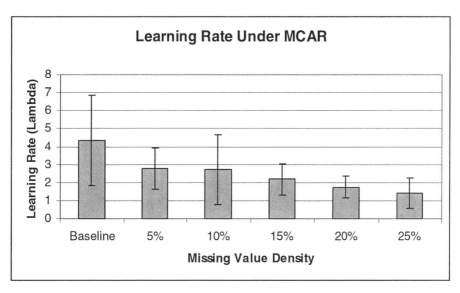

Fig. 1. Plot of learning rate (λ) for each density level of missing values, averaged over 20 trials. Error bars indicate one standard deviation.

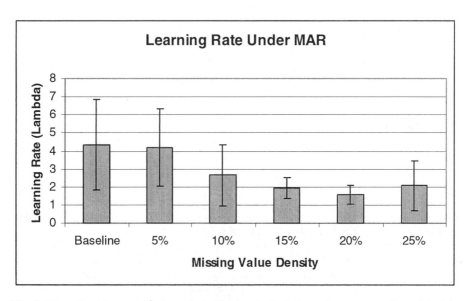

Fig. 2. Plot of learning rate (λ) for each density level of missing values, averaged over 20 trials. Error bars indicate one standard deviation.

MAR Data. The effects of MAR data on learning are demonstrated in Figure 2. Overall, the linear trend noted in MCAR data (Figure 1) appears to prevail, although there is a suggestion that at 25% density, the distribution becomes bimodal. Even so, this relationship is statistically significant (ρ=-0.83, p=0.03). The correlation of CV with density is not statistically significant for MAR data.

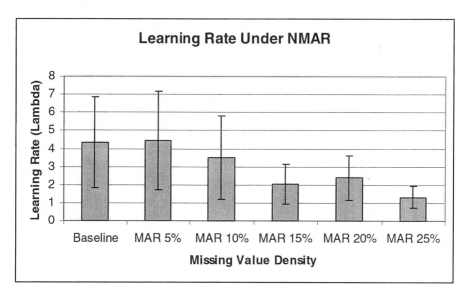

Fig. 3. Plot of learning rate (λ) for each density of missing values, averaged over 20 trials. Error bars indicate one standard deviation.

NMAR Data. While the relationship of missing value density and λ is not as linear as was seen for MCAR and MAR data (Figure 3), it is statistically significant (ρ= -0.89, p<0.05). The highest variance is still seen in the lowest densities of missing data, although the correlation of CV with missing value density is not statistically significant.

Summary of Effects of Missing Data on Learning. As shown in Table 2, the learning rate, λ, was found to be highly negatively correlated with increasing missing value density for all three missing data types. In addition, the coefficient of variation of λ was found to be generally negatively correlated with increasing density, although these correlations failed to reach statistical significance.

Table 2. Correlations (Spearman's ρ) of learning rate (λ) and its coefficient of variation with missing value density across the three missing value types.

	Learning Rate (λ)		Coefficient of Variation of λ	
	ρ	p-value	ρ	p-value
MCAR	-1.0	<0.0001	-0.14	NS
MAR	-0.83	0.04	0.09	NS
NMAR	-0.89	0.02	-0.77	NS

3.2 Effects of Missing Data on Classification Performance

The evaluation of the effect of missing data on classification performance focused on several outcomes. First, the classification accuracy of EpiCS was compared with that of See5 individually for each missing value density and type. Second, the classification performance of EpiCS, measured by the AUC and its CV, was correlated with missing value density across the three types. Third, the density of testing cases that could not be classified, or IR, with its CV, was correlated with missing value density across the three types.

Comparison of Classification Accuracy between EpiCS and See5. The AUCs obtained on testing data for EpiCS and See5 are shown below in Table 3. These AUCs were compared using the Wilcoxson nonparametric test to determine if there existed a significant difference between them at each missing value density and type.

Note that only three AUC pairs were significantly different: MAR 25%, NMAR 20% and NMAR 25%. This is remarkable only in that there may be a *dose-response relationship* (wherein performance is dependent on some way on the density of missing data) that would become evident only at higher missing value densities. It is also possible that this could be caused by artifact in the data, however.

Table 3. Areas under the receiver operating characteristic curve obtained on testing with novel data at each missing value density and type, for EpiCS and See5.

		AUC		
	Density	EpiCS	See5	p-value
	Baseline (0%)	0.9575	0.9421	NS
MCAR	5%	0.922	0.93	NS
	10%	0.896	0.898	NS
	15%	0.9097	0.904	NS
	20%	0.8995	0.904	NS
	25%	0.9016	0.87	NS
MAR	5%	0.9406	0.942	NS
	10%	0.9267	0.946	NS
	15%	0.9158	0.926	NS
	20%	0.8993	0.9322	NS
	25%	0.8912	0.946	<0.005
NMAR	5%	0.9245	0.936	NS
	10%	0.9128	0.924	NS
	15%	0.906	0.932	NS
	20%	0.8598	0.94	<0.001
	25%	0.8942	0.942	<0.001

Correlation of Classification Accuracy with Missing Value Density. Overall, both EpiCS and See5 demonstrated classification accuracies, expressed as AUC, that were highly negatively correlated with missing value density. However, as shown in Table 4, three of these were not statistically significant, MCAR data for EpiCS and MAR and NMAR for See5. It is interesting to note that the trends in correlation for EpiCS and See5 were in opposite directions; it is unclear why this would be the case.

Table 4. Correlations (Speaman's ρ) between missing value density and AUC on testing for EpiCS and See5 across the three missing value types.

	EpiCS		See5	
	ρ	p-value	ρ	p-value
MCAR	-0.60	NS	-0.94	<0.05
MAR	-1.0	<0.0000	-0.73	NS
NMAR	-.94	<0.005	-0.38	NS

Within the EpiCS runs, the coefficient of variation for the AUC obtained at testing showed a linear trend across the three types of missing data, as one moved from MCAR to MAR to NMAR. That is, as the missing values became increasingly non-ignorable, the variation in AUC became increasingly dependent on missing value density, and these correlations became increasingly statistically significant, as shown in Table 5. This indicates that the classification performance of EpiCS is dependent on the density of missing values, and that as one moves toward non-ignorable missing data, classification accuracy, as measured by the AUC, becomes increasingly variable and unstable.

Table 5. Correlations (Speaman's ρ) between the coefficient of variation of the AUC obtained on testing for EpiCS and missing value density.

	ρ	p-value
MCAR	-0.09	NS
MAR	0.60	NS
NMAR	0.83	<0.05

Effects of Missing Data on Testing Case Classifiability. The Indeterminant Rate (IR) was calculated for the EpiCS runs to indicate the proportion of novel testing cases that could not be classified, that is, not matchable within a trained macroclassifier population. The IR could not be calculated for the See5 runs, as all testing data were seemingly classifiable, according to the classification matrix provided by the software. Table 6 demonstrates that the IR was highly positively correlated with increasing missing value density, although the coefficient of variation for IR was not at all not correlated. Thus, the IR was adversely affected by the density of missing values across the three missing data types, and there is no significant variability in this phenomenon.

Table 6. Effect of missing data on the Indeterminant Rate and its coefficient of variation. Correlations (Spearman's ρ) are between the IR (or its coefficient of variation) obtained on testing for EpiCS and missing value density.

	Indeterminant Rate (IR)		Coefficient of Variation of IR	
	ρ	p-value	ρ	p-value
MCAR	1.0	<0.001	0.41	NS
MAR	1.0	<0.001	-0.85	NS
NMAR	0.95	<0.005	0.46	NS

4 Discussion

Effects of Missing Data on Learning. Figures 1-3 clearly demonstrate that missing data has a deleterious effect on the learning performance of EpiCS. This effect is dependent on the density of missing data, implying a dose-response relationship. In addition, learning is negatively affected according to the *type* of missing data, with NMAR data having the most serious effect. However, there was no statistically significant correlation of the CV of λ with increasing missing value density across the three types of missing data, as shown in Table 2.

A decrease in the variance of λ was observed in higher missing value densities, and it is not clear why this should be the case. One possible explanation could be that there is intrinsically less variance in a missing value (which can take on only a single value) than in non-missing data, which can take on either a 0 or 1 in these data. With increasing densities of missing data, there are fewer data points with the opportunity for two values.

Effects of Missing Data on Classification Accuracy. The classification accuracy, as AUC, of EpiCS was compared with that of See5 at each of the five missing value densities and for each of the three missing value types. Both systems performed very well on classification, with AUCs typically above 0.90. With the exception of three of the 16 instances, no statistically significant difference was observed between the respective AUCs. These results indicate that EpiCS classified these data as well as See5, an accepted gold standard for inducing decision rules for classification. The three occasions where they were significantly different, on 25% MAR data and at the 20% and 25% density of NMAR data, indicate that there might be a dose-response relationship in the difference between EpiCS and See5, as this pertains to the classification accuracy and density. One potentially troubling conclusion would be that EpiCS becomes less robust than See5 on classification tasks at higher missing value densities, especially for NMAR data. This could be evaluated only on pursuing an investigation similar to the current one that includes all densities up to 100%.

It was found that classification accuracy was negatively correlated with increasing density for both EpiCS and See5. The correlation for EpiCS was not significant for MCAR data, but was very high and strongly significant for MAR and NMAR data, indicating that EpiCS was extremely sensitive to the density of missing data overall, especially for data which are not MCAR. The correlation of density and AUC on testing for See5 was found to be not significant, except for MCAR data. Even so, the correlations were very high (although lowest for NMAR data), suggesting that See5 may also be sensitive to increasing missing value density across the three types. This question could be resolved by performing this investigation with a suite of many datasets, representing random samples from a large universe of data, similar to a bootstrap. Unfortunately, it is not possible in this investigation to draw any firm conclusions about the effects of missing value density on classification accuracy for See5, given that the correlations are not significant.

In looking at the CVs for the AUC data obtained on testing EpiCS with novel data, one finds a pattern of correlations suggestive of a dose-response relationship, where "dose" is the density of missing data. At this juncture, the relationship is merely suggested, owing to the lack of significant correlations for MCAR and MAR data. However, the trend toward increasing correlation of variation with increasing missing value density seems to indicate that the classification performance of EpiCS may be increasingly unstable at higher densities of missing data, and that this relationship may be strongest (and statistically significant) in NMAR data. This suggests that increasing the number of runs when using data with high densities of missing data, especially NMAR, would be a sound strategy for improving classification performance. Unfortunately, there is no way to compare EpiCS with See5 on CV, as See5 isn't an evolutionary approach and therefore doesn't give varying results from run to run on the same data. It would be interesting to compare the CVs obtained on testing with other evolutionary-based approaches, however.

The IR is extremely dependent on missing value density, suggesting that unless the classification metrics obtained for EpiCS on missing data are corrected for IR, they may overestimate the classification accuracy of the system. Another remarkable observation is that the correlation of CV for the IR with missing value density is not statistically significant for any of the three missing data types. This seems to suggest that the IR is very stable (albeit positively correlated), regardless of missing value density. Again, a larger, bootstrap-style study using many different datasets with many different missing value patterns would help to confirm this.

Limitations of This Study. While there is much in this investigation to suggest that EpiCS is sensitive to missing data in terms of learning rate and classification accuracy, there are several ways to confirm these conclusions. First, only two features in the data were used as candidates for missing data. It would be very interesting to extend the patterns of missing data to sets of features that included more than one each, such that x and/or y would have many features contained within them. It should be noted, however, that doing so would substantially increase the complexity of the analysis, due to the possibility for interactions, so these would have to be handled carefully in creating the datasets.

Second, this investigation focused on only one LCS, EpiCS. Although there is no reason to assume that they would perform significantly differently, XCS [27] and ACS [4, 25] should also be examined, as should other evolutionary computing approaches to data mining and autonomous control, such genetic programming and evolutionary strategies.

Finally, the system chosen for comparing EpiCS on classification, See5, is apparently not as robust in the presence of missing data as many have previously thought. Clearly, See5 does quite well on classification in general, yet it shows some sensitivity to the density of missing data in this regard. Further investigation should of course include See5 on the use of bootstrapped datasets, but it should also include other comparator methods, such as naïve Bayes classification, which are used extensively in data mining.

5   Conclusions

This investigation is the first report into the effects of missing data on the learning and classification performance in a learning classifier system. In general, EpiCS, and possibly other LCS paradigms as well, is sensitive to missing data, and this sensitivity is related to the degree to which such data is present in a dataset (or other environment), as well as the type of missing data. With that in mind, LCS researchers should consider these effects, and determine if missing data are a problem in their environment, whether it is a database or a real-time agent-based setting.

A future task, in addition to researching the effects of a wider range of missing value densities and patterns in a variety of dataset sizes, is to study the effects of imputation on LCS performance. Now that it is clear that missing data have a deleterious effect on LCS performance, and given that missing data are nearly always present in databases and other environments, that doesn't mean that LCS researchers are consigned to acceptance of poor performance. It has been shown in statistics that the application of various imputation methods, in an effort to reduce the density of missing data, has been a very successful endeavor in improving the accuracy and robustness of statistical inferences. Further investigation into these techniques and their possible application to the LCS may reveal a similar benefit.

References

1. Anand S.S., Bell D.A., Hughes J.G.: EDM: a general framework for data mining based on evidence theory. Data & Knowledge Engineering (1996) 18(3):189-223.
2. Bing, L., Ke, W., Lai-Fun, M., Xin-Zhi, Q.: Using decision tree induction for discovering holes in data. PRICAI'98: Topics in Artificial Intelligence. 5th Pacific Rim International Conference on Artificial Intelligence. Springer-Verlag, Berlin (1998), 182-93.
3. Bonelli, P., Parodi, A., Sen, S., Wilson, S.: NEWBOOLE: A fast GBML system, in: Porter, B. and Mooney, R. (eds.), Machine Learning: Proceedings of the Seventh International Conference. Morgan Kaufmann, San Mateo, CA (1990), 153-159.
4. Butz M.V., Goldberg, D.E., Stolzmann, W.: Investigating generalization in the anticipatory classifier system. Schoenauer M, Deb K, Rudolph G, et al (eds.): Parallel Problem Solving from Nature –PPSN VI, Proceedings of The Sixth International Conference (2000), 735-44.
5. Fengzhan, T., Hongwei, Z., Yuchang, L., Chunyi, S.: Incremental learning of Bayesian networks with hidden variables. Proceedings 2001 IEEE International Conference on Data Mining. IEEE Computing. Society, Los Alamitos, CA (2001), 651-2.
6. Holmes J.H.: Quantitative methods for evaluating learning classifier system performance In forced two-choice decision tasks. In: Wu, A. (ed.) Proceedings of the Second International Workshop on Learning Classifier Systems (IWLCS99). Morgan Kaufmann, San Francisco (1999), 250-257.
7. Holmes JH, Durbin DR, Winston FK: A new bootstrapping method to improve classification performance in learning classifier systems. Schoenauer M, Deb K, Rudolph G, et al (eds.): Parallel Problem Solving from Nature –PPSN VI, Proceedings of The Sixth International Conference (2000), 745-754.
8. Holmes JH, Durbin DR, Winston FK: The Learning Classifier System: An evolutionary computation approach to knowledge discovery in epidemiologic surveillance. Artificial Intelligence in Medicine (2000) 19(1): 53-74.
9. Holmes JH: A new representation for assessing classifier performance in mining large databases. To be published in Lecture Notes in Artificial Intelligence, 2002.
10. Jui-Chung. H., Bor-Sen, C., Wen-Sheng, H., Li-Mei, C.: Spectral estimation under nature missing data. 2001 IEEE International Conference on Acoustics, Speech, and Signal Processing. Proceedings IEEE, Piscataway, NJ (2001), 3061-4.
11. Kalousis A, Hilario M.: Supervised knowledge discovery from incomplete data. Data Mining II. Second International Conference on Data Mining. WIT Press. Southampton, UK (2000), 269-78.

12. Kryszkiewicz, M.: Association rules in incomplete databases. Methodologies for Knowledge Discovery and Data Mining. Third Pacific-Asia Conference, PAKDD-99. Springer-Verlag, Berlin (1999), 84-93.
13. Kryszkiewicz, M. and Rybinski, H.: Incomplete database issues for representative association rules. Foundations of Intelligent Systems. 11th International Symposium, ISMIS'99. Springer-Verlag, Berlin (1999), 583-91.
14. Laurikkala J., Juhola M., Lammi S., Viikki K.: Comparison of genetic algorithms and other classification methods in the diagnosis of female urinary incontinence. Methods of Information in Medicine (1999), 38(2):125-131.
15. Little R.J.A. and Rubin, D.B.: Statistical Analysis with Missing Data. John Wiley and Sons, New York, 1986.
16. Liu W.Z., White A.P., Hallissey M.T.: A learning system for gastric cancer diagnosis. Proceedings of International Conference on Neural Information Processing (ICONIP '95). Publishing House of Electron. Ind., Beijing (1995), 285-8.
17. Martinez-Trinidad J.F., Sanchez-Diaz G.. LC: a conceptual clustering algorithm. Machine Learning and Data Mining in Pattern Recognition. Second International Workshop, MLDM 2001. (Lecture Notes in Artificial Intelligence Vol.2123). Springer-Verlag, Berlin (2001), 117-27.
18. McNeil B.J. Hanley, J.A.: Statistical approaches to the analysis of receiver operating characteristic (ROC) curves. Med Decision Making (1984) 4:137-150.
19. Melli, Gabor: http://www.datasetgenerator.com/
20. Myers J.W., Laskey K.B., DeJong K.A.: Learning Bayesian networks from incomplete data using evolutionary algorithms. GECCO-99. Proceedings of the Genetic and Evolutionary Computation Conference. Joint Meeting of the Eighth International Conference on Genetic Algorithms (ICGA-99) and the Fourth Annual Genetic Programming Conference (GP-99). Morgan Kaufmann Publishers. San Francisco (1999), 458-65.
21. Ng, V. and Lee J.: Quantitative association rules over incomplete data. [Conference Paper] SMC'98 Conference Proceedings. 1998 IEEE International Conference on Systems, Man, and Cybernetics, IEEE, New York (1998), 2821-6.
22. Quinlan, J.R.: C4.5: Programs for Machine Learning. Morgan Kaufmann, San Mateo, CA (1993).
23. RuleQuest Research Pty Ltd.: See5 for Windows NT.
24. Sarle W.S.: Prediction with missing inputs. [Conference Paper] Joint Conference on Intelligent Systems 1999 (JCIS'98). Association. for Intelligent. Machinery. (1998), 399-402.
25. Stolzmann W.: Anticipatory Classifier Systems: An introduction. AIP. American Institute of Physics Conference Proceedings, no.573, (2001), 470-6.
26. Ultsch A.: A neural network learning relative distances. [Conference Paper] Proceedings of the IEEE-INNS-ENNS International Joint Conference on Neural Networks. IJCNN 2000, Neural Computing: New Challenges and Perspectives for the New Millennium. IEEE Computing Society, Los Alamitos, CA (2000), 553-8.
27. Wilson, S.W.: Classifier fitness based on accuracy, Evolutionary Computation (1995) 3:149-175.

XCS's Strength-Based Twin: Part I

Tim Kovacs

Department of Computer Science
University of Bristol
Bristol BS8 1UB, England
kovacs@cs.bris.ac.uk
http://www.cs.bris.ac.uk/~kovacs

Abstract. Wilson's XCS has rapidly become the most popular classifier system of all time, and is a major focus of current research. XCS's primary distinguishing feature is that it bases rule fitness on the accuracy with which rules predict reward, rather than the magnitude of the reward predicted (as traditional, strength-based systems do). XCS is a complex system and differs from other systems in a number of ways. In order to isolate the source of XCS's adaptive power, and, in particular to study the difference between strength and accuracy-based fitness, we introduce a system called Strength-Based XCS (SB–XCS), which is as similar to the accuracy-based XCS as we could make it, apart from being strength-based. This work provides a specification of SB–XCS and initial results for it and XCS on the 6 multiplexer and woods2 tasks. It then analyses the solutions found by the two systems and finds that each prefers a particular type of solution. A sequel paper provides further analysis.

1   Introduction

This work presents part of an ongoing comparison of strength and accuracy-based approaches to fitness calculation in Learning Classifier Systems (LCS). In order to compare strength and accuracy-based fitness, we defined Strength-Based XCS (SB–XCS), which differs as little as possible from the accuracy-based XCS, and which has been in use since [21][1]. SB–XCS was used rather than some existing strength-based LCS because the similarity of XCS and SB–XCS allows us to isolate the effects of the fitness calculation on performance in a way we cannot with any other strength LCS. Other strength-based systems differ from XCS in many ways, such as how rule strength is calculated and how actions are selected, in addition to the obvious difference in fitness calculation.

SB–XCS is not simply a straw man for XCS to outperform. It is a functional LCS, and is capable of finding optimal solutions to some tasks. SB–XCS is competitive with, for example, Wilson's Boole [32] and ZCS [35] systems, at least on the 6 multiplexer task we will use in §3. Having said this, SB–XCS lacks the fitness sharing other strength-based systems (e.g. ZCS) have, and this is bound to limit the tasks to which it can adapt. Indeed, we will see that SB–XCS cannot perform optimally on the Woods2 task.

---

[1] At one stage SB–XCS was called Goliath [22].

P.L. Lanzi et al. (Eds.): IWLCS 2002, LNAI 2661, pp. 61–80, 2003.

Why study SB–XCS when we expect it to have such limitations? SB–XCS's is intended as a tool for studying LCS, rather than as a practical alternative to XCS. SB–XCS's value is that we can study when and why it fails, and can attribute any difference between its performance and that of XCS to the difference in fitness calculation. One consequence is that we are more interested in comparing the qualitative performance on the two than their quantitative performance, and few attempts have been made to optimise SB–XCS.

Why not add fitness sharing to SB–XCS? Fitness sharing complicates the behaviour of a classifier system greatly, which limits the analysis we can perform on it. This would limit the results we have obtained with it, both those presented here and those in [24], and make their presentation far more difficult. However, the work presented here is ongoing, and the intention is to add fitness sharing to SB–XCS and to compare the resulting system to the original.

This work is organised as follows. Section 2 provides a specification of SB–XCS, and compares it to ZCS. Section 3 tests XCS, SB–XCS, and tabular Q-learning on the 6 multiplexer and Woods2 tasks. Section 4 analyses the populations evolved by XCS and SB–XCS for the 6 multiplexer. Finally, section 5 summarises the work so far, and a subsequent paper picks up with an analysis of the populations evolved by the two systems, and of the types of representations towards which they tend.

2   Specification of SB–XCS

XCS is described elsewhere [9] and we will not duplicate this material here. Instead, we assume some familiarity with XCS, and specify SB–XCS by referring to its differences with XCS. (For specification of both XCS and SB–XCS see [24].) The following sections describe the modifications made to XCS to produce SB–XCS.

2.1   Rule Fitness

To update rule strength, SB–XCS uses the same Q-learning update XCS uses to calculate a rule's prediction:

$$p_j \leftarrow p_j + \beta(P - p_j) \tag{1}$$

where p_j is the prediction of rule j, and $0 < \beta \leq 1$ is a value controlling the learning rate. For non-sequential tasks:

$$P = r_t \tag{2}$$

where r_t is the reward at time t. For sequential tasks:

$$P = r_{t-1} + \gamma \max_i P(a_i) \tag{3}$$

where $0 \leq \gamma \leq 1$ is the *discount rate* which weights the contribution of the next time step to the value of P, and $P(a_i)$ is the system prediction for action a_i (see §2.2). Note that (3) reduces to (2) when $\gamma = 0$.

That is, the strength of a rule in SB–XCS is identical to the prediction of a rule in XCS; only the name differs. However, whereas XCS goes on to calculate prediction error and other parameters involved in fitness calculation, SB–XCS simply uses strength as the rule's fitness. This simplification of the XCS updates is in fact the only major difference between XCS and SB–XCS; a number of other modifications are necessary to make SB–XCS a functional system, but all are minor.

Note 1. Since (3) is the tabular Q-learning update, SB–XCS uses Q-values for both action selection and as rule fitness in the GA.

Note 2. XCS factors a rule's numerosity into its fitness using the relative accuracy update. Since SB–XCS does not use this update, its strength/fitness does not take numerosity into account. Consequently, we must explicitly factor numerosity into fitness, unlike in XCS.

Note 3. XCS's relative accuracy update provides fitness sharing. Since SB–XCS does not use this update, it does not implement fitness sharing. SB–XCS could, of course, be modified to add fitness sharing.

2.2   System Prediction and System Strength Calculations

In XCS, a rule's contribution to the system prediction[2] for its action is a function of both its prediction and fitness:

$$P(a_i) = \frac{\sum\limits_{c \in [M]_{a_i}} F_c \cdot p_c}{\sum\limits_{c \in [M]_{a_i}} F_c} \tag{4}$$

where $[M]_{a_i}$ is the subset of the match set $[M]$ advocating action a_i, F_c is the fitness of rule c and p_c is its prediction.

In SB–XCS, however, a rule's fitness is its strength, so there is no separate fitness parameter to factor into the calculation. We do, however, need to explicitly factor numerosity into the prediction, as explained in note 2 above.

Removing fitness from equation (4) and factoring in numerosity we obtain the *System Strength*:

$$S(a_i) = \sum\limits_{c \in [M]_{a_i}} p_c \cdot numerosity(c) \tag{5}$$

In preparation for action selection, SB–XCS constructs a system strength array using (5), just as XCS constructs a system prediction array using (4). Note, however, that the two differ in that the system strength (5) for an action is *not* a prediction of the reward to be received for taking it. For example, suppose that in a given state action 1 receives a reward of 1000, and that the only matching macroclassifier advocating action 1 has strength 1000 and numerosity 2. The system strength for action 1 is $P(a_1) = 1000 \cdot 2 = 2000$, twice the actual reward since there are two copies of the rule.

---

[2] The system's estimate of the return it will receive if it takes a given action.

In order to estimate the return for an action, we must divide the system prediction by the numerosity of the rules which advocate it. For this purpose, we define the *System Prediction* in SB–XCS as:

$$P(a_i) = \frac{S(a_i)}{\displaystyle\sum_{c\in[M]_{a_i}} numerosity(c)}$$
$$= \frac{\displaystyle\sum_{c\in[M]_{a_i}} p_c \cdot numerosity(c)}{\displaystyle\sum_{c\in[M]_{a_i}} numerosity(c)} \tag{6}$$

The system prediction is needed to calculate the target for the Q-update in sequential tasks (3).

In summary, whereas XCS uses system prediction for both action selection and the Q-update, SB–XCS uses system strength for the former and system prediction only for the latter.

2.3   Subsumption Deletion

SB–XCS does not use either form of subsumption deletion [9], since these techniques make reference to a rule's accuracy. Although it might be possible to develop useful forms of subsumption deletion for strength-based systems, we will not investigate this here.

2.4   Selection for Reproduction

In preliminary tests with the 6 multiplexer function (to be introduced in §3.1) it was found that SB–XCS's rule population was swamped with overgeneral rules, and that the rules with the greatest numerosity were those with fully general conditions. Reasoning that the generalisation pressure due to the niche GA was overwhelming the selective pressure in reproduction, the roulette wheel selection inherited from XCS was replaced with tournament selection (see [2]), in which the degree of selective pressure is parameterised by the size of the tournament. Figure 1 shows SB–XCS's performance using roulette wheel selection and tournament selection with tournament sizes of 2, 4, and 16. Curves are averages of 10 runs, and a full explanation of the experimental procedure (including the performance metric $\mathcal{P}$) is given in §3.1. Figure 1 clearly shows that greater selective pressure (resulting from larger tournament sizes) results in better performance, in accord with the hypothesis that generalisation pressure swamps selective pressure using roulette selection.

It should be noted that in both roulette and tournament selection, SB–XCS factors a rule's numerosity into its probability of selection.

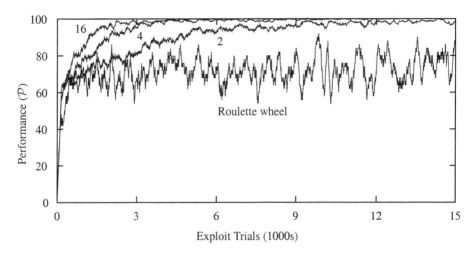

Fig. 1. SB–XCS with roulette and tournament selection on the 6 multiplexer.

2.5   Selection for Deletion

Using tournament selection SB–XCS evolved accurate, general rules for the 6 multiplexer, and achieved good performance. It was noted, however, that numerous overgeneral rules survived in the population, despite the selective pressure against them. For simplicity the preliminary tests employed random deletion, and, in order to introduce further pressure against overgeneral rules, this was replaced with tournament selection. The rule with the lowest strength of those in the tournament was deleted. This modification reduced the number of overgenerals in SB–XCS's population and improved performance on the 6 multiplexer slightly.

2.6   Comments on SB–XCS's Specification

These minor differences make the implementation of SB–XCS very close to that of XCS, which allows us to easily convert an implementation of XCS into SB–XCS. More importantly, the near identity of the algorithms allows us to attribute differences in their capacities to the difference in the fitness calculation. We will see that these minor differences – mainly the change in fitness calculation – have a major effect on how the system operates and on its capacities.

2.7   Comparison of SB–XCS and Other Strength LCS

SB–XCS makes no attempt to encourage the formation or survival of default hierarchies, although it is not unique among strength LCS in this respect. (Wilson's ZCS [35] and Boole [32] systems, for example, do not encourage them either.) The resemblance of SB–XCS and Wilson's ZCS is particularly strong, as we outline below.

ZCS was intended as a minimalist strength-based LCS, but was in many ways a precursor to XCS, which accounts for its similarity to SB–XCS. Nonetheless, the two differ in a number of ways:

- Most significantly, SB–XCS does not (currently) employ fitness sharing, whereas ZCS does.
- ZCS employs a different strength update rule ([35] p. 6)[3].
- ZCS does not employ a niche GA ([35] p. 7), though Wilson suggests a niche GA as an extension ([35] p. 21).
- ZCS employs a deletion scheme in which deletion probability is proportional to the inverse of a rule's strength ([35] p. 7), which is similar but not identical to SB–XCS's tournament deletion.
- ZCS employs a tax intended to encourage it to choose the same action consistently in a given state ([35] p. 6).
- In ZCS, GA invocation occurs with a fixed probability on each cycle ([35] p. 7).
- In ZCS, parents give half their strength to their offspring when they are created ([35] p. 7).

3   Initial Tests of XCS and SB–XCS

In this section we briefly apply XCS and SB–XCS to two problems from the LCS literature: the 6 multiplexer (a non-sequential task), and Woods2 (a sequential task). Neither the 6 multiplexer nor Woods2 is very difficult, but they are the primary tasks to which XCS has been applied in the literature, and, in any case, they provide a basic test of SB–XCS and an opportunity to compare it to XCS.

3.1   The 6 Multiplexer

The first task to which we apply the two systems is the venerable 6 multiplexer function, the most widely used test in the LCS literature [32, 29, 33, 6, 13, 5, 31, 25, 12, 14, 15, 11, 36, 16, 18, 19, 38, 10, 20, 3, 7, 8, 23]. It has also been used with other machine learning systems including neural networks [4, 1, 17, 5, 30], perceptrons [34], decision trees [28, 27], and the GPAC algorithm [26]. See [25] for a review of some of the earlier work using the multiplexer.

Definition. The 6 multiplexer is one of a family of Boolean multiplexer functions defined for strings of length $L = k + 2^k$ where k is an integer > 0. The series begins $L = 3, 6, 11, 20, 37, 70, 135, 264, 521 \ldots$. The first k bits are used to encode an address into the remaining 2^k bits, and the value of the function is the value of the addressed bit. In the 6 multiplexer ($k = 2, L = 6$), the input to the system consists of a string of six binary digits, of which the first $k = 2$ bits (the address) represent an index into the remaining $2^k = 4$ bits (the data). E.g., the value of 101101 is 0 as the first two bits 10 represent the index 2 (in base ten) which is the third bit following the address. Similarly, the value of 001000 is 1 as the 0th bit after the address is indexed.

Use as an RL Task. To use the 6 multiplexer as a test, on each time step we generate a random binary string of 6 digits which we present as input to the LCS. The LCS responds with either a 0 or 1, and receives a high reward (1000) if its output is that of the multiplexer function on the same string, and a low reward (0) otherwise.

---

[3] Page numbers refer to the electronic version of [35] which is available on the net.

Measuring Performance. We use Wilson's explore/exploit framework [36,24], in which training and testing interleave, so the learner is evaluated on-line, that is, as it is learning, rather than after it has been trained. Each time the system is presented with a new input we take the opportunity of evaluating its response and updating our statistics regarding its performance. In fact, we alternate between exploit trials (in which the system selects the action it thinks is best) and explore trials (in which it choose an action at random). Learning only occurs on explore trials, and performance statistics are generated only on exploit trials.

Wilson defines a measure of performance which he refers to simply as "performance" [36], but which we'll refer to as $\mathcal{P}$ in order to distinguish it from the more general notion of performance. $\mathcal{P}$ is defined as a moving average of the proportion of the last n trials in which the system has responded with the correct action, where n is customarily 50. That is, on each time step, we determine the proportion of the last n time steps on which the LCS has taken the correct action. The $\mathcal{P}$ curve is scaled so that when the system has acted correctly on all of the last 50 time steps it reaches the top of the figure, and when it has acted incorrectly on all these time steps it reaches the bottom of the figure.

In addition to $\mathcal{P}$, we'll monitor the number of *macro*classifiers in the population on each time step, which gives us an indication of the diversity in the rule population. In the following tests, this value is divided by 1000 in order to display it simultaneously with the $\mathcal{P}$ curve.

The macroclassifier curve initially starts at 0 since we start the LCS with an empty rule population and use covering ([36]) to generate initial rules. This curve can at most reach the population size limit, which would occur when each rule in the population had a unique condition/action pair.

Parameter		Value
Subsumption threshold	θ_{sub}	20
GA threshold	θ_{GA}	25
t3 deletion threshold	θ_{del}	25
Covering threshold	θ_{mna}	1
Low-fitness deletion threshold	δ	0.1
Population size limit	N	400
Learning rate	β	0.2
Accuracy falloff rate	α	0.1
Accuracy criterion	ε_o	0.01
Crossover rate	χ	0.8
Mutation rate	μ	0.04
Hash probability	$P_\#$	0.33

Fig. 2. Standard XCS parameter settings for the 6 multiplexer.

Parameter Settings. The standard XCS parameter settings for the 6 multiplexer used since [36, 38] were used with XCS. See figure 2. SB–XCS used the relevant subset of these settings, and used tournament sizes of 32 for selecting parents and 4 for selecting rules to delete. These two values were chosen after a brief comparison of alternative settings – no serious attempt was made to optimise them.

For this test, neither system used action set covering, instead using the original match set covering ([24]). XCS was in fact tested twice, once with neither form of subsumption, and once with GA subsumption only. SB–XCS used neither form of subsumption deletion since it is incapable of doing so (§2.3).

Results and Discussion. Figure 3 shows the $\mathcal{P}$ and population size curves for XCS and SB–XCS on the 6 multiplexer, averaged over 10 runs. The number of exploit trials is shown on the X-axis; recall that using Wilson's explore/exploit scheme we alternate explore and exploit trials so that the LCS has actually seen twice as many inputs as indicated, although it has only used the indicated number for learning.

Performance: $\mathcal{P}$. We can see that the $\mathcal{P}$ curves converge stably to the top of the figure in all three cases, suggesting the entire input/output mapping was successfully learnt. Although SB–XCS takes somewhat longer than XCS to initially reach the top, and even longer to stabilise there, we are not concerned with slight differences in performance here. What does concern us is that they both solve the problem, and do so in roughly the same amount of time.

Macroclassifiers. SB–XCS's macroclassifiers curve is the most steady of the three, showing a very gradual downward trend following the initial steep increase. With GA subsumption, XCS's curve shows a much steeper decline following the initial increase, and towards the end it has a much smaller population size than SB–XCS. Without subsumption, however, XCS's curve declines only very gradually, and its population size eventually almost exactly equals SB–XCS's.

These results suggest that while XCS with GA subsumption quickly converges on a relatively small number of useful rules, in the other two cases the population contains a large number of redundant (overly specific) and overgeneral rules. Inspection of the populations evolved by SB–XCS and XCS with subsumption bears this out. (The evolved populations are shown in §4.)

Conclusions. There are two points to note. First, XCS's ability to represent the solution with few rules is due to subsumption deletion rather than to its accuracy-based fitness. Second, XCS's $\mathcal{P}$ is somewhat better than that of SB–XCS. We might hypothesise that this is due to the larger population it allows itself in the early phase of the test. However, we'll see an argument in §4.3 that XCS's fitness update leads to more effective evolutionary search than SB–XCS's.

No major attempt was made to optimise SB–XCS, and improvements to it are likely possible. However, the results of this test indicate that it is a functional classifier system, and in fact compares favourably with other strength-based LCS on this task. Its performance on the 6 multiplexer is much superior to that of SCS ([13] p. 256), and superior to Wilson's BOOLE [32], which reached approximately 94% performance after a little more than 5000 time steps.

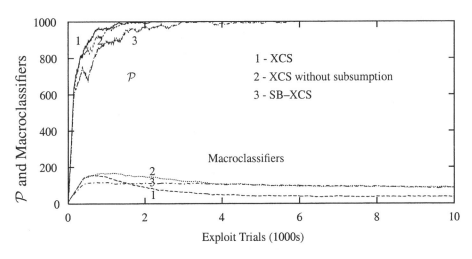

Fig. 3. XCS and SB–XCS on the 6 multiplexer.

Bonelli et al.'s NEWBOOLE [5] outperformed SB–XCS on this task, but NEW-BOOLE is a supervised learning system, so it faces an easier task than SB–XCS does. Non-LCS approaches, e.g., C4 [28] and GPAC [26], have been shown to solve this task more quickly than either XCS or SB–XCS (see [25] for a survey).

3.2 Woods2

Woods2 is a Markov sequential decision task introduced in [36], designed to allow generalisation over parts of the input space. The environment consists of a two-dimensional gridworld containing two types of rock (Q and O), two types of food (F and G) and empty cells (.). Its top and bottom and left and right edges are connected (i.e., it is toroidal).

The classifier system is used as the control system for an animat which acts in this environment, and whose goal is to reach food in as few steps as possible. On each time step, input to the classifier system consists of a 24-bit string representing the contents of the 8 cells immediately adjacent to the animat, starting with the cell to the North and moving clockwise. Each cell is coded using 3 bits as follows: F = 110, G = 111, O = 010, Q = 011, and empty cells = 000. The agent can move by 1 cell in one of 8 directions, with action 0 taking it to the North, 1 to the North East, and so on clockwise through action 7 to the North West. Actions are coded as 3-bit binary strings.

State transitions are deterministic and the animat's actions always have the intended effect, except that attempts to move into rock result in no change in position. An episode consists of placing the animat in a randomly chosen blank space (.) and allowing it to move until it reaches food, at which point the episode ends. Woods2 is shown in figure 4.

The animat receives a reward of 1000 when it takes an action which brings it to a food state (F or G), and 0 at all other times. Wilson discusses Woods2 and XCS's performance in it at some length in [36].

```
. . . . . . . . . . . . . . . . . . . . . . . . . . . .
.QQF..QQF..OQF..QQG..OQG..QQF.
.OOO..QOO..OQO..OOQ..QQO..QQQ.
.OOQ..OQQ..OQQ..QQO..OOO..QQO.
. . . . . . . . . . . . . . . . . . . . . . . . . . . .
. . . . . . . . . . . . . . . . . . . . . . . . . . . .
.QOF..QOG..QOF..OOF..OOG..QOG.
.QQO..QOO..OOO..OQO..QQO..QOO.
.QQQ..OOO..OQO..QOQ..QOQ..OQO.
. . . . . . . . . . . . . . . . . . . . . . . . . . . .
. . . . . . . . . . . . . . . . . . . . . . . . . . . .
.QOG..QOF..OOG..OQF..OOG..OOF.
.OOQ..OQQ..QQO..OQQ..QQO..OQQ.
.QQO..OOO..OQO..OOQ..OQQ..QQQ.
. . . . . . . . . . . . . . . . . . . . . . . . . . . .
```

Fig. 4. The layout of Woods2.

How Hard is Woods2? The animat is only ever at most 3 steps from food, so long sequences of actions are not needed to solve the problem; although it is a sequential task, the sequences which must be learnt are quite modest! Acting randomly, the mean number of steps to reach food is 27, while acting optimally the mean is approximately 1.7 steps.

In order to provide a baseline for comparison, a tabular Q-learning system was also tested on Woods2. (See ([24] for details of how the Q-learner was implemented.) Results for all three appear later in this section.

Measuring Performance. Although it is less than fully satisfactory for sequential tasks in general, we again use Wilson's explore/exploit framework as it has been used with XCS and Woods2 in the past [36]. The framework's inefficient exploration should not be a major problem as the number of steps to the goal tend to be relatively small, and the problem of getting stuck in loops is dealt with by simply ending episodes if they reach 100 time steps.

As Woods2 is sequential we alternate between explore and exploit *episodes* rather than trials. That is, we either select actions randomly for the entire episode, or we select the best action for the entire episode. Following Wilson [36], for Woods2 we monitor the number of macroclassifiers in the population on each time step and record a moving average of the number of time steps taken to reach food during the last 50 exploit episodes.

Parameter Settings. The settings for XCS in Woods2 [37] from the original XCS paper [36] were used for all three systems; XCS, SB–XCS and tabular Q-learning, although the last only uses a small subset of them. See figure 5. In addition, SB–XCS used tournament sizes of 16 for reproduction and 4 for deletion. XCS and SB–XCS both used action set covering [24], although more covering and less improvement result when it is used with SB–XCS than with XCS. XCS used GA subsumption but did not use action set subsumption as this was found to reduce performance on this task.

Parameter		Value
Subsumption threshold	θ_{sub}	20
GA threshold	θ_{GA}	25
t3 deletion threshold	θ_{del}	25
Covering threshold	θ_{mna}	1
Low-fitness deletion threshold δ		0.1
Population size limit	N	800
Learning rate	β	0.2
Accuracy falloff rate	α	0.1
Accuracy exponent	v	5
Accuracy criterion	ε_o	0.01
Crossover rate	χ	0.5
Mutation rate	μ	0.01
Hash probability	$P_{\#}$	0.5

Fig. 5. Standard XCS parameter settings for Woods2.

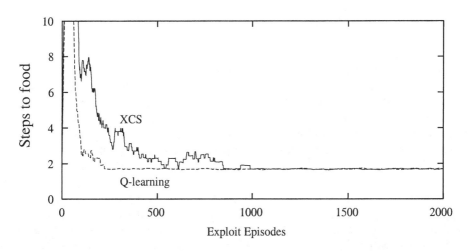

Fig. 6. Performance of XCS and tabular Q-learning on Woods2.

Results and Discussion

XCS and Q-learning. Figure 6 shows the mean steps to food for XCS and tabular Q-learning, averaged over 10 runs. Both converge to optimal performance (≈ 1.7 steps), although XCS takes longer to do so. Figure 7 shows the number of macroclassifiers in XCS's population, and the number of state-action pairs for which the Q-learner estimated Q-values. (Because the input space was immense (2^{24} syntactically possible strings), the Q-learner only allocated state-action pairs as they were needed, accounting for the initial rise in the curve.) XCS is quite effective at generalising in this task, and after 2000 episodes has less than a third as many macroclassifiers as the tabular Q-learner has state-actions.

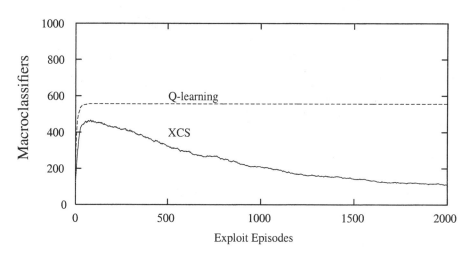

Fig. 7. Population size of XCS and tabular Q-learning on Woods2.

SB–XCS. It was found that SB–XCS's performance was very poor on Woods2. However, after some investigation this was attributed to the use of Wilson's explore/exploit framework. On exploit episodes, when the most highly advocated action is always selected, the system often gets stuck in loops and only ends the episode when it times out after 100 time steps. Because the steps-to-food curve is a moving average of the last 50 exploit episodes, and because results are averaged over 10 runs, this makes performance appear very poor, although the system in fact often behaves optimally for considerable periods.

Although XCS and the tabular Q-learner also often timed out after 100 time steps, they did so only at the outset so later performance was not affected by this problem. Because SB–XCS continued to time out throughout the run, its performance appeared worse than it really was.

To avoid the confounding effect of loops, Wilson's framework was abandoned and much better results were obtained using ϵ-greedy action selection, in which the system selects a random action with probability ϵ and the most highly advocated action otherwise. For the first 10,000 episodes ϵ was 0.1, during which the occasional random actions allowed SB–XCS to break out of loops and avoid timing out (apart from during after the initial period of adaptation). As shown in figure 8, SB–XCS achieved an average of approximately 3 steps to food, which is just how ZCS performed on the related Woods1 task [35], and a little less than twice the optimal ≈ 1.7 steps to food.

Unfortunately, the occasional random actions increase SB–XCS's average steps to food and so slightly complicate the assessment of the quality of its policy. However, we can estimate that since the random actions only added, on average, approximately 1 step to every 10 (since $\epsilon = 0.1$), and since SB–XCS averaged approximately 3 steps to food, the contribution of occasional random actions should be approximately 1/3 of a step per episode. (This estimate is approximate since when actions are chosen at random, $1/8^{th}$ of the time the same action will be chosen as when the best action is chosen. Also, in

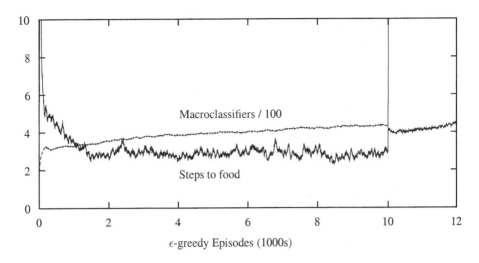

Fig. 8. SB–XCS on Woods2 with $\epsilon = 0.1$ for 10,000 episodes and $\epsilon = 0$ thereafter.

this task some actions are equally good, so choosing a random action is not necessarily inferior.)

In order to evaluate the policy learnt by SB–XCS without the effect of exploration, after 10,000 time steps ϵ was set to 0, meaning it never acted randomly. Although SB–XCS was still able to complete episodes in a few steps on some occasions, it also sometimes got stuck in loops, with episodes timing out after 100 time steps. With $\epsilon = 0$ the average steps to food jumped to approximately 28, as a result of averaging episodes which timed out with those on which SB–XCS was more successful. This indicates that SB–XCS was relying on the occasional random actions to get it out of loops, and that it had not learnt a suitable policy over the entire environment.

SB–XCS was also evaluated on Woods1, in which its performance was almost identical to that in Woods2. It would be interesting to see if ZCS performed as badly in Woods1 if we removed the non-determinism afforded by ZCS's roulette action selection.

4   Analysis of Populations Evolved by XCS and SB–XCS

In this section we return to the 6 multiplexer experiment from §3.1 and inspect sample rule populations evolved by XCS and SB–XCS. Although both systems solved the problem, and did so given a similar number of inputs, their evolved populations differ, and the differences are revealing.

4.1   SB–XCS

Figure 9 shows an extract of 26 rules from a population evolved by SB–XCS in the experiment in §3. The rules have been sorted in order of descending numerosity, and,

Rule	Strength	Numerosity	Experience
0 0 0 # # # → 0	1000	43	726
1 0 # # 1 # → 1	1000	40	900
0 1 # 0 # # → 0	1000	38	865
1 0 # # 0 # → 0	1000	37	833
1 1 # # # 1 → 1	1000	33	954
1 1 # # # 0 → 0	1000	33	675
0 0 1 # # # → 1	1000	32	971
0 1 # 1 # # → 1	1000	25	898
1 1 # 1 # 1 → 1	1000	7	112
1 1 1 # # 0 → 0	1000	6	362
1 # # # 1 # → 1	645	5	12
0 0 1 1 # # → 1	1000	4	88
1 0 0 # 0 # → 0	1000	4	40
# # 1 # # # → 1	668	4	288
# # 0 # # # → 0	640	4	96
1 # # # # 1 → 0	401	4	39
0 1 1 0 # # → 0	1000	3	54
0 # 1 1 # # → 1	1000	3	83
0 # # # # # → 1	508	3	253
# 0 # 1 0 # → 0	569	3	61
0 0 0 # 1 # → 0	1000	3	29
0 0 0 # # 1 → 0	1000	3	24
1 1 # # 0 1 → 1	1000	3	27
0 0 1 0 # # → 1	1000	3	13
0 1 1 1 # # → 1	1000	3	8
1 0 # 1 0 # → 0	1000	3	5

Fig. 9. A subset of the rules evolved by SB–XCS for the 6 multiplexer. Those above the horizontal line have high numerosity while those below have low numerosity.

to save space, only those with 3 or more copies are shown. The total number of macro-classifiers in the population was 64. What can we learn from inspecting this population of rules?

The Solution. Perhaps the first thing we might notice is that the population is split between rules with high numerosity (numerosity ≥ 25) and rules with low numerosity (numerosity ≤ 7). A horizontal line has been inserted between the two sets in order to highlight the division. Let's consider the high numerosity rules. All have high experience, reflecting both their generality and the length of time they have been in use. All have strengths of 1000, and, given their high experience, we can expect this to be an accurate estimate of the reward they will receive on use.

Clearly SB–XCS has found a number of good, general rules, produced many copies of them, and retained them in the population. In fact, these particular 8 rules constitute the unique minimal representation of the 6 multiplexer in the standard ternary language [24] (discounting the use of default hierarchies, which SB–XCS does not support). So SB–XCS has not only solved the problem, but found a representation of it which is optimal in that it consists of a minimal number of rules. Following an earlier convention [18], let us refer to this set of 8 rules as SB–XCS's *optimal solution* for the 6 multiplexer, and denote the set [O].

Subsumed Rules. If the first 8 rules suffice to solve the problem, what about the rest of the population? The remainder consists mainly of rules which also have a strength of 1000, some of which have considerable experience, and some of which do not. Inspection reveals that these rules are more specific versions of the first 8. Since each is subsumed by some more general, but not overgeneral, rule, these rules are redundant. Although they do not have as much numerosity as the first 8 rules, some of them have considerable numerosity, suggesting that SB–XCS might benefit from the introduction of pressure against such subsumed rules.

Overgeneral Rules. In addition, the population contains a number of rules whose strength is neither 1000 nor 0, which tells us they are overgeneral. The strength of these rules is alternately updated towards 1000 (when they take the correct action) and 0 (when they take the incorrect action), and so lies somewhere between the two values. Such rules are unreliable and of little or no value to the system. It would seem that SB–XCS would benefit from the introduction of further pressure against them, in order to reduce the population size. Nonetheless, SB–XCS has succeeded in finding the set of rules which represent the problem minimally, and has learnt to select the correct action for each input.

4.2   XCS

Figure 10 shows an extract of 21 rules from a population evolved by XCS for the 6 multiplexer in the experiment in §3. As before, the rules are sorted in order of numerosity and to save space only those with 2 or more copies are shown, except for the last rule, which is shown despite its numerosity of 1 because it is of special interest. The total number of macroclassifiers in the population was 44.

The Solution. Like SB–XCS's population, XCS's population is split between high and low numerosity rules, and again the two groups are separated by a horizontal line. Two points are worth noting. First, the difference in numerosity between the last member of the top group and the first member of the bottom group is greater in XCS than in SB–XCS, suggesting that XCS is better able to distinguish elements of the solution. Second, XCS has allocated high numerosity to 16 rules while SB–XCS allocated high numerosity to only 8.

Consideration of the 16 high numerosity rules reveals that they consist of the 8 rules in SB–XCS's solution and their complements, that is, the rule with the same condition but the other action. These additional 8 rules all have a prediction of 0, since they all advocate the incorrect action for the inputs they match. Why has XCS allocated high numerosity to these consistently incorrect rules? Precisely because they are consistently incorrect, that is, they accurately predict the reward they will receive, and so have low

Rule	Prediction	Accuracy	Fit.	Numerosity	Exp.
0 1 # 0 # # → 0	1000	1.0	0.981	27	839
1 0 # # 1 # → 1	1000	1.0	0.986	26	937
0 1 # 1 # # → 0	0	1.0	0.998	26	759
0 0 1 # # # → 1	1000	1.0	0.980	25	851
0 0 0 # # # → 0	1000	1.0	0.991	25	841
1 0 # # 0 # → 1	0	1.0	0.976	24	917
1 1 # # # 0 → 0	1000	1.0	0.949	24	857
0 1 # 0 # # → 1	0	1.0	0.984	24	842
0 0 0 # # # → 1	0	1.0	0.986	24	735
1 1 # # # 0 → 1	0	1.0	0.994	23	889
0 1 # 1 # # → 1	1000	1.0	0.999	23	740
1 1 # # # 1 → 0	0	1.0	0.990	21	795
1 0 # # 1 # → 0	0	1.0	0.956	20	958
1 0 # # 0 # → 0	1000	1.0	0.934	19	913
1 1 # # # 1 → 1	1000	1.0	0.989	18	823
0 0 1 # # # → 0	0	1.0	0.999	18	715
0 0 # 0 # # → 1	591	0.0	0.004	3	15
1 1 # 1 # # → 0	600	0.0	0.005	2	5
1 1 # # # # → 1	460	0.0	0.000	2	23
# 0 1 # # # → 1	804	0.0	0.000	2	19
1 # # # 0 0 → 0	1000	1.0	0.120	1	118

Fig. 10. A subset of the rules evolved by XCS for the 6 multiplexer. Those above the horizontal line have high numerosity while those below have low numerosity.

prediction errors and high prediction accuracy and fitness (as the reader can verify from consulting figure 10). To XCS it is irrelevant that these rules advocate the incorrect action and should never be used in action selection; they are accurate and so have high fitness regardless of their utility in action selection.

Following convention, let us refer to these 16 rules as XCS's optimal solution [O] to the 6 multiplexer. (Note that [O] differs depending on whether we refer to XCS or to SB–XCS.) We will investigate the difference in the two representations in the sequel to this paper.

Subsumed Rules. There is a notable lack of subsumed rules in the population evolved by XCS, suggesting it is effective at removing them. Of course, many of the rules not shown were subsumed, but they all have numerosity of only 1.

XCS's superior ability to rid its population of subsumed rules is likely due mainly to its use of GA subsumption, since without GA subsumption XCS's macroclassifier curve converged to approximately the same level as SB–XCS's (see §3). There may, however, be a small effect due to the deletion scheme (t3) XCS used, in which the deletion probability of a rule depends partly on the number of rules in the action sets in which it participates [24]. This places pressure on subsumed rules, since the rules which subsume them necessarily occur in their action sets, mutually increasing their odds of deletion. SB–XCS could easily be modified to use a similar deletion scheme and if so would likely have somewhat fewer subsumed rules in its population.

Overgeneral Rules. In addition to the high numerosity rules, XCS's population contains some overgeneral rules (whose predictions are somewhere between 1000 and 0). As figure 10 shows, these rules have low fitness and low numerosity. Furthermore, they have low experience despite their generality, indicating they have been generated relatively recently. From this we can conclude that these rules represent (inaccurate) hypotheses which XCS has recently generated and which it will likely delete in the near future.

An Extra Rule. The last rule shown in figure 10, $1 \, \# \, \# \, \# \, 0 \, 0 \rightarrow 0$, is an interesting case. It does not belong to the optimal population, nor is it subsumed by any of them. Nor is it overgeneral.

This is an accurate, general rule. In fact, it is just as accurate and general as the rules in [O]. Why is such a good rule only barely represented in the population, with a numerosity of only 1? Why has XCS given this good, general rule a fitness of only 0.12, when elements of [O] have fitness greater than 0.9? The answer is that this rule overlaps with elements of [O], and so competes with them for reproductive trials, and suffers as a result. For more on the subject of competition between overlapping rules in XCS see [24].

4.3   Learning Rate

One reason why XCS's $\mathcal{P}$ is better than SB–XCS's in figure 3 might be that it has a larger population in the early phase of the test. Another explanation is suggested by the rule fitness values shown in figures 9 and 10. The XCS rules either have fitness very close to 1 or very close to 0. In SB–XCS, in contrast, strength/fitness is often 1000, but a number of rules with fitness between 400 and 700 exist. This reflects XCS's sharp distinction between fully accurate and inaccurate rules. The accuracy k_j of rule j is given by:

$$\kappa_j = \begin{cases} 1 & \text{if } \varepsilon_j < \varepsilon_o \\ \alpha(\varepsilon_j/\varepsilon_o)^{-v} & \text{otherwise} \end{cases} \qquad (7)$$

where ε_j is the prediction error of j, and $0 < \varepsilon_o$ is the *accuracy criterion*, a constant controlling the tolerance for prediction error. Any rules with $\varepsilon < \varepsilon_o$ are considered to be equally (and fully) accurate. The *accuracy falloff rate* $0 < \alpha < 1$ and *accuracy exponent* $0 < v$ are constants controlling the rate of decline in accuracy when ε_o is exceeded. (See [36] for details.)

In XCS, fitness drops off very quickly when the accuracy criterion is exceeded. In SB–XCS, however, overgeneral rules can maintain reasonable fitness, and hence slow the convergence of $\mathcal{P}$. This explains the need for greater selection pressure in SB–XCS than XCS in order to achieve good performance (see figure 1). Adding even more selective pressure to SB–XCS might improve its performance.

5   Summary

This paper has given a detailed specification of a system called SB–XCS, which is as similar as possible to XCS while using strength-based fitness.

Empirical evaluation of the two found that although both can solve the non-sequential 6 multiplexer task, only XCS was able to achieve optimal performance on the sequential Woods2 task. Results such as these have long plagued classifier systems research. Why was SB–XCS much more able to adapt to one task than the other? That is, what is it about Woods2 that SB–XCS finds difficult? What part or parts of SB–XCS have this difficulty?

Unfortunately there is no broad theory which predicts when a given classifier system will be able to adapt to a given task. In the absence of theory, the only way to find out how (and if) a classifier system will solve a given task is to try it out. To provide such theory, we need an understanding of what types of task and what types of classifier system are possible, and how they interact. Although we have already distinguished strength and accuracy-based classifier systems, and categorised the tasks to which we might apply them as either sequential or non-sequential, we need to go deeper to provide a predictive theory. Such issues are addressed to some extent in [24].

In the sequel to this paper we will analyse XCS and SB–XCS, the populations they evolve, and the representations towards which they tend in some detail in an attempt to understand the differences between strength and accuracy-based fitness.

References

1. C. W. Anderson. *Learning and Problem solving with multilayer connectionist systems.* PhD thesis, University of Massachusetts, Amherst, MA, USA, 1986.
2. Thomas Bäck, David B. Fogel, and Zbigniew Michalewicz, editors. *Handbook of Evolutionary Computation.* Institute of Physics Publishing and Oxford University Press, 1997.
3. Alwyn Barry. *XCS Performance and Population Structure within Multiple-Step Environments.* PhD thesis, Queens University Belfast, 2000.
4. A. G. Barto, P. Anandan, and C. W. Anderson. Cooperativity in networks of pattern recognizing stochastic learning automata. In *Proceedings of the Fourth Yale Workshop on Applications of Adaptive Systems Theory*, pages 85–90, 1985.
5. Pierre Bonelli, Alexandre Parodi, Sandip Sen, and Stewart Wilson. NEWBOOLE: A Fast GBML System. In *International Conference on Machine Learning*, pages 153–159, San Mateo, California, 1990. Morgan Kaufmann.
6. Lashon B. Booker. Triggered rule discovery in classifier systems. In J. David Schaffer, editor, *Proceedings of the 3rd International Conference on Genetic Algorithms (ICGA-89)*, pages 265–274, George Mason University, June 1989. Morgan Kaufmann.
7. Martin V. Butz, David E. Goldberg, and Wolfgang Stolzmann. Investigating Generalization in the Anticipatory Classifier System. In *Proceedings of Parallel Problem Solving from Nature (PPSN VI)*, 2000. Also technical report 2000014 of the Illinois Genetic Algorithms Laboratory.
8. Martin V. Butz, Tim Kovacs, Pier Luca Lanzi, and Stewart W. Wilson. How XCS Evolves Accurate Classifiers. In Lee Spector, Erik D. Goodman, Annie Wu, W. B. Langdon, Hans-Michael Voigt, Mitsuo Gen, Sandip Sen, Marco Dorigo, Shahram Pezeshk, Max H Garzon, and Edmund Burke, editors, *GECCO-2001: Proceedings of the Genetic and Evolutionary Computation Conference*, pages 927–934. Morgan Kaufmann, 2001.
9. Martin V. Butz and Stewart W. Wilson. An Algorithmic Description of XCS. In Pier Luca Lanzi, Wolfgang Stolzmann, and Stewart W. Wilson, editors, *Advances in Learning Classifier Systems*, number 1996 in LNAI, pages 253–272. Springer–Verlag, 2001.

10. Henry Brown Cribbs III and Robert E. Smith. What Can I do with a Learning Classifier System? In C. Karr and L. M. Freeman, editors, *Industrial Applications of Genetic Algorithms*, pages 299–320. CRC Press, 1998.

11. Bart de Boer. Classifier Systems: a useful approach to machine learning? Master's thesis, Leiden University, 1994. ftp://ftp.wi.leidenuniv.nl/pub/CS/MScTheses/deboer.94. ps.gz.

12. Kenneth A. De Jong and Willliam M. Spears. Learning Concept Classification Rules Using Genetic Algorithms. In *Proceedings of the International Joint Conference on Artificial Intelligence*, pages 651–656, Sidney, Australia, 1991.

13. David E. Goldberg. *Genetic Algorithms in Search, Optimization, and Machine Learning*. Addison-Wesley, Reading, MA, 1989.

14. David Perry Greene and Stephen F. Smith. COGIN: Symbolic induction using genetic algorithms. In *Proceedings 10th National Conference on Artificial Intelligence*, pages 111–116. Morgan Kaufmann, 1992.

15. David Perry Greene and Stephen F. Smith. Using Coverage as a Model Building Constraint in Learning Classifier Systems. *Evolutionary Computation*, 2(1):67–91, 1994.

16. John H. Holmes. *Evolution-Assisted Discovery of Sentinel Features in Epidemiologic Surveillance*. PhD thesis, Drexel University, 1996.

17. R. A. Jacobs. Increased rates of convergence through learning rate adaptation. *Neural Networks*, 1:295–307, 1988.

18. Tim Kovacs. Evolving Optimal Populations with XCS Classifier Systems. Master's thesis, University of Birmingham, 1996.

19. Tim Kovacs. XCS Classifier System Reliably Evolves Accurate, Complete, and Minimal Representations for Boolean Functions. In Roy, Chawdhry, and Pant, editors, *Soft Computing in Engineering Design and Manufacturing*, pages 59–68. Springer–Verlag, London, 1997.

20. Tim Kovacs. Deletion schemes for classifier systems. In W. Banzhaf, J. Daida, A. E. Eiben, M. H. Garzon, V. Honavar, M. Jakiela, and R. E. Smith, editors, *GECCO-99: Proceedings of the Genetic and Evolutionary Computation Conference*, pages 329–336. Morgan Kaufmann, 1999.

21. Tim Kovacs. Strength or accuracy? A comparison of two approaches to fitness calculation in learning classifier systems. In Annie S. Wu, editor, *1999 Genetic and Evolutionary Computation Conference Workshop Program*, pages 258–265, 1999.

22. Tim Kovacs. Towards a theory of strong overgeneral classifiers. In Worthy Martin and William M. Spears, editors, *Foundations of Genetic Algorithms Volume 6*, pages 165–184. Morgan Kaufmann, 2001.

23. Tim Kovacs. What should a classifier system learn? In *Proceedings of the 2001 Congress on Evolutionary Computation (CEC01)*, pages 775–782. IEEE Press, 2001.

24. Tim Kovacs. *A Comparison of Strength and Accuracy-Based Fitness in Learning Classifier Systems*. PhD thesis, School of Computer Science, University of Birmingham, 2002.

25. Gunar E. Liepins and Lori A. Wang. Classifier System Learning of Boolean Concepts. In R. K. Belew and L. B. Booker, editors, *Proceedings of the Fourth International Conference on Genetic Algorithms (ICGA-91)*, pages 318–323, San Mateo, CA, 1991. Morgan Kaufmann Publishers.

26. E. M. Oblow. Implementing Valiant's Learnability Theory using Random Sets. Technical Report ORNL/TM-11512R, Oak Ridge National Laboratory, 1990.

27. G. Pagallo and D. Haussler. Boolean feature discovery in empirical learning. *Machine Learning*, 5(1):71–100, 1990.

28. J. R. Quinlan. An empirical comparison of genetic and decision-tree classifiers. In *Proceedings of the Fifth International Machine Learning Conference*, pages 135–141, 1988.

29. Sandip Sen. Classifier system learning of multiplexer function. The University of Alabama, Tuscaloosa, Alabama. Class Project, 1988.

30. Robert E. Smith and H. Brown Cribbs. Is a Learning Classifier System a Type of Neural Network? *Evolutionary Computation*, 2(1):19–36, 1994.
31. L. A. Wang. Classifier System Learning of the Boolean Multiplexer Function. Master's thesis, Computer Science Department, University of Tennessee, Knoxville, TN, 1990.
32. Stewart W. Wilson. Classifier Systems and the Animat Problem. *Machine Learning*, 2:199–228, 1987.
33. Stewart W. Wilson. Bid competition and specificity reconsidered. *Complex Systems*, 2:705–723, 1989.
34. Stewart W. Wilson. Perceptron Redux: Emergence of Structure. *Physica D*, pages 249–256, 1990.
35. Stewart W. Wilson. ZCS: A Zeroth Level Classifier System. *Evolutionary Computation*, 2(1):1–18, 1994.
36. Stewart W. Wilson. Classifier Fitness Based on Accuracy. *Evolutionary Computation*, 3(2):149–175, 1995.
37. Stewart W. Wilson. Personal communication. November 21, 1996.
38. Stewart W. Wilson. Generalization in the XCS classifier system. In John Koza, Wolfgang Banzhaf, Kumar Chellapilla, Kalyanmoy Deb, Marco Dorigo, David B. Fogel, Max H. Garzon, David E. Goldberg, Hitoshi Iba, and Rick Riolo, editors, *Genetic Programming 1998: Proceedings of the Third Annual Conference*, pages 665–674. Morgan Kaufmann, 1998.

XCS's Strength-Based Twin: Part II

Tim Kovacs

Department of Computer Science
University of Bristol
Bristol BS8 1UB, England
kovacs@cs.bris.ac.uk
http://www.cs.bris.ac.uk/~kovacs

Abstract. This sequel continues the comparison of the twins XCS and SB–XCS. We find they tend towards different representations of the solution and distinguish three types of representations which rule populations can form, namely complete maps, partial maps, and default hierarchies. Following this we evaluate the respective advantages and disadvantages of complete and partial maps at some length. We conclude that complete maps are likely to be superior for sequential tasks. For non-sequential tasks, partial maps have the advantage of parsimony whereas complete maps can take advantage of subsumption deletion. It is unclear which is more significant. We also conclude that partial maps are likely to be suitable for Pittsburgh classifier systems and supervised learning systems.

1 Introduction

This paper continues the comparison of strength and accuracy-based Learning Classifier Systems (LCS) presented in part I, using XCS and its strength-based twin SB–XCS. Section 2 distinguishes three types of representations which rule populations can form, namely complete maps, partial maps, and default hierarchies, using the 6 multiplexer as an example. We will see that while XCS evolves a complete map for the 6 multiplexer, SB–XCS evolves a partial map. Section 3 evaluates the advantages and disadvantages of complete and partial maps, and, finally, section 4 concludes.

2 Different Goals, Different Representations

Although the difference in fitness calculation between XCS and SB–XCS may seem minor – after all, most of their machinery is still identical – it has profound implications. One is the form of the *covering map* of classifiers the system maintains, that is, the set of state-actions which are matched (mapped to a strength) by some rule.

When we inspected the rule populations evolved by XCS and SB–XCS for the 6 multiplexer in the previous paper we saw that they converged on two different representations. This section explains in more detail that strength and accuracy-based systems tend towards different representations of their environment and suggests this difference indicates that the systems have different representational goals.

Like any RL system, a classifier system needs a policy which tells it how to act in any state it encounters. This means that, for each state, an LCS must contain at least

P.L. Lanzi et al. (Eds.): IWLCS 2002, LNAI 2661, pp. 81–98, 2003.

one rule which matches that state. Otherwise, how can it know what to do? Different classifier systems represent their policies, and information related to them, in different ways. The following sections investigate three ways.

2.1 Default Hierarchies

Default hierarchies [19, 24, 7, 20, 21, 5] are sets of rules in which more specific rules provide exceptions to more general default rules. Figure 1 shows a default hierarchy for the 6 multiplexer, in which the default rule # # # # # # $\rightarrow$ 1 matches all inputs, but is overruled by the other more specific rules in half of these cases. This hierarchy is notable as it is the one which represents this function with the fewest rules.

Default hierarchies were not part of Holland's original LCS formulation [10, 14], appearing only later [6, 11]. Default hierarchies have been praised as a means of increasing the number of solutions to a problem without increasing the size of the search space, and as a way of allowing LCS to adapt gradually to a problem. Consequently, they have been seen by many as an important part of the representational capacity of classifier systems, although they seem never to have been considered central to the idea of LCS. However, despite much early work, the problems of encouraging their formation and survival remain unsolved, and they have attracted little attention in recent years. (But see [12] p. 6.)

Because XCS evaluates the accuracy of each rule individually, default rules, which on their own are sometimes incorrect, are assigned low accuracy and hence low fitness. Consequently, XCS does not support default hierarchies. Although SB–XCS does not have this obstacle, it does not encourage them and indeed should not support them as it does not bias action selection towards more specific rules, as default hierarchies require.

Because of difficulties with default hierarchies, and the lack of support for them in XCS and SB–XCS, we mention them only in passing and now proceed to consider other representations.

2.2 Partial and Best Action Maps

Strength-based systems – which reproduce higher-strength rules – tend to allocate more rules to states with higher values, and to higher-valued actions within a state. In effect they attempt to find rules which advocate the best (i.e. highest valued) action for each state and in the extreme case each state would only have a single action (its best) advocated by some rule(s). Let's call this extreme case a *best action map*. Let's introduce some notation to express things more formally.

- A Boolean target function f is a total function on a binary bit string, that is $f : \{0,1\}^n \rightarrow \{0,1\}$.
- Classifiers are constant partial functions, that is, they map some subset of the domain of f to either 0 or 1. Classifiers are constant because, using the standard ternary language, they always advocate the same action regardless of their input.

Note that f merely defines the state-action space. The learning task a reinforcement learning LCS faces is defined by a reward function defined over this state-action space.

Default Hierarchy	Best Action Map	Complete Map
0 0 0 # # # → 0	0 0 0 # # # → 0	0 0 0 # # # → 0
0 1 # 0 # # → 0	0 0 1 # # # → 1	0 0 1 # # # → 0
1 0 # # 0 # → 0	0 1 # 0 # # → 0	0 1 # 0 # # → 0
1 1 # # # 0 → 0	0 1 # 1 # # → 1	0 1 # 1 # # → 0
# # # # # # → 1	1 0 # # 0 # → 0	1 0 # # 0 # → 0
	1 0 # # 1 # → 1	1 0 # # 1 # → 0
	1 1 # # # 0 → 0	1 1 # # # 0 → 0
	1 1 # # # 1 → 1	1 1 # # # 1 → 0
		0 0 0 # # # → 1
		0 0 1 # # # → 1
		0 1 # 0 # # → 1
		0 1 # 1 # # → 1
		1 0 # # 0 # → 1
		1 0 # # 1 # → 1
		1 1 # # # 0 → 1
		1 1 # # # 1 → 1

Fig. 1. Three representations of the 6 multiplexer.

As a shorthand, and to approximate Sutton and Barto's reinforcement learning notation [22], we define $\mathcal{S}$ = domain and $\mathcal{A}$ = range when dealing with classifiers and target functions. That is, a task's state is an element of $\mathcal{S}(f)$ and a classifier system's action is an element of $\mathcal{A}(f)$, where f is a target function. The states matched by a classifier c are elements of $\mathcal{S}(c)$, and the action advocated by c is $\mathcal{A}(c)$.

A set of rules C constitutes a best action map for some function f iff:

$$\forall s \in \mathcal{S}(f) \ \exists c \in C \text{ such that } s \in \mathcal{S}(c)$$

$$\text{and where } \forall c \in C, \ \forall s' \in \mathcal{S}(c) \ f(s') = c(s')$$

Figure 1 shows a best action map for the 6 multiplexer. It should be familiar, since it is SB–XCS's [O] for this function from §4 of the previous paper, and, in fact, the solution SB–XCS evolved (see figure 9 of the previous paper). Other best action maps can represent this function; a larger one consists of 32 rules each of which is fully specific, i.e., has no # s. The right side of figure 2 shows a best action map for a fragment of a sequential task – note that of all the transitions from the current state, only the state-action with the highest prediction ($P_j = 100$) is represented. Further examples of best action maps in sequential tasks are shown in §3.2.

In practice strength-based systems only tend towards best action maps – often for a given state there is more than one action advocated. We could say they maintain *partial maps*. (See, for example, SB–XCS's population in figure 9 of the previous paper.) The important point is that there tend to be states with (typically low-valued) actions unadvocated by any classifier.

Since the action selection mechanism can only make an informed choice between advocated actions, the tendency towards a best action map means the rule allocation mechanism has a hand in action selection. Best action maps are in a sense an ideal

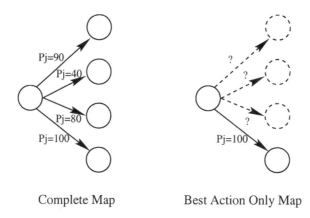

Complete Map   Best Action Only Map

Fig. 2. Complete and partial map representations of a state transition. In the best action map, only the highest valued transition is represented.

representation of the solution as they use a minimal number of rules (without using default hierarchies), but this does not imply partial maps are an ideal representation for finding solutions, as we'll see in section 3.

2.3   Complete Maps

In contrast to the partial maps of strength-based systems, the combination of XCS's accuracy-based fitness and various mechanisms which promote diversity result in a strong tendency to find a population of rules such that each action in each state is advocated by at least one rule[1]. Wilson calls this a *complete map*, and has noted that it resembles the representation of mainstream reinforcement learning systems more closely than does a partial map ([25] p. 5). More formally, a set of rules C constitutes a complete map for some function f iff:

$$\forall s \in \mathcal{S}(f), \forall a \in \mathcal{A}(f) \; \exists c \in C \text{ such that } s \in \mathcal{S}(c), a \in \mathcal{A}(c)$$

Figure 1 shows a complete map for the 6 multiplexer, which is like the best action map in that figure except that for each condition there is a rule for each of the two actions. This set of rules should look familiar as it is XCS's [O] for this function from §4 of the previous paper, and, in fact, it is the solution which XCS evolved (see figure 10 of the previous paper). An example of a complete map in a sequential tasks is shown on the left of figure 2.

When all actions are advocated, it is left entirely to the action selection mechanism to decide which action to take; the rule allocation mechanism is dissociated from action selection. This is consistent with the role of the GA in XCS, which is only to search for useful generalisations over states.

---

[1] Booker's endogenous fitness LCS favours the same representation as XCS for the 6 multiplexer [1].

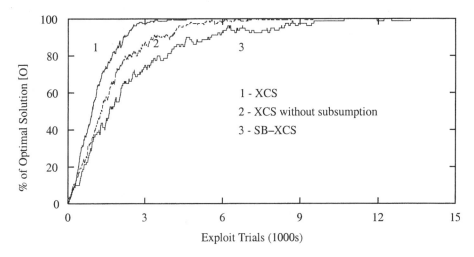

Fig. 3. Proportion of optimal solutions found by XCS and SB–XCS on the 6 multiplexer.

2.4   What Do XCS and SB–XCS Really Learn?

In the preceding sections it was argued that XCS and SB–XCS will respectively tend to-wards complete and partial maps, and the sample populations inspected in the previous paper support this. But how strong is this tendency?

Figure 3 was generated during evaluation of XCS (with and without GA subsump-tion) and SB–XCS on the 6 multiplexer and shows the percentage of the optimal so-lution found by each system on the current time step (denoted %[O]). A %[O] of 0 indicates that no rules from this set were present in the rule population, while %[O] of 100 indicates that all were present.

The curves are averages of 10 runs. That both systems converge to 100% of [O] in-dicates that *in all runs* the complete optimal set of rules is present in the rule population. This suggests XCS and SB–XCS reliably find their respective optimal solutions to the 6 multiplexer. Note that XCS finds all 16 rules in its [O] more quickly than SB–XCS finds the 8 rules in its [O]. The difference is similar to that in $\mathcal{P}$, and may be due to the same effect (see section 4.3 of the first paper).

Although the results in figure 3 were averaged over only 10 runs, XCS's ability to find [O] is highly reliable. Figure 4 shows XCS's %[O] for a set of 7 functions from the hidden parity test suite [17], each averaged over 1000 runs. Parameter settings were the standard ones for XCS [16] except that uniform crossover was used and the population size limit was 2000. That XCS found the complete [O] in all 7000 runs is indicated by the convergence of all curves to %100.

XCS is also able to find the complete [O] for much larger Boolean functions, for example the 37-bit multiplexer, for which [O] consists of 128 rules. XCS's %[O] and $\mathcal{P}$ for this test are shown in figure 5 and the population size in macroclassifiers is shown in figure 6. Parameter settings were as for the 6 multiplexer except for the following: $\theta_{sub} = 100$, $\theta_{GA} = 80$, $P_\# = 0.66$, and uniform crossover was used. Curves were averaged over 10 runs.

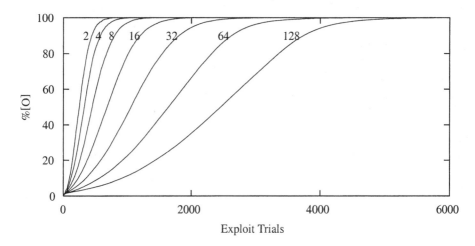

Exploit Trials

Fig. 4. Proportion of optimal solutions found by XCS on the 6-bit hidden parity suite. The number beside each curve indicates the number of rules in the [O] for that function.

In both figures, XCS was run with three different population size limits (20,000, 30,000 and 50,000 rules) to examine the effect of population size. As with other test functions performance improves with population size, although it is a case of diminishing returns. At the same time, the computational load on the system increases greatly as the population size limit increases.

With the help of a special form of reward function XCS has also learnt the 70-bit multiplexer [4], for which [O] consists of 256 rules.

3   Complete and Partial Maps Compared

In this section we weigh the pros and cons of complete and partial maps. Little is known about how they compare – the literature has nothing to say on the subject, apart from the speculation in ([25] p. 5) that complete maps may help avoid convergence to suboptimal actions, and our speculations in [15]. This is a complex subject which will require considerable effort to unravel, and this section is of necessity a basic treatment.

3.1   Advantages of Partial Maps

Partial maps use fewer rules than complete maps to represent the same input/output function, which may prove advantageous in the following ways. First, fewer rules require less memory and computing power, since fewer rules need to be stored and matched against inputs. Second, since fewer rules are involved, it may be possible to learn partial maps given less experience with the environment (although in our comparison of XCS and SB–XCS in §2.4, SB–XCS actually took longer to learn its partial map than XCS did to learn its complete map).

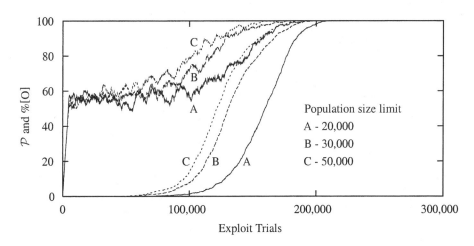

Fig. 5. $\mathcal{P}$ and %[O] for XCS on the 37-bit multiplexer for three population size limits.

How Parsimonious Are Partial Maps? Any benefit due to parsimony depends on the degree of that parsimony. So how much more parsimonious are partial maps than complete maps? We could try to compare the number of rules required in each case, but we note that the learning task used is relevant as it determines what useful generalisations, and thus what accurate rules, are possible. This makes a comparison of the number of rules needed difficult because we may be able to generalise more over one action than another, depending on the learning task. One way to deal with the relevance of the learning task is to consider a particular space of possible tasks, and give average or worst-case results for the space. We'll do this shortly, but for the moment let's ignore the issue of generalisation and, instead of considering the number of rules needed, let's consider the number of state-actions which must be represented. Using the standard ternary language this depends heavily on the number of actions available. If a actions are possible in each state, a best action map requires the value of $1/a$ state-actions be estimated per state, while a complete map requires all a actions be estimated. That is, a complete map requires the representation of a times more state-actions.

To illustrate this point, consider figure 7 which shows the reward function for a non-sequential task. Four actions are possible in each state, and each action always receives the same reward, regardless of which state it is taken in. (Consequently, the lines showing reward are flat.) Because in all states action A obtains the most reward, a best action map must represent only state-actions with action A. To emphasise this the line for action A has been drawn solid, while those for the other actions are dashed.

While a best action map represents only the most rewarding action in each state, a complete map must represent all four actions. Consequently, a complete map represents $a = 4$ times as many state-actions for this task.

The Degree of Parsimony in Representing State-Actions. For tasks with binary actions ($a = 2$), the savings of using a best action map are not terribly impressive. In many cases a will not be much larger. However, as a rises the savings of a partial map become more

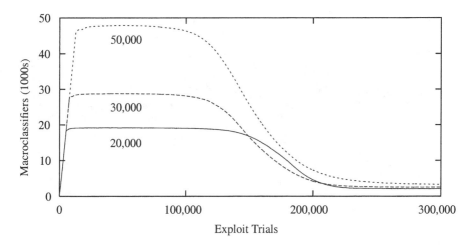

Fig. 6. Population size in macroclassifiers for XCS on the 37-bit multiplexer, using three different population size limits (20,000, 30,000 and 50,000 rules).

significant. When the action space is continuous and $a = \infty$ a partial map (or some alternative representation) is a necessity.

How Many Rules Are Needed?   Now that we've considered how many state-actions must be represented let's return to the question of how many rules are needed to represent these state-actions. As an example of the difference in the number of rules needed, let's consider the function in figure 7, which requires exactly a times as many rules for a complete map as a partial map. Note that fully general rules can accurately predict the value of the state-actions they match, which is why the ratio of rules needed is exactly the same as the ratio of state-actions to be represented. For example, the following rule constitutes a (minimal) best action map:

$$\boxed{\# \ \# \ \# \to A}$$

and the following four rules constitute a (minimal) complete map[2]:

$$\boxed{\begin{array}{l} \# \ \# \ \# \to A \\ \# \ \# \ \# \to B \\ \# \ \# \ \# \to C \\ \# \ \# \ \# \to D \end{array}}$$

The rules in both maps will be fit according to either XCS's or SB–XCS's fitness calculation.

---

[2] This map is not strictly in the standard ternary language, since its actions are not from $\{0, 1\}^l$. However, $\{A, B, C, D\}$ is effectively equivalent to $\{00, 01, 10, 11\}$.

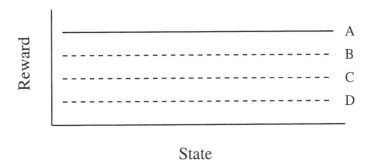

Fig. 7. A reward function for a non-sequential task with 4 actions.

Rules Needed for Binary Reward Functions. Since the learning task determines how much generalisation is possible and hence how many rules are needed, we can only compare the number of rules needed by complete and partial maps in reference to some learning task, or set of tasks. To begin, let's consider the restricted class of non-sequential tasks in which the reward function is binary, that is, ranges over only two values. (This space corresponds precisely to the space of Boolean functions when the reward function's state-action space is defined by Boolean functions, as we specified in §2.2.) In this space, the ratio of state-actions to be represented is also the ratio of rules needed, since we can generalise equally over all actions, on average. (We do not give a proof, but the space of Boolean functions has a form of symmetry which allows this.) That is, for this space, a complete map will require on average a times more rules.

Whereas the ratios for the average case depend on the number of actions possible, the worst case ratios depend on both the number of states and actions. It is possible to construct a worst case for a complete map in which a partial map requires only 1 rule while a complete map requires one rule for each state-action, although this may depend on the accuracy criterion being set unhelpfully in order to limit XCS's generalisation. In the worst case for a partial map, there is only 1 action and both maps require only 1 rule.

Rules Needed for Arbitrary Reward Functions. Now let's return to the more general class of non-sequential tasks defined by arbitrary reward functions. XCS has a difficulty generalising in this domain which SB–XCS does not, because XCS represents all actions while SB–XCS does not (as, for example, in figure 7). If an action SB–XCS does not represent results in quite different rewards in different states, XCS will have difficulty generalising over it, whereas, of course, SB–XCS will not. See [16], chapter 3 for an example. Thus, although XCS requires on average a times more rules for binary reward functions (and, as it happens, for the example in figure 7), XCS requires on average more than a times as many rules for arbitrary reward functions. We will not attempt average or worst case bounds for this class of functions.

Rules Needed for Real World Problems. Finally, let's consider "real world" problems rather than the abstract spaces of Boolean and reward functions. In the real world, the parsimony advantage of partial maps is reduced (in terms of rules needed, though not state-actions). Real-world problems generally have abundant regularity and, in practice, representations are used which can exploit this regularity. For example, the parity function is maximally difficult to represent using the standard ternary language. However, the parity function is very regular, and a little domain knowledge allows us to choose another representation which can capture this regularity.

3.2   Disadvantages of Partial Maps

The disadvantages of partial maps are that they may interfere with action selection (and exploration control more generally), and credit assignment. We discuss each of these in turn.

Partial Maps and Exploration. This section suggests that managing the explore/exploit dilemma [22] will be more difficult using a partial map since it does not allow us to record as much information on exploration as a complete map. If partial maps make exploration control more difficult, then the more difficult the exploration problem, the more of a disadvantage a partial map will be. In the following we consider exploration control using a partial map in non-sequential and sequential tasks, following which we briefly discuss non-stationary environments.

Non-sequential Tasks. In many LCS an action cannot be taken if it is not advocated by some rule, which means a partial map limits the range of actions the LCS can take and hence its ability to explore its environment. Even if we allow an LCS to take an unadvocated action, we cannot record the result (the resulting immediate reward) since we have no matching rule.

Let's return to the non-sequential task of figure 7, but now suppose that the reward function is stochastic so that the true mean reward for taking a given action in a given state must be estimated by sampling it many times. How many times should we sample a state-action?

Some simple exploration strategies, for example taking a random action 10% of the time and the highest-valued one otherwise, do not require us to keep track of the number of visits made to a given state-action. Other more sophisticated strategies, however, require us to record information such as the number of visits, the mean reward, and the variance in it. Such information is easily added to rules.

However, a problem obviously occurs in a best action map representation of this reward function, in that we have no rule which can record information concerning actions B, C, or D. Consequently we cannot use such exploration control strategies. An alternative to storing exploration control information in the rules is to use a look-up table, but if we make use of such tables there seems no point in using a classifier system rather than a tabular Q-learner. In summary, partial maps would seem to restrict us to the use of less sophisticated, and less efficient, exploration strategies.

Sequential Tasks. In sequential tasks we face the problem that we must explore not only the actions available in the current state, but the states and actions we may visit as a result of selecting an action in the current state, which makes exploration control much more difficult.

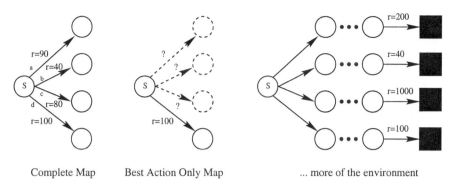

Complete Map   Best Action Only Map   ... more of the environment

Fig. 8. Complete and partial map representations of a sequential task.

If we wish to implement distal exploration control schemes [26], in which we propagate information about exploration from state-action to state-action, we need a complete map in order to propagate exploration information properly (just as with propagating Q-values) and to record any statistics (e.g., on the number of times a state-action has been taken).

Partial maps tend to allocate rules to higher-valued state-actions, but an LCS must estimate the value of state-actions and can easily get their relative values wrong. Suppose an LCS is learning the task in figure 8, and initially has a complete map of the transitions from state S, as shown on the left. This corresponds to the left of figure 2, except that this time the rewards ($r = \ldots$) associated with each transition are shown, and each transition is labelled with the action (a,b,c,d) which produces it. Now suppose the LCS tries each of the actions in state S and determines that d generates the highest immediate reward. If it deletes some of the rules which cover the other transitions to obtain a partial map, it may not represent the transition due to action c. As long as this action is unadvocated many LCS will never further explore the consequences of taking it. Now consider the right of figure 8, which shows more of the task, including the four terminal states (shown as squares). The dots ($\cdots$) are meant to suggest that part of the environment is not shown. Suppose the optimal policy involves taking action c in order to reach the terminal state with a reward of 1000. It may be difficult for the learner to find this terminal state (and the optimal policy) if it maintains a partial map, since action c may not be represented.

Globally optimal behaviour often requires that the learner take locally suboptimal actions, i.e., actions which do not return the highest possible immediate reward, like action c. Even if the system does find the highest rewarding terminal state once, it will have difficulty propagating value back from it if state-actions along the path to it are missing.

Non-stationary Environments. Hartley [8, 9] trained two classifier systems, XCS (which maintains a complete map) and NEWBOOLE (which maintains a partial map) on a binary categorisation task, then abruptly switched the category to which each stimulus belonged. XCS quickly recovered from these changes by simply adjusting the strengths of the rules involved: consistently correct rules suddenly became consistently incorrect and vice versa. NEWBOOLE, in contrast, found that its rules suddenly all had low strength, and had to engage the genetic algorithm to generate new ones as it does not maintain low strength rules.

It is important to note, however, that the changes made in this experiment were very regular, as all the inputs belonging to one category were changed to the same new category. It is unknown whether a complete map offers any advantages in adapting to less systematic changes in the environment. In fact, given the suggestion in §3.1 that it may be possible to learn partial maps more quickly, we might expect partial maps to adapt more quickly to non-stationary environments.

In Hartley's experiment the rewards were non-stationary. It is also possible for the variance in the rewards to be non-stationary, a situation which has yet to be examined.

Partial Maps and Sequential Credit Assignment. With the Temporal Difference algorithms [22] commonly used with sequential tasks we update the estimate of a state-action's value based partly on the estimated value of a state-action which is visited later. That is, we propagate value from one estimator to another. However, if the estimator for the successor state is missing (e.g., if an action is not advocated by any rule) we cannot apply the basic 1-step Temporal Difference updates (e.g., the strength/prediction update used with XCS and SB–XCS). (Of course, if we do not allow the system to take unadvocated actions this problem does not occur.) We *could* apply n-step versions of our updates [22] and propagate value from state-actions visited farther in the future (i.e., n time steps in the future), but as far as the author is aware such updates have never been used with an LCS, and they are certainly not part of standard descriptions of the bucket brigade (e.g., [11, 13, 2, 7]).

Gridworld Examples. To further illustrate how partial maps can make sequential credit assignment difficult, let us consider a number of simple gridworlds, and partial maps of them maintained by some hypothetical learning agent. In each of the following examples, the start state is marked **S** and the two terminal states are marked **T**. Upon entering a terminal state the agent receives an immediate reward and is returned to the start state to commence the next episode. The immediate reward received upon entering a state is shown in the bottom right corner of that state, or is 0 if not shown. It is possible to take the actions {North, South, East, West} in any state, although actions which would move the agent out of the maze have no effect. Let us set the discount rate to $\gamma = 0.9$.

The state-actions of the agent's partial map are shown as arrows, e.g., in example 1, in the start state the agent's map represents the values of moving North and of moving East only.

Example 1: Incomplete Paths. The gridworld in figure 9 has two terminal states, with rewards of 50 and 100 respectively. The optimal policy for the learning agent (given $\gamma = 0.9$) is to follow one of several minimal paths to the terminal state in the upper right hand corner. We'll denote this state $\mathbf{T}_{100}$.

Note that the partial map for this gridworld does not form a complete path from $\mathbf{T}_{100}$ to **S**. The first problem this causes is that some systems, XCS and SB–XCS included, cannot reach $\mathbf{T}_{100}$ if no path leads to it, since they cannot select unadvocated actions.

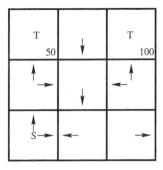

Fig. 9. A partial map forming incomplete paths.

A second problem is that even if the agent was able to reach T_{100}, an incomplete path means it is not possible to propagate value from T_{100} to **S** using the standard 1-step updates. Consequently, the credit assignment process will not be able to update the value estimates for moving North and East from **S** to take into account the existence of T_{100}, and the agent will not be aware of it. (All 1-step algorithms, including 1-step Q-learning and Bucket Brigades, will have the same problem.)

Furthermore, even if a path from T_{100} to **S** existed, the use of partial maps means an unfortunate deletion of a rule anywhere along the path would break it and disrupt the flow of value.

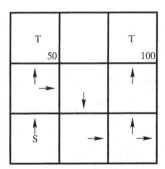

Fig. 10. A partial map with interfering local optima.

Example 2: Interfering Local Optima. The example in figure 10 is the same as the last, except that the agent's partial map differs. Now it has complete paths from **S** to both terminal states. Nonetheless, there are a number of problems with this scenario. For one, it is more difficult to reach T_{100} than T_{50} from **S** because the former is farther from it. This means both that more exploration is required to reach T_{100}, and that propagating value from T_{100} to **S** will take longer than propagating value from T_{50} to **S**, using 1-step updates. Both factors make it harder for the agent to learn to use a path to T_{100} and may cause it to converge instead on a suboptimal policy leading it to T_{50}.

Both these problems occur using complete maps, but an extra problem with the use of partial maps compounds them: since rules leading to T_{50} are likely to gain value more quickly than those leading instead to T_{100}, the latter may die out resulting in incomplete paths to T_{100}.

Example 3: Discounting and Convergence to Suboptimal Policies. A further problem in the same scenario as the last example is that the path to T_{100} is suboptimal (there exist shorter paths between **S** and T_{100}). With $\gamma = 0.9$, the value of T_{100} using this circuitous route is actually less than that of T_{50} (using a direct path), which may lead the system to converge on a policy which leads it to T_{50}. This is more likely to occur when the agent is limited to a subset of paths by a partial map.

Example 4: Interfering Negative Rewards. As a final example of how partial maps can interact harmfully with sequential credit assignment consider the maze in figure 11, in which a column of negatively rewarding states isolates T_{50} from **S**. The agent's partial map is not shown in this example.

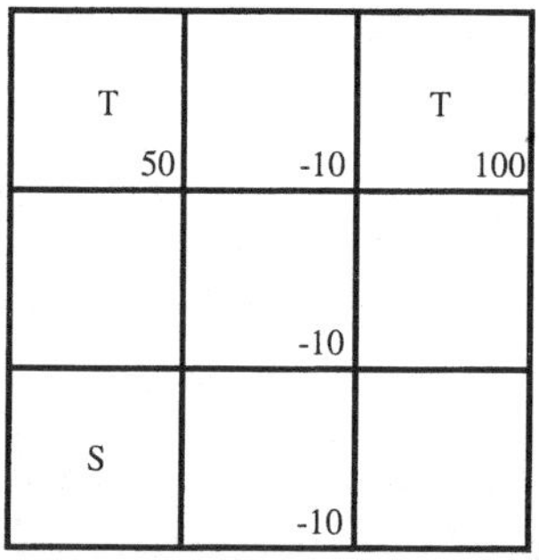

Fig. 11. A gridworld with interfering negative rewards.

The undesirable states may tend to hide T_{100} from the learning agent, since it must pass through them to reach it. This makes the task of exploring the gridworld more difficult, since the agent may prematurely learn to avoid the unpleasant states.

Although this may happen with complete maps too, an extra difficulty in using partial maps is that they may tend to become sparser around the unpleasant states, exacerbating the difficulty of reaching T_{100} and propagating value back from it.

Summary of Partial Maps and Sequential Credit Assignment. It is unclear just what the effects of partial maps are on the propagation of value, but it seems likely that any effects will be deleterious. The simplest and safest course would appear to be the maintenance of a complete map.

3.3   Complete Maps and Strength

If complete maps are useful, can we get a strength-based system like SB–XCS to maintain them? We could give rewards of 90 for incorrect actions and 100 for correct actions. If selective pressure is not too strong SB–XCS should be able to maintain classifiers for both correct and incorrect actions (i.e., a complete map). However, overgeneral rules would always have more strength (i.e., fitness) than accurate-but-incorrect rules, so the latter will be more likely to die out than the overgenerals. Such a system seems unlikely to adapt well as the overgenerals will interfere with action selection (and, of course, reproduction).

Distinguishing between Strength and Fitness. Alternatively, we could modify SB–XCS to distinguish between strength and fitness, and define a rule's fitness as:

$$\left| S_j - \frac{max - min}{2} \right|$$

where S_j is the strength of rule j, and max and min are the maximum and minimum possible rule strengths for the task. This system would give high fitness to both consistently correct and consistently incorrect rules. This system should be able to maintain complete maps for tasks which have only 2 rewards, but it will not work with arbitrary reward functions because of the problem of strong overgenerals [16].

Fitness Sharing. Another option is to introduce fitness sharing into SB–XCS. Because the strength of all rules tends towards equilibrium under fitness sharing [23, 3], the map produced with fitness sharing should be more complete. It is not clear, however, how complete it will be.

Steps towards Accuracy. The maintenance of complete maps is one of XCS's distinctive features, and attempts to get SB–XCS to maintain complete maps are steps towards making SB–XCS more XCS-like.

3.4   Contrasting Complete and Partial Maps in RL Terminology

In Reinforcement Learning terminology, while XCS maintains a complete action-value function (i.e., Q-function), SB–XCS maintains an incomplete action-value function. Best action maps map states to actions – thus, in RL terminology they represent a policy, although since they are implemented with classifiers they contain information (e.g., strength values) which policies do not. SB–XCS does not search directly in the space of complete policies, but rather in the space of policy fragments – the fragments are (generalisations over) state-action pairs (i.e., classifiers).

3.5   Summary of Comparison

Partial maps have the advantage that, in principle, they require fewer rules, and so less processing. The degree of advantage depends on the particular task being learnt, and on the number of actions available; as the number of available actions increases, so does the advantage of a partial map.

Although they require more rules, complete maps may offer advantages with sequential credit assignment and exploration control, particularly in sequential tasks. Note that tabular Q-learners employ complete maps, and that convergence proofs for them involve infinite revisits to *each* state-action. Complete maps also have the advantage of using subsumption deletion, which may outweigh the parsimony of partial maps even on non-sequential tasks.

At present it is unclear whether complete or partial maps are superior for non-sequential tasks. It remains to be seen whether subsumption deletion can be adapted to strength-based systems, and whether it matches the advantage of the parsimony of partial maps. For sequential tasks the picture is clearer; complete maps certainly seem more suitable for these tasks.

We can summarise the difference between the two by noting that partial maps provide a solution to a problem whereas complete maps, in contrast, provide a representation upon which Q-learning can operate in order to find a solution. Looked at this way, partial maps seem more suitable for systems which rely more on the GA to find solutions, i.e., those which fit the GA-view of classifier systems [16]. Consequently partial maps should suit Pittsburgh classifier systems very well. Partial maps should also suit supervised learning LCS.

Further study is needed to confirm and quantify the merits of each type of map.

4   Conclusion

This work is part of an ongoing comparison of strength and accuracy-based fitness in Michigan classifier systems.

We saw that SB–XCS is capable of learning the optimal solution to the 6 multiplexer, and is thus a non-trivial learning system. Furthermore, we saw that XCS's ability to evolve smaller populations than SB–XCS to represent Boolean functions is due to its subsumption deletion rather than its accuracy-based fitness. This also clearly demonstrated that XCS's much-valued ability to generalise on Boolean functions is not unique among classifier systems, since SB–XCS was also able to reliably find optimally general rules and optimal solutions.

XCS learned the 6 multiplexer more quickly both in terms of $\mathcal{P}$ (figure 3 of part I) and [O] (figure 3), suggesting its fitness calculation is more effective at distinguishing fit and unfit rules than that of SB–XCS (see section 4.3 of part I). We note, however, that little attempt has been made to optimise SB–XCS.

We also saw that SB–XCS was unable to obtain optimal performance on Woods2, a sequential decision task. In [16] we provide further analysis which indicates this is due to strong and fit overgeneral rules, and attempt to give an account of when these rules occur. It seems fitness sharing is needed by strength-based systems to address this problem. Although the niche GA should counter strong and fit overgenerals to some extent [16], we note that SB–XCS employs a niche GA, and so it is clearly not a solution to this problem.

We also note, however, that fitness sharing was not needed by SB–XCS to find the optimal solution for the 6 multiplexer. The next stage in our comparison of strength and accuracy will be to add fitness sharing to SB–XCS and see whether this enables it to solve sequential tasks such as Woods2, why this might be so in terms of strong and fit overgeneral rules, and what the effect of fitness sharing is on the representation favoured by the system.

The ongoing work towards which this paper has contributed is slowly building a broad characterisation of the types of classifier systems and classes of problems it is useful to distinguish for them. It is hoped that this sort of theory will lead to a better understanding of the utility of various types of classifier systems.

Acknowledgements

Thank you to Manfred Kerber, Riccardo Poli, Robert Smith and Stewart Wilson for their comments on this work.

References

1. Lashon B. Booker. Do We Really Need to Estimate Rule Utilities in Classifier Systems? In Lanzi et al. [18], pages 125–142.
2. Lashon B. Booker, David E. Goldberg, and John H. Holland. Classifier systems and genetic algorithms. *Artificial Intelligence*, 40:235–282, 1989.
3. Larry Bull and Jacob Hurst. ZCS Redux. *To appear in Evolutionary Computation*, 2002.
4. Martin V. Butz, Tim Kovacs, Pier Luca Lanzi, and Stewart W. Wilson. How XCS Evolves Accurate Classifiers. In Lee Spector, Erik D. Goodman, Annie Wu, W. B. Langdon, Hans-Michael Voigt, Mitsuo Gen, Sandip Sen, Marco Dorigo, Shahram Pezeshk, Max H Garzon, and Edmund Burke, editors, *GECCO-2001: Proceedings of the Genetic and Evolutionary Computation Conference*, pages 927–934. Morgan Kaufmann, 2001.
5. Marco Dorigo. New perspectives about default hierarchies formation in learning classifier systems. In E. Ardizzone, E. Gaglio, and S. Sorbello, editors, *Proceedings of the 2nd Congress of the Italian Association for Artificial Intelligence (AI*IA) on Trends in Artificial Intelligence*, volume 549 of *LNAI*, pages 218–227, Palermo, Italy, October 1991. Springer Verlag.
6. David E. Goldberg. *Computer-Aided Gas Pipeline Operation using Genetic Algorithms and Rule Learning*. PhD thesis, The University of Michigan, 1983.
7. David E. Goldberg. *Genetic Algorithms in Search, Optimization, and Machine Learning*. Addison-Wesley, Reading, MA, 1989.
8. Adrian Hartley. Genetics Based Machine Learning as a Model of Perceptual Category Learning in Humans. Master's thesis, University of Birmingham, 1998.
9. Adrian Hartley. Accuracy-based fitness allows similar performance to humans in static and dynamic classification environments. In W. Banzhaf, J. Daida, A. E. Eiben, M. H. Garzon, V. Honavar, M. Jakiela, and R. E. Smith, editors, *GECCO-99: Proceedings of the Genetic and Evolutionary Computation Conference*, pages 266–273. Morgan Kaufmann, 1999.
10. John H. Holland. *Adaptation in Natural and Artificial Systems*. University of Michigan Press, Ann Arbor, 1975. Republished by the MIT press, 1992.
11. John H. Holland. Escaping brittleness: The possibilities of general-purpose learning algorithms applied to parallel rule-based systems. In T. Mitchell, R. Michalski, and J. Carbonell, editors, *Machine learning, an artificial intelligence approach. Volume II*, chapter 20, pages 593–623. Morgan Kaufmann, 1986.

12. John H. Holland, Lashon B. Booker, Marco Colombetti, Marco Dorigo, David E. Goldberg, Stephanie Forrest, Rick L. Riolo, Robert E. Smith, Pier Luca Lanzi, Wolfgang Stolzmann, and Stewart W. Wilson. What is a Learning Classifier System? In Lanzi et al. [18], pages 3–32.

13. John H. Holland, Keith J. Holyoak, Richard E. Nisbett, and Paul R. Thagard. *Induction. Processes of Inference, Learning and Discovery*. The MIT Press, 1986.

14. John H. Holland and J. S. Reitman. Cognitive systems based on adaptive algorithms. In D. A. Waterman and F. Hayes-Roth, editors, *Pattern-directed inference systems*. New York: Academic Press, 1978. Reprinted in: Evolutionary Computation. The Fossil Record. David B. Fogel (Ed.) IEEE Press, 1998. ISBN: 0-7803-3481-7.

15. Tim Kovacs. Strength or Accuracy? Fitness Calculation in Learning Classifier Systems. In Lanzi et al. [18], pages 143–160.

16. Tim Kovacs. *A Comparison of Strength and Accuracy-Based Fitness in Learning Classifier Systems*. PhD thesis, School of Computer Science, University of Birmingham, 2002.

17. Tim Kovacs and Manfred Kerber. What makes a problem hard for XCS? In Pier Luca Lanzi, Wolfgang Stolzmann, and Stewart W. Wilson, editors, *Advances in Learning Classifier Systems*, number 1996 in LNAI, pages 80–99. Springer–Verlag, 2001.

18. Pier Luca Lanzi, Wolfgang Stolzmann, and Stewart W. Wilson, editors. *Learning Classifier Systems. From Foundations to Applications*, volume 1813 of *LNAI*. Springer-Verlag, Berlin, 2000.

19. Rick L. Riolo. Bucket Brigade Performance: II. Default Hierarchies. In John J. Grefenstette, editor, *Proceedings of the 2nd International Conference on Genetic Algorithms (ICGA87)*, pages 196–201, Cambridge, MA, July 1987. Lawrence Erlbaum Associates.

20. Robert E. Smith. *Default Hierarchy Formation and Memory Exploitation in Learning Classifier Systems*. PhD thesis, University of Alabama, 1991.

21. Robert E. Smith and David E. Goldberg. Variable default hierarchy separation in a classifier system. In Gregory J. E. Rawlins, editor, *Proceedings of the First Workshop on Foundations of Genetic Algorithms*, pages 148–170, San Mateo, July 15–18 1991. Morgan Kaufmann.

22. Richard S. Sutton and Andrew G. Barto. *Reinforcement Learning: An Introduction*. MIT Press, Cambridge, MA, 1998.

23. Stewart W. Wilson. Classifier Systems and the Animat Problem. *Machine Learning*, 2:199–228, 1987.

24. Stewart W. Wilson. Bid competition and specificity reconsidered. *Complex Systems*, 2:705–723, 1989.

25. Stewart W. Wilson. Classifier Fitness Based on Accuracy. *Evolutionary Computation*, 3(2):149–175, 1995.

26. Jeremy L. Wyatt. *Exploration and Inference in Learning from Reinforcement*. PhD thesis, Dept. of Artificial Intelligence, University of Edinburgh, 1997.

Further Comparison
between ATNoSFERES and XCSM

Samuel Landau[1], Sébastien Picault[2], Olivier Sigaud[1], and Pierre Gérard[1]

[1] Laboratoire d'Informatique de Paris 6
8, rue du Capitaine Scott
75 015 Paris France
{Samuel.Landau,Olivier.Sigaud,Pierre.Gerard}@lip6.fr
http://miriad.lip6.fr/~landau
http://animatlab.lip6.fr/~{sigaud,pgerard}
[2] Laboratoire d'Informatique Fondamentale de Lille
Cité Scientifique
59 655 Villeneuve d'Ascq Cedex, France
Sebastien.Picault@lifl.fr
http://www.lifl.fr/~picault

Abstract. In this paper we present ATNoSFERES, a new framework based on an indirect encoding Genetic Algorithm which builds finite-state automata controllers able to deal with perceptual aliazing. In the context of our ongoing line of research, we compare it with XCSM, a memory-based extension of the most studied Learning Classifier System, XCS, through two benchmark experiments. We focus in particular on internal state generalization, and add special purpose features to ATNoSFERES to fulfill that comparison. We then discuss the role played by internal state generalization in the experiments studied.

Keywords: Evolutionary Algorithms, Learning Classifier Systems, perceptual aliazing, internal state generalization, ATN[1]

1   Introduction

Most Learning Classifier Systems (LCS) [5] are used to tackle problems where situated and adaptive agents are involved in a sensori-motor loop with their environment. Such agents perceive situations through their sensors as vectors of several attributes, each representing a perceived feature of the environment. The task of the agents is to *learn* the optimal policy – *i.e.* which action to perform in every situation, in order to fulfill their goals the best way they can. As in the general *Reinforcement Learning* (RL) framework [18], the goal of a LCS-based agent is to maximize the scalar rewards it receives from its environment. The policy is defined by a set of rules – or classifiers – specifying the action to choose according to some *conditions* concerning the perceived situations.

In real world environments, it may happen that agents perceive the same situation in several different locations, some requiring different optimal actions, giving rise to a

---

[1] ATN stands for "Augmented Transition Networks"

P.L. Lanzi et al. (Eds.): IWLCS 2002, LNAI 2661, pp. 99–117, 2003.

perceptual aliazing problem. In such a case, the environment is said *non-Markov*, and agents cannot perform optimally if their decision at a given time step only depends on their perceptions at the same time step. Though they are more often used to solve Markov problems, there are several attempts to apply LCS to non-Markov problems ([19, 12] for instance).

Within this framework, explicit internal states were added to the classical (condition, action) pair of the classifiers, e.g. in XCSM [12, 21]. These internal states provide the additional information required to choose an action when the problem is non-Markov. The problem of properly setting the classifiers is generally devoted to *Genetic Algorithms* (GA).

In this paper, we extend our first comparison presented in [11] between XCSM and "ATNoSFERES". The latter is a new system that also uses GA to automatically design the behavior of agents facing problems in which they perceive situations as vectors of attributes, and have to select actions in order to fulfill their goals. We show in [11] that such an evolutionary approach is able to cope with non-Markov environments; in ATNoSFERES, the goals are represented by a *fitness* measure (instead of classical LCS learning techniques).

In the first section, we present the features and properties of the ATNoSFERES model. It relies upon oriented, labeled graphs (§ 2.1) for describing the behavior and the action selection procedure. The specificity of the model consists in building this graph from a bitstring (§ 2.2) that can be handled exactly like any other bitstring of a GA, with additional operators. Then we show that the graph-based representation is formally very close to LCS representations, and, in particular, to XCSM (§ 3.1). We remind the results of our previous experiments presented in [11] (§4), and the comparison we made (§5), that led us to assume that the lack of internal state generalization in ATNoSFERES explained the sub-optimality of the solutions that were found. A comparison of the performance of ATNoSFERES with and without a way to represent internal state generalization (§ 6) allows us to discuss in detail the validity of this assumption (§7). In the conclusion, we present further additions that could be made to our model so as to reach an even higher performance (§8).

2   Description of the ATNoSFERES Model

2.1   Graph-Based Expression of Behaviors

The architecture provided by the ATNoSFERES model [10, 16] involves an ATN graph [22] which is basically an oriented, labeled graph with a Start (or initial) node and an End (or final) node (see figure 5). Nodes represent states and edges represent transitions of an automaton.

Like LCSs, ATNoSFERES binds conditions expressed as a set of attributes to actions, and is endowed with the ability to generalize conditions by ignoring some attributes. But in ATNoSFERES , the conditions and actions are used in a graph structure that provides internal states. Such graphs have already been used by [10] for describing the behavior of agents. The labels on edges consist in a set of conditions (*e.g.* c1 c3 ?) that have to be fulfilled to enable the edge, and in a sequence of actions (*e.g.* a5 a2 a4 !) that are performed when the edge is chosen. We use those graphs as follows:

- At the beginning (when the agent is initialized), the agent is at the *Start* node (S).
- At each time step, the agent crosses an edge:
  1. It computes the set of eligible edges among those starting from the current node. An edge is eligible when either it has no condition label or all the conditions on its label are simultaneously true.
  2. An edge is randomly chosen in this set. If the set is empty, then an action is chosen randomly over all possible actions, the current node remains unchanged, and we do not perform the next two steps.
  3. The actions on the label of the current edge are sequentially performed by the system. Assuming that only one action can be performed by time step, only the last action is actually performed. When the action part of the label is empty, an action is chosen randomly.
  4. The new current node becomes the destination of the edge.
- The agent stops when it is at the *End* node (E). This node is a general feature of our model and may never be reached. This appears to be the case in all the following experiments (since agents reaching the *End* node stop moving and thus have a very low fitness, see § 4).

Having described how the graphs are used, we now present how they are built.

2.2   The Graph-Building Process

The graph describing the behaviors is built from a genotype by adding nodes and edges to a basic structure containing only the *Start* and *End* nodes.

There are many different evolutionary techniques to automatically design structures such as circuits [8], finite-state machines [2], neural networks [23] or program trees [7]. Very roughly, we can sketch an opposition between, on the one hand, approaches that use the genotype as an encoding of a set of parameters (like Genetic Algorithms [5, 1, 3] or Evolutionary Strategies [17]) and, on the other hand, approaches that use a single structure both as the genotype and the phenotype (such as Genetic Programming [7, 15], Evolutionary Programming [2], L-systems [13], developmental program trees, e.g. [6, 4, 14]).

In the ATNoSFERES model [9], we try to conciliate advantages from both kind of approaches: on the one hand, since the behavioral phenotype is produced by the interpretation of a graph, we want it to be of any complexity; on the other hand, we use a fine-grain genotype (a bitstring) to produce it, in order to allow a gradual exploration of the solution space through "blind" genetic operators.

Therefore, we follow a two-step process (see figure 1):

1. The bitstring (genotype) is translated into a sequence of tokens.
2. The tokens are interpreted as instructions of a robust programming language, dedicated to graph building.

Translation. Translation is a simple process that reads the bitstring genotype and decodes it into a sequence of *tokens* (symbols). It uses therefore a *genetic code*, i.e. a function $G : \{0, 1\}^n \longrightarrow \mathcal{T}$ ($|\mathcal{T}| \leq 2^n$) where $\mathcal{T}$ is the set of possible tokens (the different roles of which will be described in the next paragraph). Depending on the number of available tokens, the genetic code might be more or less redundant. Binary substrings of size n (decoded into a token each) are called "codons".

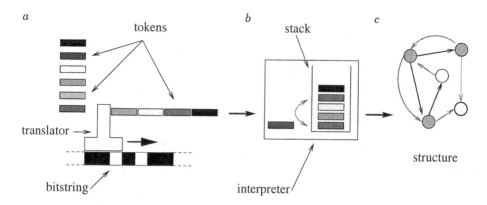

Fig. 1. Principles of the genetic expression we use to produce the behavioral graph from the bitstring genotype. The string is first decoded into tokens (*a*), which are interpreted in a second step as instructions (*b*) to create nodes, edges, and labels (*c*).

Interpretation. Tokens are instructions of the ATNoSFERES graph-building language (see table 1). They are interpreted one by one, while the interpreter is fed with the token stream produced by the translator. The interpretation of each successive token operates on a stack in which parts of the future graph are stored. The construction of the graph takes place during this interpretation process, by creating nodes and connections, and connecting them to the initial Start and End nodes. As in other stack-based languages (*e.g.* Forth, PostScript), the data in the stack can also be directly accessed by some instructions (*e.g.* connect, dup: see table 1), by other means that only push/pop operations.

In order to cope with a "blind" evolutionary process (i.e. based on random mutations on a fine-grain genotype), the graph built by the tokens sequence has to be robust to mutations [16]. For instance, the replacement of a token by another, or its deletion, should only have a *local impact*, rather than transforming the whole graph.

Therefore, if an instruction cannot be executed successfully, it is simply ignored, and when all tokens have been interpreted, the graph is made consistent, *e.g.* by linking Start to nodes without input edges (other than self-connected), or nodes without output edges to End.

Since any sequence of tokens is meaningful, the graph-building language is highly robust to any variations affecting the genotype, thus there is no specific syntactical or semantical constraint on the genetic operators. In addition, the sequence of tokens is to some extent order-independent and a given graph can be produced from very different genotypes.

The Graph-Building Language. Table 1 details the tokens that are used to build the graphs. There are three categories of token:

- stack tokens (swap, dup, ...), that manipulate the stack. They are independent from the agent abilities or the structure that is built.
- structure tokens (node, connect, ...), that perform atomic structure building steps. Here they are designed to build graphs. They are also independent from the agent abilities. Some of these tokens use tokens already in the stack.

Table 1. The graph building language. Here "first" (node, action or condition) refers to the first (node, action or condition) token encountered while going down the stack.

token	resulting actions
stack tokens	manipulate the stack
nop	no action, the token is just discarded
swap	swap the two first tokens
dup	push a copy of the first action or condition token
del	delete the first action or condition token
dupNode	push a copy of the first node token
delNode	delete the first node token[a]
popRoll	pop the token, and puts it on the bottom of the stack
pushRoll	take the token from the bottom of the stack, and push it
structure tokens	create nodes and connect them with edges
node	create a new node and push it
connect	create an edge from the first to the second node token[b], label the edge with the set of conditions token and the list of actions token until the second node, delete the action and condition tokens that were used
startConnect	create an edge from the Start node to the first node token, label the edge with the set of conditions token and the list of actions token until the node, delete the action and condition tokens that were used
endConnect	create an edge from the first node token to the End node, label the edge with the set of conditions token and the list of actions token until the node, delete the action and condition tokens that were used
agent tokens	actions and conditions tokens, specific to the agent
condition?	push the condition on the stack
action!	push the action on the stack

[a] it may be a copy: possible other copies of the node still remain in the stack
[b] they could both be copies of the same node, so it would be a self-connected edge

– agent tokens (actions, conditions), that are specific to an agent, and describe its abilities. These token are just pushed onto the stack.

2.3 Integration into an Evolutionary Framework

In this paper, the ATNoSFERES model has been applied inside an evolutionary algorithm to produce controllers for agents.

Therefore, each agent has a bitstring genotype from which it can produce a graph (the genetic code depends on the perception abilities of the agent and on the actions it can perform). The fitness of each agent is computed by evaluating its behavior in an environment. Then individuals are selected depending on their fitness and bred to produce offspring.

The genotype of the offspring is produced by a classical crossover operation between the genotypes of the parents. Additionally, we use two different mutation strate-

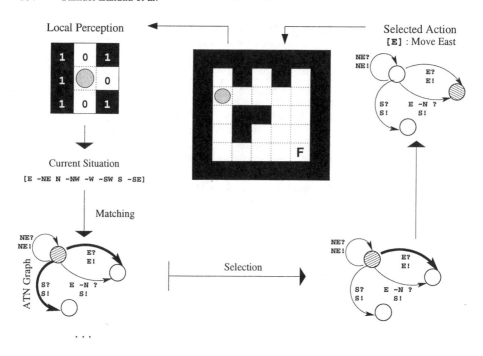

Fig. 2. In this example, the agent, located in a cell of the maze, perceives the presence/absence of blocks in each of the eight surrounding cells. It has to decide towards which of the eight adjacent cells it should move. From its current location, the agent perceives [E ¬NE N ¬NW ¬W ¬SW S ¬SE] (token E is true when the east cell is empty). From the current state (node) of its graph, two edges (in bold) are eligible, since the condition part of their label match the perceptions. One is randomly selected, then its action part (move east) is performed and the current state is updated.

gies to introduce variations into the genotype of new individuals: classical bit-flipping mutations, and random insertions or deletions of one codon. This modifies the sequence of tokens produced by translation, so that the complexity of the graph itself may change. Nodes or edges can in fact be added or removed by the evolutionary process, as can condition/action labels.

3   Learning Classifier Systems

As explained in the introduction, the problems tackled by LCS are characterized by the fact that situations are defined by several attributes representing perceivable properties of the environment. A LCS has to build classifiers, which define the behavior of the system as shown in figure 3. Within the LCS framework, the use of "#" symbols in the condition parts of the classifiers results in generalization, since *don't care* symbols make it possible to use a single description to describe several situations. Indeed, a *don't care* symbol *matches* any particular value of the considered attribute.

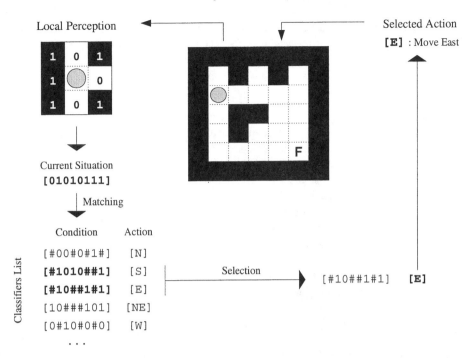

Fig. 3. The agent perceives the presence/absence (resp. 1/0) of blocks in each of the eight surrounding cells (considered clockwise, starting with the north cell). Thus from its current location, the agent perceives [01010111]. Within the list of classifiers characterizing it, the LCS first selects those matching the current situation. Then, it selects one of the matching classifiers and the corresponding action is performed.

The main issue with generalization is to figure out on which conditions can the *don't care* symbols be used so that the actions keep accurate. To do so, LCS usually call upon a GA.

In the *Pittsburg* style, the GA evolves a population of LCS with their whole lists of classifiers. The lists of classifiers are combined thanks to crossover operators and modified with mutations. The LCS are evaluated according to a fitness measure and the more efficient ones – with respect to the fitness – are kept. Thus, as in the ATNoSFERES model, a Pittsburg style LCS evolves a population of controllers.

On the contrary, in the *Michigan* style, the GA evolves a population of classifiers within the list of classifiers of a single agent. Here, this is the classifiers which are combined and modified. A fitness is associated to each classifier and the best ones are kept. Thus Michigan style LCS use GA to perform online learning: the classifiers are improved during the life time of the agent. Usually, such LCS rely on utility functions that depend on scalar rewards given by the environment, as defined in the RL framework [18].

In most of the early LCS [5], the fitness was defined directly according to the utility associated to the classifier. After having defined a very simple LCS called ZCS in [20],

Wilson found much more efficient to define the fitness according to the accuracy of the utility prediction. The resulting system, XCS [21], is now the most widely used LCS to solve Markov problems.

3.1 XCSM

Dealing with simple `Condition-Action` classifiers does not endow an agent with the ability to behave optimally in perceptually aliazed problems. In this kind of problems, it may happen that the current perception does not provide enough information to always choose the optimal action: as soon as the agent perceives the same situation in different states, it will choose the same action though this action may be inappropriate in some of these states (see figure 4).

For such problems, it is necessary to introduce internal states in the LCS. [19] proposed a way to probalistically link classifiers in order to bridge aliazed situations. In contrast, Lanzi [12] proposed XCSM, where M stands for Memory, as an extension of XCS with explicit internal states. XCSM manages an internal memory register composed of several bits that explicitly represent the internal state of the LCS. The memory register provides XCSM with more than just the environmental perceptions. Thus, dealing with perceptual aliazing is made possible by adding information from the past experience of the agent. As a result of this addition, a classifier contains four parts (see table 6): an external condition about the situation, an internal condition about the internal state, an external action to perform in the environment and an internal action that may modify the internal state.

The internal condition and the internal action contain as many attributes as there are bits in the memory register. In order to be selected by the LCS, a classifier has to match with both the external and internal conditions. When it is selected, the LCS performs the corresponding action in the environment and modifies the internal state if the internal action is not composed only of "#" symbols. When a classifier is fired, a *don't change* symbol in the internal action results in not changing the corresponding bit in the memory register. Like XCS, XCSM draws benefits from generalization in the external condition, but also in the internal condition and the internal action.

As explained in more details in [11], an ATN such as those evolved by ATNoS-FERES can be translated into a list of classifiers. The nodes of the ATN play the role of internal states in XCSM and make ATNoSFERES able to deal with perceptual aliazing. Thus it is natural to compare ATNoSFERES with XCSM. The edges of the ATN are characterized by several informations which can also be represented in classifiers: the source and destination nodes of the edge are respectively equivalent to the internal condition and the internal action; the conditions associated to the edges correspond to the external conditions of the classifiers; the actions associated to the edges correspond to the external actions of the classifiers.

4 First Experiments

4.1 The Perceptual Aliazing Problem

In [11], our purpose was to compare the evolutionary use of ATNoSFERES with XCSM with respect to their ability to deal with non-Markov problems. In order to provide that

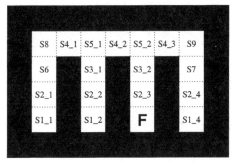

Fig. 4. The Maze10 environment. **F** represents the goal to reach (food). The agent starts from any cell of the maze; a few cells are unambiguous (S_i) but in the other ones the same perceptual situations may require either similar actions or different ones (*e.g.* go north in $S_{2\_\{1,2,4\}}$ but go south in S_{2_3}).

comparison, we experimented our model in the Maze10 environment, for which [12] provides empirical results obtained with XCSM.

4.2   Experimental Setup

We tried to reproduce an experimental setup close to that used in [12] with the Maze10 environment, with regards to the specificities of our model.

The agents used for the experiments are able to perceive the presence/absence of blocks in the eight adjacent cells of the grid. They can move in those adjacent cells (the move will be effective when the cell is empty or contains food). Thus the genetic code includes 16 condition and 8 action tokens. In order to encode 24 condition-action tokens together with 7 stack manipulation and 4 node creation/connection tokens, we need at least 6 bits to define a token ($2^6 = 64$ tokens, which means that some tokens are encoded twice).

Each experiment involves the following steps:

1. Initialize the population with $N = 300$ agents with random bitstrings.
2. For each generation, build the graph of each agent and evaluate it in the environment.
3. Select the individuals with higher fitness (namely, 20 % of the population) and produce new ones by crossing over the parents. The system performs probabilistic mutations (with a 1% rate) and insertions or deletions of codons (with a 0.5% rate) on the bitstring of the offspring.
4. Iterate the process with the new generation.

In order to evaluate the individuals, they are put into the environment, starting on a blank cell in the grid, and they have to find the food within a limited amount of time. The agent cannot perceive the food, and it can perform only one action per time step; when this action is incompatible with the environment (*e.g.* go west when the west cell contains an obstacle), it is simply discarded (the agent loses one time step and stays on the same cell). Its fitness for each run is: $F = D - K + B + 2 * R$ (*F*: fitness for the

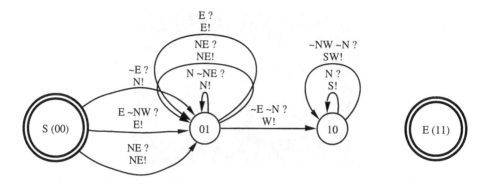

Fig. 5. Graph of the best individual in a representative experiment.

			EC					IC	EA	IA
E	NE	N	NW	W	SW	S	SE			
1	#	#	#	#	#	#	#	00	N	01
0	#	#	1	#	#	#	#	00	E	01
#	0	#	#	#	#	#	#	00	NE	01
#	1	0	#	#	#	#	#	01	N	##
#	0	#	#	#	#	#	#	01	NE	##
0	#	#	#	#	#	#	#	01	E	##
1	#	1	#	#	#	#	#	01	W	10
#	0	#	#	#	#	#	#	10	S	##
#	#	1	1	#	#	#	#	10	SW	##

Fig. 6. A LCS-like representation of the graph on figure 5. EC: external conditions, IC: internal conditions, EA: external actions, IA: internal actions.

run; D: number of blank cells that have been discovered during the run; K: time steps spent on already known cells; B: bonus when the food is found; R: remaining time if the food has been found within the time limit). Thus, the selection pressure encourages short paths to food and exploration. At each time step, the current cell is added to the set of already-known cells (in order do compute D and K). The term $2 * R$ ensures that a short path including an already-known cell is still preferred to a a longer path with only distinct cells. Each agent is evaluated 4 times starting on each empty cell, then its total fitness is the sum of the fitnesses computed for each run. In the optimal case, with $B = 30$ and a 20 time steps limit, the fitness is 4500.

The experiments reported here were carried out on various initial genotype sizes, from 300 to 540 bits. The original population genotype sizes change during evolution. Each experiment has been bounded by 10,000 generations, which is sufficient in most cases to reach high enough fitness values.

4.3   Results

Figure 5 presents a behavioral graph obtained by the best individual in a representative experiment. It has also been represented in a LCS-like formalism (fig. 6).

The agent whose graph is described in figure 5 has the following behavior: from any vertical corridor, it first reaches the horizontal corridor, then the NE corner, and finally goes straight to the food. This is a nearly optimal solution. Especially, there are clear distinctions between the bottom of vertical corridors (N ¬NE identifies cells $S_{\{1,2\}\_n}$), the top of vertical corridors (NE → S_6, S_7, S_{3_n}), the horizontal corridor (E → $S_8, S_{\{4,5\}\_n}$) and the crucial NE corner (S_9 is identified by ¬E ¬N ¬NW).

5   Discussion of the First Experiments

In [11], we presented a discussion resulting from the comparison between our model and XCSM. The main points we made were the following.

Minimality of Representation: While XCSM produces a constant size list of classifiers into which the size of the external conditions part and of the memory register must be chosen in advance, ATNoSFERES builds a graph whose number of nodes, edges, and labels on the edges can be minimal to solve the given problem (agreed that we focus on the best agent only). Hence the graph built by ATNoSFERES can be minimal while XCSM model cannot.

Reinforcement Learning and Classifier Selection: One important advantage of LCS with respect to ATNoSFERES is that the forces of classifiers are learnt through a RL algorithm. In order to remedy the fact that ATNoSFERES does not use RL, it is necessary to include into the fitness function elements that carry some information about the actual behavior of the agent (see §4.2).

Readability: As we showed in [11], one important advantage of ATNoSFERES with respect to XCSM is that the ATN resulting from the evolution is very easy to understand. Another key difference is that, in XCSM, the sequence of internal states of the agent during one run is not explicitly stated and must be derived by hand through careful examination. On the contrary, this sequence is perfectly clear when one reads an ATN. Furthermore, the internal state is very stable in ATNoSFERES. But this advantage of ATNoSFERES has its counterpart that will be discussed next: ATNoSFERES cannot easily represent Condition-Action rules that can be fired whatever the internal state is, as it is the case in XCSM with an internal condition composed of "#" only.

Generalization: In XCSM, a # in the internal condition allows the classifier to be applied whatever the internal state represented by the memory register is. This mechanism permits action regardless of the internal state. On the contrary, the tokens that have been chosen in those first experiments (see tab. 1) prevent ATNoSFERES from dealing with a default behavior, since connection tokens create edges (i.e. rules) between two nodes (i.e. two internal states). We investigate this point further in §6.

Optimality: Results given in [11] showed that the behavior obtained on Maze10 with ATNoSFERES was not completely optimal, and that obtaining the optimal graph would require a major structural change in the graph with respect to the low selective advantage.

6   New Experiments

6.1   Evaluating the Need for State Generalization

In [11], we concluded from the previous discussion by assuming that the ability of
XCSM classifiers to deal with a default behavior, regardless of the internal state was a
key advantage of XCSM over our model. Therefore we will now present our attempt
to add an internal state generalization property to our model by extending the graph
building language, with a new *defaultSelfConnect* token (see table 2).

Table 2. Extension to the graph building language (see table 1). Here "first" node refers to the
first node token encountered while going down the stack.

token	resulting actions
	...
structure tokens	create nodes and connect them with edges
	...
defaultSelfConnect	creates an edge from all the already present nodes to themselves, labels the edges with the set of conditions token and the list of actions token until the first node, deletes the action and condition tokens that were used

self transitions present on states:	IC	IA
00	00	##
00, 01	0#	##
00, 01, 10	##	##

Fig. 7. Different self-connection combinations and their translation in the XCSM formalism. IC:
internal condition, IA: internal action.

We emphasize that, since only the already created nodes will be self-connected, the
level of state generalization depends on the time when this token gets interpreted. For
example, if a *defaultSelfConnect* comes before all the internal nodes of the graph are
created, then the next nodes will not be affected by this self-connecting instruction.

As shown in figure 7, self-connecting transitions on nodes is equivalent to the presence of # in internal condition and/or internal action parts in XCSM. More precisely, as
the figure shows, if only the transition in node 00 is present, it is equivalent to a completely specified internal condition, while if the same transition is present in all nodes,
it is equivalent to a completely unspecified internal condition and internal action.

6.2   12-Candlestick Experimental Setup

In our previous experiments on Maze10, the best fitness was about 98% of the maximum
theoretic fitness. Since these results are very close to optimality, Maze10 experiments

do not provide a large enough opportunity for improvement to clearly probe the efficiency of the new encoding. Therefore, we propose a new candlestick-like maze (see figure 8) where the advantage of the *defaultSelfConnect* enabled language should be more significant with respect to the one without that token.

The agent starts from the top cells of any of the vertical corridors. We consider those starting locations only, because we are focusing on the generalization abilities, rather than searching for a general behavior to solve that maze from any starting cell. While going south along the "candles" from the 12 top cells, thanks to an empty cell on the side, the agent can determine which direction to take afterwards once it reaches the bottom of the candles. Indeed there is no ambiguity for far-right and far-left candles.

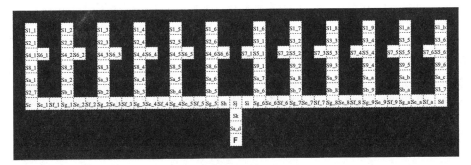

Fig. 8. The 12-Candlestick environment. **F** represents the goal to reach (food) from the 12 higher squares; 5 cells are unambiguous (S_i). In the other ones the same perceptual situations may require either similar actions or different ones (*e.g.* go west in $S_{g\text{-}\{1,2,3,4,5\}}$ but go east in $S_{g\text{-}\{6,7,8,9,a\}}$).

The internal state management strategy we have envisioned in designing this experiment is the following. The agent just needs one bit of memory. This bit is set when the agent sees an empty space on its left hand side or on its right hand side, and represents whether it is in the left part or the right part of the candlestick. This informations suffices to choose the right direction when it reaches the bottom of the candles. Given this internal state management strategy, the necessity to generalize on the internal state values becomes clear when one considers all the $\{S_{a\text{-}i}\}$ cells. In all those cells, which are represented by the same perceptual conditions, the agent must go south, *i.e.* choose the same action, *whether it is in the left part or the right part of the candlestick*. In the formalism of ATNoSFERES, this means that it must follow the same transition whatever the internal state is.

As a result of this property of the 12-Candlestick maze, only the agents following the internal state management strategy presented above can obtain an optimal performance. Any other strategy implies that the agents make additional steps in order to choose the correct directions. Indeed, disambiguating by visiting the far-left or far-right corners like the strategy obtained in Maze10 would imply a too costly detour with respect to the optimal path. But, as it will become clear in the remainder of that paper, even if this optimal behavior can be eventually obtained without using the *defaultSelf-Connect* token, it is nevertheless achieved more often with it.

The experimental setup is similar to the one in our previous Maze10 experiments, except for the genetic encoding and the fact that the agent does not start from all the empty cells. Like before, we need at least 6 bits to define a token, but this time in order to observe the influence of our special token, we use two genetic encodings. In the first encoding, we use the *nop* token, while in the second, it is replaced by the *defaultSelfConnect* token.

The agent is evaluated 6 times starting in each of the 12 top blank cells. The fitness function is the one of Maze10 experiments. In the optimal case, with $B = 50$ and a 30 time steps limit, the fitness is 6732. As for the Maze10 experiments, we made the experiments for 5 different initial genotypes length (300, 360, 420, 480 and 540 bits). During the experiments, the genetic operators might change the lengths of the genotypes.

6.3   12-Candlestick Experiment Results

Figures 9 and 11 respectively show the best solutions found with and without the *defaultSelfConnect* token. The fitness of both these individuals is 6726 for a maximum of 6732. The missing points are lost when the agent passes through the corner at the foot of the far-right candle (see figure 8, cell S_d), instead of going directly from S_{3_7} to S_{f_a}. Since there are 6 evaluation per "candle", it loses 6 times 1 point.

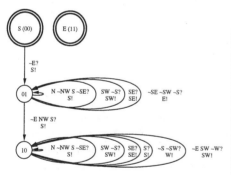

	EC							IC	EA	IA
E	NE	N	NW	W	SW	S	SE			
0	#	#	#	#	#	#	#	00	S	01
#	#	#	#	#	0	0	0	01	E	##
0	#	#	1	#	#	1	#	01	S	10
#	#	#	#	#	#	1	#	10	S	##
#	#	#	#	#	0	0	#	10	W	##
0	#	#	#	0	1	#	#	10	SW	##
#	#	1	0	#	#	1	0	##	S	##
#	#	#	#	#	1	0	#	##	SW	##
#	#	#	#	#	#	#	1	##	SE	##

Fig. 9. 12-Candlestick. Graph of the best individual using the *defaultSelfConnect* token. The token appears 3 times, after the 2 nodes were created, so there are 3 identical self-connecting edges for both nodes.

Fig. 10. A LCS-like representation of the graph on figure 9. The three last classifiers correspond to self-connecting edges in the graph. EC, IC, EA, IA: see figure 6.

6.4   Discussion of 12-Candlestick Results

As figure 13 shows, the average fitness obtained with the *defaultSelfConnect* token in the 12-Candlestick experiment is significantly better than the one obtained without that

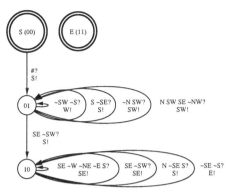

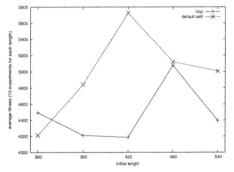

EC								IC	EA	IA
E	NE	N	NW	W	SW	S	SE			
#	#	#	#	#	#	#	#	00	S	01
#	#	#	#	#	0	0	#	01	W	##
#	#	#	#	#	#	1	0	01	S	##
#	#	0	#	#	1	#	#	01	SW	##
#	#	1	0	#	1	#	1	01	SW	##
#	#	#	#	#	0	#	1	01	S	10
0	0	#	#	0	#	1	1	10	SE	##
#	#	#	#	#	0	#	1	10	SE	##
#	#	1	#	#	#	1	0	10	S	##
#	#	#	#	#	#	0	0	10	S	##

Fig. 11. 12-Candlestick. Graph of the best individual *not* using the *defaultSelfConnect* token.

Fig. 12. A LCS-like representation of the graph on figure 11. EC, IC, EA, IA: see figure 6.

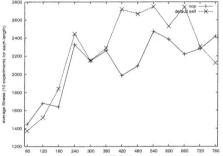

Fig. 13. 12-Candlestick. Average fitness with and without self token.

Fig. 14. Maze10. Average fitness with and without self token.

token. The difference between the performances in both cases according to the different initial lengths of the bitstrings is given on figure 15 and 16. We can clearly see from these figures that the *defaultSelfConnect* token conveys a selective advantage to our agents.

The purpose of making these experiments on the 12-Candlestick maze is to check that the *defaultSelfConnect* token is working well and provides the property for which it was designed. But, since the 12-Candlestick maze is specially designed to favor the use of the *defaultSelfConnect* token, it is also necessary to check whether or not this property can be generalized to Maze10, even if we expect less significant results.

6.5   Second Maze10 Experimental Setup

The experimental setup is that of our previous Maze10 experiments (see section 4.2), except for the genetic encoding. Like in the previous experiments, in order to observe the influence of our *defaultSelfConnect* token, both genetic encoding tested differed only by one codon: *nop* for the first, and *defaultSelfConnect* for the second, as we did in section 6.2

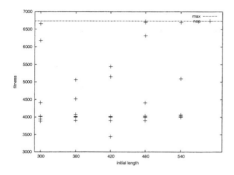

Fig. 15. 12-Candlestick. Fitness without *de-faultSelfConnect* token.

Fig. 16. 12-Candlestick. Fitness with *default-SelfConnect* token.

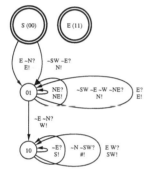

EC								IC	EA	IA
E	NE	N	NW	W	SW	S	SE			
1	#	0	#	#	#	#	#	00	E	01
0	#	#	#	#	0	#	#	00	N	01
#	1	#	#	#	#	#	#	01	NE	##
0	0	#	#	0	0	#	#	01	N	##
1	#	#	#	#	#	#	#	01	E	##
0	#	0	#	#	#	#	#	01	W	10
0	#	#	#	#	#	#	#	10	S	##
#	#	0	#	#	0	#	#	10	#	##
1	#	#	#	1	#	#	#	10	SW	##

Fig. 17. Maze10. Graph of the best individual using the *defaultSelfConnect* token for Maze 10. The token appears 1 time, and is applied on one node only.

Fig. 18. A LCS-like representation of the graph on figure 17. EC, IC, EA, IA: see figure 6.

6.6   Second Maze10 Experiment Results

The best solutions, respectively with and without the *defaultSelfConnect* token, are shown in figures 17 and 19. The best fitness for both genetic encodings (with and without the *defaultSelfConnect* token) are close to each other, respectively 4448 and 4436 for a maximum of 4500. This best fitness was found in 3 experiments for the first, and only one time for the second, over the 50 experiments run for each genetic encoding. As in our previous Maze10 experiments, most of the points are lost when reaching the NE corner when coming from the west of the maze, and other points are also lost when the agent goes in or out of some columns by passing through the cell on top of it, instead of using a diagonal move.

7   Further Discussion

From figures 13 and 14, it is clear that ATNoSFERES obtains better performance both on 12-Candlestick and on Maze10 with the *defaultSelfConnect* token than without it.

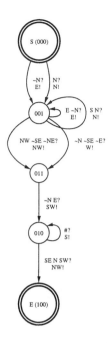

			EC					IC	EA	IA
E	NE	N	NW	W	SW	S	SE			
#	#	0	#	#	#	#	#	000	E	001
#	#	1	#	#	#	#	#	000	N	001
1	#	0	#	#	#	#	#	001	E	###
#	#	1	#	#	#	1	#	001	N	###
#	0	#	1	#	#	#	0	001	NW	011
0	#	0	#	#	#	#	0	001	W	011
1	#	0	#	#	#	#	#	011	SW	010
#	#	#	#	#	#	#	#	010	S	###
#	#	1	#	#	1	#	1	010	NW	100

Fig. 19. Maze10. Graph of the best individual *not* using the *defaultSelfConnect* token. The edge between 010 and 100 is actually never crossed.

Fig. 20. A LCS-like representation of the graph on figure 19.EC, IC, EA, IA: see figure 6.

The optimal behavior is never reached, however (the best solution is 0.1% below this optimum). The best individual on the 12-Candlestick, presented on figure 9, uses the *defaultSelfConnect* token as expected, so as to represent a completely unspecified internal state. This result seems to support our initial assumption according to which being able to generalize on the internal state is important to solve such behavioral problems, and results on Maze10 seem to confirm the generality of the assumption.

But a closer examination of the best individuals obtained through other experiments reveals that our assumption must be refined. In particular, the best individual on Maze10, presented in figure 17, uses the *defaultSelfConnect* token when there is only one node in the stack. More generally, it appears that the *defaultSelfConnect* token has been used many times to add only one self-connecting transition in the graph, or none at all (if no node is present when *defaultSelfConnect* is interpreted).

As explained in figure 7, since the interpretation of that token results in the addition of self-connecting transitions only to the nodes already present in the stack, it does not always result in the equivalent of full generalization on the internal state. In particular, when there is only one self-connecting transition in the graph, the interpretation of the *defaultSelfConnect* token results in the equivalent of a fully specified internal condition part followed by an unspecified internal action part.

Interestingly, however ATNoSFERES can obtain one self-connected node without using the *defaultSelfConnect* token. But doing so requires that much more constraints on the bitstring are fulfilled. Thus a self-connected node is much less likely to happen without the *defaultSelfConnect* token.

So it may be that ATNoSFERES gets a better performance with the *defaultSelfConnect* token than without it just because having self-connecting transitions is a beneficial property and having that token significantly increases the probability to have that property.

Hence, what this more detailled study seems to reveal is that, when several internal states are necessary to solve a non-Markov problem, it is important that the system keep the possibility to specify (condition, action) transitions without being compelled to change its internal state.

As a result of these new findings, we still cannot definitively conclude yet on whether it is having the ability to generalize on the internal state or having the ability to represent stable internal state that is the most beneficial property in the problems studied in this paper.

8   Conclusion and Future Work

In the context of a comparison between XCSM and ATNoSFERES, we have studied in this paper the importance of the ability to represent generalized internal states. In order to do so, we have introduced a new *defaultSelfConnect* token which adds a self-connecting transition to all the nodes already present in the stack. We have also presented a new maze experiment specially designed to advantage systems able to generalize on the internal state.

Our experiments have shown that the performance of our system is significantly better with this addition. But, while this result seems to support the conclusion that being able to generalize on the internal state is a significant property of adaptive algorithms, a closer examination of what really happened during the experiments reveals that our *defaultSelfConnect* token has also been used for a different purpose than just generalizing on the internal state. That token seems to have another interesting property than the one for which it was designed.

In order to be able to conclude more accurately on the relative role played by the internal state generalization property and the stable internal state property, more experiments will be necessary. We believe that going into an even more detailed comparison between XCSM and ATNoSFERES on the two experiments presented above will help identifying further what is really necessary to reach an optimal behavior. In particular, we should try to assess the distinctive roles of generalization on the internal condition and on the internal action parts, by adding one or two specialized tokens representing each property independently of the other.

References

1. K. A. DE JONG, *An Analysis of the Behavior of a Class of Genetic Adaptive Systems*, PhD thesis, Dept. of Computer and Communication Sciences, University of Michigan, 1975.
2. L. J. FOGEL, A. J. OWENS, AND M. J. WALSH, *Artificial Intelligence through Simulated Evolution*, John Wiley & Sons, 1966.
3. D. E. GOLDBERG, *Genetic Algorithms in Search, Optimization, and Machine Learning*, Addison-Wesley, 1989.

4. F. GRUAU, *Neural Network Synthesis Using Cellular Encoding and the Genetic Algorithm*, Ph.D. thesis, ENS Lyon – Université Lyon I, 1994.
5. J. H. HOLLAND, *Adaptation in Natural and Artificial Systems: An Introductory Analysis with Applications to Biology, Control, and Artificial Intelligence*, University of Michigan Press, Ann Arbor, MI, 1975.
6. J. KODJABACHIAN AND J.-A. MEYER, *Evolution and Development of Neural Controllers for Locomotion, Gradient-Following, and Obstacle-Avoidance in Artificial Insects*, IEEE Transactions on Neural Networks, 9 (1998), pp. 796–812.
7. J. R. KOZA, *Genetic Programming: On the Programming of Computers by Means of Natural Selection*, MIT Press, Cambridge, MA, 1992.
8. J. R. KOZA, F. H. BENNETT III, D. ANDRE, AND M. A. KEANE, *Automated Design of Both the Topology and Sizing of Analog Electrical Circuits Using Genetic Programming*, in Artificial Intelligence in Design'96, J. S. Gero and F. Sudweeks, eds., 1996, pp. 151–170.
9. S. LANDAU AND S. PICAULT, *Stack-Based Gene Expression*, Technical Report LIP6 2002/011, LIP6, Paris, 2002.
10. S. LANDAU, S. PICAULT, AND A. DROGOUL, *ATNoSFERES: a Model for Evolutive Agent Behaviors*, in Proceedings of the AISB'01 Symposium on Adaptive Agents and Multi-Agent Systems, 2001.
11. S. LANDAU, S. PICAULT, O. SIGAUD, AND P. GÉRARD, *A Comparison between AT-NoSFERES and XCSM*, in Proc. of the Genetic and Evolutionary Computation Conference (GECCO 2002), W. Langdon, E. Cantu-Paz, K. Mathias, R. Roy, D. Davis, R. Poli, K. Balakrishnan, V. Honavar, G. Rudolph, J. Wegener, L. Bull, M. A. Potter, A. Schultz, J. F. Miller, E. Burke, and N. Jonoska, eds., New York, july 9-13 2002, Morgan Kaufmann, pp. 926–933.
12. P. L. LANZI, *An Analysis of the Memory Mechanism of XCSM*, in Proceedings of the Third Annual Conference on Genetic Programming, J. R. Koza, W. Banzhaf, K. Chellapilla, K. Deb, M. Dorigo, D. B. Fogel, M. H. Garzon, D. E. Goldberg, H. Iba, and R. Riolo, eds., University of Wisconsin, Madison, Wisconsin, USA, 1998, Morgan Kaufmann.
13. A. LINDENMAYER, *Mathematical Models for Cellular Interaction in Development, parts I and II*, Journal of theoretical biology, 18 (1968).
14. S. LUKE AND L. SPECTOR, *Evolving Graphs and Networks with Edge Encoding: Preliminary Report*, in Late Breaking Papers at the Genetic Programming 1996 Conference, J. R. Koza, ed., Stanford University, CA, july 1996, Stanford Bookstore, pp. 117–124.
15. D. J. MONTANA, *Strongly Typed Genetic Programming*, in Evolutionary Computation, vol. 3, 1995.
16. S. PICAULT AND S. LANDAU, *Ethogenetics and the Evolutionary Design of Agent Behaviors*, in Proceedings of the 5th World Multi-Conference on Systemics, Cybernetics and Informatics (SCI'01), N. Callaos, S. Esquivel, and J. Burge, eds., vol. III, 2001, pp. 528–533.
17. H.-P. SCHWEFEL, *Evolution and Optimum Seeking*, John Wiley and Sons, Inc., 1995.
18. R. S. SUTTON AND A. G. BARTO, *Reinforcement Learning, an introduction*, MIT Press, Cambridge, MA, 1998.
19. A. TOMLINSON AND L. BULL, *CXCS*, in Learning Classifier Systems: from Foundations to Applications, P. Lanzi, W. Stolzmann, and S. Wilson, eds., Springer Verlag, Heidelberg, 2000, pp. 194–208.
20. S. W. WILSON, *ZCS, a Zeroth level Classifier System*, Evolutionary Computation, 2 (1994), pp. 1–18.
21. S. W. WILSON, *Classifier Fitness Based on Accuracy*, Evolutionary Computation, 3 (1995), pp. 149–175.
22. W. A. WOODS, *Transition Networks Grammars for Natural Language Analysis*, Communications of the Association for the Computational Machinery, 13 (1970), pp. 591–606.
23. X. YAO, *Evolving Artificial Neural Networks*, Proceedings of the IEEE, 87 (1999).

Accuracy, Parsimony, and Generality in Evolutionary Learning Systems via Multiobjective Selection

Xavier Llorà[1], David E. Goldberg[1], Ivan Traus[2], and Ester Bernadó[2]

[1] Illinois Genetic Algorithms Laboratory (IlliGAL)
National Center for Supercomputing Applications,
University of Illinois at Urbana-Champaign,
104 S. Mathews Ave, Urbana, IL 61801
{xllora,deg}@illigal.ge.uiuc.edu
[2] Enginyeria i Arquitectura La Salle,
Universitat Ramon Llull,
Psg. Bonanova 8, 08022, Barcelona,
Catalonia, Spain, European Union
{is06376,esterb}@salleURL.edu

Abstract. Evolutionary learning systems (also known as *Pittsburgh* learning classifier systems) need to balance accuracy and parsimony for evolving high quality general hypotheses. The learning process used in evolutionary learning systems is based on a set of training instances that sample the target concept to be learned. Thus, the learning process may overfit the learned hypothesis to the given set of training instances. In order to address some of these issues, this paper introduces a multiobjective approach to evolutionary learning systems. Thus, we translate the selection of promising hypotheses into a two-objective problem that looks for: (1) *accurate* (low error), and (2) *compact* (low complexity) solutions. Using the proposed multiobjective approach a set of compromise hypotheses are spread along the Pareto front. We also introduce a theory of the impact of noise when sampling the target concept to be learned, as well as the appearance of overfitted hypotheses as the result of perturbations on high quality generalization hypotheses in the Pareto front.

1 Introduction

This paper deals with a learning classifier system (LCS) [1–4] known as an evolutionary learning system (ELS), or *Pittsburgh* classifier system [5–8]. Among other characteristics, evolutionary learning systems use variable-size individuals. The main reason for using this kind of individual is because an individual must be a complete solution to the classification problem. That is, an individual codifies an hypothesis of the target concept to be learned. In order to perform the learning, ELSs use a set of instances that are a sample of the target concept to be learned. Thus, like other machine learning algorithms, ELSs assume that the target concept do not change over time. Some variable-size knowledge representation of hypotheses often used in ELSs include rule sets, instance sets, or decision trees [9].

P.L. Lanzi et al. (Eds.): IWLCS 2002, LNAI 2661, pp. 118–142, 2003.

Traditionally, the evolutionary-driven learning process of ELSs has focused on the evolution of accurate hypotheses that correctly classify the available training instances. However, this approach does not solve some relevant issues of machine learning algorithms [10]. The first one is described by *Occam's razor*. Given two equally accurate hypotheses, we prefer the simplest one. Thus, if the hypotheses are represented as a set of rules, we prefer the one with fewer rules, or in other words, the most general and accurate hypothesis that describes the target concept. The second issue is the quality of the evolved hypothesis in terms of generalization accuracy (accuracy of an hypothesis given unseen instances of the target concept). Since ELSs use a training set that is a sample set of the target concept, an ELS may evolve an overfitted hypotheses to the given training data set. This is a critical issue in real-world learning problems. Therefore, the evolved hypotheses, in order to achieve a high quality generalized accuracy on the target concept, must avoid over-adapted solutions. If not, the hypotheses may have poor performance when tested on unseen instances of the target concept.

Another problem that ELSs have to address is the *bloat* phenomenon. *Bloat* can be defined as the individual size growth without fitness improvement. This problem is well-known in the genetic programming (GP) community [11–22], as well as in ELSs [23–25], especially when the ELSs are used for solving data-mining tasks.

Some efforts to address *Occam's razor* and *bloat* introduce direct penalties also known as *parsimony pressure*. The goal of parsimony pressure is to bias the evolution of the hypotheses toward solutions that balance accuracy and size. Introducing explicit selection bias toward generalization, a common parsimony pressure introduces a static (or adaptive) tradeoff between the accuracy and the size of the evolved hypotheses, constraining the search path of the evolutionary algorithm. This fact often guides the learning algorithm toward a collapsed population where all the individuals represent the most general hypothesis. In other words, if the hypotheses are represented using a set of rules, the individuals codify hypotheses that contain only one rule that matches everything.

In order to address the generalization issues discussed previously, here we address parsimony and generality by transforming an ELS into a two-objective problem. This multiobjective approach uses two different objectives for a given hypothesis: (1) *accuracy* (low error), and (2) *compactness* (low complexity hypotheses under the *Occam's razor*). The first one guarantees that we solve the problem accurately, whereas the second introduces generalization pressure toward compact solutions. Our proposal is based on the concept of a Pareto optimal set [26–29]. Roughly explained, we want to spread the evolved hypotheses over the Pareto front of the learning problem. Thus, the multiobjective selection pressure coevolves different solutions with different tradeoffs between accuracy and complexity. Therefore, once the evolutionary learning process is done, we will be able to choose among the different hypotheses (and their associated tradeoff). Moreover, the Pareto front of the evolved population lets us gain some theoretical insights on the behavior of the proposed multiobjective ELSs. Our analysis is twofold. On one hand, we study the effect of noise when sampling the target concept. On the other hand, we also make some considerations about the overfitting of the evolved hypothesis in terms of the Pareto front of the population.

The paper is structured as follows. Section 2 presents some related work from GP and ELSs efforts for controlling *bloat*, as well as some work done using multiobjective optimization. Then, section 3 presents a description of the multiobjective fitness evaluation proposed to achieve the goals of this paper. Section 4 describes how the multiobjective fitness evaluation is used in two learning systems (the first one based on genetic algorithms (GA), whereas the second relies on evolution strategies (ES)). Some experiments using both algorithms are summarized in section 5. Finally, section 6 discusses the conclusions of this work, as well as some future work.

2   Related Work

One of the main problems that arises with the evolution of variable-size individuals is the *bloat* phenomenon [30]. *Bloat* is usually defined (in GP terms) as the code growth of individuals without any fitness improvement. Unfortunately ELSs that use variable-size representations also suffer from *bloat*. In ELSs, this phenomenon may appear in two different forms: (1) the addition of useless rules, or (2) the evolution of over-specific rules.

Early works in GP reported unexpected code growth of individuals that did not improve fitness [11–13,30]. This phenomenon was called *bloat* [30]. Banzhaf and Langdon [21] categorize being of *bloat* as two disputed types. The first is known as "fitness causes *bloat*" [16], whereas the second is referred as "natural code is protective" [15]. Fitness selection bias favors individuals with the same fitness regardless of their size. This means that given an individual, there is a set of individuals (almost infinite) that share the same fitness value, but with a larger code. Therefore, once a given fitness value has been reached, the search becomes a random walk among these bigger individuals without an improvement in fitness. On the other hand, *bloat* also appears as neutral code that does not take part in fitness computation. This neutral code increases the size of the individual and as a consequence it reduces the probability that the genetic operators disrupt useful code.

Many different approaches and studies to control code growth have been developed in the GP community [14, 17–19, 22]. Some of them impose a *parsimony pressure* toward compact individuals by varying fitness or through specially tailored operators, among others. Recently, an approach has been proposed by Bleuler, Brack, Thiele, and Zitzler [20] in which they address *bloat* as a multiobjective optimization problem. The two objectives are to: (1) maximize fitness, and (2) minimize size. In order to achieve this goal, they used a multiobjective evolutionary algorithm known as SPEA2 [31–33].

Several authors have studied the growth of individuals in Pittsburgh classifier systems, but they have not addressed this problem from a multiobjective point of view. The most common approach is to introduce a parsimony pressure in the fitness function, in such a way that the fitness of larger individuals is decreased [24,25,23]. For example, in [23] the *bloat* is controlled by a step fitness function: when the number of rules of an individual exceeds a certain maximum, its fitness is decreased abruptly. One problem of this approach is to set this thresholds value appropriately. Bacardit and Garrell [25] define a similar fitness function, as well as a set of operators for the deletion of introns[1]

---

[1] Non-coding segments. In GP literature this concept has also been termed *non-effective code* [21].

[34] (rules that are not used in the classification) and a tournament-based selection operator that considers the size of individuals. The authors argue that the *bloat* control has an influence over the generalization capability of the solutions. It has been observed that shorter rule sets tend to have more generalization capabilities [35, 25, 34].

Therefore, the use of a parsimony pressure has beneficial effects: it controls the unlimited growth of individuals, increases the efficiency in the search process and leads to solutions with better generalization. Nevertheless, the parsimony pressure must be balanced appropriately. An excessive pressure toward small individuals could result in premature convergence leading to compact solutions but with suboptimal fitness [34], or even in a total population failure (population collapses with individuals of minimal size). Soule and Foster [17] showed that the effect of parsimony pressure can be measured by calculating explicitly the relationship between the size and the performance of individuals within the population. Based on these results, it seems that a multiobjective approach may overcome some of these difficulties. Instead of balancing the parsimony pressure, a multiobjective approach based on the concept of the Pareto front [26–29] can coevolve a set of solutions with different tradeoffs between size and accuracy. Spreading these solutions among the Pareto front implicitly balances the relationship between the generality and the performance of individuals within the population. Doing so may also have the benefit of providing a richer set of diverse rules to enhance the search capability of the scheme.

In the field of evolutionary fuzzy models, there have been some proposals with the use of multiobjective techniques. Gómez-Skarmeta, Jiménez, and Ibáez [36] use a multiobjective evolutionary algorithm to generate and tune fuzzy models. The system obtains a collection of fuzzy rule sets along the discovered Pareto front, which is defined by the minimization of two objectives: the quadratic mean error and the number of rules. Although the minimization of the number of rules is an objective included in the evolutionary search, the number of rules is previously limited by a parameter tuned by the user. In their work, the multiobjective algorithm is used as a tool for providing multiple solutions to the decision maker, who has to decide *a posteriori* the best solution according to the problem environment. Jiménez, Gómez-Skarmeta, Roubos, and Robert [37] also define a multiobjective evolutionary algorithm to obtain fuzzy models. They identify several objectives such as the accuracy, the similarity between fuzzy sets, and the number of rules, but their final approach does not include the number of rules as an objective to minimize because, according to the authors, it led to sub-optimal solutions.

Our proposal uses a multiobjective evolutionary approach which minimizes the classification accuracy and the size (number of rules). Besides controlling the number of rules (*bloat*) dynamically, this would allow the formation of compromise hypotheses. This explicit tradeoff formation let us explore the generalization capabilities of the hypotheses that form the Pareto front. In certain environments like data mining, where the extraction of explanatory models is desirable, high quality general solutions (in terms of accuracy out of sample, or compactness of hypotheses) are useful. For instance, the presence of noise in the data set may lead to accurate but overfitted solutions. Maintaining a Pareto front of compromise solutions we can identify the overfitted perturbations of high quality general hypotheses. Therefore, evolving a set of different compromise solutions between accuracy and generalization, we can postpone the decision of picking the "best rule set" to the final user (decision maker), or combine them all using some *bagging* technique [38, 39, 9].

3 Multiobjective Evolution and Evolutionary Learning Systems

Since multiobjective optimization plays a central role in the work presented here, this section summarizes some relevant issues. First, we briefly summarize some multiobjective optimization definitions in subsection 3.1. Then, subsection 3.2 presents how we can use a multiobjective approach to address the *bloat* phenomenon that usually appears on variable-size individuals evolved in some learning systems. Finally, subsection 3.3 discusses the usefulness of evolving a classification front in a learning system.

3.1 Multiobjective Optimization

In a multiobjective optimization problem (MOP) [29] a solution $\vec{x} \in \Omega$ is represented as a vector of n decision variables $\vec{x} = (x_1, \ldots, x_n)$, where Ω is the decision variable space. We want to optimize k objectives which are defined as $f_i(\vec{x})$, with $i = 1 \ldots k$. These objectives are grouped in a vector function denoted as $F(\vec{x}) = (f_1(\vec{x}), \ldots, f_k(\vec{x}))$, where $F(\vec{x}) \in \Lambda$. F is a function which maps points from the decision variable space Ω to the objective function space Λ:

$$F : \Omega \longmapsto \Lambda$$
$$\vec{x} \longmapsto \vec{y} = F(\vec{x}) \tag{1}$$

Without loss of generality, we can define a MOP as the problem of minimizing a set of objectives $F(\vec{x}) = (f_1(\vec{x}), \ldots, f_k(\vec{x}))$, subject to some constraints $g_i(\vec{x}) \leq 0$, $i = 1, \ldots, m$. These constraints are necessary for problems where there are invalid solutions in Ω. Although the MOP's definition addresses a minimization problem, MOP is not limited exclusively to minimization. MOP can be applied to maximization problems as well as to problems where some objectives must be minimized and some others maximized. Nevertheless, in the rest of this section we will assume a minimization MOP.

A solution that minimizes all the objectives and satisfies all constraints may not exist. Sometimes, the minimization of a certain objective implies a degradation in another objective. Then, there is not a global optimum that minimizes all the objectives simultaneously. In this context, the concept of optimality must be redefined. Vilfredo Pareto [26] introduced the concept of dominance and Pareto optimum to deal with this issue.

In general terms, a vector $\vec{u}$ *dominates* another vector $\vec{v}$, written as $\vec{u} \preceq \vec{v}$, if and only if every component u_i is less or equal than v_i, and at least there is one component in $\vec{u}$ which is strictly less than the corresponding component in $\vec{v}$. This can be formulated as follows:

$$\vec{u} \preceq \vec{v} \iff \forall i \in 1, \ldots, k, \, u_i \leq v_i \wedge \exists i \in 1, \ldots, k : u_i < v_i \tag{2}$$

For example, given a MOP with three objectives and the vectors $\vec{u} = F(\vec{x}_1) = (1, 1, 2)$ and $\vec{v} = F(\vec{x}_2) = (1, 2, 2)$, we notice that $\vec{u} \preceq \vec{v}$. However, if $\vec{u} = (1, 1, 2)$ and $\vec{v} = (1, 2, 1)$, neither $\vec{u}$ dominates $\vec{v}$ nor $\vec{v}$ dominates $\vec{u}$.

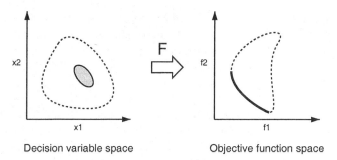

Decision variable space   Objective function space

Fig. 1. In this hypothetical example we have a two objective problem with two decision variables. Solutions are mapped from the decision variable space to the objective function space. The shadowed area in decision variable space represents the Pareto optimal set and the continuous line in objective function space the Pareto front. A simple mathematical example of this kind of behavior can be displayed using $f_1(x_1) = (x_1 - 2)^2$ and $f_2(x_2) = (x_2 - 4)^2$.

The concept of *Pareto optimality* is based on the dominance definition. Thus, a solution $\vec{x} \in \Omega$ is Pareto optimal if there is not any other solution $\vec{x}' \in \Omega$ whose objective vector $\vec{u}' = F(\vec{x}')$ dominates $\vec{u} = F(\vec{x})$. In other words, a solution whose objectives can not be improved simultaneously by any other solution is Pareto optimum.

The set of all solutions whose objective vectors are not dominated by any other objective vector is called the Pareto optimal set $\mathcal{P}^*$:

$$\mathcal{P}^* := \left\{ \vec{x}_1 \mid \nexists\, \vec{x}_2 : \vec{F}(\vec{x}_2) \preceq \vec{F}(\vec{x}_1) \right\} \tag{3}$$

Analogously, the set of all vectors $\vec{u} = F(\vec{x})$ such that $\vec{x}$ belongs to the Pareto optimal set is called the Pareto Front $\mathcal{PF}^*$:

$$\mathcal{PF}^* := \left\{ \vec{u} = \vec{F}(\vec{x}) = (f_1(\vec{x}), \dots, f_k(\vec{x})) \mid \vec{x} \in \mathcal{P}^* \right\} \tag{4}$$

Figure 1 represents a two objective problem in the decision space (left) and the objective space (right). The shadowed area on the left represents the optimal solutions in the decision space, also called as Pareto optimal set. The thick curve in the objective function space represents the Pareto Front. It is constituted by the objective vectors which are not dominated by any other objective vectors. These solutions represent compromise solutions, i.e., solutions with different tradeoffs between the objectives. We cannot improve an objective without penalizing the other one. Among these compromise solutions, we have to choose the desired tradeoff between the different objectives in order to take the best solution to the problem. This decision is done by a *decision maker*, a human or an expert system with some knowledge about the problem.

3.2 Classification and Multiobjective Optimization

The goal of our multiobjective approach introduced in ELSs is to trade off two objectives: (1) the accuracy of an individual, and (2) its size. In particular, we are interested in evolving accurate (with a reduced classification error) general solutions to the classification problem. This means that we prefer maximally general solutions [3] describing the knowledge pattern behind that classification data. In an ELS where an individual is a complete solution to the classification problem, this can be achieved biasing the evolution toward compact (small sized) individuals. Therefore, we have two different objectives to optimize at the same time, accuracy and size.

Let's define $\vec{x}$ as an individual that is a complete solution to the classification problem; $\mathcal{D}$ the training data set for the given problem; $|\mathcal{D}|$ number of instances in $\mathcal{D}$; $miss(\vec{x}, \mathcal{D})$ the number of incorrectly classified instances of $\mathcal{D}$ performed by $\vec{x}$; and finally, $size(\vec{x})$ a measure of the current size of $\vec{x}$ (e.g. the number of rules it contains). Using this notation, a simple multiobjective approach can be defined as follows:

$$\min F(\vec{x}) = (f_e(\vec{x}), f_s(\vec{x})) \tag{5}$$

$$f_e(\vec{x}) = \frac{miss(\vec{x}, \mathcal{D})}{|\mathcal{D}|} \tag{6}$$

$$f_s(\vec{x}) = size(\vec{x}) \tag{7}$$

Thus, our multiobjective approach minimizes $F(\vec{x})^2$. With this simple multiobjective definition, the evolution is biased toward the hypotheses that form the Pareto optimal set. Therefore, the population may evolve hypotheses with different tradeoffs between accuracy and generality. Besides, the *bloat* phenomenon is also addressed due to the bias toward the Pareto front. For implementation purposes f_s was divided by the data set size (number of available instances).

3.3   What Is the Purpose of the Classification Front?

The main purpose of the evolved Pareto front (or classification front) is to keep solutions with different tradeoffs between accuracy and size. Coevolving these compromise solutions, we can delay the need of choosing a solution until the evolution is over and the classification front is provided. However, this decision is critical for achieving a high quality accuracy generalization when tested with unseen instances of the target concept.

The *decision maker* has several hypotheses among which to choose, all provided by the classification front. The *decision maker* can be a human or an expert system with some knowledge about the problem. However, there are other approaches already explored in the ML and GBML community. Among others, some interesting approaches are based on the *bagging* technique [38, 39]. The goal is to combine different hypotheses (e.g. the ones that form the classification front) into a new single classification hypothesis. The goal is to obtain a new combined hypothesis that reduce the impact of the overfitting of the used hypotheses, producing a high quality general hypothesis. This technique tends to reduce the deviation among runs, and it often improves the generalization capability of the combined solution [9].

However, in this paper we use a simpler approach. In order to test unseen instances, we pick only one solution from the evolved classification front. This solution may be

---

[2] We used error instead of accuracy for simplifying the implementation details.

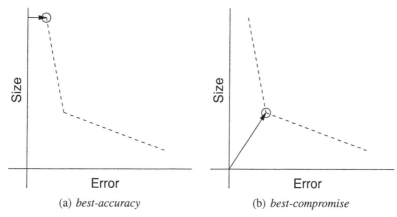

(a) *best-accuracy*   (b) *best-compromise*

Fig. 2. Selected hypotheses, using two different strategies, among the Pareto front compromise solutions for testing unseen instances.

chosen using one of the two different strategies, shown in figure 2. The first one (*best-accuracy*) chooses the solution $\vec{x}$ of the front with the best accuracy, that is, the one that minimizes $f_e(\vec{x})$. On the other hand, the second one (*best-compromise*) picks the hypothesis of the front that minimizes the objective vector $\vec{u} = F(\vec{x})$. Thus, the selected solution is the one that balances equally both objectives. In other words, the solution $\vec{x}$ that minimizes $|F(\vec{x})| = \sqrt{f_e(\vec{x})^2 + f_s(\vec{x})^2}$. For further insight about this approach is provided on section 5.3.

4   Multiobjective Learning Systems

There are several approaches to LCSs [2, 8, 9]. Among the different alternatives, we chose to implement our multiobjective approach, presented in section 3, using two different ELSs. The first one uses an evolutionary model based on genetic algorithms (MOLS-GA), whereas the second exploits an evolutionary learning approach based on evolution strategies (MOLS-ES) [40]. Both ELSs share some common elements, mainly related to the multiobjective mechanisms. This section describes briefly the two systems, and afterwards it focuses on the evaluation phase where the multiobjective techniques are introduced.

4.1   MOLS-GA

MOLS-GA is a learning system based on genetic algorithms. The knowledge representation is based on rule sets or instance sets [9, 41, 42]. If the problem's attributes are nominal, MOLS-GA uses rule sets, represented by the ternary alphabet (0, 1, #) often used in other LCSs [1–3]. Otherwise, if the problem is defined by continuous-valued attributes, instance sets—based on a nearest neighbor classification—are used.

The GA learning cycle works as follows. First, the fitness of each individual in the population is computed. This is done on a multiobjective basis, taking into account the misclassification error and the size of each individual. This phase is explained in details in section 4.3. Then, selection is applied using a tournament selection algorithm [43–45] with elitism. Elitism is often applied in evolutionary multiobjective optimization algorithms and it usually consists in keeping the solutions of the Pareto Front evolved in each generation [29]. MOLS-GA performs similarly: it keeps all the distinct solutions of the evolved Pareto Front, and also a 30% of the individuals with the lowest error. This guarantees that the best compromise solutions evolved so far are not lost, as well as the best low-error solutions which are important to drive the evolution toward accurate solutions.

After selection, crossover and mutation are applied. The crossover operator is based on the operator described in [6]. It is a variant of the classical two-point crossover, adapted to deal with variable-size individuals. It works in the following way. The crossover point can occur anywhere (i.e., both on the rule/instance boundaries as well as within a rule/instance). The only requirement is that the crossover points in the two parents must be equivalent in order to produce valid solutions. That is, if one parent is cut on a rule/instance boundary, then the other parent must also be cut on a rule/instance boundary. Similarly, if one parent is cut within a rule/instance, then the other parent must be cut in a similar spot. The mutation consists in generating a random new gene value.

4.2   MOLS-ES

MOLS-ES [40] is a learning system that uses an evolution strategy scheme [46–48] instead of a genetic algorithm. Each individual of the population codifies a set of rules. The rules are represented in the ternary alphabet if the attributes are binary, and in a (n+1)-alphabet if the attributes are nominal (where n is the number of nominal values). If the attributes are real-valued, the hyper-rectangle codification proposed by Wilson [49] is used.

The multiobjective approach has been introduced in MOLS-ES in the same way as in MOLS-GA. It is described in the following section. Besides the fitness computation stage, the other phases of MOLS-ES differ from MOLS-GA, since MOLS-ES is based on an Evolution Strategy approach. MOLS-ES uses a $(\mu + \lambda)$ selection scheme, which means that from the recombination and mutation of μ parents λ children are obtained. From the resulting overlapping population, the best μ individuals are selected for the next generation, where the concept of *best* is defined according to the multiobjective evaluation algorithm. It can be noticed that this selection also induces a kind of elitism.

The crossover operator applied to the solutions is the same as in MOLS-GA, which is a two-point crossover adapted to the variable size of individuals. The mutation is applied according to Evolution Strategies. For each gen x_i, there is a standard deviation σ_i associated with it which is used to mutate the gen. Both the solutions and the standard deviations are mutated as follows:

$$\sigma_i' = \sigma_i \cdot \exp(\tau' \cdot N(0,1) + \tau \cdot N_i(0,1)) \tag{8}$$

$$x_i' = x_i + \sigma_i' \cdot N_i(0,1) \tag{9}$$

where $N(0,1)$ and $N_i(0,1)$ are random numbers distributed normally with mean 0 and standard deviation 1 and τ and τ' are set as recommended in [47]. Thus, the solutions

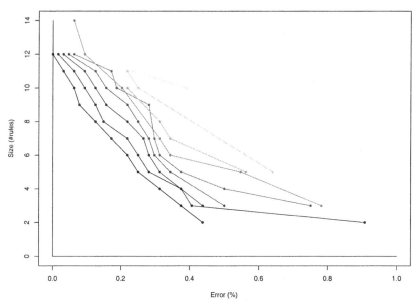

Fig. 3. Sorted population fronts at a given iteration of MOLS in the mux problem.

and their standard deviations are adapted along the evolution process. For real-valued attributes, this scheme fits perfectly. Nevertheless, for nominal attributes the mutation of x_i has to be modified. In this case, σ_i is proportional to the mutation probability. The new mutated x_i value is chosen randomly among the available symbols.

4.3   Multiobjective Fitness in MOLS-GA and MOLS-ES

In both systems, the multiobjective fitness scheme is introduced in the same way. The procedure is inspired by NSGA [50, 51] and NSGA-II [52] and it works as follows.

The individuals of the population are sorted in equivalent classes. These classes are determined by the Pareto Fronts that can be defined among the population. That is, given a population of individuals $\mathcal{I}$, the first equivalence class $\mathcal{I}^0$ is the set of individuals which belongs to the evolved Pareto optimal set $\mathcal{I}^0 = \mathcal{P}^*(\mathcal{I})$. The next equivalence class $\mathcal{I}^1$ is computed without considering the individuals in $\mathcal{I}^0$, as $\mathcal{I}^1 = \mathcal{P}^*(\mathcal{I} \setminus \mathcal{I}^0)$, and so forth. Figure 3 shows an example of the different equivalence classes, presented using the fronts that appear in a population at a given iteration. This plot is obtained with the mux problem. In this example, the population is classified into nine different fronts. The left front is $\mathcal{I}^0$, which corresponds to the non-dominated vectors of the population. The next front to the right represents $\mathcal{I}^1$ and so on.

Once the population of individuals $\mathcal{I}$ is sorted, fitness values are assigned. Since the evolution must bias the population toward non-dominated solutions, we impose the constraint:

$$fitness(\mathcal{I}^i) > fitness(\mathcal{I}^{i+1}) \tag{10}$$

Thus, the evolution will try to guide the population toward the left part of the plot, i.e., the real Pareto Front. The fitness of each individual depends on the front where the individual belongs. That is, all the individuals of the same equivalence class $\mathcal{I}^i$ receive the same constant value $(n-i)\delta$, where n is the number of equivalence classes and δ is a constant. Moreover, in order to spread the population along the Pareto Front, a *sharing* function is applied. Thus, the final fitness of an individual j in a given equivalence class $\mathcal{I}^i$ is:

$$fitness(\mathcal{I}_j^i) = \frac{(n-i)\delta}{\sum_{k \in \mathcal{I}} \phi(d_{\mathcal{I}_j^i \mathcal{I}_k})} \tag{11}$$

where $\phi(d_{\mathcal{I}_j^i \mathcal{I}_k})$ is the sharing function [53]. The *sharing* function is computed using the phenotipical distance between the individuals; that is, the Euclidean distance between their multiobjective vectors. The radius of the *sharing* function σ_{sh} was set to $\sigma_{sh} = 0.1$.

5   Experiments

This section discusses the results obtained using the multiobjective ELSs presented in section 4. The experiments explore different facets of the behavior of the proposed ELSs. Both ELSs were used to solve artificial and real-world problems, paying special attention to their performance in terms of the evolved Pareto fronts. The section starts describing briefly the data sets and algorithms used in the experiments (subsection 5.1). Then subsection 5.2 presents the fronts obtained on two artificial problems where the optimal Pareto front is known. After presenting these results, subsection 5.3 shows some interesting properties of the Pareto front evolved by the proposed ELS in the presence of noise in the data set. These results let us justify the results obtained in real-world problems. Thus, subsection 5.4 analyzes some interesting facets of the behavior of both ELSs on these real-world problems.

5.1   Test Suite

In order to evaluate the performances of the proposed multiobjective ELSs on different domains, we performed experiments on nine data sets. These data sets can be grouped into two different categories: artificial and real-world. Table 1 describes their characteristics.

We used two *artificial data sets* to tune both ELSs, because we knew their solutions in advance. Mux is the eleven input multiplexer, widely used by the LCS community [3]. Led is the seven-segments problem [54]. Given seven light emitting diodes that represent a digit (seven binary input attributes), the goal of the led problem is to identify the digit represented by the active diodes (the ten available classes). The data set used in the Led problem was generated using the program provided by the UCI repository [55].

The *public data sets* were obtained from the UCI repository [55]. We chose seven data sets: *Bupa Liver Disorders* (bpa), *Wisconsin Breast Cancer* (bre), *Glass* (gls), *Ionosphere* (ion), *Iris* (irs), *Primary Tumor* (prt), and *Sonar* (son). These data sets contain categorical and numeric attributes, as well as binary and n-ary classification tasks.

We also run several evolutionary and non-evolutionary classifier schemes on the previous data sets. The evolutionary classifier schemes were GALE [39, 41, 42, 9] and XCS [3, 56], whereas the non-evolutionary ones were IB1 [57], C4.5 [58, 59], and PART [60]. The non-evolutionary schemes were obtained from the *Weka* package [61] developed at the University of Waikato in New Zealand. The code is available from the http address: http://www.cs.waikato.ac.nz/ml/weka. These algorithms were run with the default configuration provided by their authors.

In order to allow the replication of the results presented in this section, we briefly summarize the settings used in MOLS-GA and MOLS-ES. The parameter values used in MOLS-GA were: σ_{sh}=0.1, δ=1000, pop_size=285, crossover probability p_χ=0.4, probability of mutation of an individual p_{mut}=0.25, and the gene perturbation probability p_{gen}=0.02. On the other hand, the parameter values used in MOLS-ES as follows: σ_{sh}=0.1, δ=1000, μ=50, λ=250, and ϵ_σ=0.01 (in the son ϵ_σ=0.0001). In the led, mux and prt, p_χ=0.5, σ_0=0.75, whereas in the rest of the problems p_χ=1, σ_0=1. The maximum number of iterations allowed in both ELSs were 250 iterations, exception made in the led, mux and prt problems where it was extended to 1000.

Table 1. Summary of the data sets used in the experiments.

id	Data set	Size	Missing values(%)	Numeric Attributes	Nominal Attributes	Classes
bpa	*Bupa Liver Disorders*	345	0.0	6	-	2
bre	*Wisconsin Breast Cancer*	699	0.3	9	-	2
gls	*Glass*	214	0.0	9	-	6
ion	*Ionosphere*	351	0.0	34	-	2
irs	*Iris*	150	0.0	4	-	3
led	*Led (10% noise)*	2000	0.0	-	7	10
mux	*Multiplexer (11 inputs)*	2048	0.0	-	1	2
prt	*Primary Tumor*	339	3.9	-	17	22
son	*Sonar*	208	0.0	60	-	2

5.2   Spreading the Population along the Pareto Front

The first results we present are obtained using both multiobjective ELSs on the two artificial data sets (mux and led). Initially, we used a version of the led data set free of noise, leaving noise considerations for the next subsection. In order to identify the optimal Pareto front, we analyze first the optimal solutions that should be obtained in each problem. These optimal solutions are shown in figure 4. For each problem, the optimal Pareto front can be obtained removing one rule iteratively. Each time we remove a rule, we compute the accuracy of the resulting rule set. Therefore the resulting objective vector $F(\vec{x})$ is represented as a point in the optimal Pareto front. The computed optimal Pareto fronts are printed in figure 5.

s_0	s_1	s_2	s_3	s_4	s_5	s_6		Class
1	1	1	1	1	1	0	:	0
0	0	0	0	1	1	0	:	1
1	0	1	1	0	1	1	:	2
1	0	0	1	1	1	1	:	3
0	1	0	0	1	1	1	:	4
1	1	0	1	1	0	1	:	5
1	1	1	1	1	0	1	:	6
1	0	0	0	1	1	0	:	7
1	1	1	1	1	1	1	:	8
1	1	0	0	1	1	1	:	9

(a) led problem

a_2	a_1	a_0	i_0	i_1	i_2	i_3	i_4	i_5	i_6	i_7		o
0	0	0	0	#	#	#	#	#	#	#	:	0
0	0	1	#	0	#	#	#	#	#	#	:	0
0	1	0	#	#	0	#	#	#	#	#	:	0
0	1	1	#	#	#	0	#	#	#	#	:	0
1	0	0	#	#	#	#	0	#	#	#	:	0
1	0	1	#	#	#	#	#	0	#	#	:	0
1	1	0	#	#	#	#	#	#	0	#	:	0
1	1	1	#	#	#	#	#	#	#	0	:	0
#	#	#	#	#	#	#	#	#	#	#	:	1

(b) mux problem

Fig. 4. Optimal solutions for the led and mux problems. The mux problem has two optimal solutions using ordered activation of classifiers. We only show one of these solutions; the other can be obtained swapping the 0s for 1s of the i_j and o attributes.

Figure 5 also shows the results obtained using both multiobjective ELSs. As it can be seen, both ELSs evolve the perfect Pareto front in the noise-free led problem. However, the results obtained in the mux problem are slightly different. The evolved Pareto fronts clearly approximate the optimal front. The evolved fronts differ in their top-left part, showing that some generalization of the solutions trapped in that part of the front are still needed. Inspecting the evolved solutions contained in the front, the differences are the result of still having (see the optimal solution in figure 4) more than one rule codifying class 1. These extra rules can be removed if we increase the number of iterations of both ELSs.

Figure 6 shows the evolution of the learning performed by both multiobjective ELSs, averaged across five different runs. The error is the best-so-far obtained at a given iteration, whereas the size of the individuals (number of rules) is the average size of the population along the different runs. As it can be seen, the multiobjective approach easily balances the pressure toward accurate and compact (general) solutions. This approach can efficiently reduce at the same time both objectives.

5.3 Noise in the Data Set

Recently, Llorà and Goldberg [62, 63] have shown the relevance of performing accurate noise analyses in ELSs theoretically. This kind of theoretical analyses helps in bounding the performance of ELSs. The remainder of this section introduces these results, focussing on the ELSs presented in this paper. This background becomes useful in the later analysis of the results obtained by the proposed ELSs when solving real-world problems.

The next experiment done introduced 10% noise in the led problem. Noise was introduced by swapping the antecedent values of the instances of the training data set with a probability equal to 0.1. This procedure is explained in detail elsewhere [62]. The instances of the noisy data set were generated using the program provided by the UCI repository [55]. The goal of this experiment was twofold. First, we were interested in the impact of the added noise on the performance of the two proposed multiobjective ELSs. Thus, when we solve real-world problems we easily would be able to understand

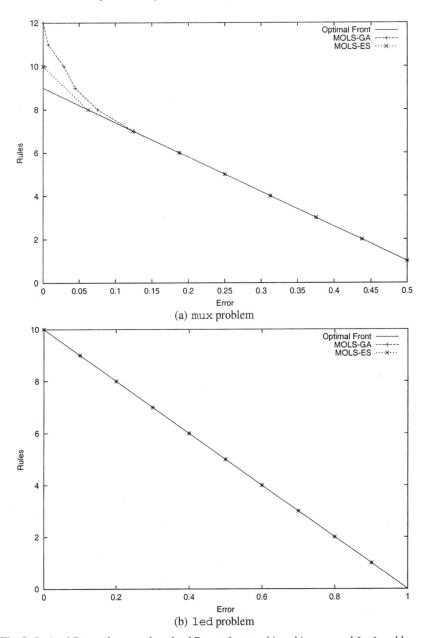

Fig. 5. Optimal Pareto fronts and evolved Pareto fronts achieved in mux and led problems.

the results that we obtained. The second reason for this experiment was to display the impact of the noise on the evolved Pareto front.

Before discussing the results, we need to introduce some theoretical results obtained for the noisy led problem. Detailed descriptions of these results can be found in [62,

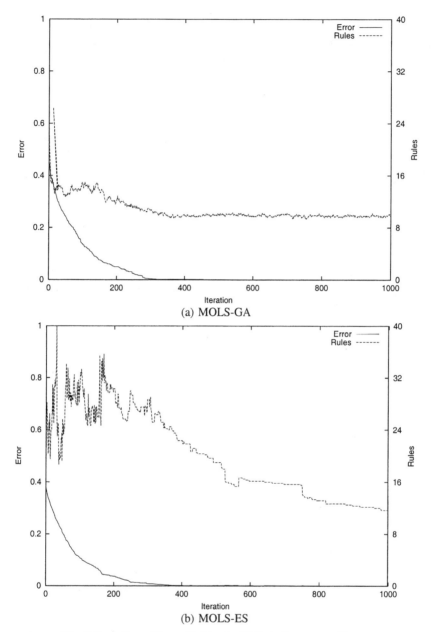

Fig. 6. Evolution of the multiobjective ELSs in the mux problem.

63]. The optimal subset of instances $\mathcal{O}$ for the LED problem was shown in figure 4.a. The number of possible antecedents in the led problem is $2^7 = 128$. In the noise-free led problem, only ten of all the possible antecedents are part of $\mathcal{O}$, and thus part of the available data set $\mathcal{D}$. The remaining 118 antecedents only appear in $\mathcal{D}$ as the effect of the presence of noise. Therefore, we can intuitively understand the addition of noise as a disruptive element toward the appearance of inconsistencies[3] in $\mathcal{D}$.

As it has been proved elsewhere [62], the inconsistencies introduced by the noise addition bound the *minimal achievable error* (MAE) that a learning algorithm can reach on the noisy led problem. The main issue is that MAE only depends on the added noise ratio ϵ. MAE can be computed theoretically as follows. In order to simplify the notation we assume that each antecedent is indexed by the number it codifies (its binary number representation). Moreover, d_{ij} is the Hamming distance between antecedents i and j and ϵ is the noise ratio added to the data set. The first step is computing the *jumping matrix* $\mathcal{J}$. This matrix contains the jumping probabilities between antecedents. Rows represent the original antecedent (one of the ten that appear in $\mathcal{O}$, indexed by the instance's class $\chi(i)$), whereas the columns show the final antecedent of the instance after noise perturbation. This matrix $\mathcal{J}$ is then defined as

$$\mathcal{J}_{\chi(i)j} = \epsilon^{d_{ij}} \cdot (1 - \epsilon)^{(7-d_{ij})}. \tag{12}$$

Using the jumping matrix $\mathcal{J}$, we can compute the probability distribution of the appearance of all possible antecedents α. Where α_a is the probability of appearance of the antecedent a on the noisy led data set $\mathcal{D}$. Moreover, using $\mathcal{J}$ we can also obtain the minimal classification achievable error e_a for a given antecedent a. The error e_a is the result of the inconsistencies that the noise ϵ introduces for each antecedent a. Thus, the minimal classification error is achieved only when we assign the majority class of the inconsistencies to the antecedent a. Having computed α and e, MAE is defined as follows:

$$MAE = \sum_i \alpha_i e_i \tag{13}$$

Figure 7 shows the empirical validation of the MAE model for the led problem. The empirical data were obtained using different noisy $\mathcal{D}_\epsilon$ data sets sizes (500, 1,000, 2,000, 5,000, and 500,000 noisy instances) and computing the error based on the degree of inconsistencies.

There are two interesting observations that arise from the data shown in figure 7. The first one is that, when enough instances are provided to the $\mathcal{D}_\epsilon$ data set, the theoretical model and the experimental results match perfectly (e.g. 500,000 instances). The second interesting observation provided by the results appears when we analyze the results achieved for the sizes of the $\mathcal{D}_\epsilon$ data set: 500, 1,000, 2,000, and 5,000. The empirical results using these small data sets show smaller MAE values that the ones theoretically predicted, showing some interesting deviations. These are the result of the random number generator bias used and the led instances distribution. Therefore, the experimental noise ratio ϵ is different than that theoretically expected, since not enough instances are generated. This fact leads to data sets that maintain some regularities that reduce the number of inconsistencies in $\mathcal{D}_\epsilon$.

Using these theoretical results we can now explain the Pareto front achieved in the noisy led problem. The data set contained 2,000 instances. These instances were generated using a noise ratio $\epsilon = .1$, that theoretically leads to a MAE equal to 0.26

---

[3] Two instances are inconsistent if they have the same antecedent, but different consequents.

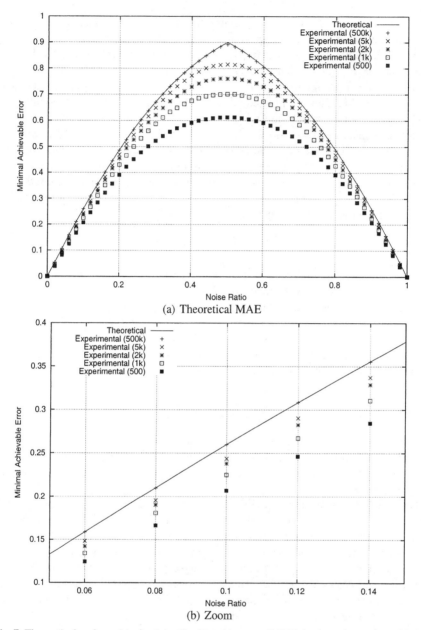

(a) Theoretical MAE

(b) Zoom

Fig. 7. Theoretical and empirical *minimal achievable error* (MAE) in the noisy `led` problem.

(see figure 7.b). However, the empirical MAE obtained from the $\mathcal{D}_\epsilon$ used is 0.23. Figure 8 presents the Pareto front achieved by both multiobjective ELSs proposed. The figure also shows the theoretical and empirical MAE boundaries, as well as the optimal non-noisy Pareto front and size of $\mathcal{O}$. Let us call *rupture point* the point defined as (MAE($\epsilon =$

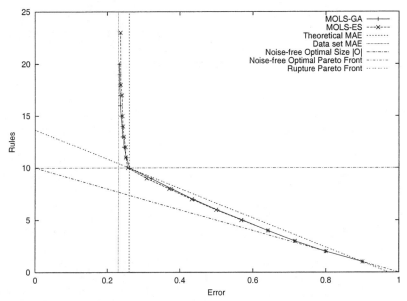

Fig. 8. Pareto fronts achieved in `led` problem. The data set contains 2000 instances perturbed with a noise ratio $\epsilon = 0.1$.

$0.1), |\mathcal{O}|)=(0.26,10)$. This point would be the performing point of $\mathcal{O}$ on a data set $\mathcal{D}_\epsilon$ with an experimental MAE equal to the theoretical one.

The *rupture point* indicates the place where the evolved Pareto front abruptly changes its slope. The front that appears to the left of the *rupture point* is the result of the deviation of the empirical MAE from its theoretical value. This has an interesting interpretation. All the points that define this segment of the front are over-fitted solutions. This means that they are learning some misleading noisy pattern as the result of the MAE value deviation. Therefore, if any of these points is tested using a different randomly generated $\mathcal{D}_\epsilon$ data set, they would experience a significant drop in accuracy. Thus, this leads to a reduction of the generalization capabilities (in terms of classification accuracy) of the solutions kept in that part of the front. Moreover, these solutions are closer to the *bloat* phenomenon, because very small (misleading) improvements require a large individual growth. All these problems disappear when we force the theoretical and the empirical MAE to be the same. This constraint removes the part of the front that appears at the left of the *rupture point*. Moreover, the optimal noisy Pareto front is bounded by the optimal noise-free front and the *rupture front* that appears between the *rupture point* and the *random guess point*. The *random guess point* is defined by the majority rule that describes solutions like $F(\vec{x}) = (0.9, 1)$.

5.4   Some Real-World Problems

The last kind of experiments are focused on the real-world problems summarized in table 1. The results, shown in table 2, were obtained from *stratified ten-fold cross-validations runs* [10,61] using the different learning algorithms on the selected data sets. MOLS-GA used a *best-accuracy* strategy for the test phase, whereas MOLS-ES used *best-compromise* (see figure 2). The main interest in these results is the fact that they prove the competence of the multiobjective approach. Moreover, for some particular data sets (like bpa or prt) some interesting improvements were achieved.

Table 2. Results obtained using the data sets presented in table 1. The table shows the mean and standard deviation of the *stratified ten-fold cross-validation runs* done using each system.

id	MOLS-GA	MOLS-ES	GALE	XCS	C4.5	PART	IB1
bpa	76.5±13.4	68.7±6.7	68.4±6.7	65.4±6.9	65.8±6.9	65.8±10.0	64.2±9.1
bre	96.0±1.1	96.1±2.2	95.7±2.2	96.7±2.5	95.4±1.6	95.3±2.2	95.9±1.5
gls	67.1±9.3	63.4±7.3	65.6±11.9	70.5±8.5	68.5±10.4	69.0±10.0	66.4±10.9
ion	91.5±3.6	92.8±2.7	94.0±3.3	89.6±3.1	89.8±0.5	90.6±0.9	90.9±3.8
irs	99.3±1.9	95.3±3.1	98.7±2.8	94.7±5.3	95.3±3.2	95.3±3.2	95.3±3.3
led	74.9±13.7	74.4±3.4	75.0±0.0	74.5±0.2	74.9±0.2	75.1±0.3	74.3±3.7
mux	100.0±0.0	100.0±0.0	100.0±0.0	100.0±0.0	99.9±0.2	100.0±0.0	99.8±0.2
prt	51.2±15.8	40.6±5.7	37.0±8.3	39.8±6.6	41.6±6.4	41.6±6.4	42.5±6.3
son	90.8±9.1	71.6±12.5	79.3±6.1	77.5±3.6	71.5±0.5	73.5±2.2	83.6±9.6

Another interesting issue that can be drawn from the results achieved using the selected real-world problems is related to the Pareto front behavior. Figure 9 plots the fronts evolved in two real-world problems (bre and prt). Looking at the results presented in table 2, it may seem that, for instance, MOLS-GA and MOLS-ES had a similar behavior in the bre data set in terms of classification accuracy. If we analyze the evolved Pareto fronts printed in figure 9.a, we realize that they are spreading the population in quite a different way. MOLS-GA achieves its performance through the evolution of bigger hypotheses than the ones obtained by MOLS-ES. These results were achieved using the same amount of iterations. Nevertheless, in other problems (see figure 9.b.) MOLS-ES produce bigger hypotheses than MOLS-GA. Further analysis should be done about this problem dependences.

The Pareto fronts presented in figure 9 also suggest another interesting vision of the analysis of the results. For instance, the front presented in figure 9.b shows an interesting resemblance to the fronts obtained in the noisy led problem (see figure 8). This clearly suggests the presence of inconsistencies in the prt data set that bounds the MAE. A preliminary inspection of the data set shows that 8.8% of the instances were replicated, and that only the 83.2% have different antecedents. However, the experimental MAE equals to .085. In fact in this data set we can identify some extra elements that force the appearance of large fronts. One of these is the large number of classes contained in the prt problem. For instance, in the noisy led data set the *instances/classes* ratio (r_{ic}) was r_{ic}=200, whereas in the prt problem this ratio drops to r_{ic}=15.4. This fact suggest interesting connections to some results obtained in the *probably approximately correct* models in the *computational learning theory* field [10]. These models compute a theoretical bound to the number of training examples required for successful learning. Therefore, some new interesting questions arise for further research.

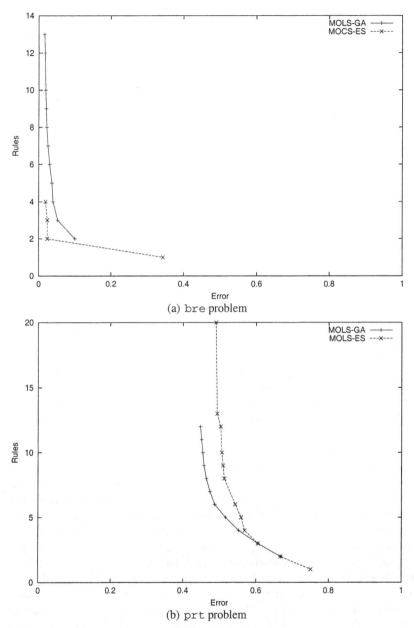

(a) bre problem

(b) prt problem

Fig. 9. Pareto fronts achieved in real-world problems.

6   Conclusions and Further Work

In this paper we have presented a multiobjective optimization approach to evolutionary learning systems. The main motivation was twofold. On one hand we aimed to minimize simultaneously the classification error and the number of rules of a given individual. On the other hand, we were also interested in the relation among generalization and overfitting capabilities of hypotheses. Given this scenario, multiobjective optimization was an elegant solution for achieving the desired goals. In order to validate our approach, we used two different multiobjective learning classifier systems. The first one uses an evolutionary model based on genetic algorithms (MOLS-GA), whereas the second exploits a learning approach based on evolution strategies (MOLS-ES). Both multiobjective learning classifier systems were tested using different data sets. The results obtained show that this multiobjective tradeoff is beneficial to searching for points of appropriate parsimony and accuracy. Moreover, the *bloat* phenomenon is no longer an issue in these systems. Results also show the competence of this approach when compared to previous evolutionary and non-evolutionary learning algorithms.

The multiobjective approach also let us gain some theoretical notions on the effect of noise in the data set. When properly obtained, the Pareto front of the evolved population let us identify overfitting conditions. As we have shown, when the noise in the data set is smaller than the theoretical *minimal achievable error*, the Pareto front shows a *rupture* point. All the trapped solutions are located at left-hand side of the *rupture* point, clearly represented in terms of overfitted hypotheses of the optimal generalization achievable of the classification performance. We also provided a theoretical model to compute this *rupture* point for the led data set, given a noise ratio ϵ. Moreover, if the theoretical and the empirical *minimal achievable error* are equal, then the overfitted part of the front disappears.

The work presented in this paper has opened some new directions for further research. The first one is to perform a statistical comparison between the proposed multiobjective learning systems and the other evolutionary and non-evolutionary learning algorithms (see [56]). This comparison should include more data sets, and analyse the impact on accuracy generalization of the *best-accuracy* and *best-compromise* picking strategies. The second one is related to the *minimal achievable error* measure. This measure was computed theoretically only for the led problem. The main question that should be investigated is if in a given problem we can compute this measure theoretically, since it is possible to compute it empirically. Unfortunately, it seems that for computing the theoretical MAE model we require extra background knowledge about the problem (for the led problem we used the optimal solution $\mathcal{O}$) in addition to the corresponding data set. This background knowledge is not usually available on real-world problems. The results obtained in the prt problem also show that in some real-world problems, with few data available and a large set of possible classes, the *minimal achievable error* should include some extra facets like the *instances/classes* ratio r_{ic}. Finally, some further research should be conducted in order to bring some of the theoretical models obtained in the *computational learning theory* field over the learning classifier systems discipline. The initial goal should be to determine how many instances are required for an ELS in order to obtain high quality general hypotheses of the target concept.

Acknowledgments

This work was sponsored by the Air Force Office of Scientific Research, Air Force Materiel Command, USAF, under grant F49620-00-0163, and by the Technology Research Center (TRECC), a program of the University of Illinois at Urbana-Champaign, administered by the National Center for Supercomputing Applications (NCSA) and funded by the Office of Naval Research under grant N00014-01-1-0175. Research funding for this work was also provided by a grant from the National Science Foundation under grant DMI-9908252. The US Government is authorized to reproduce and distribute reprints for Government purposes notwithstanding any copyright notation thereon.

The views and conclusions contained herein are those of the authors and should not be interpreted as necessarily representing the official policies or endorsements, either expressed or implied, of the Air Force Office of Scientific Research, the National Science Foundation, or the U.S. Government.

References

1. Holland, J.H.: Adaptation in Natural and Artificial Systems: An Introductory Analysis with Applications to Biology, Control and Artificial Intelligence. MIT Press/ Bradford Books edition (1975)
2. Goldberg, D.E.: Genetic Algorithms in Search, Optimization and Machine Learning. Addison-Wesley Publishing Company, Inc. (1989)
3. Wilson, S.W.: Classifier Fitness Based on Accuracy. Evolutionary Computation **3** (1995) 149–175
4. Butz, M.V.: Anticipatory learning classifier systems. Genetic Algorithms and Evolutionary Computation. Kluwer Academic Publishers, Boston, MA (2002)
5. Smith, S.F.: Flexible Learning of Problem Solving Heuristics through Adaptive Search. In: Proceedings of the 8th International Joint Conference on Artificial Intelligence. (1983) 422–425
6. De Jong, K.A., Spears, W.M.: Learning Concept Classification Rules Using Genetic Algorithms. In: Proceedings of the International Joint Conference on Artificial Intelligence, Sidney, Australia (1991) 651–656
7. Janikow, C.: Inductive Learning of Decision Rules in Attribute-Based Examples: a Knowledge-Intensive Genetic Algorithm Approach. PhD thesis, University of North Carolina at Chapel Hill (1991)
8. Michalewicz, Z.: Genetic Algorithms + Data Structures = Evolution Programs. Springer-Verlag (1992)
9. Llorà, X.: Genetic Based Machine Learning using Fine-grained Parallelism for Data Mining. PhD thesis, Enginyeria i Arquitectura La Salle. Ramon Llull University, Barcelona, Catalonia, European Union (February, 2002)
10. Mitchell, T.M.: Machine Learning. McGraw-Hill (1997)
11. Koza, J.R.: Genetic Programing: On the Programing of Computers by Means of Natural Selection (Complex Adaptive Systems). MIT Press (1992)
12. Altenberg, L.: Emergent phenomena in genetic programming. Proceedings of the Third Annual Conference on Evolutionary Programming (1994) 233–241
13. Blickle, T., Thiele, L.: Genetic programming and redundancy. Genetic Algorithms within the Framework of Evolutionary Computation: Proceedings of the KI-94 Workshop (1994) 33–38

14. Blickle, T.: Evolving compact solutions in genetic programming: A case study. Parallel Problem Solving from Nature, PPSN IV (1996) 564–573
15. Angeline, P.J.: Subtree crossover causes bloat. Genetic Programming 98 (1998) 745–752
16. Langdon, W.B., Poli, R.: Fitness causes bloat: Mutation. Genetic Programming: First European Conference (1998) 37–48
17. Soule, T., Foster, J.A.: Effects of code growth and parsimony pressure on populations in genetic programming. Evolutionary Computation 6 (1998) 293–309
18. Langdon, W.B.: Quadratic bloat in genetic programming. Proceedings of the Genetic and Evolutionary Computation Conference 2000 (2000) 451–458
19. Podgorelec, V., Kokol, P.: Fighting program bloat with the fractal complexity measure. Genetic Programming: Third European Conference (2000) 326–337
20. Bleuler, S., Brack, M., Thiele, L., Zitzler, E.: Multiobjective genetic programming: Reducing bloat using SPEA2. In: Proceedings of the 2001 Congress on Evolutionary Computation CEC2001, COEX, World Trade Center, 159 Samseong-dong, Gangnam-gu, Seoul, Korea, IEEE Press (2001) 536–543
21. Banzhaf, W., Langdon, W.B.: Some Considerations on the Reason for Bloat. Genetic Programming and Evolvable Hardware 3 (2002) 81–91
22. Soule, T.: Exons and code growth in genetic programming. In Lutton, E., Foster, J.A., Miller, J., Ryan, C., Tettamanzi, A.G.B., eds.: Proceedings of the 4th European Conference on Genetic Programming, EuroGP 2002. Volume 2278 of LNCS., Kinsale, Ireland, Springer-Verlag (2002) 143–152
23. Garrell, J.M., Golobardes, E., Bernadó, E., Llorà, X.: Automatic Diagnosis with Genetic Algorithms and Case-Based Reasoning. AIENG 13 (1999) 367–372
24. Bassett, J.K., De Jong, K.A.: Evolving Behaviors for Cooperating Agents. In: Proceedings of the Twelfth International Symposium on Methodologies for Intelligent Systems, Springer-Verlag Berlin Heidelberg, LNAI 1932 (2000)
25. Bacardit, J., Garrell, J.M.: Métodos de generalización para sistemas clasificadores de Pittsburgh. In: Primer Congreso Espaol de Algoritmos Evolutivos y Bioinspirados (AEB'02). (2002) 486–493
26. Pareto, V.: Cours d'Economie Politique, volume I and II. F. Rouge, Lausanne (1896)
27. Van Veldhuizen, D.A., Lamont, G.B.: Evolutionary computation and convergence to a pareto front. In Koza, J.R., ed.: Late Breaking Papers at the Genetic Programming 1998 Conference, Madison, WI, Omni Press (1998) 221–228
28. Coello-Coello, C.A.: An updated survey of GA-Based Multiobjective Optimization Techniques. Technical report lania-rd-09-08, Laboratorio Nacional de Informática Avanzada (LANIA), Xalapa, Veracruz, México (December, 1998)
29. Van Veldhuizen, D.A., Lamont, G.B.: Multiobjective evolutionary algorithms: Analyzing the state-of-the-art. Evolutionary Computation 8 (2000) 125–147
30. Tackett, W.A.: Recombination, selection, and the genetic construction of computer programs. Unpublished doctoral dissertation, University of Southern California (1994)
31. Zitzler, E.: Evolutionary Algorithms for Multiobjective Optimization: Methods and Applications. PhD thesis, Swiss Federal Institute of Technology (ETH) Zurich (1999)
32. Zitzler, E., Deb, K., Thiele, L.: Comparison of Multiobjective Evolutionary Algorithms: Empirical Results. Evolutionary Computation 8 (2000) 173–195
33. Zitzler, E.: SPEA2: Improving the Strength Pareto Evolutionary Algorithm. Technical report 103, Swiss Federal Institute of Technology (ETH) Zurich, Gloriastrasse 35, CH-8092 Zurich (May, 2001)
34. Nordin, P., Banzhaf, W.: Complexity Compression and Evolution. In: Proceedings of the Sixth International Conference on Genetic Algorithms. (1995)

35. Bernadó, E., Mekaouche, A., Garrell, J.M.: A Study of a Genetic Classifier System Based on the Pittsburgh Approach on a Medical Domain. In: 12th International Conference on Industrial and Engineering Applications of Artificial Intelligence and Expert Systems, IEA/AIE-99. (1999) 175–184

36. Gómez-Skarmeta, A.F., Jiménez, F., Ibáez, J.: Pareto-optimality in fuzzy modeling. In: 6th European Congress on Intelligent Techniques and Soft Computing (EUFIT'98). (1998) 694–700

37. Jiménez, F., Gómez-Skarmeta, A.F., Roubos, H., Robert, B.: Accurate, transparent, and compact fuzzy models for function approximation and dynamic modelling through multiobjective evolutionary optimization. In: First International Conference on Evolutionary Multi-Criterion Optimization, Springer-Verlag. Lecture Notes in Computer Science No. 1993 (2001) 653–667

38. Breiman, L.: Bagging predictors. Machine Learning **24** (1996) 123–140

39. Llorà, X., Garrell, J.M.: Automatic Classification and Artificial Life Models. In: Proceedings of Learning00 Workshop, IEEE and Univesidad Carlos III (2000)

40. Traus, I., Bernadó, E.: Sistema Classificador Pittsburgh basat en Estratègies Evolutives. Technical Report TR-ISRG-2002/0001, Enginyeria i Arquitectura La Salle, Universitat Ramon Llull, Barcelona, European Union (2002)

41. Llorà, X., Garrell, J.M.: Evolving Partially-Defined Instances with Evolutionary Algorithms. In: Proceedings of the 18th International Conference on Machine Learning (ICML'2001), Morgan Kaufmann Publishers (2001) 337–344

42. Llorà, X., Garrell, J.M.: Knowledge-Independent Data Mining with Fine-Grained Parallel Evolutionary Algorithms. In: Proceedings of the Genetic and Evolutionary Computation Conference (GECCO'2001), Morgan Kaufmann Publishers (2001) 461–468

43. Oei, C.K., Goldberg, D.E., Chang, S.J.: Tournament selection, niching, and the preservation of diversity. IlliGAL Report No. 91011, University of Illinois at Urbana-Champaign, Urbana, IL (1991)

44. Bäck, T.: Generalized convergence models for tournament- and (μ, λ)-selection. Proceedings of the Sixth International Conference on Genetic Algorithms (1995) 2–8

45. Miller, B.L., Goldberg, D.E.: Genetic algorithms, tournament selection, and the effects of noise. Complex Systems **9** (1995) 193–212

46. Schwefel, H.P.: Kybernetische Evolution als Strategie der experimentellen Forschung in der Strömungstechnik. Technical report, Diplomarbeit, Technische Universität Berlin (1965)

47. Schwefel, H.P.: Numerische Optimierung von Computer-Modellen mittels der Evolutionsstrategie. In: Interdisciplinary Systems Research. Volume 26., Birkhäuser. Basel (1977)

48. Bäck, T.: Evolutionary algorithms in theory and practice. Oxford University Press, New York (1996)

49. Wilson, S.W.: Get real! XCS with continuous-valued intpus. In Booker, L., Forrest, S., Mitchell, M., Riolo, R.L., eds.: Festschrift in Honor of John H. Holland, Center for the Study of Complex Systems (1999) 11–121

50. Srinivas, N., Deb, K.: Multiobjective optimization using nondominated sorting in genetic algorithms. submitted to EC (1994)

51. Srinivas, N., Deb, K.: Multiobjective optimization using nondominated sorting in genetic algorithms. Evolutionary Computation **2** (1995) 221–248

52. Deb, K., Agrawal, S., Pratab, A., Meyarivan, T.: A Fast Elitist Non-Dominated Sorting Genetic Algorithm for Multi-Objective Optimization: NSGA-II. KanGAL report 200001, Indian Institute of Technology (2000)

53. Goldberg, D.E., Richardson, J.: Genetic algorithms with sharing for multimodal function optimization. In: Proceedings of the Second International Conference on Genetic Algorithms. (1987) 41–49

54. Breiman, L., Friedman, J., Olshen, R., Stone, C.: Classification and Regression Trees. Wadsworth International Group (1984)
55. Merz, C.J., Murphy, P.M.: UCI Repository for Machine Learning Data-Bases [http://www.ics.uci.edu/~mlearn/MLRepository.html]. Irvine, CA: University of California, Department of Information and Computer Science (1998)
56. Bernadó, E., Llorà, X., Garrell, J.M.: XCS and GALE: a Comparative Study of Two Learning Classifier Systems with Six Other Learning Algorithms on Classification Tasks. In: Proceedings of the 4th International Workshop on Learning Classifier Systems (IWLCS-2001), *to appear*, Springer-Verlag (2001)
57. Aha, D., Kibler, D.: Instance-based learning algorithms. Machine Learning **6** (1991) 37–66
58. Quinlan, R.: Induction of decision trees. Machine Learning **1** (1986) 81–106
59. Quinlan, R.: C4.5: Programs for Machine Learning. Morgan Kaufmann Publishers (1993)
60. Frank, E., Witten, I.H.: Generating Accurate Rule Sets Without Global Optimization. In Shavlik, J., ed.: Machine Learning: Proceedings of the Fifteenth International Conference, Morgan Kaufmann (1998) 144–151
61. Witten, I.H., Eibe, F.: Data Mining. Practical Machine Learning Tools and Techniques with Java Implementations. Morgan Kaufmann (2000)
62. Llorà, X., Goldberg, D.E.: Minimal Achievable Error in the LED problem. IlliGAL Report No. 2002015, University of Illinois at Urbana-Champaign, Illinois Genetic Algorithms Laboratory, Urbana, IL (2002)
63. Llorà, X., Goldberg, D.E.: Bounding the effect of noise in Multiobjective Learning Classifier Systems. Evolutionary Computation (2003) In press

Anticipatory Classifier System Using Behavioral Sequences in Non-Markov Environments

Marc Métivier and Claude Lattaud

Laboratoire d'Intelligence Artificielle de Paris 5
UFR de Mathématiques et d'Informatique
Centre Universitaire des Saints-Pères
45, rue des Saints-Pères – 75006 Paris
{metivier,lattaud}@math-info.univ-paris5.fr

Abstract. Learning in non-Markov environments presents difficulties for Learning Classifier Systems. The presence of perceptually aliased situations induces the system to consider some distinct states of the environment as identical. The system, therefore, may not be able to decide the best action in each situation. An alternative, presented by Stolzmann (1999), is to use classifiers with behavioral sequences in the Anticipatory Classifier System (ACS). This method allows ACS to learn latently a non-Markov environment in mobile robot simulations. This paper presents a study of ACS reward and latent learning capacities in some non-Markov environments when using behavioral sequences. An ACS, based on Stolzmann's work and using some enhancements introduced by Butz, Goldberg and Stolzman (2000), is detailed. This system is tested in several woods environments in order to highlight the learning effectiveness of this method according to the environmental properties.

1 Introduction

The Anticipatory Classifier System (ACS) is a Learning Classifier System (LCS) developed by Stolzmann in 1997 [1]. ACS learns by using the psychological learning mechanism of "anticipatory behavioral control" [2]. In this system, the structure of stimulus-response rules in LCSs is enhanced by an effect part representing an anticipation of the perceptive consequences of its action on an environment. This effect part, associated with a learning process called the Anticipatory Learning Process (ALP), enables the ACS to learn latently complete internal representation of an environment. The ALP represents the application of the anticipatory behavioral control into the system. Therefore, the ACS combines the idea of learning by anticipation with that of the LCS framework [3].

The learning capabilities of LCSs rely on their perception of the environment. There are cases in which the system perceives all the relevant information necessary to decide the best action in every situation. There are other cases in which perceptions are aliased because the sensors perceive only *partial* information about the environment. When the system observes its environment only partially, there might be *distinct* situations which appear *identical* to the LCS but which require different actions. So when the system perceives such a situation, it cannot decide which action is the

P.L. Lanzi et al. (Eds.): IWLCS 2002, LNAI 2661, pp. 143–162, 2003.

best. This problem is known as the "perceptual aliasing problem" [4]. The condition according to which an environment does not contain any aliased situation is called the *Markov* property [5]. Environments that satisfy the Markov property are called *Markov environments*, and those which do not *non-Markov environments*.

Learning in non-Markov environments is a major problem in the LCS framework, and, more generally, in the reinforcement learning field. An approach to cope with perceptual aliasings is to add an internal memory mechanism to the system [4]. This has been performed and studied with ZCS [6] and XCS [7] classifiers systems. With ACS, another alternative to learn non-Markov environments is to use classifiers with "behavioral sequences". This approach has been presented by Stolzmann in 1999 [8]. In his work, he defines a behavioral sequence as a succession of actions. A classifier with a behavioral sequence is, thus, a classifier whose action part consists on several actions which are to be executed sequentially. He showed that this mechanism, associated with an action-planning mechanism, permits a high number of simulated Khepera robots to latently learn a non-Markov environment. Above all, the system has presented capacities to avoid "non-Markov states" (i.e. situations of perceptual aliasing).

This paper presents a study of ACS capacities in different types of non-Markov environments when using behavioral sequences. The system used is an ACS provided with enhancements presented by Butz [9] which were not used by Stolzmann in his experiments on behavioral sequences. In opposition to Stolzmann's work, the system does not use action-planning. Latent learning performance and reward optimization capacities are both studied in order to highlight the advantages and limitations of the use of behavioral sequences with respect to the environment. Above all, the objective of the study is to determine the different properties of non-Markov environments that enable the use of behavioral sequences to cope with perception aliasing.

In the first part, the characteristics of the ACS classifier system are presented, and a description of the system used in this study is done.

Then, in the second part, the management of classifiers with behavioral sequences is presented. Several mechanisms are described permitting to detect aliased situations, to create classifiers with behavioral sequences and to take them into account in the framework of ACS.

The next part describes experiments of latent learning and reward optimization in a Markov environment and in several non-Markov environments. Results are presented and, in the last part, discussed.

2   The Anticipatory Classifier System

This section firstly presents a summary of related works about the ACS structure and similar systems in order to place the ACS version used in this paper among existing versions. Then, the system's structure is detailed.

2.1   A Brief Presentation of ACS

The basic structure of the ACS with its anticipatory learning process (ALP) was introduced by Stolzmann in 1997 [1].

In 1999, Stolzmann published an additional mechanism using a mark in each classifier permitting the ALP to execute a *specification of unchanging components* [8]. This work also presents the use of behavioral sequences and action-planning.

Action-planning has been studied in ACS by Butz in 1999, without using behavioral sequences but using the mark mechanism [10].

In 2000, Butz, Goldberg, and Stolzmann [9] introduced an enhancement of the ALP application and a genetic algorithm (GA) for the ACS. The basic structure of this version differs from the previous one by the absence of a message list mechanism. The ALP, provided with the mark mechanism, is enhanced by being applied on a whole set of classifiers at each behavioral act instead of being applied on a unique classifier as in the previous systems. Moreover, the system is improved by a genetic algorithm and a subsumption method. The use of a genetic algorithm has also been studied in [11, 12].

In [13], Butz introduces a probability-enhancement in the ACS predictions to enable the system to handle different kinds of non-determinism in an environment.

Nevertheless, new LCSs based on the ACS anticipation mechanism have been published. It is, thus, the case of ACS2 developed by Butz [14], and YACS developed by Gerard and Sigaud [15].

Among all these papers about anticipatory LCSs, Stolzmann's paper about behavioral sequences [8] is the only one presenting a mechanism to cope with non-Markov states.

The anticipatory classifier system used in this work is based on the ACS developed by Stolzmann with some enhancements presented by Stolzmann and by Butz since the first version of ACS. Thus, the system uses the mark mechanism and applies the ALP on a whole set of classifiers instead of on a unique classifier. Moreover, it does not use a message list. In fact, this system is similar to the ACS version presented by Butz in [9], but without the genetic algorithm and with another action-selection mechanism. The next section gives a detailed description of the system. The formalism used in this description is based on the formalism used by Butz in his paper.

2.2 Basic Elements

The system is composed of three basics components: an input interface, an output interface and a classifier list.

The *input interface* acts as sensors for the system. At an instant t, it receives a string $\sigma(t)$ representing the actual situation perceived by the system in the environment, and a payoff $\rho(t)$. Such a situation is defined as a string of discrete values: $\sigma(t) \in S^L$ with L the length of the string and $S = \{s_1,...,s_m\}$ a set of possible values, m being its cardinality. A payoff $\rho(t)$ is a simple real value.

The *output interface* acts as actuators for the system. It receives an action $\alpha(t)$ and executes it in the environment. Actions are also coded with discrete values: $\alpha(t) \in \{a_1,...,a_n\}$ where n is the number of different actions and $a_1,...,a_n$ are the different actions.

The *classifier list* is the basic knowledge of the system and is represented by a population of rules. The rules, named classifiers, are presented in the next section.

2.3 Classifiers

The classifier definition used in our model is the one proposed by Butz in [Butz 2000]. Each classifier of the classifier list consists of the following parts:

- The condition part (C) specifies the perception prerequisites for the application of the rule.
- The action part (A) specifies an action to execute.
- The effect part (E) anticipates the perceptive changes caused by the action A under the condition C.
- The mark (M) specifies all different attributes where the classifier did not antici-pate correctly.
- The quality q measures the accuracy of the anticipations.
- The reward measure r predicts the payoff from the environment after the execution of A.

The condition and effect parts are represented by a string of L discrete values be-longing to $S \cup \{\#\}$. Thus, $C, E \in \{s_1, \ldots, s_m, \#\}^L$. The '#'-symbol is a particular symbol whose signification is proper to each part. In the condition part, the '#'-symbol is called a "don't-care" symbol and matches any perceived value in this attribute. In the effect part, the '#'-symbol is called a "pass-through" symbol and predicts that the cor-responding value of this attribute in the perception does not change after the execution of an action. The action part is represented by any of the n possible actions in the environment, i.e. $A \in \{a_1, \ldots, a_n\}$. Notice that this is the classical way to represent the action part in ACS. Later, section 3.1 presents classifiers whose action part may con-sist of a behavioral sequence, i.e. a succession of actions. The mark has the following structure: $M \in (S_1, \ldots, S_L)$ with each $S_{i=1,\ldots,L}$ a subset of S containing the values of the ith attribute of the situations where the classifier did not work correctly.

Figure 1 presents a typical classifier.

$$\#\#\#.O\#\#\# \ — \ N \ — \ \#\#\#O.\#\#\# \ \rightarrow \ \{\{.\}, \{.\}, \{.,O\}, \{.\}, \{O\}, \{.,O\}, \{.\}, \{.\}\}$$

Fig. 1. This classifier matches all situations with a '.' in the fourth attribute and a 'O' in the fifth attribute. It predicts that after the execution of the action A='N', the '.' will change to 'O' and the 'O' will change to '.'. The other attributes will stay the same. The mark specifies that the classi-fier did not anticipate correctly in certain states.

2.4 A Behavioral Act

The ACS used in this work does not use a message list. All the information needed, at a time t, is the couple $(\sigma(t), \rho(t))$ obtained by the input interface during the perception.

A behavioral act, at a time t, is composed of the following steps:

- **Step 1: Perception at t.** The system perceives information $(\sigma(t), \rho(t))$ from the environment.
- **Step 2: Match Set Creation.** A match M_t is formed out of the current population of classifiers. This set contains all classifiers whose conditions are satisfied by $\sigma(t)$.

- **Step 3: Action Selection.** A classifier is selected from M_t. The policy used to select this classifier is the following: with an exploration probability p_x the classifier
is selected randomly, otherwise the classifier is selected by *roulette-wheel selection*
[16] with a strength (r * q). This selection mechanism has been used with ACS by
Butz in [17]. The selected classifier is considered as the "active" classifier. Finally,
the action selected to be executed is the one represented by the action part of the
active classifier. This mechanism is different from the one used by Butz in [9]: the
e-greedy policy[4]. In the e-greedy policy, with a probability e, a random action,
among the n possible ones, is selected (and not a random classifier among the
whole match set), otherwise the best classifier is chosen. Such a distinction has
been made to enable the use of behavioral sequences (see section 3.1).

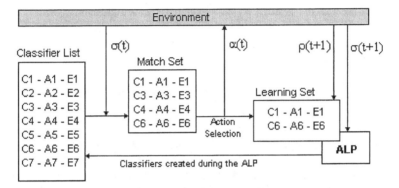

Fig. 2. A behavioral act.

- **Step 4: Learning Set Creation.** A learning set L_t is formed out of M_t. This set
contains all classifiers whose action part is the same as the active classifier's one.
In fact, while the system does not use behavioral sequences (see section 3), the
learning set is defined as an *action set*.
- **Step 5: Interaction with This Environment.** The selected action is sent to the
output interface, which executes it in the environment.
- **Step 6: Perception at t+1.** The system perceives information $(\sigma(t+1), \rho(t+1))$ from
the environment.
- **Step 7: RLP.** The Reinforcement Learning Process (RLP) is applied on L_t with the
reward $\rho(t+1)$.
- **Step 8: ALP.** The Anticipatory Learning Process (ALP) is applied on L_t taking
$\sigma(t+1)$ into account. New classifiers that may have been created during the ALP
are added in the current population of classifiers. Nevertheless, a new behavioral
act begins in step 2 with the couple $(\sigma(t+1), \rho(t+1))$ as a new perception.

2.5 The Anticipatory Learning Process

The Anticipatory Learning Process (ALP) is derived from the psychological theory of
"anticipatory behavioral control" [2]. This theory has been translated into an artificial
system under the form of the ALP in ACS by Stolzmann [1].

The learning begins with a complete general knowledge: for each possible action there is one classifier, whose C and E parts contain only '#'-symbols. Thus, before its first behavioral act, the population contains only n classifiers: one for each of the n possible actions. These n original classifiers have a particular status in the system. They cannot be deleted and they cannot be marked.

The ALP always occurs on a learning set. It must have two data points: $\sigma(t)$, the situation matched by the C part of all classifiers of the set, and $\sigma(t+1)$, the situation perceived after the action proposed by the classifiers, has been executed (all classifiers of the set propose the same action).

The ALP applies to all classifiers in the set. For each classifier, the ALP distinguishes the following cases:

- The *useless case*: the situation has not changed between time t and time t+1, which means that $\sigma(t)$ and $\sigma(t+1)$ are identical. In this case, the quality of the classifier is decreased and the classifier is marked by $\sigma(t)$.
- The classifier anticipates the situation $\sigma(t+1)$ incorrectly. The quality of the classifier is decreased and the classifier is marked by $\sigma(t)$. Then, two sub-cases are distinguished:

  - The *correctable case:* the rule of the classifier can be further specified in the condition and effect parts to involve a correct anticipation with the situation-consequence couple $(\sigma(t), \sigma(t+1))$. This case represents classifiers whose effect parts contain a '#'-symbol in at least one changing attribute between $\sigma(t)$ and $\sigma(t+1)$. The ALP generate a new classifier which is more specific in such *changing components*: each '#'-symbol (in both C and E parts) on a changing attribute is specified according to $\sigma(t)$ for the C part and $\sigma(t+1)$ for the E part.

    For instance, the classifier (###.O### - N - ###O.###) would be incorrect in the following case: $\sigma(t)$ = ...O.... and $\sigma(t+1)$= ...O.O.. (the sixth attribute does not stay the same as predicted by the classifier). Therefore, the classifier (###.O.## - N - ###O.O##) is created and added to the list.
  - The *not correctable case:* the rule of the classifier cannot be made more specific. This means that an attribute already specified in the E part is different with $\sigma(t+1)$. In this case, the ALP does not generate a new classifier.

- The *expected case*: the classifier anticipates the situation $\sigma(t+1)$ correctly. Its quality is increased. If the classifier is marked, then a new classifier may be generated. As a matter of fact, the presence of a mark means that the classifier has been incorrect in a particular situation. Thus, if the classifier contains attributes in the C part that are marked with at least one value differing from that of the corresponding attribute in $\sigma(t)$, a new classifier is generated specifying these attributes with the value of $\sigma(t)$ in both the C and E parts.
  For instance, the classifier (###.O### - N - ###O.###) anticipates correctly the following situation-consequence couple $(\sigma(t) = ...O..., \sigma(t+1) = ...O....)$. If this classifier contains the mark {{.}, {.}, {.}, {.}, {O}, {.}, {.,O}, {.,O}}, then the classifier (###.O#.. - N - ###O.#..) is created and added to the list.

In this version of the ALP, it is important to note that every specialization of an attribute in a classifier occurs in both the C and E parts. Therefore, for all the classifiers of the population, if a classifier contains a "don't-care" symbol in the C part, it contains a "pass-trough" symbol at the same place in the E part. Conversely, if a classifier contains a "pass-trough" symbol in the E part, it contains a "don't-care" symbol at the same place in the C part.

The quality q of a classifier is increased and decreased by using the Widrow-Hoff delta rule [18] with learning rate $b_q \in [0, 1]$:

$$\text{Increase: } q = (1 - b_q) * q + b_q \tag{1}$$

$$\text{Decrease: } q = (1 - b_q) * q \tag{2}$$

The quality of all new classifiers is initialized to 0.5. If the quality increases over the threshold $\theta_r = 0.9$, the classifier is considered to be reliable. The environmental model is represented by all reliable classifiers.

Nevertheless, the system assumes that all classifiers of the list are distinct. Therefore, when a classifier already existing in the list has to be added, the classifier is not added, and the q value of the identical classifier in the list is increased.

Moreover, the system uses a subsumption method to avoid the creation of over-specialized classifiers. This method is inspired by the subsumption method introduced by Wilson [19] in XCS. The use of this method has been introduced in ACS by Butz [9]. When a new classifier is created, it is not added if an already existing classifier *subsumes* the new one. A classifier cl_1 subsumes a classifier cl_2 if cl_1 is reliable, is not marked, and is more general than cl_2. Thus, if cl_1 subsumes cl_2, then cl_2 is not added and the quality of cl_1 is increased.

2.6 The Reinforcement Learning Process

To enable reward learning, the ACS adapts the Q-learning idea in reinforcement learning [20].

In order to learn an optimal policy in ACS, the reward prediction r of each classifier of the learning set, at a time t, is updated according to the equation (3).

$$R = (1 - b_r) * R + b_r * (\gamma * \max_{cl \in Mt+1}(q_{cl} * r_{cl}) + \rho(t)) \tag{3}$$

The parameter $b_r \in [0, 1]$ is the learning rate and $\gamma \in [0, 1]$ the discount factor similar to Q-learning . M_{t+1} is the match set at a time t+1 and $\rho(t+1)$ is the reward at t+1.

3 The Non-Markov States Problem

A non-Markov environment is an environment containing aliased situations for the sensors of the system. This means that at least two distinct situations in the environments appear to be identical for the system. Therefore, if the optimal behavior consists of different actions in these situations, the system will not be able to choose the best action. It will not be able to distinguish between the two situations and therefore determine the action it has to perform. Aliased situations are also called "non-Markov states" [8]. Several examples of non-Markov environments are presented in section 4.

To avoid such aliased situations, the alternative developed in this work is to take into account the last action, or succession of actions, that bring the system in the current environmental situation. When the system encounters such non-Markov states, the developed method consists in creating a classifier that associates previous actions with a possible action in its action part.

3.1 Behavioral Sequence Classifiers

A behavioral sequence is defined as a succession of actions. A behavioral sequence classifier is a classifier with an action part composed of several ordered actions. The definition of the action part A of this kind of classifier is the following:

$$A = (\alpha_i)_{1 < i \leq bsl} \text{ with } 1 < bsl \leq BS_{max} \tag{4}$$

$(\alpha_i)_{1 < i \leq bsl}$ is a succession of actions. BS_{max} is a parameter specifying the maximal size of behavioral sequences in the system, bsl is the number of actions in the sequence A , and $\alpha_i \in \{a_1,...,a_n\}$ are actions among the n possible actions of the system.

Behavioral sequence classifiers are used in the classifier list in the same way as classical classifiers are used. They may be selected as active classifiers by the selection mechanism used in the behavioral act and, so, provide a succession of actions instead of a unique action. In this case, the system executes all actions before selecting a new active classifier. In the behavioral act description made in section 2.4, this means that step 3 is executed only if the last active classifier was not a behavioral sequence classifier or if all the actions of the sequence have been performed.

The action selection mechanism of the system must take the possible presence of behavioral sequence classifiers in the classifier list into account. The *e-greedy* policy [4] explores different behaviors by choosing a proportion of action randomly (cf. 2.4). With such a mechanism, a behavioral sequence may be selected only if the best classifier is selected and, moreover, if this classifier provides a behavioral sequence. No exploration may be executed on behavioral sequence classifiers, only exploitation. To enable the exploration with the selection of successions of actions, the mechanism used does exploration by selecting a random classifier among the match set, instead of choosing a random action. The selected classifier becomes the active classifier and the system performs the action or the succession of actions represented by the action part of the classifier. Notice that the exploration could be done by choosing a random behavioral sequence among all possible successions of actions, but this mechanism would allow the choice of behavioral sequences not represented in the classifier list. This is not desirable, the objective being not to develop all possible behavioral sequence classifiers. The intention is to develop only classifiers that are able to cope with non-Markov states.

The next section presents how behavioral sequence classifiers are generated. The application of the RLP and the ALP on behavioral sequence classifiers is described in section 3.3.

3.2   Creation of Behavioral Sequence Classifiers

In order to avoid non-Markov states, the system has to be provided with the capacity to detect them in the environment. In [8], Stolzmann proposes a method for ACS to detect a non-Markov state: if a marked classifier reaches the *expected case* of the ALP, and if the *specification of unchanging components* fails, then the ACS assumes that this situation is a non-Markov state. As a matter of fact, the *specification of unchanging components* fails if the mark contains only one situation and if this situation is identical to the current one. This would mean that the classifier sometimes anticipates correctly in this situation (it has reached the expected case) and sometimes not (it is marked with the situation). This phenomenon is only possible, in static environments, if the situation is a non-Markov state.

The creation of new behavioral sequence classifiers occurs in the *expected case* of the ALP. If a classifier reaches this case, is marked, and cannot be specified, then a new classifier is created gathering the previous active classifier and the current classifier as a new behavioral sequence classifier.

For instance, consider $c = (C - A - E)$ as a marked classifier that reached the expected case and cannot be specified. Let $c_{active-1} = (C_{active-1} - A_{active-1} - E_{active-1})$ be the previous active classifier, i.e. the classifier that brings the system to the state that c had matched to be updated. Then a new behavioral sequence classifier $c_{new} = (C_{new} - A_{new} - E_{new})$ is generated. c_{new} consists of:

- $C_{new} = passthrough\ (\ C, C_{active-1}\ )$
- $E_{new} = passthrough\ (\ E_{active-1}, E)$
- $A_{new} = A_{active-1}\ A$

The *passthrough* operator has been defined by Stolzmann in [1]. It applies to two strings with a same number of attributes which may contain '#'-symbols. *passthrough* (A, B) returns a string C of the same size as A and B, with its attributes initialized as follows:

```
C ← PASSTHROUGH (A , B):
        FOR i FROM 1 TO L DO
            If ( B[i]='#' )
            THEN C[i] ← A[i]
            ELSE C[i] ← B[i]
```

L is the number of attributes in A, B and C. A[i], B[i] and C[i] are the ith attributes of, respectively, A, B and C.

$A_{active-1}A$ is a behavioral sequence constituted in order with the action or succession of actions of $A_{active-1}$ followed by the action or succession of actions of A.

3.3 Classifiers Update

If a behavioral sequence classifier is active, the ALP does not take place until the last action of the sequence has been executed. Therefore the step 8 of behavioral acts is not applied while a sequence is not finished.

The RLP and ALP are applied on a learning set. Classically, the learning set is an action set: a set containing all the classifiers of the match that have the executed action as action part. If the system executed a behavioral sequence instead of a unique action, the learning set is formed with all the behavioral sequence classifiers of the match set that have the executed behavioral sequence as action part.

If an ACS uses behavioral sequences, then it can produce classifiers with an action part representing a looping behavioral sequence. It is the case, for example, when a behavioral sequence consists on moving forward and then backward. To prevent such a looping behavior, the system uses a *situations list* during the execution of a behavioral sequence. The quality of every classifier that provides a looping behavioral sequence is decreased. The algorithm used to perform such a mechanism has been presented by Stolzmann [8]. This algorithm was originally used to update a unique classifier. Here, the algorithm is applied on all classifiers providing the current executed behavioral sequence. The algorithm is the following:

EXECUTION OF A BEHAVIORAL SEQUENCE BS = $(\alpha_i)_{1 < i < m}$:

> L ← {S_0}
>
> FOR i FROM 1 TO m DO
>
> > Execute α_i
> >
> > Perceive S_i
> >
> > IF $S_i \in$ L THEN
> >
> > > FOR each classifier with BS as action part DO
> > >
> > > q ← (1 - b_q) * q
> >
> > L ← L $\cup$ {S_i}

In this algorithm, m is the size of the executed behavioral sequence BS. $\alpha_{i=1,...,m}$ are the m actions of BS. L is the situations list. $S_{i=0,...,m}$ are the perceived situations. q is the quality parameter of classifiers and b_q the learning rate (the equation used to update q corresponds to the equation (2) presented in section 2.5).

4   Experiments in Woods Environments

4.1   The Woods Environments

The Woods environments are discrete two-dimensional environments containing two kinds of objects: obstacles and food. Each position in this grid is coded either as a tree, represented by 'O' for the sensors, as food, 'F', or as a free position '.'.

In each cycle of experiment, each behavioral act, the system perceives the eight nearest cells of the environment as shown in the figure 3. Moreover, it can act by moving toward one of the eight nearest cells. Therefore, the possible actions of the system are these eight movements. Moving toward an obstacle cell is impossible.

The environment used by Stolzmann to study behavioral sequences is the "T-Maze environment" [8]. It consists on a two-dimensional grid containing some obstacles and food. The difference with woods environments is that Stolzmann's system is not provided with the same sensors and actuators than in the classical woods context. As a matter of fact, the Stolzmann's ACS controls simulated khepera robots which cannot perceive the environment as in the figure 3. Due to this distinction, the T-Maze provides different properties. In Stolzmann experiments, the environment is a non-Markov environment while in the present context the T-Maze would be a Markov one. Thus, results would not be comparable. For this reason, the T-Maze is not used here. Moreover, Stolzmann focused on latent learning capacities of the system while this study focuses on reward learning ones.

7	0	1
6	A	2
5	4	3

Fig. 3. Perception and actions of the system. The 'A' represents the position of the system. It perceives the eight nearest cells of its position, numbered from 0 to 7. It can act by moving to one of the eight cells.

In this work, four environments are studied: one Markov environment and three non-Markov ones. The first one, Woods1, is studied as a reference environment. Butz, Goldberg and Stolzamnn presented ACS performances in Woods1 in [11, 17]. These experiments have been made to validate the system's basic behaviors as conform with some already presented results. The following environments are non-Markov environments with different properties to permit the study of the system's performances in several distinct contexts.

4.2 The Experiments

Two types of experiments are made: latent learning tests and reward learning tests. All experiments follow a same principle: the system is placed in a random free cell and acts until it enters in a food cell. When the system is in a food cell, it is replaced in a random free cell.

In the latent learning experiments, the system does not receive any reward when finding the food. Every 200 steps, the knowledge is tested. The knowledge is represented by the *reliable* classifiers of the classifier list (i.e. the classifier that have a quality more than θ_r). In each free position, and so in each possible situation of the environment, each possible movement is tested. If a reliable classifier matches a situation, induces a given action, and predicts correctly the consequent situation, then this situation-reaction-consequence is considered as known by the system. Its knowledge is, thus, the percentage of situation-reaction-consequence known among all possible ones in the environment. When a classifier contains a behavioral sequence, then all the situation-reaction-consequence which form a chain correctly matched by the C, A and E parts of the classifier are considered as known.

In the reward learning experiments, the system receives a reward of 1000 when it enters into a food cell. To test the performance, the steps to food averaged over 50 trials are recorded. This corresponds to the method used by Wilson to test ZCS[21] and XCS[19] performances in woods environment. After 1000 trials, the system switches to pure exploitation but learning processes are not stopped. Reward learning performances are compared to optimal performances in each environment. These optimal performances are computed as the best performances the system could obtain if it had a complete perception of the environment. Therefore, in the non-Markov environments, the system cannot reach these optimal performances. These optima values have been used as reference because the computation of optimal performances according to the system perception may be a hard problem in certain non-Markov environments (especially in the E2 environment presented later).

The parameter values used in the experiments are the following:

- $b_r = 0.05$
- $b_q = 0.05$
- $\theta_r = 0.9$
- $p_x = 0.8$
- BS_{max} depends on the studied environment (see below).

These values, except for BS_{max}, are the ones used by Butz to test ACS in Woods1 [9, 17].

4.3   Experiments in Woods1

Woods1 is a Markov environment introduced by Wilson to test ZCS [21]. Due to its Markov property, this environment does not represent a real challenge for ACS. In particular, the use of behavioral sequences is not needed to obtain optimal perform-ances. Butz [17] demonstrated that after 17000 steps of latent learning, a complete model of the environment is developed by ACS. In [11] he showed that the complete model is obtained faster if the ALP is applied on a whole action set. The number of situation-reaction-consequence constellations represented in Woods1 is of 101 (i.e. 16 positions * 8 movements – 27 impossible movements).

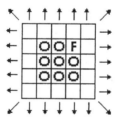

Fig. 4. The Woods1 environment. This configuration is repeated indefinitely in the horizontal and vertical directions.

In the present work, experiments in Woods1 have been made to confirm that the system obtains similar results than Butz in [11], in this environment. The action selec-tion mechanism used by Butz is not the one used in this work. Therefore, the system has been tested with the two selection mechanisms to permit a result comparison of both approaches.

As in Butz results [9], the system developed a complete internal model of the envi-ronment. The size of the classifier list converges to a value around 190 with both selection mechanisms. The two mechanisms provides similar results in Woods1. In reward learning experiments, the system converges to optimal performances when it switches to exploitation.

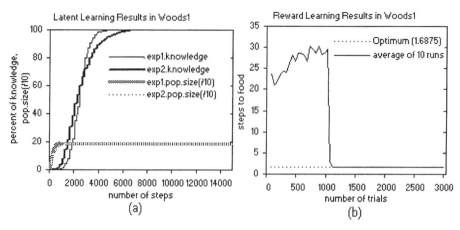

Fig. 5. (a) Latent learning results the Woods1 environment according to two different action selection mechanism. In the fist experiment, exp1, the system uses the e-greedy policy with e = 0 (i.e. all actions are selected randomly). In the second, exp2, the system uses the classifier selection mechanism used in later with behavioral sequences experiments (cf. 2.4) with p_x = 0.8. (b) Reward learning results in Woods1. The system uses the classifier selection mechanism and switches to exploitation after 1000 trials. All curves (in (a) and (b)) are averages of 10 runs.

4.4 Experiments in Woods100

Woods100 has been used by Lanzi to study reinforcement learning whith internal memory [5]. It consists on a minimalist non-Markov environment presenting two non-Markov-states (cl. Fig. 6). The number of situation-reaction-consequence constellations represented in Woods100 is of 10 (i.e. 6 positions * 8 movements – 38 impossible movements).

O	O	O	O	O	O	O	O
O		N		F		N		O
O	O	O	O	O	O	O	O

Fig. 6. The Woods100 environment. In the figure the 'N' symbols marks the two aliased situations of the environment.

Note that, in reward learning results with BS_{max} of 1, the steps to food value increases tremendously after the system switches to exploitation. It does not converge to a stable value but, rather, increases during all the experiment. At the 10000th trials the system needs a mean of 400 steps to get to the food.

In order to test the system in environments of increasing complexity, two environments, E1 and E2, have been created.

4.5 Experiments in E1

Compared to Woods100, E1 is a non-Markov Environment which contains many different non-Markov states instead of two aliased states. Indeed, it presents 20 aliased situations, among the 44 possible positions of the environment, perceived by the system as 9 distinct situations. In this environment, the system has to take different configurations of non-Markov states into account. As a matter of fact, all aliased situations are contiguous with, at least, one other aliased situations. Nevertheless, in this environment, any contiguous non-Markov states are perceived as distinct by the system.

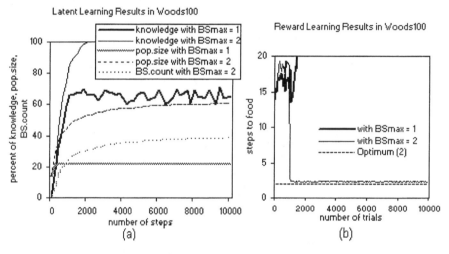

Fig. 7. (a) Latent learning results in the Woods100 environment according to the BS_{max} value. The BS.count result represents the number of behavioral sequence classifiers in the classifier list. (b) Reward learning results in Woods100. All curves (in (a) and (b)) are averages of 10 runs.

O	O	O	O	O	O	O	O
O	N_1				N_1		O
O	W_1	O	W_2	X	E_2	O E_1	O
O	N_2				N_2		O
O	X		**F**		X		O
O	S_2				S_2		O
O	W_1	O	W_2	X	E_2	O E_1	O
O	S_1				S_1		O
O	O	O	O	O	O	O	O

Fig. 8. The E1 environment. Aliased situations are represented by the 'N1', 'N2', 'E1', 'E2', 'W1', 'W2', 'S1', 'S2' and 'X' symbols. Two states marked with a same symbol are perceived as identical by the system.

Results show that if E1 provides an increase of the non-Markov states configuration complexity in the environment, it represents a challenge less difficult than Woods100. Indeed, compared to the system performances in Woods100, the system does not need to use behavioral sequences to converge to stable reward performance. Nevertheless, behavioral sequences of length 2 enable the system to develop a complete internal model of the environment and to improve the "step to food" performance.

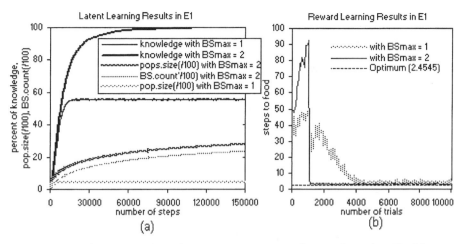

Fig. 9. (a) Latent learning results in the E1 environment according to BS_{max} value. The BS.count result represents the number of behavioral sequence classifiers in the classifier list. (b) Reward learning results in E1. With $BS_{max} = 1$, it converges to a performance around 4. With $BS_{max} = 2$, it converges to a performance around 3.3. All curves (in (a) and (b)) are averages of 10 runs.

4.6 Experiments in E2

As E1, E2 contains different non-Markov states, 36 aliased situations among the 48 possible positions of the environment. These non-Markov states are perceived as 5 distinct situations by the system. This environment may be considered as more complex than E1 in the non-Markov state configuration because the number of Markov states is lower than the number of non-Markov ones. Moreover, a major difference with E1 is that this environment provides contiguous aliased situations perceived as identical by the system.

O	O	O	O	O	O	O	O
O		N	N	N	N	N		O
O	W	C	C	C	C	C	E	O
O	W	C				C	E	O
O	W	C		F		C	E	O
O	W	C				C	E	O
O	W	C	C	C	C	C	E	O
O		S	S	S	S	S		O
O	O	O	O	O	O	O	O

Fig. 10. The E2 environment. The 'N', 'E', 'S', 'W' and 'C' symbols mark the aliased situation of the environment. Two states marked with a same symbol are perceived as identical by the system.

Latent learning results (see figure 11) show that the system needs behavioral sequence length 3 to be able to develop a complete internal model of the environment. Moreover the size of the classifier list increases to 2500 with the use of behavioral sequence classifiers instead of 280 without them.

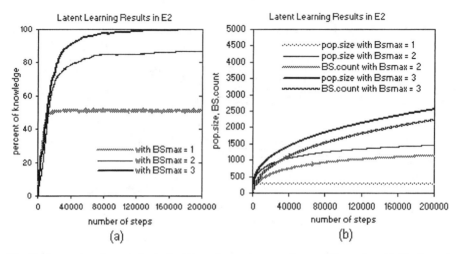

(a)   (b)

Fig. 11. Latent learning results in the E2 environment according to BS_{max} value. (a) The knowledge performances of the system. It shows that the system needs behavioral sequence of length 3 to develop a complete internal model of the environment. (b) The classifier list size variations. The BS.count result represents the number of behavioral sequence classifiers in the classifier list. All curves (in (a) and (b)) are averages of 10 runs.

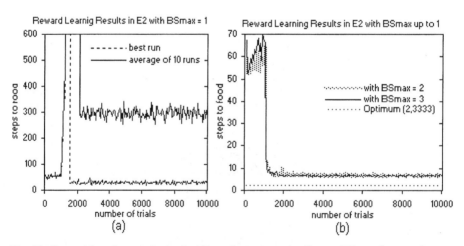

(a)   (b)

Fig. 12. Reward learning results in the E2 environment according to BS_{max} value. (a) Steps to food performances when no behavioral sequence classifier is used. The "best run" curve presents the performances of the only run among ten which converges to stable performances with a steps to food value around 30. (b) (a) Steps to food performances with BS_{max} values of 2 and 3. Whatever BS_{max} value, the system converges to performance around 6.5. All curves (in (a) and (b)) are averages of 10 runs.

Reward learning results (see figure 12) show that behavioral sequences of length 2 are enough to converge to stable performances. Without behavioral sequences, a stable policy is reachable by the system but only one run among ten has converged to it. The performance obtained with this stable policy is of 30. With behavioral sequence of length 2, the system converge, in every run, to stable performances around 6.5. The use of behavioral sequences of length 3 does not improve these "steps to food" performances. Whatever the maximal length, the system obtains performances up to twice the absolute optimum.

5 Discussion

Results of the experiments show that the use of behavioral sequence classifiers improves the system's performances in non-Markov environments either in reward or latent learning experiments. In the environments Woods100, E1 and E2, the system develops a stable strategy to get the food, i.e. it converges to stable reward learning performances. In latent learning tests, behavioral sequence classifiers permit the system to develop a complete model of all environments. These results do not have the same importance in the three environments. Indeed, if Woods100, E1 and E2 all satisfy the properties to be non-Markov environments, they do not represent equivalent challenges for the system.

In Woods100, the system is not able to converge to stable reward learning performances when it does not use behavioral sequences. Moreover, it obtains performances worse than a random action strategy. In this context, the use of behavioral sequence classifiers provides the system with the capacity to develop a stable strategy. Obtained performances are close to the optimal.

The case of the E1 environment is different. Stable reward learning performances may be reached without using behavioral sequences. The use of behavioral sequence classifiers just improves the performances. As in Woods100, the obtained performances are close to the optimal.

At least, in E2, stable reward learning performances may be reached without behavioral sequences, but only one experiment among ten has converged to it. Latent learning results show that the system needs a BS_{max} value of 3 to develop a complete model of the environment. The use of behavioral sequence classifiers enables the system to converge to stable reward learning performances in every experiment. But, whatever the BS_{max} value is , between 2 and 3, the obtained performances are the same. If these performances are better than without behavioral sequences, they stay, however, up to twice the optimal.

The ability of the system to cope with non-Markov states heavily relies on the number and the disposition of the Markov states. As a matter of fact, a behavioral sequence classifier may be efficient if it is only applicable to a non-ambiguous situation as in a Markov state. Otherwise, the classifier cannot be reliable because it cannot anticipate correctly the resulting situation, and it has thus a small chance to be more useful than a classifier with a simple action. Thus, in the majority of E2 experiments, when the system has converged to stable reward learning performances, the only states where a behavioral sequence is performed are the four corners. In most states of the environment, behavioral sequences are not used, and the system develops a strategy based on classifiers with simple action to find Markov states. For instance, it will go along the tree cells, while avoiding the chaining of two states perceived as identical, until it encounters a corner and, only in such a state, a behavioral sequence will be used to reach one of the Markov states close to the food cell (cf. fig. 10). This may explain why the system's reward learning performances stay up to twice the optimal in

E2 when using behavioral sequence classifiers. Moreover, this highlights why using a BS_{max} value of 3, which enables the system to develop a complete model of the environment, does not improve reward learning performances obtained with a BS_{max} value of 2. Indeed, using behavioral sequences of three actions allows to take into account non-Markov states that were not reachable from Markov states with smaller sequences. But the strategy to get the food still stays the same as with sequences of two actions.

The usefulness of behavioral sequences in the system is, thus, dependent on the position of Markov states in the environment. Therefore, it may be possible to have non-Markov environments where the use of behavioral sequences have no interest whatever is the BS_{max} value. As a matter of fact, non-Markov environments in which the only Markov states are near the food, may present difficulties. This result highlights a major difficulty of non-Markov environments for reinforcement learning systems. Indeed, any mechanism permitting to cope with non-Markov states need non-aliased states as reference to raise aliasing. Thus, actual LCSs using a memory mechanism, like a memory register, may suffer from same difficulties observed here. Their reward performances should depend on the position of Markov states.

The ACS version used in this study does not have any generalization mechanism. As shown by Butz [11], this provides the system with a tendency to over-specialize the classifiers and to therefore develop a population size higher than necessary. For example, the population size converges to 190 in Woods1 while only 101 classifiers are necessary. However, the size of the classifier list increases tremendously with the use of behavioral sequence classifiers. Results of latent learning experiments show that a very high number of behavioral sequence classifiers are generated. To limit this population increase, the system may need a more sophisticated mechanism to select the classifiers that will be used to create a behavioral sequence classifier. Above all, the system may use a reliable classifier instead of using the previous active classifier. To avoid over-specialization and to generate maximally general classifiers, the system may also use a genetic algorithm[16]. Such an enhancement has been studied by Butz[9, 11, 12].

6 Conclusion

This paper presented a study of ACS performances in different non-Markov environments when using behavioral sequences. A version of ACS is detailed based on Stolzmann's ACS [1], and using enhancements proposed by Stolzmann [8] and Butz[9, 11, 13, 17]. Latent learning and reward learning experiments have been made in four distinct environments, one Markov and three non-Markov, in order to test the system's performances when using behavioral sequences and when not using it.

The reward and latent learning results in the Markov-environment show that the performances of the system match former results obtained by Butz, Goldberg and Stolzmann in a same environment [17, 11].

Experiments in non-Markov environments showed that using behavioral sequences permit an improvement of the system's performances. In latent learning experiments, the use of behavioral sequence classifiers enables the system to develop a complete model of the environments. In reward learning experiments, the system converges to a stable policy in the three non-Markov environments.

Nevertheless, the study highlights a relation between the system's ability to cope with aliased situations and the position of Markov states (i.e. non aliased situations) in the environment. Indeed, any system provided with a mechanism to cope with non-Markov states needs non-aliased states to develop stable policies in non-Markov environments. ACS with behavioral sequences needs non-aliased states to develop reliable behavioral sequence classifiers able to avoid aliased situations. The proportion of Markov states, and their disposition among aliased ones, have a strong impact on the system behavioral sequence classifiers use. Thus, if this method provides the system with the capacity to develop stable strategies close to the optimal in certain non-Markov environments, it is not adapted to all non-Markov environments. Such results may permit to develop a categorization of non-Markov environments based on the applicability of behavioral sequences to cope with aliased situations.

As future work, generalization mechanisms should be added to the system in order to avoid its tendency to over-specialize its classifiers. Butz, Goldberg and Stolzmann introduced the use of a genetic algorithm in ACS [9, 11, 13] and showed that this method enables the system to develop maximally general reliable classifiers. The use of behavioral sequence increases tremendously the classifier list size. This method may be enhanced with more sophisticated mechanisms to select the classifiers used to form new behavioral sequence classifiers. Moreover, this method has to be tested in non-Markov environments used to test ZCS and XCS with internal memory, in order to enable a comparison of the two approaches. A comparison may permit to further highlight the dependencies of this method with particular properties of each non-Markov environment.

Acknowledgments

The authors would like to thank the LIAP5 laboratory, University René Descartes, and Elsa Serfaty for her useful corrections.

References

1. Stolzmann W.: Anticipatory Classifier Systems. In Koza, John R., Banzhaf, Wolfgang, Chellapilla, Kumar, Deb, Kalyanmoym Dorigo, Marco, Fogel, David B., Garzon, Max H., Goldberg, David E., Iba, Hitoshi, and Riolo, Rick. (editors). Genetic Programming 1998: Proceedings of the Third Annual Conference, July 22-25, 1998, University of Wisconsin, Madison, Wisconsin, 658-664. San Francisco, CA: Morgan Kaufmann (1998)
2. Hoffmann J.: Vorhersage und Erkenntnis [Anticipation and Cognition]. Goettingen, Germany: Hogrefe (1993).
3. Booker, L. B., Goldberg, D. E., Holland, J. H.: Classifier systems and genetic algorithms. Artificial Intelligence (1989), 40, 235-282.
4. Pier Luca Lanzi. Adaptive Agents with Reinforcement Learning and Internal Memory. In Sixth International Conference on the Simulation of Adaptive Behavior (SAB2000), pages 333-342. MIT Press, 2000.
5. Sutton, R. S., Barto, A. G.: Reinforcement Learning: An Introduction. Cabridge: The MITPress (1998)

6. Cliff, Dave, Ross, Susi, 1995, Adding Temporary Memory to ZCS, Adaptive Bahavior Vol.3, No. 2, 101-150.
7. Lanzi, Pier Luca, 1998, An Analysis of the Memory Mechanism of XCSM, in Koza, John R., et al. (editors), Genetic Programming 1998: Proceedings of the Third Annual Conference, July 22-25, 11998, University of Wisconsin, Madison, Wisconsin, San Francisco, CA: Morgan Kaufmann, 643-651.
8. Stolzmann W.: Latent Learning in Khepera Robots with Anticipatory Classifier Systems. In A.S. Wu (Ed.), Proceedings of the 1999 Genetic and Evolutionary Computation Conference Workshop Program (1999), pp. 290-297.
9. Butz, M., Goldberg, D. E., Stolzmann, W., 2000, The Anticipatory Classifier System and Genetic Generalization, in the Illigal Report No. 200032
10. Martin Butz & Wolfgang Stolzmann (1999): Action-Planning in Anticipatory Classifier Systems. In A.S. Wu (Ed.), Proceedings of the 1999 Genetic and Evolutionary Computation Conference Workshop Program, pp. 242-249.
11. Butz, Martin V., Goldberg, David E., and Stolzmann, Wolfgang, Introducing a genetic generalization pressure to the Anticipatory Classifier System Part 1: Theoretical approach, in Proceedings of the Genetic and Evolutionary Computation Conference (GECCO-2000)
12. Butz, Martin V., Goldberg, David E., and Stolzmann, Wolfgang, Introducing a genetic generalization pressure to the Anticipatory Classifier System Part 2: Performance Analysis, in Proceedings of the Genetic and Evolutionary Computation Conference (GECCO-2000).
13. Butz, M., Goldberg, M., Stolzmann W., 2000, Probability-Enhanced Predictions in the Anticipatory Classifier System, in the Illigal Report No. 200015
14. Butz, M.V. (2001) Anticipations, Anticipatory Classifier Systems, and Genetic Generalization. A Diploma Thesis from the University of Wuerzburg, German, in the IlliGAL Report No. 2001025
15. Gérard, P., Stolzmann, W. and Sigaud, O. (to appear) YACS : a new Learning Classifier System using Anticipation. Journal of Soft Computing : Special Issue on Learning Classifier Systems. Springer Verlag.
16. Goldberg, D. E., 1989, Genetic Algorithms in search, optimization and machine learning. Reading, Massachusetts: Addison-Wesley.
17. Butz, M., Goldberg, D. E., Stolzmann, W. (1999): New Challenges for an Anticipatory Classifier System : Hard Problems and Possible Solutions, in the Illigal Report No. 99019
18. Widrow, B., Hoff, M.: Adaptive switching circuits. Western Electronics Show and Convention 1960. 4. 96-104.
19. Wilson, S. W.: Classifier fitness based on accuracy, Evolutionary Computation, 3(2), 149-175, 1995.
20. Watkins, C. J. C. H., Dayan, P.: Qlearning. Machine Learning. 1992. 8(3). 272-292.
21. Wilson, S. W.: ZCS: A zeroth level classifier system. Evolutionary Computation, 2(1):1-18, 1994.

Mapping Artificial Immune Systems into Learning Classifier Systems

Patrícia A. Vargas, Leandro N. de Castro, and Fernando J. Von Zuben

[1] Department of Computer Engineering and Industrial Automation,
School of Electrical and Computer Engineering, State University of Campinas (Unicamp),
Campinas-SP, Brazil
{pvargas,lnunes,vonzuben}@dca.fee.unicamp.br
http://www.dca.fee.unicamp.br

Abstract. This paper presents one form of mapping Artificial Immune Systems (AIS) into Learning Classifier Systems (LCS). Artificial Immune Systems can be defined as adaptive systems inspired by theoretical models and principles of the biological immune system and applied to solve problems in the most diverse domains, from biology to computing. Similar to Learning Classifier Systems, already used to model complex adaptive systems, a better understanding of Artificial Immune Systems can be obtained when they are analysed under the perspective of complex adaptive systems. One of the goals here is to determine complementary features of both systems (LCS and AIS), aiming at providing a novel mapping conception. The formal treatment proposed along the paper may then be used to integrate models for complex adaptive systems.

1 Introduction

Nature abounds with complexity. All natural systems have to be capable of coping with continuous changes in environmental conditions so as to maintain life. This survival capability requires some fundamental features, such as adaptability, interactivity, self-maintenance and diversity. Complex adaptive system (CAS) is a terminology originally proposed to denote any system, either natural or artificial, that presents these characteristics [21]. One of the greatest challenges in designing artificial complex adaptive systems lies in the adaptability and flexibility of the models. There are several ways of implementing such models. One is to look for a single model encompassing all the necessary features. Another is by combining complementary attributes of distinct conceptual devices or practical tools, giving rise to hybrid models. These models are always motivated by the absence of a single device capable of properly supporting all the requirements under consideration.

Learning classifier systems (LCS) have for long been used to solve a number of complex computational and engineering problems, such as pattern classification and decision making [35],[36]. Concurrently, artificial immune systems (AIS), have also been successfully applied to these domains [11]. Given that LCS have already been proposed as a framework to model CAS [21], and noting that LCS and AIS share

P.L. Lanzi et al. (Eds.): IWLCS 2002, LNAI 2661, pp. 163–186, 2003.

similar domains of application, the main aspects to be considered here are preliminary steps toward the integration of LCS and AIS in the context of CAS.

To accomplish this task, this paper has two main goals: determining and highlighting complementary features of artificial immune systems and learning classifier systems; and, as an extension of the first effort, proposing a mapping between these two approaches. Both initiatives may then provide the necessary understanding to be explored in a near future for fully integrating both approaches.

These goals will be reached by means of four distinct steps. First, the identification of common aspects between both systems. Second, the establishment of correspondence rules between AIS and LCS by associating elements of one system with elements of the other and analysing their complementary features. Third, the presentation of the suggested mapping together with an application example. Finally, a discussion about the outcomes of the proposal.

The framework to be proposed for AIS also brings some similarities with the framework introduced by Holland [20] to model adaptation in natural and artificial systems. Holland suggested that such a framework might be composed of an environment undergoing adaptation, an adaptive plan that determines successive structural modifications in response to the environment, and a performance measure of different structures in the environment. According to de Castro & Timmis [11], AIS can be designed using a layered framework composed of three main parts: a representation scheme, some adaptation procedures, and a set of mechanisms to evaluate interactions.

Therefore, even considering the existence of distinctive aspects among the many frameworks for problem solving and modelling complex adaptive systems, in general terms the following requirements are always involved: an environment in which the systems are built, a given representation scheme for individuals that inhabit the environment, some evaluation mechanisms to allow for a qualitative distinction of individuals, and adaptation strategies to change the configuration (structure or parameters) of the system.

This paper is organised as follows. Section 2 shows the foundations of LCS, introducing one of the most popular views of complex adaptive systems. In Section 3, learning classifier systems and adaptive agents to model CAS are briefly described, with a historical overview of other models of classifier systems. Section 4 provides a discussion of the vertebrate immune system, claiming why it can be characterised as a CAS, together with a broader outline of the artificial immune systems. Previous proposals dealing with the resemblance of learning classifier systems and artificial immune systems are reviewed in Section 5, followed by the presentation of a novel mapping conception and an application example. Section 6 presents a discussion and analyses the possible outcomes of this research.

2   Foundations for Complex Adaptive Systems (CAS)

Complex Adaptive Systems (CAS) is a terminology used to describe all natural (biological and social) systems, together with their many properties, interactions and resultant emergent behaviours. The work proposed by Holland [21] starts with a discussion of how these systems are formed and self-sustained, explaining how the (complex) behaviour of the whole is more than a simple sum of individual behaviours. One of the main questions raised is that of how a decentralised – with no central planning – system is self-organised. Note that there is a strong similarity between the concept of a CAS and the concept of *emergent systems* [22], [30]. Indeed, complex adaptive systems exhibit emergent phenomena, but this is not the focus of the discussion to be presented here.

As an instance of a CAS, one can think of the immune system, with its sheer diversity of cells, molecules and organs, all working in concert to provide security against foreign attacks and to aid in sustaining life. Several other examples can be given, such as all bodily systems (e.g., the nervous system, and the endocrine system), insect societies (e.g., ant and termite colonies), trading in commerce (e.g., the stock market), and so forth. A common aspect is that there is no central control. Every element composing the system plays its individual role and sometimes adapts itself and interacts with other elements (and even whole systems) with the aim of generating and sustaining its integrity and the life of the organism.

Despite the differences among the many complex adaptive systems, in every single case the persistence of the system relies on three main aspects: 1) interactions of components, 2) diversity, and 3) adaptation. According to Holland [21], the choice of the name *Complex Adaptive Systems* is more than a terminology "[i]t signals our intuition that general principles rule CAS behaviour, principles that point to ways of solving attendant problems." (p. 4)

Holland [21] propositions were delineated to uncover general principles associated with the synthesis of refined CAS behaviours from simple laws. The core idea is to develop a well-designed mathematical model for CAS, i.e. a formal theory. The steps taken toward this goal were to initially select *seven basics* – four properties (*aggregation, nonlinearity, flows,* and *diversity*) and three mechanisms (*tagging, internal models,* and *building blocks*) – common to all CAS, and then to devise a framework and implement a computer-based model to study CAS. In the following, we attempt to summarise the main parts of Holland's *seven basics*.

Seven Basics
As described above, Holland's seven basics are divided into four properties: aggregation, nonlinearity, flows and diversity; and three mechanisms: tagging, internal models and building blocks.

Properties
Aggregation in complex adaptive systems occurs in static and dynamic senses. The first sense states how to describe the inherent structure of CAS (a standard way of modelling a CAS), and the second is related to what CAS do aggregate, i.e., how complex large-scale behaviours *emerge* from the aggregate interactions of less complex elements. More precisely, in the first sense, basically, there is an aggregation of categories that afterwards will turn into building blocks for the models. In the second sense, aggregation is a basic characteristic of all complex adaptive systems, where each category aggregates with another category forming a more complex category, thus yielding to more complex hierarchical aggregations.

Non-linearity is present in complex adaptive systems in several distinct levels, defining how non-linear dynamics almost always make the behaviour of the aggregate more complicated. Therefore, the behaviour of a system containing non-linear components is harder to model and to predict.

Flows concern how data (e.g., information, stimuli, electric impulses, resources etc.) propagate through a system and vary over time. The effects of such flows are of two kinds: the multiplier effect, which spreads an injected resource or information at a given node or agent throughout the network; and the recycling effect, as the name suggests, helps to maintain the equilibrium by adapting the data to a new use or function, by passing it through a cycle again, as for further treatment, or just by starting a different cycle.

The last property, diversity, is viewed as a necessary feature to generate and maintain a CAS. In fact, perpetual novelty is a hallmark of CAS. It indicates that the diversity is the product of progressive adaptations, as signalised by Charles Darwin [9], when he observed that the principles of evolution that operated to generate the species, like competition, variation and selection, arise from the diversity of species.

Mechanisms

The first mechanism, denoted tagging, refers to tag-based interactions (i.e., labelled identified, and/or classified interactions) that provide a sound basis for filtering, specialisation, co-operation, competition, formation of aggregates, manipulation of symmetries, and selective interactions.

The internal models mechanism is the terminology used to refer to mechanisms for anticipation (the act of considering something beforehand, i.e. foreknowledge) and prediction (the act of reasoning about future events or possibilities, especially on the basis of special knowledge, i.e. foresight). In fact, internal models distinguish CAS from other complex systems. They balance exploration with exploitation [21], providing the make of careful systematic searches of profitable and useful resources. There are two kinds of internal models, *tacit* - that simply prescribes a current action, and *overt* - that explores alternatives (looks ahead), allowing inferences to be accomplished.

The last mechanism, named building blocks or generators, constitute basic elements or parts that compose internal models. In fact, relevant building blocks are combined to model new situations, therefore, to generate internal models or a completely novel CAS.

3 Learning Classifier Systems and Adaptive Agents for CAS

Learning classifier systems (LCS) were introduced by J. Holland in mid 1970s [20]. Basically, they refer to a methodology for creating and updating rules, named classifiers, which encode alternative specific actions according to the purpose of the system and the current state of the environment [5]. There have been a number of variants to the standard (original) LCS introduced by Holland. This section presents the standard learning classifier system, describes how LCS can be used to model agents for CAS, and reviews some of its most well known variants.

3.1 Holland's Learning Classifier System

The learning classifier system communicates with the environment through its message detectors. These detectors are responsible for the reception and proper encoding of the messages received by the system. The system acts on the environment through its effectors, which decode the systems' proposed actions. The appropriate reward applied to the active classifier is determined by the nature of the outcome of each action, that is, the environmental feedback. Figure 1 summarises the interaction of a LCS with the environment and depicts its main component parts.

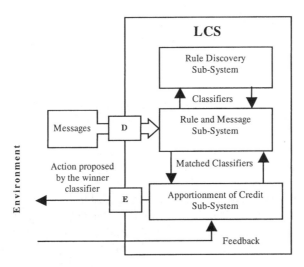

Fig. 1. Simplified flow of the interaction of a learning classifier system with the environment. D: detectors; E: effectors

A classifier is composed of an antecedent and a consequent part, similarly to a production rule, with a condition and an action part. The antecedent part is usually a string composed of the ternary alphabet { 1, 0, # }, and the consequent part is encoded as a binary string. The "#" symbol corresponds to a 'don't care', that is, it can be interpreted either as a '1' or as a '0'.

Associated with each classifier there is a value, named *strength*, used to express the energy or power of the classifier during the adaptive process. The matching of the classifier's antecedent part with the messages of the environment defines which classifiers will compete to act on the environment. This competition is based on the strength of the selected classifiers.

Another important concept is the *specificity* of each classifier, which is a measure inversely proportional to the number of don't care symbols "#" on the antecedent part of the classifier.

The interaction between the LCS and the environment happens as follows:

- when the message detectors perceive the presence of a message from the environment, this message is sent to the *Rule and Message Sub-System* (see Figure 1). Then, all the classifiers try to match its antecedent part with the message received from the environment. This phase is called the *matching phase* and can be performed in a bit-to-bit basis, according to specific operators.
- given a message from the environment, the classifiers that have the highest level of matching will be allowed to take part in the competition. The winner is recognised by a parameter called *bid*, which is calculated taking the strength and specificity of the classifier and modulating it by a signal with Gaussian distribution. The winner will be allowed to act on the environment.
- when using the *Bucket Brigade* algorithm, instead of directly acting on the environment, the winner classifier posts its message (i.e. the consequent part) to a message list, which afterwards will activate other classifiers that might also post their messages, creating a cascade of actions stimulated by actions already adopted.
- the environment will provide a feedback to the learning classifier system in response to the action commanded by the effectors. It is the responsibility of the *Apportionment of Credit Sub-System* to incorporate a reward or punishment value, based on the feedback from the environment, to the strength of the classifier or subset of classifiers responsible for an action or sequence of actions.
- once feedback is received from the environment, and the credit is attributed to the pertinent classifiers, a new message will be provided by the environment, describing its new current state. Then, once again the Rule and Message Sub-System receives and processes the environmental message. The process continues for one epoch of iteration, defined as a sequence of actions adopted by the learning classifier system between adaptive phases.

At the end of each epoch, the learning classifier system takes part in another adaptive process: the discovery of new rules at the *Rule Discovery Sub-System*. At this stage, evolutionary operators, such as crossover and mutation, are applied to produce the next generation of rules. This evolutionary process aims at producing a learning classifier system with improved performance. Basically, a *genetic algorithm* is used to evolve the set of classifiers, taking the strengths as the fitness values. Those classifiers with greater strength are selected, reproduced, and suffer genetic variation through crossover and mutation. The generated offspring classifiers are introduced into the population at the next generation, replacing the weakest individuals (the ones with the lowest strengths).

3.2 LCS to Model Agents for CAS

Although the term CAS has different meanings for different researchers [8], we particularly adopted John Holland's idea because he was the proponent of the first framework to develop adaptive agents for CAS. The framework proposed by Holland [21] for developing adaptive agents for CAS was introduced as consisting of three major built-in stages, to be described in what follows.

In the *performance system* stage, agents are viewed as a collection of message processing rules. The syntax of the rules depends on their interaction with the environment. A set of detectors and a set of effectors manage this system-environment interaction. Additionally, the *performance system* specifies the agents' capabilities at a fixed point in time, and it prepares these agents to novel situations without having all rules a priori.

In the *credit-assignment* stage, the core idea is to provide the agents with the capability of adapting to the environment. In the performance system, a number of rules can be fired simultaneously according to the interactions of the system. As a consequence, these rules must compete with one another in order to have a single rule being selected to determine the output of the system. Each rule has a *strength* assigned, which is modified via *credit-assignment* on the basis of experience (e.g., a Bucket Brigade algorithm [5]). Credit-assignment is performed in response (reward – reinforcement or punishment) to a 'payoff' received from the environment.

The *rule-discovery* stage describes another way of endowing agents with adaptability by allowing the system to automatically generate 'plausible' rules. It should be done always taking the past experience into account. The author uses the notion of schemas (likened to building blocks) and genetic algorithms as tools for rule discovery.

The framework described above for modelling agents for CAS is reminiscent of Learning Classifier Systems. Indeed, Classifier Systems have already been used to model CAS [20]. For instance, the set of detectors/effectors plus the IF/THEN rules (classifiers) correspond to the performance system. The rule discovery and credit apportionment systems are equivalent to the rule discovery and credit assignment algorithms, respectively. Table 1 summarises the direct mapping between the LCS and the proposed framework to model adaptive agents for complex adaptive systems.

Table 1. Mapping Learning Classifier Systems (LCS) into the Holland's framework to describe adaptive agents for CAS

Learning Classifier Systems	Adaptive Agents for CAS
Set of detectors/effectors plus the classifiers	Performance system
Rule discovery system	Rule discovery system
Credit apportionment system	Credit assignment system

3.3 Other Types of Classifier Systems

The learning classifier system previously described corresponds to the standard framework proposed by Holland [23], [20]. Based on previous studies, it is possible to claim that learning classifier systems constitute a sufficiently flexible tool for self-adaptation to time-varying contexts. Also, they have shown effectiveness on the production of secondary responses to previously presented stimuli and are able to react promptly to changes in the environment due to their diversity preservation mechanisms [47]. However, there have been also a number of other well-succeeded variants to the standard learning classifier system [35],[36], as summarised in Table 2.

Table 2. Already proposed variant models of classifier systems (adapted from Kovacs (2000))

Date	Model	Brief description	Authors
1975	CS	Classifier System	John Holland [20]
1986	LCS	Learning CS	John Holland [23]
1985	CSM	CS with Memory	Hayong Harry Zhou [53]
1989	HCS	Hierarchical CS	Lingyan Shu and Jonathan Schaeffer [41]
1989	SCS	Simple CS	David Goldberg [17]
1989	VCS	Variable CS	Lingyan Shu and Jonathan Schaeffer [41]
1990	PCS	Predictive CS	Piet Spiessens (Spiessens (1990) in [32])
1994	FCS	Fuzzy CS	Takeshi Furuhashi, Ken Nakaoka and Yoshiki Uchikawa [15]
1994	ZCS	Zeroth-level CS	Stewart W. Wilson [51]
1995	OCS	Organizational CS	Jason Wilcox [50] e Takadama and collaborators. [44]
1995	XCS	Special CS	Stewart W. Wilson [52]
1996	ACS	Anticipatory CS	Wolfgang Stolzmann [43]
1997	EpiCS	Departed from NEWBOOLE (Bonelli et al, 1990)	John H. Holmes [24]
1999	CCS	Corporate CS	Andy Tomlinson and Larry Bull [45]

Despite the existence of several variations of the standard learning classifier system and many new models, there are still open challenges in the field of LCS. Aspects such as generalisation, scalability and anticipation have not yet been fully examined. According to Holmes et al. [25], these three challenges are part of the many interesting research directions to be explored. However, not only the recently developed models should be further investigated and/or improved, but also new propositions should be considered.

In the present paper, an attempt will be made to compare artificial immune systems (AIS) and learning classifier systems (LCS), under various perspectives. The intent is to provide enough background for a further combination of their potentialities, based mainly on the existence of complementary features, both in terms of properties and mechanisms. Next section presents a discussion of the vertebrate immune system, claiming why it can be characterised as a CAS, together with a broader outline of the field of AIS.

4   The Vertebrate Immune System and Artificial Immune Systems

Together with many other bodily systems, the immune system plays an important role in maintaining life. One of its primary goals is to provide the organism with a notion of self, so that disease causing agents (viruses, bacteria, funguses and parasites) and abnormal self-cells are detected and eliminated before major damages are caused to the body [11].

The immune system, in particular the vertebrate immune system, is composed of a large variety and number of cells, molecules, and organs distributed all over the body. Therefore, the number of theories, principles and processes used to explain the behaviour of the immune system or portions of it is vast. This section reviews some basic aspects of the vertebrate immune system (IS) together with its computational counterpart, namely, the artificial immune system (AIS).

4.1 Fundamentals of Immunology

The immune system can be decomposed into innate and adaptive, where the innate immune system constitutes the first line of defence against a wide variety of disease causing agents, namely antigens, without requiring any previous exposure to them. The innate immune system is also crucial for the regulation of immune responses. Cells and molecules of the adaptive immune system "adapt" to previously seen pathogenic (disease-causing) agents, thus resulting in immunity against future infections by the same or similar agents. This happens by altering the concentration and molecular structure of those immune cells responsible for successfully recognising and fighting against infection.

The adaptability of the immune system is easily illustrated by the vaccination procedures. An attenuated or dead sample of a pathogenic agent is inoculated into the organism so that those immune cells responsible for recognising this specific agent are stimulated to proliferate, according to a process known as *clonal selection and expansion* [6]. This agent does not cause any harm to the organism because it is attenuated or dead. However, the stimulation it provides results in the increase of those clones (specific sets) of cells that recognise this agent. In addition, during proliferation some cells have their molecular structure altered by regulated processes of mutation. Those cells with mutated receptors of high affinity with the eliciting antigens are selected for survival. Therefore, the immune system "learns" to deal with a certain pathogenic agent by altering the concentration and molecular structure of individual cells and molecules successful in combating specific diseases.

In addition to this clonal selection theory of immunity, there are others, such as the immune network theory that has great potentiality for engineering applications [12]. Basically, the immune network theory proposes that the immune system is composed of sets of cells and molecules dynamically connected with each other through molecular structures. The dynamics of this network is an intrinsic property of the immune system that results from the mutual recognition between immune cells and molecules. As such, disease-causing agents, termed pathogens, are responsible for disturbing the internal network of cells and molecules.

One important feature of immune cells for the promotion of immune responses and understanding of the network theory is the presence of surface receptor molecules responsible for recognising and binding with molecular structures of pathogens, known as antigens. Particularly, one class of immune cells, termed as B-cells, can alter in number (increase their concentration level) and modify the structures of their receptor molecules, named *antibodies*, so as to provide a better recognition of and defence against previously encountered antigens.

Antigenic recognition is performed by matching molecules on antigens with a receptor molecule on the surface of an immune cell. The matching is a result of physical, chemical and electrical interactions between a portion of the receptor and a portion of the antigen. The degree of match between the molecules is termed *affinity*. The better the match, the higher the affinity, and thus the stronger the binding (recognition). Figure 2 illustrates how an antibody molecule on the surface of a B-cell matches an antigen.

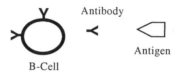

Fig. 2. Recognition of an antigen by an antibody molecule on a B-cell. The shapes adopted in the illustration provide only a pictorial view

In the *immune network theory*, originally proposed by Jerne [28], antibodies are capable of recognising not only antigens, but also other antibodies. This way, antibodies were assumed to have some molecular patterns on their surfaces, named *idiotopes*, which play the role of antigens and could thus be recognised by other antibodies, as illustrated in Figure 3.

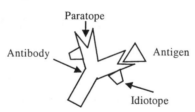

Fig. 3. The antibodies with their molecular portions and antigenic recognition. The portion of an antibody that can recognise an antigen is called paratope, and the portion that can be recognised by another antibody is named idiotope

As antibodies can recognise and be recognised by other antibodies, this interaction forms a network of communication (interaction) within the immune system. An interesting aspect of this immune network theory is that it does not depend upon the presence of external (or "foreign") antigens to stimulate the immune system. Thus, the presence of immune cells and molecules is sufficient to endow the immune system with a dynamic behaviour associated with the interactions of immune cells and molecules. The recognition of an antibody by another antibody causes the stimulation of the recognising antibody. In contrast, when an antibody is recognised by another antibody, the former is suppressed. Antibody stimulation and suppression are illustrated in Figure 4.

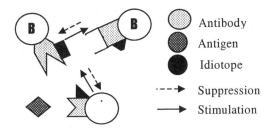

Antibody

Antigen

Idiotope

- - - ➤ Suppression

———➤ Stimulation

Fig. 4. The immune network theory. When an antibody, present at the surface of a B-cell, recognises an antigen or another antibody it is stimulated; when it is recognised, it is suppressed

Another important concept is the network *metadynamics*: insertion of new cells and molecules into the network and removal of non-stimulated cells from the network. The network metadynamics models a natural tendency of the immune system to be always producing new cells and removing useless, damaged or dead cells from the organism.

To determine if one of the generated cells is going to be allowed to enter the network, it is necessary to determine the *sensitivity* (stimulation and suppression) level of each new cell with relation to the cells already in the network. One main problem with the immune network theory is the lack of a more explicit account of phenomena like network suppression and stimulation. Many theoretical models have been developed, and each of these models treats stimulation and suppression in different forms.

4.2   The Vertebrate Immune System as a Complex Adaptive System

It is possible to identify the seven basics of CAS in the vertebrate immune system. Here we provide our own perspective of how the seven basics can be observed in the vertebrate immune system, briefly described above. Further concepts about the immune system will be presented as required.

Properties

1) *Aggregation* – There is a large variety of cells composing the immune system. Among them, lymphocytes are the most important ones, from a biological and computational perspective. These cells can be naturally categorised according to their physiology and function, mainly into B- and T-cells. They all act together to protect our bodies against foreign attacks by pathogens, and against malfunctioning self-cells. The physiology and functions that lead to an aggregation of immune cells can be easily exemplified. For instance, those naïve lymphocytes that mature within the bone marrow are termed B-cells, and those that mature into the thymus are named T-cells. Macrophages are different from B- and T-cells for they act by scavenging infected cells and other debris found in the blood stream and lymph. Interactions among cells and molecules in the immune system are not only abundant, but also necessary for its functioning. Without the help of T-cells, B-cells cannot detect pathogens hidden inside and causing damage to our own cells. Also, chemical products released by B- and T-cells stimulate and signal to other cells,

such as macrophages and even other B- and T-cells. Aggregation is thus pervasive in the immune system.

2) *Nonlinearity* – In the case of the immune system, there are, among others, the effects of saturation in antibody production and lymphokine secretion. Regardless of the number of pathogens invading the organism, antibody production and lymphokine secretion cannot raise above a certain level. Nonlinearity is also evident when one considers that, for example, two antibodies acting together have a different effect in an antigen than if we sum the effect of both of them acting individually. This holds true for all elements in the immune system, from lymphokines to macrophages.

3) *Flows* – Similarly to nonlinearity, several levels of flow can be identified in the immune system. From the flow of immune cells throughout the organism, to the flow of its secreted chemicals (e.g., lymphokines).

4) *Diversity* – In the immune system, B-cells, T-cells, macrophages, granulocytes, chemokines (lymphokines), etc., all contribute to a suitable immune functioning. Diversity in the immune system can also be studied in different levels. For instance, there are different types of cells (e.g., B-cells, T-cells and macrophages); there are different types of molecules (e.g., antibodies and lymphokines); and there are different organs (e.g., bone marrow, thymus, and lymph nodes).

Mechanisms

1) *Tagging* – Each immune cell has its particular design; not a single element is the perfect copy of another one. Nevertheless, all elements of a given type (e.g., B-cells) share some common features (tags) that allow them to be categorised as B-cells. The same is true for other cell types and molecules in the immune system.

2) *Internal models* – When the immune system is primed with a type of pathogen, it builds a repertoire of cells and molecules that is specialised in recognising this type of pathogen. The immune system thus builds an internal model that allows it to recognise and fight against previously seen pathogens. The idea of internal models in the immune system is largely studied in theories of immune networks. In the original immune network theory, introduced by Jerne [28], individual cells and molecules are capable of recognising each other and antigens as well. As an outcome, the immune system naturally generates and maintains a network of immune cells and molecules that interact with each other even in the absence of external stimuli. The same immune cell that can recognise another immune cell can also recognise an antigen. The immune cell recognised has similar attributes to the antigen and is thus called an *internal image* of the antigen.

3) *Building blocks* - A clear example of the presence of building blocks in the immune system is the use of genes, selected from gene libraries, to construct lymphocyte receptor molecules. Individual genes and the libraries themselves can be considered as building blocks to generate receptor molecules. This perspective can also be expanded to the level of immune receptors and cells. Different immune cells carry receptors responsible for recognising specific sets of disease-causing agents. Therefore, these sets of immune cells correspond to building blocks that contribute to the construction of the whole "immune memory".

4.3   Artificial Immune Systems

Artificial immune systems (AIS) are composed of computational intelligence methodologies, inspired by the natural immune system for the solution of real-world problems [10]. AIS can also be defined as adaptive systems inspired by theoretical immunology and observed immune functions, principles and models, which are applied to problem solving [11]. According to the later authors, AIS can be designed using a layered framework composed of three main parts:

1) a *representation scheme* for the components of the system;
2) a set of *mechanisms to evaluate the interactions* of individuals with the environment and each other; and
3) some *adaptation procedures*.

Within each of these layers there are various strategies. For instance, in layer 1 – representation – shape-spaces [40] play a major role. A shape-space may be understood as a (search) space where attribute strings are used as abstract models to represent immune cells and molecules. The idea is to define metrics in the shape-space as means of quantifying the degree of recognition (affinity) between immune cells, and between them and antigens. For instance, if using binary strings to represent the immune receptors, a metric such as the Hamming distance is a candidate to be used to quantify the degree of dissimilarity (recognition) between two bit strings (two points in the shape-space).

In layer 2 – interactions – the environment may be simulated by a set of input stimuli, and fitness and/or affinity functions. The existence of a metric space and the determination of an affinity function allow the definition of the (relative) quality of the individuals composing the population.

The procedures of adaptation govern how the behaviour of the system varies with time, and are usually simplified models of an immune function, process, or theory. For instance, clonal selection [6], negative selection [34], immune networks [28],[29], and so forth, have been largely used by the AIS community. These procedures usually take the affinity/fitness measures of layer 2 as part of their processing.

As a modelling example using the proposed framework, consider the immune network theory, where several immune network models have been proposed to account for how the cells and molecules of the immune system vary their concentration level and molecular structure. The aim is to control how the cells of the immune network have their concentration and molecular structure (attributes) varied with time; processes known as the network *dynamics*.

These models usually assume an attribute string to represent the cells and molecules, and use ordinary differential equations, difference equations or iterative procedures of adaptation to control the network dynamics and metadynamics.

In a specific model proposed by Watanabe et al. [49], the immune cells and molecules (antibodies) are represented by binary attribute strings of fixed length. Only B-cells and antibodies are modelled, and as each B-cell has a single type of antibody on its surface, no distinction is made between a network cell and its antibody. Equation 1 is used to control the dynamics of the network model used in this paper. Based on this equation, the concentration a_i of each antibody is determined by considering the similarity of each antibody with the current antigen, the connections among antibodies (that can be stimulatory or suppressive), and the natural death of antibodies.

$$\frac{da_i(t)}{dt} = \left(\sum_{j=1}^{N} m_{ji} a_j(t) - \sum_{k=1}^{N} m_{ik} a_k(t) + m_i - k_i \right) a_i(t) \tag{1}$$

$$a_i(t+1) = \frac{1}{1 + \exp(0.5 - a_i(t))} \tag{2}$$

where:

- N is the number of antibodies that compose the network;
- m_i is the affinity between the antibody i and a given antigen;
- m_{ji} represents the affinity between the antibody j and antibody i, in other words, the degree of stimulation;
- m_{ik} represents the affinity between the antibody k and antibody i, in other words, the degree of suppression;
- k_i is the natural death rate of a_i.

Equation 2 is a squashing function used to impose an upper limit on the concentration level of each antibody.

The network model described above is a clear example of an artificial immune system designed using the already proposed framework. Immune cells and molecules are represented using binary attribute strings, their affinity is determined by a distance metric between two bit strings, and the adaptation procedure follows an ordinary differential equation (Equation 1).

Note that this framework is not different in essence from the one proposed by Michalewicz and Fogel [37] when describing heuristic problem solving techniques. They suggest that three main concepts are involved in problem solving: representation, the definition of an objective function, and the choice of an evaluation function.

As already mentioned, the proposed framework for AIS also brings some similarities with the framework introduced by Holland [20] to model adaptation in natural and artificial systems: an environment undergoing adaptation, an adaptive plan, and a performance measure.

There are also many similarities between the AIS framework discussed and some basic design principles of other biologically inspired techniques, such as neural networks and evolutionary algorithms. Artificial neural networks require a model for an artificial neuron and a network structure (representation), some connectivity pattern (interactions), and a learning algorithm (adaptation procedure). Evolutionary algorithms also require some sort of data structure (representation), fitness function (interactions), and (genetic) variation operators to be used in the adaptation procedures.

Therefore, though there might be slight differences among the many frameworks for modelling complex adaptive systems, it is possible to stress a set of basic components (building blocks) from which some of them may be useful in a particular context: an environment, a representation scheme, some evaluation mechanisms, and adaptation strategies to change the configuration (state) of the system.

Summing up, among all the AIS main properties, we can stress uniqueness, self-identity, diversity, self-organisation, autonomy, multilayered structure, robustness, learning and memory ability. Due to its wide intrinsic properties, the AIS has also a wide range of applications, from the biosciences, to computational intelligence, to computer science and software engineering (see de Castro & Timmis [11] for more details).

4.4 Artificial Immune Systems as Complex Adaptive Systems

After identifying Holland's seven basics for all CAS in the vertebrate immune system, and having briefly discussed the fundamentals of artificial immune systems, we are now going to claim that AIS also provides models to be interpreted as agents for CAS. To give support to our claim, we will first map AIS into the framework for adaptive agents for CAS introduced by Holland. In the following section we will map artificial immune systems into learning classifier systems. Table 3 summarises the mapping between AIS and the framework for CAS.

Table 3. Mapping artificial immune systems into the Holland's framework for adaptive agents to model CAS

Artificial Immune Systems	Adaptive Agents for CAS
Immune cells and molecules representation (shape-spaces) together with their structural relationship	Performance system
Procedures of adaptation	Rule discovery system
Mechanisms to evaluate interactions	Credit assignment system

5 Mapping Artificial Immune Systems into Learning Classifier Systems

The vertebrate immune system and artificial immune systems have already been placed in the broader context of complex adaptive systems [48]. So far, AIS and learning classifier systems have both been demonstrated capable of modelling agents for CAS. Table 4 proposes the same three stages for building agents for CAS into these two different contexts: AIS and LCS.

The next and second step is to establish a rule of correspondence between the two systems that associates each element of one system with an element of the other system. This is accomplished by first providing a general comparison between both systems, i.e., placing the framework for engineering AIS introduced in de Castro & Timmis [11] in the context of learning classifier systems, and then determining complementary features of artificial immune systems and learning classifier systems.

Table 4. The same three stages in the contexts of AIS and LCS

Stages for creating adaptive agents for CAS	AIS	LCS
First Stage (performance)	Immune cells and molecules	Classifiers
Second Stage (credit assignment)	Affinity (fitness) evaluation	Strength
Third Stage (rule discovery)	Procedures of adaptation	Genetic algorithm

5.1 AIS and LCS: A Survey and a General Framework Comparison

A Survey

Many researches have already attempted to compare the similarities and differences between LCS and AIS. However, all these comparisons were made under specific scenarios. Among others, it is possible to highlight the works of Farmer et al. [14], Kauffman [31], Varela et al. [46], Bersini & Varela [1], Bersini [2], Hunt & Cooke [26] and Hofmeyr & Forrest [19].

The first work to look for similarities and differences between both systems was proposed by Farmer et al. [14]. Basically, the authors wrote both systems in the form of a dynamical system, resulting in equations of motion to describe their dynamics, i.e. behaviour with time. A classifier system was used to model the immune system by drawing an analogy between individual classifiers and antibodies. The authors pointed out that the main difference between both systems is the nature of the nonlinearity in the proposed dynamical equations. They also stressed other differences, like the interaction with the external environment and the system of message passing used in the classifier system. Furthermore, the authors stated that "...it is an accident that there is any similarity at all between the immune and classifier systems. The classifier system does not have to satisfy any of the constraints of nature, since ultimately its only function is to provide a general purpose scheme for adaptive problem solving." (p. 201-202). Some similarities were presented, such as the generation of new solutions that act in precisely the same manner in both systems (providing novelty). It was also argued that both systems are strongly non-linear dynamical systems.

For Bersini & Varela [1], the immune system is more like Holland's Classifier System (either escape 'brittleness' (fragility) or 'semantic closure'). The 'problem solving' qualities belong to an evolving, adaptive and self-organising population of interactive individuals. The authors suggest that a complete comparison between CS and an immune network model covers the whole cognitive domain: search, adaptability, memory and learning.

In Hunt & Cooke's [26] point of view, their immune network model combines the advantages of learning classifier systems with some of the advantages of neural networks, machine induction and case-based retrieval. The authors believe that although their AIS has similarities with both systems, it differs from both in a number of significant aspects. These differences have the potential to make their AIS applicable in situations where neural networks or learning classifier systems are not appropriate, e.g. learning classifier systems find it difficult to deal with problems which lack of separation between global solutions or have many locally optimal rules. This was claimed not to be the case for their AIS.

Hofmeyr & Forrest [19] referred to their AIS for network intrusion detection as a resemblance to the architecture of a classifier system. The mapping between their AIS and CS was suggested not to be 1 to 1. In their implementation nothing corresponded to the action part of a classifier. Furthermore, the authors were the first ones to suggest that their AIS could be added to the repertoire of CAS.

General Framework Comparison

To design an AIS, de Castro & Timmis [11] proposed a layered framework with three main parts. The comparison of specific AIS with classifier systems can be extended to a more general comparison of AIS in the light of the framework proposed as follows.

The classifiers correspond to the attribute strings, in a given shape-space, representing immune cells and molecules. These strings can be simple structures such as binary strings or more complex structures such as one containing symbolic values. The communication with the environment is performed via a set of input stimuli, or one or more fitness/affinity measure. A detector in a classifier system corresponds to a receptor in an immune cell, and the effector might be likened to lymphokines secreted by the immune cells. Other types of effectors can also be available in an AIS depending on their rationale (e.g., the elimination or classification of given patterns). The strength of a classifier might correspond to the affinity value of a given immune cell or molecule, which in turn will be responsible for determining an action of or to be acted upon this cell or molecule. Though most AIS do not employ wild cards (don't cares) in their representation, works employing this type of data structure can also be found in the literature (e.g., Hart and Ross [18]).

In a higher level, it is also possible to link AIS with classifier systems. The rule and message sub-system can be likened to the set of attribute strings representing immune cells and molecules. The apportionment of credit sub-system can be equated to the set of mechanisms to evaluate the interactions of individuals with the environment. Finally, the rule discovery sub-system corresponds to the procedures of adaptation for AIS. Table 5 summarises the high-level comparison between AIS and learning classifier systems.

Table 5. General framework comparison between AIS and LCS

AIS	LCS
Representation (shape-spaces)	Rule and message sub-system
Mechanisms to evaluate interactions	Apportionment of credit sub-system
Procedures of adaptation	Rule discovery sub-system

5.2 AIS and LCS: Determining Complementary Features

After providing a general comparison between both systems, this section concerns the end of the second and final step towards the new mapping conception, i.e., the determination of the complementary features of AIS and LCS.

Consider the most important open challenges in the field of LCS namely, generalisation, scalability and anticipation.

- **Generalisation.** The ability of a system to represent in a compact form what it has learned and to apply it to previously unseen situations. According to Holmes et al. [25] this aspect raises several questions such as: What triggers the evolution of accurate and maximally general classifiers? What are the system requirements that insure effective generalisation? What are the difficult classes of problems? Should we look for alternative ways to implement generalisation? Or are genetic algorithms the best solution? Many of these questions can be answered by considering some of the AIS main properties, in particular, diversity maintenance through mutation and receptor editing [16], cross-reactivity [42], and memory. Receptor editing is a mechanism the immune system developed to replace receptors with very low degrees of recognition by receptors randomly generated. Cross-reactivity corresponds to the immune capability of recognising molecular patterns similar to those previously seen. Editing, cross-reactivity and memory can all be found in some AIS algorithms [11], and these may be useful for combination (hybridisation) with LCS.

- **Scalability.** It refers to how rapidly the learning time or the system size grows as the problem complexity increases. As generalization is directly related to scalability, a system that can generalise properly can learn complex tasks rapidly and with limited memory resources. These aspects can be directly addressed by the same AIS properties enumerated above, in addition to others, like the multilayered structure, self-organisation ability, self-assertion [3] and autonomy. These four properties together allow the AIS to react promptly and rapidly to environmental changes. The notion of self that naturally emerges in the immune system (self-assertion) promotes the creation of an immune repertoire that appropriately constitutes an internal image of the universe we inhabit. This way, it is always possible to create parsimonious representations of structured environments.

- **Anticipation.** The ability of a system to predict or anticipate the effect of their actions, raised another question [25]: Despite the current models based on the work of Stolzmann [43], are there other feasible approaches for adding anticipations to LCS? The answer is yes, the anticipatory capacity of the immune system and some artificial immune systems can be taken into account, for example, when creating new classifiers through gene recombination. Only now researchers from the AIS community are beginning to realise that gene libraries [39] carrying useful information about a given problem can be used to generate receptor molecules embodying prior information of specific domains. This endows AIS (and possibly LCS) with enhanced potentiality for dealing with novel situations.

5.3   AIS and LCS: A Suggested Mapping

In addition to the general framework comparison made above, there are some equivalencies between both systems that must be emphasised. These equivalencies may be associated with theoretical issues or just practical aspects, and have already been pointed out along the presentation of previous applications of AIS and LCS performed by the authors [7],[47],[11],[12]. However, this paper is the first one to aggregate all the equivalencies and to perform a complete mapping in a common framework.

The equivalencies are the following:

- both systems employ tags in their inside and outside interactions;
- there is an intrinsic willingness to cooperate and/or to compete (combat);
- the matching processes are isomorphic in function; and
- both systems are frequently updating their internal models.

Table 6 summarises our proposal for a mapping from AIS into LCS.

Table 6. AIS into LCS: a suggested mapping

AIS	mapping into	LCS
Attribute strings	→	Classifiers
Fitness/affinity	→	Strength of a classifier
Receptors	→	Detectors
Signals	→	Effectors
Don't cares	→	Don't cares

This mapping was proposed by placing the framework for engineering AIS (Section 4.3) introduced in de Castro & Timmis [11] in the context of learning classifier systems. The next section summarises a mapping example by implementing an AIS for a robot autonomous navigation problem.

5.4   AIS and LCS: A Mapping Example

One of the most challenging problems in machine learning is robot autonomous navigation. The literature associated with LCS is full of initiatives to implement control devices for autonomous navigation [13]. Similar approaches based on AIS, particularly based on the immune network theory, have also been proposed in the literature [27],[49],[38], though not with the same perspective as the one adopted here. As a preliminary investigation of the proposed mapping, the work of Michelan & Von Zuben [38] will be considered.

The work was based on the immune network theory for the navigation control and the task consists of a robot that needs to collect garbage without running out of energy. This navigation task has already been addressed by Ishiguro et al. [27]. However, though using the same fixed rules that govern the robot navigation, the work presented by Michelan and Von Zuben [38] proposes an automatic determination of immune network connections via evolutionary techniques. Under this scenario, not only the dynamics but also the metadynamics of the immune network is being considered.

As a sum up, we illustrate in Table 7 the main features of the immune device for autonomous navigation.

Table 7. A summary of an application of an AIS to robot autonomous navigation by Michelan & Von Zuben [38]

Robot Autonomous Navigation	AIS
Navigation control system	Immune network
System performance	On-line fitness evaluation
Dynamic behaviour	Network dynamics via antibody concentration level
Condition/action behaviour	Antigen/antibody interaction (response)
Sensors	Antigens
Actuators	Idiotopes

The final step in this work is to present a mapping example of an AIS implementation. Table 8 shows our mapping proposal for the robot autonomous navigation case just described.

Table 8. A proposed mapping of AIS into LCS for the robot autonomous navigation case of Table 7

AIS	mapping into	LCS
Antibodies	→	Classifiers
On-line fitness evaluation	→	Classifiers fitness ([1])
Antibodies concentration level	→	Classifiers strength
Antigen/antibody interaction	→	Condition/action matching
Antigens	→	Detectors of environment messages
Idiotopes	→	Effectors

6 Discussion and Future Work

Together with a terminology to encompass all natural and artificial systems presenting a set of specific properties, Holland also introduced a general framework to model

---

[1] While observing the mapping proposal of Table 8, it is possible to state that the standard LCS proposed by John Holland (1992) does not explicit accounts for the fitness evaluation of the rules. Indeed this kind of metric was proposed later on by Wilson (1995) in his seminal work on a well established LCS model, named XCS (Special Classifier System).

agents for such systems. The potentiality of this proposal, broadly termed *classifier systems*, has led to its study, development, improvement, and application by researchers on the most varied fields. Another field of research that presents some features in common with and complementary to classifier systems are the so called *artificial immune systems*. In both areas of investigation much has been done to evaluate their true potentiality for problem solving, main domain of applications, formal aspects, drawbacks and limitations.

This conceptual paper introduces both fields with a reasonable level of detail, investigates the similarities and differences between them, highlights their main features, maps one into the other, and suggests avenues for hybridising them so as to overcome individual limitations. The focus is on how AIS can be used to improve LCS performance. Furthermore, a survey from the literature contrasting AIS with LCS is provided, and some speculative application examples are given to illustrate the conceptual proposal presented here.

We are currently working on the development of a hybrid system between classifier systems and artificial immune systems with a view of applying it to robotic autonomous navigation. It characterises an extension of the work performed by Michelan and Von Zuben [38], briefly described in Section 5.4, and whose complexity might suffice to validate the utility of the hybrid system.

References

1. Bersini, H. & Varela, F. (1990). Hints for Adaptive Problem Solving Gleaned from Immune Networks. Proceedings of the First Conference on Parallel Problem Solving from Nature, pp. 343-354.
2. Bersini, H. (1991). Immune Network and Adaptive Control. Proceedings of the First European Conference on Artificial Life, MIT Press, pp. 217-226.
3. Bersini, H. (2002). Self-Assertion versus Self-Recognition: A Tribute to Francisco Varela, *Proc. of ICARIS 2002*, pp. 107-112.
4. Bonelli, P.; Parodi, A.; Sen, S.; Wilson, S. (1990). NEWBOOLE: A fast GBML system. Porter, B.; Mooney, R. Machine Learning: Proceedings of the Seventh International Conference; 1990 Jun 21; Texas. Morgan Kaufmann Publishers, Inc.; 153-159.
5. Booker, L. B., Goldberg, D. E. & Holland, J. H. (1989). Classifier Systems and Genetic Algorithms. Artificial Intelligence, vol. 40, pp. 235-282.
6. Burnet, F. M. (1959), *The Clonal Selection Theory of Acquired Immunity*, Cambridge University Press.
7. Costa, A. M. , Vargas, P. A., Von Zuben, F. J. & França, P. M.. Makespan Minimization on Parallel Processors: An Immune-Based Approach. Proceedings of the 2002 Congress on Evolutionary Computation (CEC'2002), vol.1, pp.920-925, Honolulu, Hawaii, May 12-17, 2002.
8. Cowan, G. A., Pines, D. & Meltzer, D. (eds.) (1994), *Complexity: metaphors, models and reality,* Proceedings Vol. XIX, Santa Fe Institute, Studies in the Sciences of Complexity, Addison-Wesley Pub. Co., MA 01867.
9. Darwin, C. (1859), *On the Origin of Species By Means of Natural Selection*, 6th Edition, [Online Book] www.literature.org/authors/darwin.

10. Dasgupta, D.(Ed.) (1999), *Artificial Immune Systems and their Applications*, Springer-Verlag.
11. de Castro, L. N. & Timmis, J. I. (2002). *Artificial Immune Systems: A New Computational Intelligence Approach*, Springer-Verlag: London.
12. de Castro, L. N. & Von Zuben, F. J. (2001), "aiNet: An Artificial Immune Network for Data Analysis", In *Data Mining: A Heuristic Approach*, H. A. Abbass, R. A. Sarker, and C. S. Newton (eds.), Idea Group Publishing, USA, Chapter XII, pp. 231-259.
13. Dorigo, M. and Colombetti, M. (1997). Robot Shaping: An Experiment in Behavior Engineering (Intelligent Robotics and Autonomous Agents), MIT Press.
14. Farmer, J. D., Packard, N. H. & Perelson, A. S. (1986). "The Immune System, Adaptation and Machine Learning", Physica 22D, pp. 187-204.
15. Furuhashi, T. , Nakaoka, K. e Uchikawa, Y. (1994). "A Study on Fuzzy Classifier System for Finding Control Knowledge of Multi-Input Systems", pag. 489-502, Genetic Algorithms And Soft Computing.
16. George, A. J. T. & Gray, D. (1999), "Receptor Editing During Affinity Maturation", *Imm. Today*, **20**(4), pp. 196.
17. Goldberg, D. E. (1989). *Genetic Algorithms in Search Optimization, and Machine Learning*. Addison-Wesley, Inc.
18. Hart, E. & Ross, P. (1999), "The Evolution and Analysis of a Potential Antibody Library for Use in Job-Shop Scheduling", In *New Ideas in Optimization*, D. Corne, M. Dorigo & F. Glover (eds.), McGraw Hill, London, pp. 185-202.
19. Hofmeyr, S. A. & Forrest, S. (2000). Architecture for an Artificial Immune System, Evolutionary Computation, 8(4), pp. 443-473.
20. Holland, J. H. (1992). *Adaptation in Natural and Artificial Systems : an Introductory Analysis with Applications to Biology, Control, and Artificial Intelligence*. The MIT Press, Ann Arbor, MI.91.
21. Holland, J. H. (1995). *Hidden Order: How Adaptation Builds Complexity*. Addison-Wesley, Inc.
22. Holland, J. H. (1998). *Emergence: From Chaos to Order*. Addison-Wesley, Inc.
23. Holland, J.H. (1986). "Escaping Brittleness: The possibilities of general-purpose learning algorithms applied to parallel rule-based systems". In: R.S. Michalski, J.G. Carbonell & T.M. Mitchell (eds), Machine Learning: An Artificial Intelligence approach, Vol II, 593-623, Los Altos, CA: Morgan Kaufman.
24. Holmes, J. H. (1997). "Discovering Risk of Disease with a Learning Classifier System", "http://cceb.med.upenn.edu/holmes/icga97.ps.gz", ICGA97.
25. Holmes, J. H., Lanzi, P. L., Stolzmann, W., and Wilson, S. W. (2000). "Learning classifier systems: new models, successful applications", Information Processing Letters, to appear.
26. Hunt, J. E. & Cooke, D. E. (1996). "Learning Using an Artificial Immune System", Journal of Network and Computer Applications, 19, pp. 189-212.
27. Ishiguro, A., Kondo, T., Watanabe, Y., Shirai, Y. and Uchikawa, H.(1996). "Immunoid: A Robot with a Decentralized Consensus-Making Mechanism Based on the Immune System", *Presented at ICMAS Workshop on Immunity-Based Systems*, December, pp.82-92.
28. Jerne, N. K. (1974). "Towards a Network Theory of the Immune System", Ann. Immunol. (Int. Pasteur) 125C, pp. 373-389.
29. Jerne, N. K. (1984). "Idiotypic Networks and other preconceived ideas," *Immunological Rev.*,Vol.79, pp. 5-24.
30. Johnson, S. (2002), *Emergence: The Connected Lives of Ants, Bains, Cities and Software*, Penguim Books.

31. Kauffman, S. A. (1989). Principles of Adaptation in Complex Systems, in D. Stein (ed.), Lectures in the Sciences of Complexity, Addison Wesley.

32. Kovacs, T. & Lanzi, P.L. (1999). "A Learning Classifier Systems Bibliograph", Technical Report: CSRP-99-19, University of Birmingham, United Kingdom. http://www.cs.bris.ac.uk/~kovacs/lcs/search.html

33. Kovacs, T. (2000). "A Learning Classifier Systems Bibliograph". http://www.cs.bris.ac.uk/~kovacs/lcs/search.html.

34. Kruisbeek, A. M. (1995), "Tolerance", *The Immunologist*, 3/5-6, pp. 176-178.

35. Lanzi, P. L., Stolzmann, W. and Wilson, S. W. , editors (2000). Learning Classifier Systems. From Foundations to Applications, volume 1813 of LNAI. Springer-Verlag, Berlin.

36. Lanzi, P. L., Stolzmann, W. and Wilson, S. W., editors (2001). Advances in Learning Classifier Systems, volume 1996 of LNAI. Springer-Verlag, Berlin.

37. Michalewicz, Z. and Fogel, D. B. (2000). *How to solve it: Modern Heuristics*. Springer-Verlag Berlin Heidelberg, New York.

38. Michelan, R. and Von Zuben, F.J. (2002). Decentralized Control System for Autonomous Navigation based on an Evolved Artificial Immune Network. Proceedings of the 2002 Congress on Evolutionary Computation (CEC'2002), vol. 2, pp. 1021-1026, Honolulu, Hawaii, May 12-17.

39. Oprea, L.M. (1999). Antibody repertoires and pathogen recognition: the role of germline diversity and somatic hypermutation. PhD. Thesis, University of New Mexico.

40. Perelson, A. S. & Oster, G. F. (1979). "Theoretical Studies of Clonal Selection: Minimal Antibody Repertoire Size and Reliability of Self-Nonself Discrimination", *J. theor.Biol.*, 81, pp. 645-670.

41. Shu, L. and Schaeffer, J. (1989). "VCS: Variable Classifier System", pag. 334-339, ICGA89.

42. Smith, D. J., Forrest, S., Hightower, R. R. & Perelson, A. S. (1998), "Deriving Shape Space Parameters from Immunological Data", *Journal of Theoretical Biology*, **189**, pp. 141-150.

43. Stolzmann, W. (1996). "Learning Classifier Systems using the Cognitive Mechanism of Anticipatory Behavioural Control, detailed version.", Proceedings of the First European Workshop on Cognitive Modelling, pag. 82-89, Berlin.

44. Takadama, K., Terano, T., Shimohara, K., Hori, K. and Nakasuka, S. (1999). Making Organizational Learning Operational: Implications from Learning Classifier System, Computational and Mathematical Organization Theory (CMOT), Kluwer Academic Publishers, Vol. 5, No. 3, pp. 229-252.

45. Tomlinson, A. e Bull, L. (1999). "On Corporate Classifier Systems: Increasing the Benefits of Rule Linkage", pag.649-656, GECCO99.

46. Varela, F., Sanchez, V. & Coutinho, A. (1989). Adaptive Strategies Gleaned from Immune Networks in B. Goodwin and P. Saunders (eds.), Evolutionary and Epigenetic Order from Complex Systems: A Waddington Memorial Volume. Edinburgh U. Press.

47. Vargas, P. A., Lyra, C. & Von Zuben, F. J. (2002a). On-line Approach for Loss Reduction in Electric Power Distribution Networks Using Learning Classifier Systems, in *Lecture Notes in Artificial Intelligence* (LNAI 2321), Springer-Verlag, pp. 181-196.

48. Vargas, P. A., de Castro, L. N. & Von Zuben, F. J. (2002b). Artificial Immune Systems as Complex Adaptive Systems. Proceedings of the 1st International Conference on Artificial Immune Systems (ICARIS-2002), pp.115-123, University of Kent at Canterbury, England, September 9-11, 2002.

49. Watanabe, Y., Ishiguro, A. and Uchikawa, H. (1999). "Decentralized Behaviour Arbitration Mechanism for Autonomous Mobile Robot Using Immune Network", In D. Dasgupta (Editor), Artificial Immune Systems and their Applications, Springer.
50. Wilcox, J. R. (1995). "Organisational Learning within a Learning Classifier System", University of Illinois", Technical Report No. 95003 IlliGAL.
51. Wilson, S. W. (1994). "ZCS: A zeroth level classifier system", Evolutionary Computation,1, Vol. 2, pag.1-18.
52. Wilson, S. W. (1995)."Classifier Fitness Based on Accuracy", Evolutionary Computation, 2, Vol. 3, pag.149-175.
53. Zhou, H. H. (1985). "Classifier systems with long term memory", pag. 178-182, International Conference on Genetic Algorithms.

The 2003 Learning Classifier Systems Bibliography

Tim Kovacs

Department of Computer Science
The University of Bristol
Bristol BS8 1UB England
kovacs@cs.bris.ac.uk
http://www.cs.bris.ac.uk/~kovacs

Abstract. With over 700 entries, this is the most comprehensive bibliography of the machine learning systems introduced by John Holland.

Introduction

Learning classifier systems have a long and rich history. We hope this bibliography will both illustrate this point and prove a useful resource for researchers. Although the first classifier system, CS-1, was reported in 1978 [350], the development of LCS was foreshadowed by some of Holland's earlier work [334–336] dating back as far as 1971. In the early 80's much progress was in the form of PhD theses [612, 60, 291, 556, 257] (but see also [696, 697]), following which LCS papers began to appear steadily in conferences. Later landmarks include the publication of books by Holland in 1986 [348] and Goldberg in 1989 [294], and the series of International Workshops on LCS (IWLCS), in 1992, and yearly from 1999 to 2003.

Acknowledgements

We are grateful to Alwyn Barry for the contribution of his large LCS bibliography to ours, and to the many other individuals who have contributed.

P.L. Lanzi et al. (Eds.): IWLCS 2002, LNAI 2661, pp. 187–229, 2003.

References

1. Emergent Computation. Proceedings of the Ninth Annual International Conference of the Center for Nonlinear Studies on Self-organizing, Collective, and Cooperative Phenomena in Natural and Artificial Computing Networks. A special issue of Physica D. Stephanie Forrest (Ed.), 1990.

2. *Collected Abstracts for the First International Workshop on Learning Classifier System (IWLCS92)*, 1992. October 6–8, NASA Johnson Space Center, Houston, Texas.

3. *Proceedings of the 2000 Congress on Evolutionary Computation (CEC00).* IEEE Press, 2000.

4. Proceedings of the International Workshop on Learning Classifier Systems (IWLCS-2000), in the Joint Workshops of SAB 2000 and PPSN 2000, 2000. Pier Luca Lanzi, Wolfgang Stolzmann and Stewart W. Wilson (workshop organisers).

5. *Proceedings of the 2001 Congress on Evolutionary Computation (CEC01).* IEEE Press, 2001.

6. Jose Aguilar and Mariela Cerrada. Fuzzy classifier system and genetic programming on system identification problems. In Lee Spector, Erik D. Goodman, Annie Wu, W.B. Langdon, Hans-Michael Voigt, Mitsuo Gen, Sandip Sen, Marco Dorigo, Shahram Pezeshk, Max H. Garzon, and Edmund Burke, editors, *Proceedings of the Genetic and Evolutionary Computation Conference (GECCO-2001)*, pages 1245–1251, San Francisco, California, USA, 7-11 July 2001. Morgan Kaufmann.

7. Jose L. Aguilar and Mariela Cerrada. Reliability-Centered Maintenance Methodology-Based Fuzzy Classifier System Design for Fault Tolerance. In Koza et al. [423], page 621. One page paper.

8. Manu Ahluwalia and Larry Bull. A Genetic Programming-based Classifier System. In Banzhaf et al. [22], pages 11–18.

9. Rudolf F. Albrecht, Nigel C. Steele, and Colin R. Reeves, editors. *Proceedings of the International Conference on Artificial Neural Nets and Genetic Algorithms.* Spring-Verlag, 1993.

10. Peter J. Angeline, Zbyszek Michalewicz, Marc Schoenauer, Xin Yao, and Ali Zalzala, editors. *Proceedings of the 1999 Congress on Evolutionary Computation CEC99*, Washington (DC), 1999. IEEE Press.

11. W. Brian Arthur, John H. Holland, Blake LeBaron, Richard Palmer, and Paul Talyer. Asset Pricing Under Endogenous Expectations in an Artificial Stock Market. Technical report, Santa Fe Institute, 1996. This is the original version of LeBaron1999a.

12. Jaume Bacardit and Josep M. Garrell. Evolution of adaptive discretization intervals for A rule-based genetic learning system. In W. B. Langdon, E. Cantú-Paz, K. Mathias, R. Roy, D. Davis, R. Poli, K. Balakrishnan, V. Honavar, G. Rudolph, J. Wegener, L. Bull, M. A. Potter, A. C. Schultz, J. F. Miller, E. Burke, and N. Jonoska, editors, *GECCO 2002: Proceedings of the Genetic and Evolutionary Computation Conference*, page 677. Morgan Kaufmann Publishers, 2002.

13. Jaume Bacardit and Josep Maria Garrell. Evolving multiple discretizations with adaptive intervals for a Pittsburgh rule-based learning classifier system. In E. Cantú-Paz, J. A. Foster, K. Deb, D. Davis, R. Roy, U.-M. O'Reilly, H.-G. Beyer, R. Standish, G. Kendall, S. Wilson, M. Harman, J. Wegener, D. Dasgupta, M. A. Potter, A. C. Schultz, K. Dowsland, N. Jonoska, and J. Miller, editors, *Genetic and Evolutionary Computation – GECCO-2003*, pages 1818–1831, Berlin, 2003. Springer-Verlag.

14. Thomas Bäck, editor. *Proceedings of the 7th International Conference on Genetic Algorithms (ICGA97).* Morgan Kaufmann, 1997.

15. Thomas Bäck, David B. Fogel, and Zbigniew Michalewicz, editors. *Handbook of Evolutionary Computation*. Institute of Physics Publishing and Oxford University Press, 1997. http://www.iop.org/Books/Catalogue/.

16. Thomas Bäck, Ulrich Hammel, and Hans-Paul Schwefel. Evolutionary computation: Comments on the history and current state. *IEEE Transactions on Evolutionary Computation*, 1(1):3–17, 1997.

17. Jalal Baghdadchi. A Classifier Based Learning Model for Intelligent Agents. In Whitely et al. [699], page 870. One page poster paper.

18. Anthony J. Bagnall. A Multi-Adaptive Agent Model of Generator Bidding in the UK Market in Electricity. In Whitely et al. [699], pages 605–612.

19. Anthony J. Bagnall and G. D. Smith. An Adaptive Agent Model for Generator Company Bidding in the UK Power Pool. In *Proceedings of Artificial Evolution*, 1999.

20. Anthony J. Bagnall and G. D. Smith. Using an Adaptive Agent to Bid in a Simplified Model of the UK Market in Electricity. In Banzhaf et al. [22], page 774. One page poster paper.

21. N. R. Ball. Towards the Development of Cognitive Maps in Classifier Systems. In Albrecht et al. [9], pages 712–718.

22. Wolfgang Banzhaf, Jason Daida, Agoston E. Eiben, Max H. Garzon, Vasant Honavar, Mark Jakiela, and Robert E. Smith, editors. *Proceedings of the Genetic and Evolutionary Computation Conference (GECCO-99)*. Morgan Kaufmann, 1999.

23. Alwyn Barry. The Emergence of High Level Structure in Classifier Systems - A Proposal. *Irish Journal of Psychology*, 14(3):480–498, 1993.

24. Alwyn Barry. Hierarchy Formulation Within Classifiers System – A Review. In Goodman et al. [300], pages 195–211.

25. Alwyn Barry. Aliasing in XCS and the Consecutive State Problem: 1 – Effects. In Banzhaf et al. [22], pages 19–26.

26. Alwyn Barry. Aliasing in XCS and the Consecutive State Problem: 2 – Solutions. In Banzhaf et al. [22], pages 27–34.

27. Alwyn Barry. Specifying Action Persistence within XCS. In Whitely et al. [699], pages 50–57.

28. Alwyn Barry. *XCS Performance and Population Structure within Multiple-Step Environments*. PhD thesis, Queens University Belfast, 2000.

29. Alwyn Barry. Limits in long path learning with XCS. In E. Cantú-Paz, J. A. Foster, K. Deb, D. Davis, R. Roy, U.-M. O'Reilly, H.-G. Beyer, R. Standish, G. Kendall, S. Wilson, M. Harman, J. Wegener, D. Dasgupta, M. A. Potter, A. C. Schultz, K. Dowsland, N. Jonoska, and J. Miller, editors, *Genetic and Evolutionary Computation – GECCO-2003*, volume 2724 of *LNCS*, pages 1832–1843. Springer-Verlag, 2003.

30. Alwyn M. Barry. The stability of long action chains in xcs. *Journal of Soft Computing*, 6(3–4):183–199, 2002.

31. Dr. Alwyn Barry. A hierarchical xcs for long path environments. In Lee Spector, Erik D. Goodman, Annie Wu, W.B. Langdon, Hans-Michael Voigt, Mitsuo Gen, Sandip Sen, Marco Dorigo, Shahram Pezeshk, Max H. Garzon, and Edmund Burke, editors, *Proceedings of the Genetic and Evolutionary Computation Conference (GECCO-2001)*, pages 913–920, San Francisco, California, USA, 7-11 July 2001. Morgan Kaufmann.

32. Richard J. Bauer. *Genetic Algorithms and Investment Strategies*. Wiley Finance Editions. John Wiley & Sons, 1994.

33. Eric Baum. Towards a model of intelligence as an economy of agents. *Machine Learning*, 35(2):155–185, 1999.

34. Eric Baum and Igor Durdanovic. An Evolutionary Post Production System. In *Proceedings of the International Workshop on Learning Classifier Systems (IWLCS-2000), in the Joint Workshops of SAB 2000 and PPSN 2000* [4]. Extended abstract.

35. Eric Baum and Igor Durdanovic. An Artificial Economy of Post Production Systems. In Lanzi et al. [448], pages 3–20.
36. Richard K. Belew and Stephanie Forrest. Learning and Programming in Classifier Systems. *Machine Learning*, 3:193–223, 1988.
37. Richard K. Belew and Michael Gherrity. Back Propagation for the Classifier System. In Schaffer [563], pages 275–281.
38. Ester Bernadó, Xavier Llorà, and Josep M. Garrell. XCS and GALE: a Comparative Study of Two Learning Classifier Systems with Six Other Learning Algorithms on Classification Tasks. In *Proceedings of the 4th International Workshop on Learning Classifier Systems (IWLCS-2001)*, pages 337–341, 2001. Short version publishe in Genetic and Evolutionary Compution Conference (GECCO2001).
39. Ester Bernadó, Xavier Llorà, and Josep M. Garrell. Xcs and gale: A comparative study of two learning classifier systems on data mining. In Lanzi et al. [448], pages 115–132.
40. Hugues Bersini and Francisco J. Varela. Hints for Adaptive Problem Solving Gleaned From Immune Networks. In Schwefel and Männer [572], pages 343–354.
41. Janine Beunings, Ludwig Bölkow, Bernd Heydemann, Biruta Kresling, Claus-Peter Lieckfeld, Claus Mattheck, Werner Nachtigall, Josef Reichholf, Bertram J. Schmidt, Veronika Straa, and Reinhard Witt. *Bionik: Natur als Vorbild*. WWF Dokumentationen. PRO FUTURA Verlag, Mnchen, 1993.
42. J. Biondi. Robustness and evolution in an adaptive system application on classification task. In Albrecht et al. [9], pages 463–470.
43. Andrea Bonarini. ELF: Learning Incomplete Fuzzy Rule Sets for an Autonomous Robot. In Hans-Jürgen Zimmermann, editor, *First European Congress on Fuzzy and Intelligent Technologies – EUFIT'93*, volume 1, pages 69–75, Aachen, D, September 1993. Verlag der Augustinus Buchhandlung.
44. Andrea Bonarini. Evolutionary Learning of General Fuzzy Rules with Biased Evaluation Functions: Competition and Cooperation. *Proc. 1st IEEE Conf. on Evolutionary Computation*, pages 51–56, 1994.
45. Andrea Bonarini. Learning Behaviors Represented as Fuzzy Logic Controllers. In Hans-Jürgen Zimmermann, editor, *Second European Congress on Intelligent Techniques and Soft Computing - EUFIT'94*, volume 2, pages 710–715, Aachen, D, 1994. Verlag der Augustinus Buchhandlung.
46. Andrea Bonarini. Extending Q-learning to Fuzzy Classifier Systems. In Marco Gori and Giovanni Soda, editors, *Proceedings of the Italian Association for Artificial Intelligence on Topics in Artificial Intelligence*, volume 992 of *LNAI*, pages 25–36, Berlin, 1995. Springer.
47. Andrea Bonarini. Delayed Reinforcement, Fuzzy Q-Learning and Fuzzy Logic Controllers. In Herrera and Verdegay [336], pages 447–466.
48. Andrea Bonarini. Delayed Reinforcement, Fuzzy Q-Learning and Fuzzy Logic Controllers. In F. Herrera and J. L. Verdegay, editors, *Genetic Algorithms and Soft Computing, (Studies in Fuzziness, 8)*, pages 447–466, Berlin, D, 1996. Physica-Verlag.
49. Andrea Bonarini. Evolutionary Learning of Fuzzy rules: competition and cooperation. In W. Pedrycz, editor, *Fuzzy Modelling: Paradigms and Practice*, pages 265–284. Norwell, MA: Kluwer Academic Press, 1996. ftp://ftp.elet.polimi.it/pub/Andrea.Bonarini/ELF/ELF-Pedrycz.ps.gz.
50. Andrea Bonarini. Anytime learning and adaptation of fuzzy logic behaviors. *Adaptive Behavior*, 5(3–4):281–315, 1997.
51. Andrea Bonarini. Reinforcement Distribution to Fuzzy Classifiers. In *Proceedings of the IEEE World Congress on Computational Intelligence (WCCI) – Evolutionary Computation*, pages 51–56. IEEE Computer Press, 1998.
52. Andrea Bonarini. Comparing reinforcement learning algorithms applied to crisp and fuzzy learning classifier systems. In Banzhaf et al. [22], pages 52–59.

53. Andrea Bonarini. An Introduction to Learning Fuzzy Classifier Systems. In Lanzi et al. [446], pages 83–104.

54. Andrea Bonarini and Filippo Basso. Learning to compose fuzzy behaviors for autonomous agents. *Int. Journal of Approximate Reasoning*, 17(4):409–432, 1997.

55. Andrea Bonarini, Claudio Bonacina, and Matteo Matteucci. Fuzzy and crisp representation of real-valued input for learning classifier systems. In Wu [739], pages 228–235.

56. Andrea Bonarini, Claudio Bonacina, and Matteo Matteucci. Fuzzy and Crisp Representations of Real-valued Input for Learning Classifier Systems. In Lanzi et al. [446], pages 107–124.

57. Andrea Bonarini, Marco Dorigo, V. Maniezzo, and D. Sorrenti. AutonoMouse: An Experiment in Grounded Behaviors. In *Proceedings of GAA91 – Second Italian Workshop on Machine Learning, Bari, Italy*, 1991.

58. Pierre Bonelli and Alexandre Parodi. An Efficient Classifier System and its Experimental Comparison with two Representative learning methods on three medical domains. In Booker and Belew [72], pages 288–295.

59. Pierre Bonelli, Alexandre Parodi, Sandip Sen, and Stewart W. Wilson. NEWBOOLE: A Fast GBML System. In *International Conference on Machine Learning*, pages 153–159, San Mateo, California, 1990. Morgan Kaufmann.

60. Lashon B. Booker. *Intelligent Behavior as an Adaptation to the Task Environment*. PhD thesis, The University of Michigan, 1982.

61. Lashon B. Booker. Improving the performance of genetic algorithms in classifier systems. In Grefenstette [305], pages 80–92.

62. Lashon B. Booker. Classifier Systems that Learn Internal World Models. *Machine Learning*, 3:161–192, 1988.

63. Lashon B. Booker. Triggered rule discovery in classifier systems. In Schaffer [563], pages 265–274.

64. Lashon B. Booker. Instinct as an Inductive Bias for Learning Behavioral Sequences. In Meyer and Wilson [476], pages 230–237.

65. Lashon B. Booker. Representing Attribute-Based Concepts in a Classifier System. In Rawlins [519], pages 115–127.

66. Lashon B. Booker. Viewing Classifier Systems as an Integrated Architecture. In *Collected Abstracts for the First International Workshop on Learning Classifier System (IWLCS-92)* [2]. October 6–8, NASA Johnson Space Center, Houston, Texas.

67. Lashon B. Booker. Do We Really Need to Estimate Rule Utilities in Classifier Systems? In Wu [739], pages 236–241.

68. Lashon B. Booker. Classifier systems, endogenous fitness, and delayed reward: A preliminary investigation. In *Proceedings of the International Workshop on Learning Classifier Systems (IWLCS-2000), in the Joint Workshops of SAB 2000 and PPSN 2000* [4]. Extended abstract.

69. Lashon B. Booker. Do We Really Need to Estimate Rule Utilities in Classifier Systems? In Lanzi et al. [446], pages 125–142.

70. Lashon B. Booker. Classifier systems, endogenous fitness, and delayed rewards: A preliminary investigation. In Lee Spector, Erik D. Goodman, Annie Wu, W.B. Langdon, Hans-Michael Voigt, Mitsuo Gen, Sandip Sen, Marco Dorigo, Shahram Pezeshk, Max H. Garzon, and Edmund Burke, editors, *Proceedings of the Genetic and Evolutionary Computation Conference (GECCO-2001)*, pages 921–926, San Francisco, California, USA, 7-11 July 2001.

71. Lashon B. Booker. A new approach to encoding actions in classifier systems. 2001.

72. Lashon B. Booker and Richard K. Belew, editors. *Proceedings of the 4th International Conference on Genetic Algorithms (ICGA91)*. Morgan Kaufmann, July 1991.

73. Lashon B. Booker, David E. Goldberg, and John H. Holland. Classifier Systems and Genetic Algorithms. *Artificial Intelligence*, 40:235–282, 1989.

74. Lashon B. Booker, Rick L. Riolo, and John H. Holland. Learning and Representation in Classifier Systems. In Vassant Honavar and Leonard Uhr, editors, *Artificial Intelligence and Neural Networks*, pages 581–613. Academic Press, 1994.

75. Will Browne. *The Development of an Industrial Learning Classifier System for Application to a Steel Hot Strip Mill*. PhD thesis, University of Wales, Cardiff, 1999.

76. Will Browne, Karen Holford, and Carolynne Moore. An Industry Based Development of the Learning Classifier System Technique. Submitted to: 4th International Conference on Adaptive Computing in Design and Manufacturing (ACDM 2000).

77. Will Browne, Karen Holford, Carolynne Moore, and John Bullock. The implementation of a learning classifier system for parameter identification by signal processing of data from steel strip downcoilers. In A. T. Augousti, editor, *Software in Measurement. IEE Computer and Control Division*, 1996.

78. Will Browne, Karen Holford, Carolynne Moore, and John Bullock. A Practical Application of a Learning Classifier System for Downcoiler Decision Support in a Steel Hot Strip Mill. *Ironmaking and Steelmaking*, 25(1):33–41, 1997. Engineering Doctorate Seminar '97. Swansea, Wales, Sept. 2nd, 1997.

79. Will Browne, Karen Holford, Carolynne Moore, and John Bullock. A Practical Application of a Learning Classifier System in a Steel Hot Strip Mill. In Smith et al. [597], pages 611–614.

80. Will Browne, Karen Holford, Carolynne Moore, and John Bullock. An Industrial Learning Classifier System: The Importance of Pre-Processing Real Data and Choice of Alphabet. *To appear in: Engineering Applications of Artificial Intelligence*, 1999.

81. Larry Bull. *Artificial Symbiology: evolution in cooperative multi-agent environments*. PhD thesis, University of the West of England, 1995.

82. Larry Bull. On ZCS in Multi-agent Environments. In A. E. Eiben, T. Baeck, M. Schoenauer, and H.-P. Schwefel, editors, *Proceedings Parallel Problem Solving From Nature (PPSN-V)*, volume 1498 of *Lecture Notes in Computer Science*, pages 471–480. Springer–Verlag, 1998.

83. Larry Bull. On Evolving Social Systems. *Computational and Mathematical Organization Theory*, 5(3):281–298, 1999.

84. Larry Bull. On using ZCS in a Simulated Continuous Double-Auction Market. In Banzhaf et al. [22], pages 83–90.

85. Larry Bull. Simple markov models of the genetic algorithm in classifier systems: Accuracy-based fitness. In *Proceedings of the International Workshop on Learning Classifier Systems (IWLCS-2000), in the Joint Workshops of SAB 2000 and PPSN 2000* [4]. Extended abstract.

86. Larry Bull. Simple markov models of the genetic algorithm in classifier systems: Multi-step tasks. In *Proceedings of the International Workshop on Learning Classifier Systems (IWLCS-2000), in the Joint Workshops of SAB 2000 and PPSN 2000* [4]. Extended abstract.

87. Larry Bull. Lookahead and latent learning in ZCS. In W. B. Langdon, E. Cantú-Paz, K. Mathias, R. Roy, D. Davis, R. Poli, K. Balakrishnan, V. Honavar, G. Rudolph, J. Wegener, L. Bull, M. A. Potter, A. C. Schultz, J. F. Miller, E. Burke, and N. Jonoska, editors, *GECCO 2002: Proceedings of the Genetic and Evolutionary Computation Conference*, pages 897–904, New York, 9-13 July 2002. Morgan Kaufmann Publishers.

88. Larry Bull. On accuracy-based fitness. *Journal of Soft Computing*, 6(3–4):154–161, 2002.

89. Larry Bull and Terence C. Fogarty. Coevolving Communicating Classifier Systems for Tracking. In Albrecht et al. [9], pages 522–527.

90. Larry Bull and Terence C. Fogarty. Evolving Cooperative Communicating Classifier Systems. In A. V. Sebald and L. J. Fogel, editors, *Proceedings of the Third Annual Conference on Evolutionary Programming*, pages 308–315, 1994.

91. Larry Bull and Terence C. Fogarty. Parallel Evolution of Communicating Classifier Systems. In *Proceedings of the 1994 IEEE Conference on Evolutionary Computing*, pages 680–685. IEEE, 1994.

92. Larry Bull and Terence C. Fogarty. Evolutionary Computing in Cooperative Multi-Agent Systems. In Sandip Sen, editor, *Proceedings of the 1996 AAAI Symposium on Adaptation, Coevolution and Learning in Multi-Agent Systems*, pages 22–27. AAAI, 1996.

93. Larry Bull and Terence C. Fogarty. Evolutionary Computing in Multi-Agent Environments: Speciation and Symbiogenesis. In H-M. Voigt, W. Ebeling, I. Rechenberg, and H.-P. Schwefel, editors, *Parallel Problem Solving from Nature – PPSN IV*, pages 12–21. Springer-Verlag, 1996.

94. Larry Bull, Terence C. Fogarty, S. Mikami, and J. G. Thomas. Adaptive Gait Acquisition using Multi-agent Learning for Wall Climbing Robots. In *Automation and Robotics in Construction XII*, pages 80–86, 1995.

95. Larry Bull, Terence C. Fogarty, and M. Snaith. Evolution in Multi-agent Systems: Evolving Communicating Classifier Systems for Gait in a Quadrupedal Robot. In Eshelman [227], pages 382–388.

96. Larry Bull and O. Holland. Internal and External Representations: A Comparison in Evolving the Ability to Count. In *Proceedings of the First Annual Society for the Study of Artificial Intelligence and Simulated Behaviour Robotics Workshop*, pages 11–14, 1994.

97. Larry Bull and Jacob Hurst. Self-Adaptive Mutation in ZCS Controllers. In *Proceedings of the EvoNet Workshops - EvoRob 2000*, pages 339–346. Springer, 2000.

98. Larry Bull, Jacob Hurst, and Andy Tomlinson. Mutation in Classifier System Controllers. In et al. [228], pages 460–467.

99. Larry Bull and Toby O'Hara. Accuracy-based neuro and neuro-fuzzy classifier systems. In W. B. Langdon, E. Cantú-Paz, K. Mathias, R. Roy, D. Davis, R. Poli, K. Balakrishnan, V. Honavar, G. Rudolph, J. Wegener, L. Bull, M. A. Potter, A. C. Schultz, J. F. Miller, E. Burke, and N. Jonoska, editors, *GECCO 2002: Proceedings of the Genetic and Evolutionary Computation Conference*, pages 905–911. Morgan Kaufmann Publishers, 9-13 July 2002.

100. Larry Bull and Matt Studley. Consideration of multiple objectives in neural learning classifier systems. In H.-P. Schwefel J.-J. Merelo Guervós, P. Adamidis, H.-G. Beyer, J.-L. Fernández-Villacañas, editor, *Parallel Problem Solving from Nature - PPSN VII, 7th International Conference, Granada, Spain, September 7-11, 2002. Proceedings*, number 2439 in Lecture Notes in Computer Science, LNCS, page 549 ff. Springer-Verlag, 2002.

101. Larry Bull, Dave Wyatt, and Ian Parmee. Towards the use of XCS in interactive evolutionary design. In W. B. Langdon, E. Cantú-Paz, K. Mathias, R. Roy, D. Davis, R. Poli, K. Balakrishnan, V. Honavar, G. Rudolph, J. Wegener, L. Bull, M. A. Potter, A. C. Schultz, J. F. Miller, E. Burke, and N. Jonoska, editors, *GECCO 2002: Proceedings of the Genetic and Evolutionary Computation Conference*, page 951. Morgan Kaufmann Publishers, 2002.

102. Martin Butz, David E. Goldberg, and Wolfgang Stolzmann. New challenges for an ACS: Hard problems and possible solutions. Technical Report 99019, University of Illinois at Urbana-Champaign, Urbana, IL, October 1999.

103. Martin Butz, David E. Goldberg, and Wolfgang Stolzmann. The anticipatory classifier system and genetic generalization. Technical Report 2000032, Illinois Genetic Algorithms Laboratory, 2000.

104. Martin Butz and Wolfgang Stolzmann. Action-Planning in Anticipatory Classifier Systems. In Wu [739], pages 242–249.

105. Martin V. Butz. An Implementation of the XCS classifier system in C. Technical Report 99021, The Illinois Genetic Algorithms Laboratory, 1999.

106. Martin V. Butz. XCSJava 1.0: An Implementation of the XCS classifier system in Java . Technical Report 2000027, Illinois Genetic Algorithms Laboratory, 2000.

107. Martin V. Butz. An Algorithmic Description of ACS2. In Lanzi et al. [448], pages 211–229.
108. Martin V. Butz. Biasing Exploration in an Anticipatory Learning Classifier System. In Lanzi et al. [448], pages 3–22.
109. Martin V. Butz and David E. Goldberg. Bounding the population size in XCS to ensure reproductive opportunities. In E. Cantú-Paz, J. A. Foster, K. Deb, D. Davis, R. Roy, U.-M. O'Reilly, H.-G. Beyer, R. Standish, G. Kendall, S. Wilson, M. Harman, J. Wegener, D. Dasgupta, M. A. Potter, A. C. Schultz, K. Dowsland, N. Jonoska, and J. Miller, editors, *Genetic and Evolutionary Computation – GECCO-2003*, volume 2724 of *LNCS*, pages 1844–1856. Springer-Verlag, 2003.
110. Martin V. Butz, David E. Goldberg, and Wolfgang Stolzmann. Introducing a Genetic Generalization Pressure to the Anticipatory Classifier System – Part 1: Theoretical Approach. In Whitely et al. [699], pages 34–41. Also Technical Report 2000005 of the Illinois Genetic Algorithms Laboratory.
111. Martin V. Butz, David E. Goldberg, and Wolfgang Stolzmann. Introducing a Genetic Generalization Pressure to the Anticipatory Classifier System – Part 2: Performance Analysis. In Whitely et al. [699], pages 42–49. Also Technical Report 2000006 of the Illinois Genetic Algorithms Laboratory.
112. Martin V. Butz, David E. Goldberg, and Wolfgang Stolzmann. Investigating Generalization in the Anticipatory Classifier System. In *Proceedings of Parallel Problem Solving from Nature (PPSN VI)*, 2000. Also technical report 2000014 of the Illinois Genetic Algorithms Laboratory.
113. Martin V. Butz, David E. Goldberg, and Wolfgang Stolzmann. Probability-enhanced predictions in the anticipatory classifier system. In *Proceedings of the International Workshop on Learning Classifier Systems (IWLCS-2000), in the Joint Workshops of SAB 2000 and PPSN 2000* [4]. Extended abstract.
114. Martin V. Butz, Tim Kovacs, Pier Luca Lanzi, and Stewart W. Wilson. How XCS Evolves Accurate Classifiers. In Lee Spector, Erik D. Goodman, Annie Wu, W. B. Langdon, Hans-Michael Voigt, Mitsuo Gen, Sandip Sen, Marco Dorigo, Shahram Pezeshk, Max H Garzon, and Edmund Burke, editors, *GECCO-2001: Proceedings of the Genetic and Evolutionary Computation Conference*, pages 927–934. Morgan Kaufmann, 2001.
115. Martin V. Butz and Martin Pelikan. Analyzing the evolutionary pressures in xcs. In Lee Spector, Erik D. Goodman, Annie Wu, W.B. Langdon, Hans-Michael Voigt, Mitsuo Gen, Sandip Sen, Marco Dorigo, Shahram Pezeshk, Max H. Garzon, and Edmund Burke, editors, *Proceedings of the Genetic and Evolutionary Computation Conference (GECCO-2001)*, pages 935–942, San Francisco, California, USA, 7-11 July 2001. Morgan Kaufmann.
116. Martin V. Butz, Kumara Sastry, and David E. Goldberg. Tournament selection: Stable fitness pressure in XCS. In E. Cantú-Paz, J. A. Foster, K. Deb, D. Davis, R. Roy, U.-M. O'Reilly, H.-G. Beyer, R. Standish, G. Kendall, S. Wilson, M. Harman, J. Wegener, D. Dasgupta, M. A. Potter, A. C. Schultz, K. Dowsland, N. Jonoska, and J. Miller, editors, *Genetic and Evolutionary Computation – GECCO-2003*, volume 2724 of *LNCS*, pages 1857–1869. Springer-Verlag, 2003.
117. Martin V. Butz and Stewart W. Wilson. An Algorithmic Description of XCS. Technical Report 2000017, Illinois Genetic Algorithms Laboratory, 2000.
118. Martin V. Butz and Stewart W. Wilson. An Algorithmic Description of XCS. In Lanzi et al. [447], pages 253–272.
119. Martin V. Butz and Stewart W. Wilson. An algorithmic description of xcs. *Journal of Soft Computing*, 6(3–4):144–153, 2002.
120. Alessio Camilli. Classifier systems in massively parallel architectures. Master's thesis, University of Pisa, 1990. (In Italian).
121. Alessio Camilli and Roberto Di Meglio. Sistemi a classificatori su architetture a parallelismo massiccio. Technical report, Univ. Delgi Studi di Pisa, 1989.

122. Alessio Camilli, Roberto Di Meglio, F. Baiardi, M. Vanneschi, D. Montanari, and R. Serra. Classifier System Parallelization on MIMD Architectures. Technical Report 3/17, CNR, 1990.

123. Y. J. Cao, N. Ireson, L. Bull, and R. Miles. Distributed Learning Control of Traffic Signals. In *Proceedings of the EvoNet Workshops - EvoSCONDI 2000*, pages 117–126. Springer, 2000.

124. Y. J. Cao, N. Ireson, Larry Bull, and R. Miles. Design of a Traffic Junction Controller using a Classifier System and Fuzzy Logic. In *Proceedings of the Sixth International Conference on Computational Intelligence, Theory, and Applications*. Springer-Verlag, 1999.

125. A. Carbonaro, G. Casadei, and A. Palareti. Genetic Algorithms and Classifier Systems in Simulating a Cooperative Behavior. In Albrecht et al. [9], pages 479–483.

126. Brian Carse. Learning Anticipatory Behaviour Using a Delayed Action Classifier System. In Fogarty [246], pages 210–223.

127. Brian Carse and Terence C. Fogarty. A delayed-action classifier system for learning in temporal environments. In *Proceedings of the 1st IEEE Conference on Evolutionary Computation*, volume 2, pages 670–673, 1994.

128. Brian Carse and Terence C. Fogarty. A Fuzzy Classifier System Using the Pittsburgh Approach. In Davidor and Schwefel [169], pages 260–269.

129. Brian Carse, Terence C. Fogarty, and A. Munro. Distributed Adaptive Routing Control in Communications Networks using a Temporal Fuzzy Classifier System. In *Proceedings of the Fifth IEEE Conference on Fuzzy Systems*, pages 2203–2207. IEEE, 1996.

130. Brian Carse, Terence C. Fogarty, and A. Munro. Evolutionary Learning of Controllers using Temporal Fuzzy Classifier Systems. In I. C. Parmee, editor, *Proceedings of the Second Conference on Adaptive Computing in Engineering Design and Control*, pages 174–180, 1996.

131. Brian Carse, Terence C. Fogarty, and A. Munro. Evolving fuzzy rule based controllers using genetic algorithms. *International Journal for Fuzzy Sets and Systems*, 80:273–293, 1996.

132. Brian Carse, Terence C. Fogarty, and A. Munro. The Temporal Fuzzy Classifier System and its Application to Distributed Control in a Homogeneous Multi-Agent ecology. In Goodman et al. [300], pages 76–86.

133. Brian Carse, Terence C. Fogarty, and Alistair Munro. Evolving Temporal Fuzzy Rule-Bases for Distributed Routing Control in Telecommunication Networks. In Herrera and Verdegay [336], pages 467–488.

134. Brian Carse, Terence C. Fogarty, and Alistair Munro. Artificial evolution of fuzzy rule bases which represent time: A temporal fuzzy classifier system. *International Journal of Intelligent Systems*, 13(issue 10-11):905–927, 1998.

135. G. Casadei, A. Palareti, and G. Proli. Classifier System in Traffic Management. In Albrecht et al. [9], pages 620–627.

136. Keith Chalk and George D. Smith. Multi-Agent Classifier Systems and the Iterated Prisoner's Dilemma. In Smith et al. [597], pages 615–618.

137. Keith W. Chalk and George D. Smith. The Co-evolution of Classifier Systems in a Competitive Environment. Poster presented at AISB94. Authors were from the University of East Anglia, U.K.

138. Sin Man Cheang, Kin Hong Lee, and Kwong Sak Leung. Data classification using genetic parallel programming. In E. Cantú-Paz, J. A. Foster, K. Deb, D. Davis, R. Roy, U.-M. O'Reilly, H.-G. Beyer, R. Standish, G. Kendall, S. Wilson, M. Harman, J. Wegener, D. Dasgupta, M. A. Potter, A. C. Schultz, K. Dowsland, N. Jonoska, and J. Miller, editors, *Genetic and Evolutionary Computation – GECCO-2003*, volume 2724 of *LNCS*, pages 1918–1919. Springer-Verlag, 2003.

139. Hung-Ming Chen and Shinn-Ying Ho. Designing an optimal evolutionary fuzzy decision tree for data mining. In Lee Spector, Erik D. Goodman, Annie Wu, W.B. Langdon, Hans-Michael Voigt, Mitsuo Gen, Sandip Sen, Marco Dorigo, Shahram Pezeshk, Max H. Garzon, and Edmund Burke, editors, *Proceedings of the Genetic and Evolutionary Computation Conference (GECCO-2001)*, pages 943–950, San Francisco, California, USA, 7-11 July 2001. Morgan Kaufmann.

140. Pawel Cichosz. Reinforcement learning algorithms based on the methods of temporal differences. Master's thesis, Institute of Computer Science, Warsaw University of Technology, 1994.

141. Pawel Cichosz. *Reinforcement Learning by Truncating Temporal Differences*. PhD thesis, Department of Electronics and Information Technology, Warsaw University of Technology, 1997.

142. Pawel Cichosz and Jan J. Mulawka. GBQL: A novel genetics-based reinforcement learning architecture. In *Proceedings of the Third European Congress on Intelligent Techniques and Soft Computing (EUFIT'95)*, 1995.

143. Pawel Cichosz and Jan J. Mulawka. Faster temporal credit assignment in learning classifier systems. In *Proceedings of the First Polish Conference on Evolutionary Algorithms (KAE-96)*, 1996.

144. Dave Cliff and Seth G. Bullock. Adding 'Foveal Vision' to Wilson's Animat. *Adaptive Behavior*, 2(1):47–70, 1993.

145. Dave Cliff, Philip Husbands, Jean-Arcady Meyer, and Stewart W. Wilson, editors. *From Animals to Animats 3. Proceedings of the Third International Conference on Simulation of Adaptive Behavior (SAB94)*. A Bradford Book. MIT Press, 1994.

146. Dave Cliff and Susi Ross. Adding Temporary Memory to ZCS. *Adaptive Behavior*, 3(2):101–150, 1994. Also technical report: ftp://ftp.cogs.susx.ac.uk/pub/reports/csrp/csrp347.ps.Z.

147. Dave Cliff and Susi Ross. Adding Temporary Memory to ZCS. Technical Report CSRP347, School of Cognitive and Computing Sciences, University of Sussex, 1995. ftp://ftp.cogs.susx.ac.uk/pub/reports/csrp/csrp347.ps.Z.

148. H. G. Cobb and John J. Grefenstette. Learning the persistence of actions in reactive control rules. In *Proceedings 8th International Machine Learning Workshop*, pages 293–297. Morgan Kaufmann, 1991.

149. Philippe Collard and Cathy Escazut. Relational Schemata: A Way to Improve the Expressiveness of Classifiers. In Eshelman [227], pages 397–404.

150. Marco Colombetti and Marco Dorigo. Learning to Control an Autonomous Robot by Distributed Genetic Algorithms. In Roitblat and Wilson [545], pages 305–312.

151. Marco Colombetti and Marco Dorigo. Robot Shaping: Developing Situated Agents through Learning. Technical Report TR-92-040, International Computer Science Institute, Berkeley, CA, 1993.

152. Marco Colombetti and Marco Dorigo. Training Agents to Perform Sequential Behavior. Technical Report TR-93-023, International Computer Science Institute, Berkeley, CA, September 1993.

153. Marco Colombetti and Marco Dorigo. Training agents to perform sequential behavior. *Adaptive Behavior*, 2(3):247–275, 1994. ftp://iridia.ulb.ac.be/pub/dorigo/journals/IJ.06-ADAP94.ps.gz.

154. Marco Colombetti and Marco Dorigo. Verso un'ingegneria del comportamento. *Rivista di Automatica, Elettronica e Informatica*, 83(10), 1996. In Italian.

155. Marco Colombetti and Marco Dorigo. Evolutionary Computation in Behavior Engineering. In *Evolutionary Computation: Theory and Applications*, chapter 2, pages 37–80. World Scientific Publishing Co.: Singapore, 1999. Also Technical Report. TR/IRIDIA/1996-1, IRIDIA, Université Libre de Bruxelles.

156. Marco Colombetti, Marco Dorigo, and G. Borghi. Behavior Analysis and Training: A Methodology for Behavior Engineering. *IEEE Transactions on Systems, Man and Cybernetics*, 26(6):365–380, 1996.

157. Marco Colombetti, Marco Dorigo, and G. Borghi. Robot shaping: The HAMSTER Experiment. In M. Jamshidi et al., editor, *Proceedings of ISRAM'96, Sixth International Symposium on Robotics and Manufacturing, May 28–30, Montpellier, France*, 1996.

158. M. Compiani, D. Montanari, R. Serra, and P. Simonini. Asymptotic dynamics of classifier systems. In Schaffer [563], pages 298–303.

159. M. Compiani, D. Montanari, R. Serra, and P. Simonini. Learning and Bucket Brigade Dynamics in Classifier Systems. In *Special issue of Physica D (Vol. 42)* [1], pages 202–212.

160. M. Compiani, D. Montanari, R. Serra, and G. Valastro. Classifier systems and neural networks. In *Parallel Architectures and Neural Networks–First Italian Workshop*, pages 105–118. World Scientific, Teaneck, NJ, 1989.

161. Clare Bates Congdon. Classification of epidemiological data: A comparison of genetic algorithm and decision tree approaches. In *Proceedings of the 2000 Congress on Evolutionary Computation (CEC00)* [3], pages 442–449.

162. O. Cordón, F. Herrera, E. Herrera-Viedma, and M. Lozano. Genetic Algorithms and Fuzzy Logic in Control Processes. Technical Report DECSAI-95109, University of Granada, Granada, Spain, 1995.

163. Oscar Cordón, Francisco Herrera, Frank Hoffmann, and Luis Magdalena. *Genetic Fuzzy Systems*. World Scientific, 2001.

164. H. Brown Cribbs III and Robert E. Smith. Classifier System Renaissance: New Analogies, New Directions. In Koza et al. [425], pages 547–552.

165. Henry Brown Cribbs III and Robert E. Smith. What Can I do with a Learning Classifier System? In C. Karr and L. M. Freeman, editors, *Industrial Applications of Genetic Algorithms*, pages 299–320. CRC Press, 1998.

166. Walling Cyre. Learning grammars with a modified classifier system. In David B. Fogel, Mohamed A. El-Sharkawi, Xin Yao, Garry Greenwood, Hitoshi Iba, Paul Marrow, and Mark Shackleton, editors, *Proceedings of the 2002 Congress on Evolutionary Computation CEC2002*, pages 1366–1371. IEEE Press, 2002.

167. Martin Danek and Robert E. Smith. XCS applied to mapping FPGA architectures. In W. B. Langdon, E. Cantú-Paz, K. Mathias, R. Roy, D. Davis, R. Poli, K. Balakrishnan, V. Honavar, G. Rudolph, J. Wegener, L. Bull, M. A. Potter, A. C. Schultz, J. F. Miller, E. Burke, and N. Jonoska, editors, *GECCO 2002: Proceedings of the Genetic and Evolutionary Computation Conference*, pages 912–919. Morgan Kaufmann Publishers, 2002.

168. Dipankar Dasgupta and Fabio A. Gonzalez. Evolving complex fuzzy classifier rules using a linear tree genetic representation. In Lee Spector, Erik D. Goodman, Annie Wu, W.B. Langdon, Hans-Michael Voigt, Mitsuo Gen, Sandip Sen, Marco Dorigo, Shahram Pezeshk, Max H. Garzon, and Edmund Burke, editors, *Proceedings of the Genetic and Evolutionary Computation Conference (GECCO-2001)*, pages 299–305, San Francisco, California, USA, 7-11 July 2001. Morgan Kaufmann.

169. Y. Davidor and H.-P. Schwefel, editors. *Parallel Problem Solving From Nature – PPSN III*, volume 866 of *Lecture Notes in Computer Science*, Berlin, 1994. Springer Verlag.

170. Lawrence Davis. Mapping Classifier Systems into Neural Networks. In *Proceedings of the Workshop on Neural Information Processing Systems 1*, pages 49–56, 1988.

171. Lawrence Davis, editor. *Genetic Algorithms and Simulated Annealing*, Research Notes in Artificial Intelligence. Pitman Publishing: London, 1989.

172. Lawrence Davis. Mapping Neural Networks into Classifier Systems. In Schaffer [563], pages 375–378.

173. Lawrence Davis. Covering and Memory in Classifier Systems. In *Collected Abstracts for the First International Workshop on Learning Classifier System (IWLCS-92)* [2]. October 6–8, NASA Johnson Space Center, Houston, Texas.

174. Lawrence Davis, Chunsheng Fu, and Stewart W. Wilson. An incremental multiplexer problem and its uses in classifier system research. In Lanzi et al. [448], pages 23–31.

175. Lawrence Davis and David Orvosh. The Mating Pool: A Testbed for Experiments in the Evolution of Symbol Systems. In Eshelman [227], pages 405–412.

176. Lawrence Davis, Stewart W. Wilson, and David Orvosh. Temporary Memory for Examples can Speed Learning in a Simple Adaptive System. In Roitblat and Wilson [545], pages 313–320.

177. Lawrence Davis and D. K. Young. Classifier Systems with Hamming Weights. In *Proceedings of the Fifth International Conference on Machine Learning*, pages 162–173. Morgan Kaufmann, 1988.

178. Devon Dawson. Improving extended classifier system performance in resource-constrained configurations. Master's thesis, California State University, Chico, 2002.

179. Devon Dawson. Improving performance in size-constrained extended classifier systems. In E. Cantú-Paz, J. A. Foster, K. Deb, D. Davis, R. Roy, U.-M. O'Reilly, H.-G. Beyer, R. Standish, G. Kendall, S. Wilson, M. Harman, J. Wegener, D. Dasgupta, M. A. Potter, A. C. Schultz, K. Dowsland, N. Jonoska, and J. Miller, editors, *Genetic and Evolutionary Computation – GECCO-2003*, pages 1870–1881, Berlin, 2003. Springer-Verlag.

180. Devon Dawson and Benjoe Juliano. Modifying xcs for size-constrained systems. *International Journal on Neural and Mass-Parallel Computing and Information Systems*, 2003.

181. Bart de Boer. Classifier Systems: a useful approach to machine learning? Master's thesis, Leiden University, 1994. ftp://ftp.wi.leidenuniv.nl/pub/CS/MScTheses/deboer.94.ps.gz.

182. Kenneth A. De Jong. Learning with Genetic Algorithms: An Overview. *Machine Learning*, 3:121–138, 1988.

183. Michael de la Maza. A SEAGUL Visits the Race Track. In Schaffer [563], pages 208–212.

184. Daniel Derrig and James Johannes. Deleting End-of-Sequence Classifiers. In John R. Koza, editor, *Late Breaking Papers at the Genetic Programming 1998 Conference*, University of Wisconsin, Madison, Wisconsin, USA, July 1998. Stanford University Bookstore.

185. Daniel Derrig and James D. Johannes. Hierarchical Exemplar Based Credit Allocation for Genetic Classifier Systems. In Koza et al. [423], pages 622–628.

186. L. Desjarlais and Stephanie Forrest. Linked learning in classifier systems: A control architecture for mobile robots. In *Collected Abstracts for the First International Workshop on Learning Classifier System (IWLCS-92)* [2]. October 6–8, NASA Johnson Space Center, Houston, Texas.

187. John C. Determan and James A. Foster. A genetic algorithm for expert system rule generation. In Lee Spector, Erik D. Goodman, Annie Wu, W.B. Langdon, Hans-Michael Voigt, Mitsuo Gen, Sandip Sen, Marco Dorigo, Shahram Pezeshk, Max H. Garzon, and Edmund Burke, editors, *Proceedings of the Genetic and Evolutionary Computation Conference (GECCO-2001)*, page 757, San Francisco, California, USA, 7-11 July 2001. Morgan Kaufmann.

188. P. Devine, R. Paton, and M. Amos. Adaptation of Evolutionary Agents in Computational Ecologies. In *BCEC-97, Sweden*, 1997.

189. Federico Divina and Elena Marchiori. Evolutionary concept learning. In W. B. Langdon, E. Cantú-Paz, K. Mathias, R. Roy, D. Davis, R. Poli, K. Balakrishnan, V. Honavar, G. Rudolph, J. Wegener, L. Bull, M. A. Potter, A. C. Schultz, J. F. Miller, E. Burke, and N. Jonoska, editors, *GECCO 2002: Proceedings of the Genetic and Evolutionary Computation Conference*, pages 343–350, New York, 9-13 July 2002. Morgan Kaufmann Publishers.

190. Phillip William Dixon, David W. Corne, and Martin John Oates. A preliminary investigation of modified xcs as a generic data mining tool. In Lanzi et al. [448], pages 133–150.

191. Jean-Yves Donnart. *Cognitive Architecture and Adaptive Properties of an Motivationally Autonomous Animat.* PhD thesis, Université Pierre et Marie Curie. Paris, France, 1998.

192. Jean-Yves Donnart and Jean-Arcady Meyer. A hierarchical classifier system implementing a motivationally autonomous animat. In Cliff et al. [145], pages 144–153.

193. Jean-Yves Donnart and Jean-Arcady Meyer. Hierarchical-map Building and Self-positioning with MonaLysa. *Adaptive Behavior*, 5(1):29–74, 1996.

194. Jean-Yves Donnart and Jean-Arcady Meyer. Learning Reactive and Planning Rules in a Motivationally Autonomous Animat. *IEEE Transactions on Systems, Man and Cybernetics - Part B: Cybernetics*, 26(3):381–395, 1996.

195. Jean-Yves Donnart and Jean-Arcady Meyer. Spatial Exploration, Map Learning, and Self-Positioning with MonaLysa. In Maes et al. [468], pages 204–213.

196. Marco Dorigo. Message-Based Bucket Brigade: An Algorithm for the Apportionment of Credit Problem. In Y. Kodratoff, editor, *Proceedings of European Working Session on Learning '91, Porto, Portugal*, number 482 in Lecture notes in Artificial Intelligence, pages 235–244. Springer-Verlag, 1991.

197. Marco Dorigo. New perspectives about default hierarchies formation in learning classifier systems. In E. Ardizzone, E. Gaglio, and S. Sorbello, editors, *Proceedings of the 2nd Congress of the Italian Association for Artificial Intelligence (AI*IA) on Trends in Artificial Intelligence*, volume 549 of *LNAI*, pages 218–227, Palermo, Italy, October 1991. Springer Verlag.

198. Marco Dorigo. Using Transputers to Increase Speed and Flexibility of Genetic-based Machine Learning Systems. *Microprocessing and Microprogramming*, 34:147–152, 1991.

199. Marco Dorigo. Alecsys and the AutonoMouse: Learning to Control a Real Robot by Distributed Classifier Systems. Technical Report 92-011, Politecnico di Milano, 1992.

200. Marco Dorigo. *Optimization, Learning and Natural Algorithms.* PhD thesis, Politecnico di Milano, Italy, 1992. (In Italian).

201. Marco Dorigo. Genetic and Non-Genetic Operators in ALECSYS. *Evolutionary Computation*, 1(2):151–164, 1993. Also Technical Report TR-92-075 International Computer Science Institute.

202. Marco Dorigo. Gli Algoritmi Genetici, i Sistemi a Classificatori e il Problema dell'Animat. *Sistemi Intelligenti*, 3(93):401–434, 1993. In Italian.

203. Marco Dorigo. Alecsys and the AutonoMouse: Learning to Control a Real Robot by Distributed Classifier Systems. *Machine Learning*, 19:209–240, 1995.

204. Marco Dorigo. The Robot Shaping Approach to Behavior Engineering. Thèse d'Agrégation de l'Enseignement Supérieur, Faculté des Sciences Appliquées, Université Libre de Bruxelles, pp.176, 1995.

205. Marco Dorigo and Hugues Bersini. A Comparison of Q-Learning and Classifier Systems. In Cliff et al. [145], pages 248–255.

206. Marco Dorigo and Marco Colombetti. Robot shaping: Developing autonomous agents through learning. *Artificial Intelligence*, 2:321–370, 1994. ftp://iridia.ulb.ac.be/pub/dorigo/journals/IJ.05-AIJ94.ps.gz.

207. Marco Dorigo and Marco Colombetti. The Role of the Trainer in Reinforcement Learning. In S. Mahadevan et al., editor, *Proceedings of MLC-COLT '94 Workshop on Robot Learning, July 10th, New Brunswick, NJ*, pages 37–45, 1994.

208. Marco Dorigo and Marco Colombetti. Précis of Robot Shaping: An Experiment in Behavior Engineering. *Special Issue on Complete Agent Learning in Complex Environments, Adaptive Behavior*, 5(3–4):391–405, 1997.

209. Marco Dorigo and Marco Colombetti. Reply to Dario Floreano's "Engineering Adaptive Behavior". *Special Issue on Complete Agent Learning in Complex Environments, Adaptive Behavior*, 5(3–4):417–420, 1997.

210. Marco Dorigo and Marco Colombetti. *Robot Shaping: An Experiment in Behavior Engineering*. MIT Press/Bradford Books, 1998.
211. Marco Dorigo and V. Maniezzo. Parallel Genetic Algorithms: Introduction and Overview of Current Research. In J. Stenders, editor, *Parallel Genetic Algorithms: Theory and Applications*, Amsterdam, 1992. IOS Press.
212. Marco Dorigo, V. Maniezzo, and D. Montanari. Classifier-based robot control systems. In *IFAC/IFIP/IMACS International Symposium on Artificial Intelligence in Real-Time Control*, pages 591–598, Delft, Netherlands, 1992.
213. Marco Dorigo, Mukesh J. Patel, and Marco Colombetti. The effect of Sensory Information on Reinforcement Learning by a Robot Arm. In M. Jamshidi et al., editor, *Proceedings of ISRAM'94, Fifth International Symposium on Robotics and Manufacturing, August 14–18, Maui, HI*, pages 83–88. ASME Press, 1994.
214. Marco Dorigo and U. Schnepf. Organisation of Robot Behaviour Through Genetic Learning Processes. In *Proceedings of ICAR'91 – Fifth IEEE International Conference on Advanced Robotics, Pisa, Italy*, pages 1456–1460. IEEE Press, 1991.
215. Marco Dorigo and U. Schnepf. Genetics-based Machine Learning and Behaviour Based Robotics: A New Synthesis. *IEEE Transactions on Systems, Man and Cybernetics*, 23(1):141–154, 1993.
216. Marco Dorigo and E. Sirtori. A Parallel Environment for Learning Systems. In *Proceedings of GAA91 – Second Italian Workshop on Machine Learning, Bari, Italy*, 1991.
217. Marco Dorigo and Enrico Sirtori. Alecsys: A Parallel Laboratory for Learning Classifier Systems. In Booker and Belew [72], pages 296–302.
218. Barry B. Druhan and Robert C. Mathews. THIYOS: A Classifier System Model of Implicit Knowledge in Artificial Grammars. In *Proc. Ann. Cog. Sci. Soc.*, 1989.
219. D. Dumitrescu, B. Lazzerini, L. C. Jain, and A. Dumitrescu. *Evolutionary Computation*. CRC Press International, 2000.
220. Daniel Eckert and Johann Mitlöhner. Modelling individual and endogenous learning in games: the relevance of classifier systems. In *Complex Modelling for Socio-Economic Systems, SASA, Vienna*, 1997.
221. Daniel Eckert, Johann Mitlöhner, and Makus Moschner. Evolutionary stability issues and adaptive learning in classifier systems. In *OR'97 Conference on Operations Research, Vienna*, 1997.
222. G. Enee and C. Escazut. Classifier systems evolving multi-agent system with distributed elitism. In Angeline et al. [10], pages 1740–1745.
223. G. Enee and C. Escazut. A minimal model of communication for a multi-agent classifier system. In Lanzi et al. [448], pages 32–42.
224. Cathy Escazut and Philippe Collard. Learning Disjunctive Normal Forms in a Dual Classifier System. In Nada Lavrač and Stefan Wrobel, editors, *Proceedings of the 8th European Conference on Machine Learning*, volume 912 of *LNAI*, pages 271–274. Springer, 1995.
225. Cathy Escazut, Philippe Collard, and Jean-Louis Cavarero. Dynamic Management of the Specificity in Classifier Systems. In Albrecht et al. [9], pages 484–491.
226. Cathy Escazut and Terence C. Fogarty. Coevolving Classifier Systems to Control Traffic Signals. In John R. Koza, editor, *Late Breaking Papers at the 1997 Genetic Programming Conference*, Stanford University, CA, USA, July 1997. Stanford Bookstore.
227. Larry J. Eshelman, editor. *Proceedings of the 6th International Conference on Genetic Algorithms (ICGA95)*. Morgan Kaufmann Publishers, 1995.
228. J. A. Meyer et al., editor. *From Animals to Animats 6: Proceedings of the Sixth International Conference on Simulation of Adaptive Behavior*, 2000.
229. Andrew Fairley and Derek F. Yates. Improving Simple Classifier Systems to alleviate the problems of Duplication, Subsumption and Equivalence of Rules. In Albrecht et al. [9], pages 408–416.

230. Andrew Fairley and Derek F. Yates. Inductive Operators and Rule Repair in a Hybrid Genetic Learning System: Some Initial Results. In Fogarty [246], pages 166–179.

231. I. De Falco, A. Iazzetta, E. Tarantino, and A. Della Cioppa. An evolutionary system for automatic explicit rule extraction. In *Proceedings of the 2000 Congress on Evolutionary Computation (CEC00)* [3], pages 450–457.

232. William Joseph Falke II and Peter Ross. Dynamic strategies in a real-time strategy game. In E. Cantú-Paz, J. A. Foster, K. Deb, D. Davis, R. Roy, U.-M. O'Reilly, H.-G. Beyer, R. Standish, G. Kendall, S. Wilson, M. Harman, J. Wegener, D. Dasgupta, M. A. Potter, A. C. Schultz, K. Dowsland, N. Jonoska, and J. Miller, editors, *Genetic and Evolutionary Computation – GECCO-2003*, LNCS, pages 1920–1921. Springer-Verlag, 2003.

233. J. Doyne Farmer. A Rosetta Stone for Connectionism. In *Special issue of Physica D (Vol. 42)* [1], pages 153–187.

234. J. Doyne Farmer, N. H. Packard, and A. S. Perelson. The Immune System, Adaptation & Learning. *Physica D*, 22:187–204, 1986.

235. Francine Federman. NEXTNOTE: A Learning Classifier System. In Annie S. Wu, editor, *Proceedings of the Genetic and Evolutionary Computation Conference Workshop Program*, pages 136–138, 2000.

236. Francine Federman and Susan Fife Dorchak. Information Theory and NEXTPITCH: A Learning Classifier System. In Bäck [14], pages 442–449.

237. Francine Federman and Susan Fife Dorchak. Representation of Music in a Learning Classifier System. In Rad and Skowron, editors, *Foundations of Intelligent Systems: Proceedings 10th International Symposium (ISMIS'97)*. Springer-Verlag: Heidelberg, 1997.

238. Francine Federman and Susan Fife Dorchak. A Study of Classifier Length and Population Size. In Koza et al. [423], pages 629–634.

239. Francine Federman, Gayle Sparkman, and Stephanie Watt. Representation of Music in a Learning Classifier System Utilizing Bach Chorales. In Banzhaf et al. [22], page 785. One page poster paper.

240. Thomas Fent. *Applications of Learning Classifier Systems for Simulating Learning Organizations*, volume 10 of *Fortschrittsberichte Simulation*. ARGESIM / ASIM–Verlag, Wien, September 2001.

241. Rhonda Ficek. Genetic Algorithms. Technical Report NDSU-CS-TR-90-51, North Dakota State University. Computer Science and Operations Research, 1997.

242. M. V. Fidelis, H. S. Lopes, and A. A. Freitas. Discovering comprehensible classification rules with a genetic algorithm. In *Proceedings of the 2000 Congress on Evolutionary Computation (CEC00)* [3], pages 805–810.

243. Gary William Flake. *The Computational Beauty of Nature*. MIT Press, 1998. (Contains a chapter on ZCS).

244. Peter Fletcher. Simulating the use of 'fiat money' in a simple commodity economy. Master's thesis, Schools of Psychology and Computer Science, University of Birmingham, 1996.

245. Terence C. Fogarty. Co-evolving Co-operative Populations of Rules in Learning Control Systems. In *Evolutionary Computing, AISB Workshop Selected Papers* [246], pages 195–209.

246. Terence C. Fogarty, editor. *Evolutionary Computing, AISB Workshop Selected Papers*, number 865 in Lecture Notes in Computer Science. Springer-Verlag, 1994.

247. Terence C. Fogarty. Learning new rules and adapting old ones with the genetic algorithm. In G. Rzevski, editor, *Artificial Intelligence in Manufacturing*, pages 275–290. Springer-Verlag, 1994.

248. Terence C. Fogarty. Optimising Individual Control Rules and Multiple Communicating Rule-based Control Systems with Parallel Distributed Genetic Algorithms. *IEE Journal of Control Theory and Applications*, 142(3):211–215, 1995.

249. Terence C. Fogarty, Larry Bull, and Brian Carse. Evolving Multi-Agent Systems. In J. Periaux and G. Winter, editors, *Genetic Algorithms in Engineering and Computer Science*, pages 3–22. John Wiley & Sons, 1995.

250. Terence C. Fogarty, Brian Carse, and Larry Bull. Classifier Systems – recent research. *AISB Quarterly*, 89:48–54, 1994.

251. Terence C. Fogarty, Brian Carse, and Larry Bull. Classifier Systems: selectionist reinforcement learning, fuzzy rules and communication. Presented at the First International Workshop on Biologically Inspired Evolutionary Systems, Tokyo, 1995.

252. Terence C. Fogarty, Brian Carse, and A. Munro. Artificial evolution of fuzzy rule bases which represent time: A temporal fuzzy classifier system. *International Journal of Intelligent Systems*, 13(10–11):906–927, 1998.

253. Terence C. Fogarty and Luis Miramontes Hercog. Social simulation using a multi-agent model based on classifier systems: The emergence of switching agents in the dual pub problem. In Erik D. Goodman, editor, *2001 Genetic and Evolutionary Computation Conference Late Breaking Papers*, pages 87–94, 2001.

254. Terence C. Fogarty, N. S. Ireson, and Larry Bull. Genetic-based Machine Learning – Applications in Industry and Commerce. In Vic Rayward-Smith, editor, *Applications of Modern Heuristic Methods*, pages 91–110. Alfred Waller Ltd, 1995.

255. David B. Fogel. *Evolutionary Computation. The Fossil Record. Selected Readings on the History of Evolutionary Computation*, chapter 16: Classifier Systems. IEEE Press, 1998. This is a reprint of (Holland and Reitman, 1978), with an added introduction by Fogel.

256. Stephanie Forrest. *A study of parallelism in the classifier system and its application to classification in KL-ONE semantic networks*. PhD thesis, University of Michigan, Ann Arbor, MI, 1985.

257. Stephanie Forrest. Implementing semantic network structures using the classifier system. In Grefenstette [305], pages 24–44.

258. Stephanie Forrest. The Classifier System: A Computational Model that Supports Machine Intelligence. In *International Conference on Parallel Processing*, pages 711–716, Los Alamitos, Ca., USA, August 1986. IEEE Computer Society Press.

259. Stephanie Forrest. *Parallelism and Programming in Classifier Systems*. Pittman, London, 1991.

260. Stephanie Forrest, editor. *Proceedings of the 5th International Conference on Genetic Algorithms (ICGA93)*. Morgan Kaufmann, 1993.

261. Stephanie Forrest and John H. Miller. Emergent behavior in classifier systems. In *Special issue of Physica D (Vol. 42)* [1], pages 213–217.

262. Stephanie Forrest, Robert E. Smith, and A. Perelson. Maintaining diversity with a genetic algorithm. In *Collected Abstracts for the First International Workshop on Learning Classifier System (IWLCS-92)* [2]. October 6–8, NASA Johnson Space Center, Houston, Texas.

263. Richard Forsyth. *Machine Learning: Applications in expert systems and information retrival*, chapter Evolutionary Learning Strategies, pages 78–95. Ellis Horwood Limited, 1986.

264. Peter W. Frey and David J. Slate. Letter Recognition Using Holland-Style Adaptive Classifiers. *Machine Learning*, 6:161–182, 1991.

265. Chunsheng Fu and Lawrence Davis. A modified classifier system compaction algorithm. In W. B. Langdon, E. Cantú-Paz, K. Mathias, R. Roy, D. Davis, R. Poli, K. Balakrishnan, V. Honavar, G. Rudolph, J. Wegener, L. Bull, M. A. Potter, A. C. Schultz, J. F. Miller, E. Burke, and N. Jonoska, editors, *GECCO 2002: Proceedings of the Genetic and Evolutionary Computation Conference*, pages 920–925. Morgan Kaufmann Publishers, 2002.

266. Chunsheng Fu, Stewart W. Wilson, and Lawrence Davis. Studies of the xcsi classifier system on a data mining problem. In Lee Spector, Erik D. Goodman, Annie Wu, W.B. Langdon, Hans-Michael Voigt, Mitsuo Gen, Sandip Sen, Marco Dorigo, Shahram Pezeshk, Max H. Garzon, and Edmund Burke, editors, *Proceedings of the Genetic and Evolutionary Computation Conference (GECCO-2001)*, page 985, San Francisco, California, USA, 7-11 July 2001. Morgan Kaufmann.

267. Leeann L. Fu. The XCS Classifier System and Q-learning. In John R. Koza, editor, *Late Breaking Papers at the Genetic Programming 1998 Conference*, University of Wisconsin, Madison, Wisconsin, USA, 1998. Stanford University Bookstore.

268. Leeann L. Fu. What I have come to understand about classifier systems, 1998. Unpublished document. Dept. of Electrical Engineering and Computer Science. University of Michigan.

269. Takeshi Furuhashi. A Proposal of Hierarchical Fuzzy Classifier Systems. In Forrest [260].

270. Takeshi Furuhashi, Ken Nakaoka, Koji Morikawa, and Yoshiki Uchikawa. Controlling Excessive Fuzziness in a Fuzzy Classifier System. In Forrest [260], pages 635–635.

271. Takeshi Furuhashi, Ken Nakaoka, and Yoshiki Uchikawa. A Study on Fuzzy Classifier System for Finding Control Knowledge of Multi-Input Systems. In Herrera and Verdegay [336], pages 489–502.

272. Michelle Galea and Qiang Shen. Evolutionary approaches to fuzzy rule induction. In Jonathan M. Rossiter and Trevor P. Martin, editors, *Proceedings of the 2003 UK Workshop on Computational Intelligence (UKCI-03)*, pages 205–216, 2003.

273. Santiago Garcia, Fermin Gonzalez, and Luciano Sanchez. Evolving Fuzzy Rule Based Classifiers with GAP: A Grammatical Approach. In Riccardo Poli, Peter Nordin, William B. Langdon, and Terence C. Fogarty, editors, *Genetic Programming, Proceedings of EuroGP'99*, volume 1598 of *LNCS*, pages 203–210, Goteborg, Sweden, May 1999. Springer-Verlag.

274. Chris Gathercole. A Classifier System Plays a Simple Board Game. Master's thesis, Department of AI, University of Edinburgh, U.K., 1993.

275. Pierre Gerard and Olivier Sigaud. Combining Anticipation and Dynamic Programming in Classifier Systems. In *Proceedings of the International Workshop on Learning Classifier Systems (IWLCS-2000), in the Joint Workshops of SAB 2000 and PPSN 2000* [4]. Extended abstract.

276. Pierre Gerard and Olivier Sigaud. Adding a generalization mechanism to YACS. In Lee Spector, Erik D. Goodman, Annie Wu, W.B. Langdon, Hans-Michael Voigt, Mitsuo Gen, Sandip Sen, Marco Dorigo, Shahram Pezeshk, Max H. Garzon, and Edmund Burke, editors, *Proceedings of the Genetic and Evolutionary Computation Conference (GECCO-2001)*, pages 951–957, San Francisco, California, USA, 7-11 July 2001. Morgan Kaufmann.

277. Pierre Gerard and Olivier Sigaud. YACS: Combining dynamic programming with generalization in classifier systems. In *Advances in Classifier Systems*, volume 1996 of *LNAI*, pages 52–69. Springer-Verlag, 2001.

278. Pierre Gérard and Olivier Sigaud. Designing efficient exploration with MACS: Modules and function approximation. In E. Cantú-Paz, J. A. Foster, K. Deb, D. Davis, R. Roy, U.-M. O'Reilly, H.-G. Beyer, R. Standish, G. Kendall, S. Wilson, M. Harman, J. Wegener, D. Dasgupta, M. A. Potter, A. C. Schultz, K. Dowsland, N. Jonoska, and J. Miller, editors, *Genetic and Evolutionary Computation – GECCO-2003*, volume 2724 of *LNCS*, pages 1882–1893. Springer-Verlag, 2003.

279. Pierre Gerard, Wolfgang Stolzmann, and Olivier Sigaud. YACS, a new LCS using anticipation. *Journal of Soft Computing*, 6(3–4):216–228, 2002.

280. Andreas Geyer-Schulz. Fuzzy Classifier Systems. In Robert Lowen and Marc Roubens, editors, *Fuzzy Logic: State of the Art*, Series D: System Theory, Knowledge Engineering and Problem Solving, pages 345–354, Dordrecht, 1993. Kluwer Academic Publishers.

281. Andreas Geyer-Schulz. *Fuzzy Rule-Based Expert Systems and Genetic Machine Learning*. Physica Verlag, 1995. Book review at: http://www.apl.demon.co.uk/aplandj/fuzzy.htm. 2nd edition appeared in 1997.

282. Andreas Geyer-Schulz. Holland Classifier Systems. In *Proceedings of the International Conference on APL (APL'95)*, volume 25, pages 43–55, New York, NY, USA, June 1995. ACM Press.

283. Antonella Giani. A Study of Parallel Cooperative Classifier Systems. In John R. Koza, editor, *Late Breaking Papers at the Genetic Programming 1998 Conference*, University of Wisconsin, Madison, Wisconsin, USA, July 1998. Stanford University Bookstore.

284. Antonella Giani, Fabrizio Baiardi, and Antonina Starita. Q-Learning in Evolutionary Rule-Based Systems. In Davidor and Schwefel [169], pages 270–289.

285. Antonella Giani, Fabrizio Baiardi, and Antonina Starita. PANIC: A parallel evolutionary rule based system. In John R. McDonnell, Robert G. Reynolds, and David B. Fogel, editors, *Evolutionary Programming IV. Proceedings of the Fourth Annual Conference on Evolutionary Programming*, pages 753–771, 1995.

286. Antonella Giani, A. Sticca, F. Baiardi, and A. Starita. Q-learning and Redundancy Reduction in Classifier Systems with Internal State. In Claire Ndellec and Cline Rouveirol, editors, *Proceedings of the 10th European Conference on Machine Learning (ECML-98)*, volume 1398 of *LNAI*, pages 364–369. Springer, 1998.

287. A. H. Gilbert, Frances Bell, and Christine L. Valenzuela. Adaptive Learning of Process Control and Profit Optimisation using a Classifier System. *Evolutionary Computation*, 3(2):177–198, 1995.

288. Attilio Giordana and G. Lo Bello. Learning classification programs: The genetic algorithm approach. In A. E. Eiben and Z. Michalewicz, editors, *Evolutionary Computation*, pages 163–177. IOS Press, 1999.

289. Attilio Giordana and Filippo Neri. Search-Intensive Concept Induction. *Evolutionary Computation*, 3:375–416, 1995.

290. Attilio Giordana and L. Saitta. REGAL: An integrated system for learning relations using genetic algorithms. In *Proc. 2nd International Workshop on Multistrategy Learning*, pages 234–249, 1993.

291. Attilio Giordana and L. Saitta. Learning disjunctive concepts by means of genetic algorithms. In *Proc. Int. Conf. on Machine Learning*, pages 96–104, 1994.

292. David E. Goldberg. *Computer-Aided Gas Pipeline Operation using Genetic Algorithms and Rule Learning*. PhD thesis, The University of Michigan, 1983.

293. David E. Goldberg. Dynamic System Control using Rule Learning and Genetic Algorithms. In *Proceedings of the 9th International Joint Conference on Artificial Intelligence (IJCAI-85)*, pages 588–592. Morgan Kaufmann, 1985.

294. David E. Goldberg. Genetic algorithms and rules learning in dynamic system control. In Grefenstette [305], pages 8–15.

295. David E. Goldberg. *Genetic Algorithms in Search, Optimization, and Machine Learning*. Addison-Wesley, Reading, Mass., 1989.

296. David E. Goldberg. Probability Matching, the Magnitude of Reinforcement, and Classifier System Bidding. *Machine Learning*, 5:407–425, 1990. (Also TCGA tech report 88002, U. of Alabama).

297. David E. Goldberg. Some Reflections on Learning Classifier Systems. Technical Report 2000009, Illinois Genetic Algorithms Laboratory, University of Illinois at Urbana-Champaign, 2000. This appeared as part of Holland2000a.

298. David E. Goldberg, Jeffrey Horn, and Kalyanmoy Deb. What Makes a Problem Hard for a Classifier System? In *Collected Abstracts for the First International Workshop on Learning Classifier System (IWLCS-92)* [2]. (Also technical report 92007 Illinois Genetic Algorithms Laboratory, University of Illinois at Urbana-Champaign). Available from ENCORE (ftp://ftp.krl.caltech.edu/pub/EC/Welcome.html) in the section on Classifier Systems.

299. S. Y. Goldsmith. *Steady state analysis of a simple classifier system*. PhD thesis, University of New Mexico, Albuquerque, USA, 1989.

300. E. G. Goodman, V. L. Uskov, and W. F. Punch, editors. *Proceedings of the First International Conference on Evolutionary Algorithms and their Application EVCA'96*, Moscow, 1996. The Presidium of the Russian Academy of Sciences.

301. David Perry Greene and Stephen F. Smith. COGIN: Symbolic induction using genetic algorithms. In *Proceedings 10th National Conference on Artificial Intelligence*, pages 111–116. Morgan Kaufmann, 1992.

302. David Perry Greene and Stephen F. Smith. Competition-based induction of decision models from examples. *Machine Learning*, 13:229–257, 1993.

303. David Perry Greene and Stephen F. Smith. Using Coverage as a Model Building Constraint in Learning Classifier Systems. *Evolutionary Computation*, 2(1):67–91, 1994.

304. A. Greenyer. The use of a learning classifier system JXCS. In P. van der Putten and M. van Someren, editors, *CoIL Challenge 2000: The Insurance Company Case*. Leiden Institute of Advanced Computer Science, June 2000. Technical report 2000-09.

305. John J. Grefenstette, editor. *Proceedings of the 1st International Conference on Genetic Algorithms and their Applications (ICGA85)*. Lawrence Erlbaum Associates: Pittsburgh, PA, July 1985.

306. John J. Grefenstette. Multilevel Credit Assignment in a Genetic Learning System. In *Proceedings of the 2nd International Conference on Genetic Algorithms (ICGA87)* [307], pages 202–207.

307. John J. Grefenstette, editor. *Proceedings of the 2nd International Conference on Genetic Algorithms (ICGA87)*, Cambridge, MA, July 1987. Lawrence Erlbaum Associates.

308. John J. Grefenstette. Credit Assignment in Rule Discovery Systems Based on Genetic Algorithms. *Machine Learning*, 3:225–245, 1988.

309. John J. Grefenstette. A System for Learning Control Strategies with Genetic Algorithms. In Schaffer [563], pages 183–190.

310. John J. Grefenstette. Lamarckian Learning in Multi-Agent Environments. In Booker and Belew [72], pages 303–310. http://www.ib3.gmu.edu/gref/publications.html.

311. John J. Grefenstette. Learning decision strategies with genetic algorithms. In *Proc. Intl. Workshop on Analogical and Inductive Inference*, volume 642 of *Lecture Notes in Artificial Intelligence*, pages 35–50. Springer-Verlag, 1992. http://www.ib3.gmu.edu/gref/.

312. John J. Grefenstette. The Evolution of Strategies for Multi-agent Environments. *Adaptive Behavior*, 1:65–89, 1992. http://www.ib3.gmu.edu/gref/.

313. John J. Grefenstette. Using a genetic algorithm to learn behaviors for autonomous vehicles. In *Proceedings American Institute of Aeronautics and Astronautics Guidance, Navigation and Control Conference*, pages 739–749. AIAA, 1992. http://www.ib3.gmu.edu/gref/.

314. John J. Grefenstette. Evolutionary Algorithms in Robotics. In M. Jamshedi and C. Nguyen, editors, *Robotics and Manufacturing: Recent Trends in Research, Education and Applications, v5. Proc. Fifth Intl. Symposium on Robotics and Manufacturing, ISRAM 94*, pages 65–72. ASME Press: New York, 1994. http://www.ib3.gmu.edu/gref/.

315. John J. Grefenstette and H. G. Cobb. User's guide for SAMUEL, Version 1.3. Technical Report NRL Memorandum Report 6820, Naval Research Laboratory, 1991.

316. John J. Grefenstette, C. L. Ramsey, and Alan C. Schultz. Learning Sequential Decision Rules using Simulation Models and Competition. *Machine Learning*, 5(4):355–381, 1990. http://www.ib3.gmu.edu/gref/publications.html.

317. John J. Grefenstette and Alan C. Schultz. An evolutionary approach to learning in robots. In *Machine Learning Workshop on Robot Learning*, New Brunswick, NJ, 1994. http://www.ib3.gmu.edu/gref/.

318. T. Nakashima H. Ishibuchi and T. Kuroda. A fuzzy genetics-based machine learning method for designing linguistic classification systems with high comprehensibility. In *Proceedings 6th Int. Conf. on Neural Information Processing*, volume 2, pages 597–602, 1999.

319. T. Nakashima H. Ishibuchi and T. Kuroda. A hybrid fuzzy gbml algorithm for designing compact fuzzy rule-based classification systems. In *Proc. 9th IEEE Int. Conf. on Fuzzy Systems (FUZZ IEEE 2000)*, volume 2, pages 706–711, 2000.

320. T. Nakashima H. Ishibuchi and T. Murata. Genetic-algorithm-based approaches to the design of fuzzy systems for multi-dimensional pattern classification problems. In *Proc. 1996 IEEE Int. conf on Evolutionary Computation*, pages 229–234, 1996.

321. T. Nakashima H. Ishibuchi and T. Murata. Performance evaluation of fuzzy classifier systems for multidimensional pattern classification problems. *IEEE Transactions on Systems, Man and Cybernetics, Part B*, 29(5):601–618, 1999.

322. Hisashi Handa, Takashi Noda, Tadataka Konishi, Osamu Katai, and Mitsuru Baba. Coevolutionary fuzzy classifier system for autonomous mobile robots. In Takadama [640].

323. Adrian Hartley. Genetics Based Machine Learning as a Model of Perceptual Category Learning in Humans. Master's thesis, University of Birmingham, 1998. ftp://ftp.cs.bham.ac.uk/pub/authors/T.Kovacs/index.html.

324. Adrian Hartley. Accuracy-based fitness allows similar performance to humans in static and dynamic classification environments. In Banzhaf et al. [22], pages 266–273.

325. U. Hartmann. Efficient Parallel Learning in Classifier Systems. In Albrecht et al. [9], pages 515–521.

326. U. Hartmann. On the Complexity of Learning in Classifier Systems. In Davidor and Schwefel [169], pages 280–289. Republished in: ECAI 94. 11th European Conference on Artificial Intelligence. A Cohn (Ed.), pp.438–442, 1994. John Wiley and Sons.

327. Marianne Haslev. A Classifier System for the Production by Computer of Past Tense Verb-Forms. Presented at a Genetic Algorithms Workshop at the Rowland Institute, Cambridge MA, Nov 1986, 1986.

328. Mozart Hasse and Aurora R. Pozo. Using Phenotypic Sharing in a Classifier Tool. In Whitely et al. [699], page 392. One page poster paper.

329. Akira Hayashi and Nobuo Suematsu. Viewing Classifier Systems as Model Free Learning in POMDPs. In *Advances in Neural Information Processing Systems (NIPS) 11*, pages 989–995, 1999.

330. Luis Miramontes Hercog. Hand-eye coordination: An evolutionary approach. Master's thesis, Department of Artificial Intelligence. University of Edinburgh, 1998.

331. Luis Miramontes Hercog and Terence C. Fogarty. XCS-based inductive intelligent multi-agent system. In *Late Breaking Papers at the 2000 Genetic and Evolutionary Computation Conference (GECCO-2000)*, pages 125–132, 2000.

332. Luis Miramontes Hercog and Terence C. Fogarty. XCS-based Inductive Multi-Agent System. In *Proceedings of the International Workshop on Learning Classifier Systems (IWLCS-2000), in the Joint Workshops of SAB 2000 and PPSN 2000* [4]. Extended abstract.

333. Luis Miramontes Hercog and Terence C. Fogarty. Analysis of inductive intelligence in xcs-based multi-agent system (maxcs). In J.Periaux, P. Joly, and E. Onate, editors, *Innovative Tools for Scientific Computation in Aeronautical Engineering*, pages 351–366. CIMNE, Barcelona, 2001. ISBN: 84-90025-78-X.

334. Luis Miramontes Hercog and Terence C. Fogarty. Co-evolutionary classifier systems for multi-agent simulation. In David B. Fogel, Mohamed A. El-Sharkawi, Xin Yao, Garry Greenwood, Hitoshi Iba, Paul Marrow, and Mark Shackleton, editors, *Proceedings of the 2002 Congress on Evolutionary Computation CEC2002*, pages 1798–1803. IEEE Press, 2002.

335. Luis Miramontes Hercog and Terence C. Fogarty. Social simulation using a Multi-Agent Model based on Classifier Systems: The Emergence of Vacillating Behaviour in the "El Farol" Bar Problem. In Lanzi et al. [448], pages 88–111.

336. F. Herrera and J. L. Verdegay, editors. *Genetic Algorithms and Soft Computing, (Studies in Fuzziness, 8)*. Physica-Verlag, Berlin, 1996.

337. E. Herrera-Viedma. Sistemas Clasificadores de Aprendizaje. Aproximaciones Difusas. Technical Report DECSAI-95132, Dept. of Computer Science and A.I., University of Granada, 1995.

338. M. R. Hilliard, G. E. Liepins, Mark Palmer, Michael Morrow, and Jon Richardson. A classifier based system for discovering scheduling heuristics. In Grefenstette [307], pages 231–235.

339. John H. Holland. Processing and processors for schemata. In E. L. Jacks, editor, *Associative Information Processing*, pages 127–146. New York: American Elsevier, 1971.

340. John H. Holland. *Adaptation in Natural and Artificial Systems*. University of Michigan Press, Ann Arbor, 1975. Republished by the MIT press, 1992.

341. John H. Holland. Adaptation. In R. Rosen and F. M. Snell, editors, *Progress in Theoretical Biology*. New York: Plenum, 1976.

342. John H. Holland. Adaptive algorithms for discovering and using general patterns in growing knowledge bases. *International Journal of Policy Analysis and Information Systems*, 4(3):245–268, 1980.

343. John H. Holland. Genetic Algorithms and Adaptation. Technical Report 34, University of Michigan. Department of Computer and Communication Sciences, Ann Arbor, 1981.

344. John H. Holland. Escaping brittleness. In *Proceedings Second International Workshop on Machine Learning*, pages 92–95, 1983.

345. John H. Holland. Properties of the bucket brigade. In Grefenstette [305], pages 1–7.

346. John H. Holland. A Mathematical Framework for Studying Learning in a Classifier System. In Doyne Farmer, Alan Lapedes, Norman Packard, and Burton Wendroff, editors, *Evolution, Games and Learning: Models for Adaptation in Machines and Nature*, pages 307–317, Amsterdam, 1986. North-Holland.

347. John H. Holland. A Mathematical Framework for Studying Learning in Classifier Systems. *Physica D*, 22:307–317, 1986.

348. John H. Holland. Escaping Brittleness: The Possibilities of General-Purpose Learning Algorithms Applied to Parallel Rule-Based Systems. In Mitchell, Michalski, and Carbonell, editors, *Machine Learning, an Artificial Intelligence Approach. Volume II*, chapter 20, pages 593–623. Morgan Kaufmann, 1986.

349. John H. Holland. Genetic Algorithms and Classifier Systems: Foundations and Future Directions. In Grefenstette [307], pages 82–89.

350. John H. Holland. Concerning the Emergence of Tag-Mediated Lookahead in Classifier Systems. In *Special issue of Physica D (Vol. 42)* [1], pages 188–201.

351. John H. Holland, Lashon B. Booker, Marco Colombetti, Marco Dorigo, David E. Goldberg, Stephanie Forrest, Rick L. Riolo, Robert E. Smith, Pier Luca Lanzi, Wolfgang Stolzmann, and Stewart W. Wilson. What is a Learning Classifier System? In Lanzi et al. [446], pages 3–32.

352. John H. Holland and Arthur W. Burks. Adaptive Computing System Capable of Learning and Discovery. Patent 4697242 United States 29 Sept., 1987.

353. John H. Holland, Keith J. Holyoak, Richard E. Nisbett, and P. R. Thagard. *Induction: Processes of Inference, Learning, and Discovery*. MIT Press, Cambridge, 1986.

354. John H. Holland, Keith J. Holyoak, Richard E. Nisbett, and Paul R. Thagard. Classifier Systems, Q-Morphisms, and Induction. In Davis [171], pages 116–128.

355. John H. Holland and J. S. Reitman. Cognitive systems based on adaptive algorithms. In D. A. Waterman and F. Hayes-Roth, editors, *Pattern-directed Inference Systems*. New York: Academic Press, 1978. Reprinted in: Evolutionary Computation. The Fossil Record. David B. Fogel (Ed.) IEEE Press, 1998. ISBN: 0-7803-3481-7.

356. John H. Holmes. *Evolution-Assisted Discovery of Sentinel Features in Epidemiologic Surveillance*. PhD thesis, Drexel University, 1996.
http://cceb.med.upenn.edu/holmes/disstxt.ps.gz.

357. John H. Holmes. A genetics-based machine learning approach to knowledge discovery in clinical data. *Journal of the American Medical Informatics Association Supplement*, 1996.

358. John H. Holmes. Discovering Risk of Disease with a Learning Classifier System. In Bäck [14]. http://cceb.med.upenn.edu/holmes/icga97.ps.gz.

359. John H. Holmes. Differential negative reinforcement improves classifier system learning rate in two-class problems with unequal base rates. In Koza et al. [423], pages 635–642. http://cceb.med.upenn.edu/holmes/gp98.ps.gz.

360. John H. Holmes. Evaluating Learning Classifier System Performance In Two-Choice Decision Tasks: An LCS Metric Toolkit. In Banzhaf et al. [22], page 789. One page poster paper.

361. John H. Holmes. Quantitative Methods for Evaluating Learning Classifier System Performance in Forced Two-Choice Decision Tasks. In Wu [739], pages 250–257.

362. John H. Holmes. Applying a Learning Classifier System to Mining Explanatory and Predictive Models from a Large Database. In *Proceedings of the International Workshop on Learning Classifier Systems (IWLCS-2000), in the Joint Workshops of SAB 2000 and PPSN 2000* [4]. Extended abstract.

363. John H. Holmes. Learning Classifier Systems Applied to Knowledge Discovery in Clinical Research Databases. In Lanzi et al. [446], pages 243–261.

364. John H. Holmes. A representation for accuracy-based assessment of classifier system prediction performance. In Lanzi et al. [448], pages 43–56.

365. John H. Holmes, Dennis R. Durbin, and Flaura K. Winston. A New Bootstrapping Method to Improve Classification Performance in Learning Classifier Systems. In *Proceedings of Parallel Problem Solving from Nature (PPSN VI)*, 2000.

366. John H. Holmes, Dennis R. Durbin, and Flaura K. Winston. The learning classifier system: an evolutionary computation approach to knowledge discovery in epidemiologic surveillance. *Artificial Intelligence In Medicine*, 19(1):53–74, 2000.

367. Keith J. Holyoak, K. Koh, and Richard E. Nisbett. A Theory of Conditioning: Inductive Learning within Rule-Based Default Hierarchies. *Psych. Review*, 96:315–340, 1990.

368. Jeffrey Horn. *The Nature of Niching: Genetic Algorithms and the Evolution of Optimal, Cooperative Populations*. PhD thesis, University of Illinois at Urbana-Champaign (UMI Dissertation Service No. 9812622, 1997.

369. Jeffrey Horn and David E. Goldberg. Natural Niching for Cooperative Learning in Classifier Systems. In Koza et al. [425], pages 553–564.

370. Jeffrey Horn and David E. Goldberg. A Timing Analysis of Convergence to Fitness Sharing Equilibrium. In *Parallel Problem Solving from Nature (PPSN)*, 1998.

371. Jeffrey Horn and David E. Goldberg. Towards a Control Map for Niching. In *Foundations of Genetic Algorithms (FOGA)*, pages 287–310, 1998.

372. Jeffrey Horn, David E. Goldberg, and Kalyanmoy Deb. Implicit Niching in a Learning Classifier System: Nature's Way. *Evolutionary Computation*, 2(1):37–66, 1994. Also IlliGAL Report No 94001, 1994.

373. Dijia Huang. A framework for the credit-apportionment process in rule-based systems. *IEEE Transactions on Systems, Man and Cybernetics*, 1989.

374. Dijia Huang. *Credit Apportionment in Rule-Based Systems: Problem Analysis and Algorithm Synthesis*. PhD thesis, University of Michigan, 1989.

375. Dijia Huang. The Context-Array Bucket-Brigade Algorithm: An Enhanced Approach to Credit-Apportionment in Classifier Systems. In Schaffer [563], pages 311–316.

376. Jacob Hurst and Larry Bull. A Self-Adaptive Classifier System. In *Proceedings of the International Workshop on Learning Classifier Systems (IWLCS-2000), in the Joint Workshops of SAB 2000 and PPSN 2000* [4]. Extended abstract.

377. Jacob Hurst and Larry Bull. A Self-Adaptive XCS. In Lanzi et al. [448], pages 57–73.

378. Francesc Xavier Llorà i Fàbrega. Automatic Classification using genetic algorithms under a Pittsburgh approach. Master's thesis, Enginyeria La Salle - Ramon Llull University, 1998. http://www.salleurl.edu/~xevil/Work/index.html.

379. Francesc Xavier Llorà i Fàbrega and Josep Maria Garrell i Guiu. GENIFER: A Nearest Neighbour based Classifier System using GA. In Banzhaf et al. [22], page 797. One page poster paper appeared at GECCO. The full version is available at http://www.salleurl.edu/~xevil/Work/index.html.

380. Francesc Xavier Llorà i Fàbrega, Josep Maria Garrell i Guiu, and Ester Bernadó i Mansilla. A Classifier System based on Genetic Algorithm under the Pittsburgh approach for problems with real valued attributes. In Viceng Torra, editor, *Proceedings of Artificial Intelligence Catalan Workshop (CCIA98)*, volume 14–15, pages 85–93. ACIA Press, 1998. In Catalan http://www.salleurl.edu/~xevil/Work/index.html.

381. Josep Maria Garrell i Guiu, Elisabet Golobardes i Ribé, Ester Bernadó i Mansilla, and Francesc Xavier Llorà i Fàbrega. Automatic Classification of mammary biopsy images with machine learning techniques. In E. Alpaydin, editor, *Proceedings of Engineering of Intelligent Systems (EIS'98)*, volume 3, pages 411–418. ICSC Academic Press, 1998. http://www.salleurl.edu/~xevil/Work/index.html.

382. Josep Maria Garrell i Guiu, Elisabet Golobardes i Ribé, Ester Bernadó i Mansilla, and Francesc Xavier Llorà i Fàbrega. Automatic Diagnosis with Genetic Algorithms and Case-Based Reasoning. *To appear in AIENG Journal*, 1999. (This is an expanded version of Guiu98a).

383. H. Iba, H. de Garis, and T. Higuchi. Evolutionary Learning of Predatory Behaviors Based on Structured Classifiers. In Roitblat and Wilson [545], pages 356–363.

384. H. Inoue, K. Takadama, M. Okada, K. Shimohara, , and O. Katai. Agent architecture based on self-reflection learning classifier system. In *The 5th International Symposium on Artificial Life and Robotics (AROB'2000)*, pages 454–457, 2000.

385. H. Inoue, K. Takadama, and K. Shimohara. Inference of user's internal states and its agent's architecture. In *The 20th System Engineering Meeting of SICE (The Society of Instrument and Control Engineers)*, pages 55–60, 2000.

386. N. Ireson, Y. J. Cao, L. Bull, and R. Miles. A Communication Architecture for Multi-Agent Learning Systems. In *Proceedings of the EvoNet Workshops - EvoTel 2000*, pages 255–266, 2000.

387. Hisao Ishibuchi and Tomoharu Nakashima. Linguistic Rule Extraction by Genetics-Based Machine Learning. In Whitely et al. [699], pages 195–202.

388. Hisao Ishibuchi and Takashi Yamamoto. Fuzzy rule selection by data mining criteria and genetic algorithms. In W. B. Langdon, E. Cantú-Paz, K. Mathias, R. Roy, D. Davis, R. Poli, K. Balakrishnan, V. Honavar, G. Rudolph, J. Wegener, L. Bull, M. A. Potter, A. C. Schultz, J. F. Miller, E. Burke, and N. Jonoska, editors, *GECCO 2002: Proceedings of the Genetic and Evolutionary Computation Conference*, pages 399–406, New York, 9-13 July 2002. Morgan Kaufmann Publishers.

389. Yasushi Ishikawa and Takao Terano. Co-evolution of multiagents via organizational-learning classifier system and its application to marketing simulation. In *Proc. 4th Pacific-Asia Conf. on Information Systems (PACIS-2000)*, pages 1114–1127, 2000.

390. Jacob Hurst, Larry Bull and Chris Melhuish. TCS learning classifier system controller on a real robot. In H.-P. Schwefel J.-J. Merelo Guervós, P. Adamidis, H.-G. Beyer, J.-L. Fernández-Villacañas, editor, *Parallel Problem Solving from Nature - PPSN VII, 7th International Conference, Granada, Spain, September 7-11, 2002. Proceedings*, number 2439 in Lecture Notes in Computer Science, LNCS, page 588 ff. Springer-Verlag, 2002.

391. Kenneth A. De Jong and William M. Spears. Learning Concept Classification Rules using Genetic Algorithms. In *Proceedings of the Twelfth International Conference on Artificial Intelligence IJCAI-91*, volume 2, 1991.

392. K. Takadama, T. Terano, K. Shimohara, K. Hori and S. Nakasuka. Towards a multiagent design principle - analyzing an organizational-learning oriented classifier system. In V. Loia and S. Sessa, editors, *Soft Computing Agents: New Trends for Designing Autonomous Systems*, Series of Studies in Fuzziness and Soft Computing. Springer–Verlag, 2001.

393. Daisuke Katagami and Seiji Yamada. Real robot learning with human teaching. In Takadama [640].

394. Hiroharu Kawanaka, Tomohiro Yoshikawa, and Shinji Tsuruoka. A Study of Parallel GA Using DNA Coding Method for Acquisition of Fuzzy Control Rules. In *Late Breaking Papers at the 2000 Genetic and Evolutionary Computation Conference (GECCO-2000)*, pages 431–436, 2000.

395. Yeong-Joon Kim and Christoph F. Eick. Multi-rule-set decision-making schemes for a genetic algorithm learning environment for classification tasks. In John R. McDonnell, Robert G. Reynolds, and David B. Fogel, editors, *Evolutionary Programming IV. Proceedings of the Fourth Annual Conference on Evolutionary Programming*, pages 773–788, 1995.

396. Hiroaki Kitano, Stephen F. Smith, and Tetsuya Higuchi. GA-1: A Parallel Associative Memory Processor for Rule Learning with Genetic Algorithms. In Booker and Belew [72], pages 311–317.

397. Leslie Knight and Sandip Sen. PLEASE: A Prototype Learning System using Genetic Algorithms. In Eshelman [227], pages 429–435.

398. Gabriella Kókai, Zoltán Tóth, and Szilvia Zvada. An experimental comparison of genetic and classical concept learning methods. In W. B. Langdon, E. Cantú-Paz, K. Mathias, R. Roy, D. Davis, R. Poli, K. Balakrishnan, V. Honavar, G. Rudolph, J. Wegener, L. Bull, M. A. Potter, A. C. Schultz, J. F. Miller, E. Burke, and N. Jonoska, editors, *GECCO 2002: Proceedings of the Genetic and Evolutionary Computation Conference*, page 952. Morgan Kaufmann Publishers, 2002.

399. Kostyantyn Korovkin and Robert Richards. Visual Auction: A Classifier System Pedagogical and Researcher Tool. In Scott Brave and Annie S. Wu, editors, *Late Breaking Papers at the 1999 Genetic and Evolutionary Computation Conference (GECCO-99)*, pages 159–163, 1999.

400. Tim Kovacs. Evolving Optimal Populations with XCS Classifier Systems. Master's thesis, School of Computer Science, University of Birmingham, Birmingham, U.K., 1996. Also technical report CSR-96-17 and CSRP-96-17 ftp://ftp.cs.bham.ac.uk/pub/tech-reports/1996/CSRP-96-17.ps.gz.

401. Tim Kovacs. Steady State Deletion Techniques in a Classifier System. Unpublished document – partially subsumed by Kovacs1999a 'Deletion Schemes for Classifier Systems', 1997.

402. Tim Kovacs. XCS Classifier System Reliably Evolves Accurate, Complete, and Minimal Representations for Boolean Functions. In Roy, Chawdhry, and Pant, editors, *Soft Computing in Engineering Design and Manufacturing*, pages 59–68. Springer-Verlag, London, 1997. ftp://ftp.cs.bham.ac.uk/pub/authors/T.Kovacs/index.html.

403. Tim Kovacs. XCS Classifier System Reliably Evolves Accurate, Complete, and Minimal Representations for Boolean Functions. Technical Report Version. Technical Report CSRP-97-19, School of Computer Science, University of Birmingham, Birmingham, U.K., 1997. http://www.cs.bham.ac.uk/system/tech-reports/tr.html.

404. Tim Kovacs. Deletion schemes for classifier systems. In Banzhaf et al. [22], pages 329–336. Also technical report CSRP-99-08, School of Computer Science, University of Birmingham.

405. Tim Kovacs. Strength or accuracy? A comparison of two approaches to fitness calculation in learning classifier systems. In Wu [739], pages 258–265.

406. Tim Kovacs. Strength or Accuracy? Fitness calculation in learning classifier systems. In Lanzi et al. [446], pages 143–160.

407. Tim Kovacs. Towards a theory of strong overgeneral classifiers. In Worthy Martin and William M. Spears, editors, *Foundations of Genetic Algorithms (FOGA) Volume 6*, pages 165–184. Morgan Kaufmann, 2000. Also technical report CSRP-00-20, School of Computer Science, University of Birmingham.

408. Tim Kovacs. Trends in learning classifier systems publication. Technical Report CSRP-00-21, School of Computer Science, University of Birmingham, 2000.

409. Tim Kovacs. What should a classifier system learn? In *Proceedings of the 2001 Congress on Evolutionary Computation (CEC01)* [5], pages 775–782.

410. Tim Kovacs. *A Comparison and Strength and Accuracy-based Fitness in Learning Classifier Systems*. PhD thesis, University of Birmingham, 2002.

411. Tim Kovacs. Learning Classifier Systems Resources. *Journal of Soft Computing*, 6(3–4):240–243, 2002.

412. Tim Kovacs. Performance and population state metrics for rule-based learning systems. In David B. Fogel, Mohamed A. El-Sharkawi, Xin Yao, Garry Greenwood, Hitoshi Iba, Paul Marrow, and Mark Shackleton, editors, *Proceedings of the 2002 Congress on Evolutionary Computation CEC2002*, pages 1781–1786. IEEE Press, 2002.

413. Tim Kovacs. Two views of classifier systems. In Lanzi et al. [448], pages 74–87.

414. Tim Kovacs. What should a classifier system learn and how should we measure it? *Journal of Soft Computing*, 6(3–4):171–182, 2002.

415. Tim Kovacs. *Strength or Accuracy: Credit Assignment in Learning Classifier Systems*. Springer, 2004.

416. Tim Kovacs and Manfred Kerber. Some dimensions of problem complexity for XCS. In Annie S. Wu, editor, *Proceedings of the 2000 Genetic and Evolutionary Computation Conference Workshop Program*, pages 289–292, 2000.

417. Tim Kovacs and Manfred Kerber. What makes a problem hard for XCS? In *Proceedings of the International Workshop on Learning Classifier Systems (IWLCS-2000), in the Joint Workshops of SAB 2000 and PPSN 2000* [4]. Extended abstract.

418. Tim Kovacs and Manfred Kerber. What makes a problem hard for XCS? In Lanzi et al. [447], pages 80–99.

419. Tim Kovacs and Pier Luca Lanzi. A Learning Classifier Systems Bibliography. Technical Report 99.52, Dipartimento di Elettronica e Informazione, Politecnico di Milano, 1999.

420. Tim Kovacs and Pier Luca Lanzi. A Learning Classifier Systems Bibliography. In Lanzi et al. [446], pages 321–347.

421. Tim Kovacs and Pier Luca Lanzi. A Bigger Learning Classifier Systems Bibliography. In Lanzi et al. [447], pages 213–249.

422. Yuhsuke Koyama. The emergence of the cooperative behaviors in a small group. In Takadama [640].

423. John R. Koza, Wolfgang Banzhaf, Kumar Chellapilla, Kalyanmoy Deb, Marco Dorigo, David B. Fogel, Max H. Garzon, David E. Goldberg, Hitoshi Iba, and Rick Riolo, editors. *Genetic Programming 1998: Proceedings of the Third Annual Conference.* Morgan Kaufmann, 1998.

424. John R. Koza, Kalyanmoy Deb, Marco Dorigo, David B. Fogel, Max H. Garzon, Hitoshi Iba, and Rick Riolo, editors. *Genetic Programming 1997: Proceedings of the Second Annual Conference.* Morgan Kaufmann, 1997.

425. John R. Koza, David E. Goldberg, David B. Fogel, and Rick L. Riolo, editors. *Genetic Programming 1996: Proceedings of the First Annual Conference,* Stanford University, CA, USA, 1996. MIT Press.

426. Samuel Landau, Sébastien Picault, Oliver Sigaud, and Pierre Gérard. A comparison between ATNoSFERES and XCSM. In W. B. Langdon, E. Cantú-Paz, K. Mathias, R. Roy, D. Davis, R. Poli, K. Balakrishnan, V. Honavar, G. Rudolph, J. Wegener, L. Bull, M. A. Potter, A. C. Schultz, J. F. Miller, E. Burke, and N. Jonoska, editors, *GECCO 2002: Proceedings of the Genetic and Evolutionary Computation Conference,* pages 926–933. Morgan Kaufmann Publishers, 2002.

427. Pier Luca Lanzi. A Model of the Environment to Avoid Local Learning (An Analysis of the Generalization Mechanism of XCS). Technical Report 97.46, Politecnico di Milano. Department of Electronic Engineering and Information Sciences, 1997. http://ftp.elet.polimi.it/people/lanzi/report46.ps.gz.

428. Pier Luca Lanzi. A Study of the Generalization Capabilities of XCS. In Bäck [14], pages 418–425. http://ftp.elet.polimi.it/people/lanzi/icga97.ps.gz.

429. Pier Luca Lanzi. Solving Problems in Partially Observable Environments with Classifier Systems (Experiments on Adding Memory to XCS). Technical Report 97.45, Politecnico di Milano. Department of Electronic Engineering and Information Sciences, 1997. http://ftp.elet.polimi.it/people/lanzi/report45.ps.gz.

430. Pier Luca Lanzi. Adding Memory to XCS. In *Proceedings of the IEEE Conference on Evolutionary Computation (ICEC98).* IEEE Press, 1998. http://ftp.elet.polimi.it/people/lanzi/icec98.ps.gz.

431. Pier Luca Lanzi. An analysis of the memory mechanism of XCSM. In Koza et al. [423], pages 643–651. http://ftp.elet.polimi.it/people/lanzi/gp98.ps.gz.

432. Pier Luca Lanzi. Generalization in Wilson's XCS. In A. E. Eiben, T. Bäck, M. Shoenauer, and H.-P. Schwefel, editors, *Proceedings of the Fifth International Conference on Parallel Problem Solving From Nature – PPSN V,* number 1498 in LNCS. Springer Verlag, 1998.

433. Pier Luca Lanzi. *Reinforcement Learning by Learning Classifier Systems.* PhD thesis, Politecnico di Milano, 1998.

434. Pier Luca Lanzi. An Analysis of Generalization in the XCS Classifier System. *Evolutionary Computation,* 7(2):125–149, 1999.

435. Pier Luca Lanzi. Extending the Representation of Classifier Conditions Part I: From Binary to Messy Coding. In Banzhaf et al. [22], pages 337–344.

436. Pier Luca Lanzi. Extending the Representation of Classifier Conditions Part II: From Messy Coding to S-Expressions. In Banzhaf et al. [22], pages 345–352.

437. Pier Luca Lanzi. Adaptive Agents with Reinforcement Learning and Internal Memory. In *Sixth International Conference on the Simulation of Adaptive Behavior (SAB2000),* pages 333–342, 2000.

438. Pier Luca Lanzi. Learning Classifier Systems from a Reinforcement Learning Perspective . Technical Report 00-03, Dipartimento di Elettronica e Informazione, Politecnico di Milano, 2000.

439. Pier Luca Lanzi. Mining interesting knowledge from data with the xcs classifier system. In Lee Spector, Erik D. Goodman, Annie Wu, W.B. Langdon, Hans-Michael Voigt, Mitsuo Gen, Sandip Sen, Marco Dorigo, Shahram Pezeshk, Max H. Garzon, and Edmund Burke, editors, *Proceedings of the Genetic and Evolutionary Computation Conference (GECCO-2001)*, pages 958–965, San Francisco, California, USA, 7-11 July 2001. Morgan Kaufmann.

440. Pier Luca Lanzi. Learning classifier systems from a reinforcement learning perspective. *Journal of Soft Computing*, 6(3–4):162–170, 2002.

441. Pier Luca Lanzi. Estimating classifier generalization and action's effect: A minimalist approach. In E. Cantú-Paz, J. A. Foster, K. Deb, D. Davis, R. Roy, U.-M. O'Reilly, H.-G. Beyer, R. Standish, G. Kendall, S. Wilson, M. Harman, J. Wegener, D. Dasgupta, M. A. Potter, A. C. Schultz, K. Dowsland, N. Jonoska, and J. Miller, editors, *Genetic and Evolutionary Computation – GECCO-2003*, volume 2724 of *LNCS*, pages 1894–1905. Springer-Verlag, 2003.

442. Pier Luca Lanzi. Using raw accuracy to estimate classifier fitness in XCS. In E. Cantú-Paz, J. A. Foster, K. Deb, D. Davis, R. Roy, U.-M. O'Reilly, H.-G. Beyer, R. Standish, G. Kendall, S. Wilson, M. Harman, J. Wegener, D. Dasgupta, M. A. Potter, A. C. Schultz, K. Dowsland, N. Jonoska, and J. Miller, editors, *Genetic and Evolutionary Computation – GECCO-2003*, volume 2724 of *LNCS*, pages 1922–1923. Springer-Verlag, 2003.

443. Pier Luca Lanzi and Marco Colombetti. An Extension of XCS to Stochastic Environments. Technical Report 98.85, Dipartimento di Elettronica e Informazione - Politecnico di Milano, 1998.

444. Pier Luca Lanzi and Marco Colombetti. An Extension to the XCS Classifier System for Stochastic Environments. In Banzhaf et al. [22], pages 353–360.

445. Pier Luca Lanzi and Rick L. Riolo. A Roadmap to the Last Decade of Learning Classifier System Research (from 1989 to 1999). In Lanzi et al. [446], pages 33–62.

446. Pier Luca Lanzi, Wolfgang Stolzmann, and Stewart W. Wilson, editors. *Learning Classifier Systems. From Foundations to Applications*, volume 1813 of *LNAI*. Springer-Verlag, Berlin, 2000.

447. Pier Luca Lanzi, Wolfgang Stolzmann, and Stewart W. Wilson, editors. *Advances in Learning Classifier Systems*, volume 1996 of *LNAI*. Springer-Verlag, Berlin, 2001.

448. Pier Luca Lanzi, Wolfgang Stolzmann, and Stewart W. Wilson, editors. *Advances in Learning Classifier Systems*, volume 2321 of *LNAI*. Springer-Verlag, Berlin, 2002.

449. Pier Luca Lanzi and Stewart W. Wilson. Optimal classifier system performance in non-Markov environments. Technical Report 99.36, Dipartimento di Elettronica e Informazione - Politecnico di Milano, 1999. Also IlliGAL technical report 99022, University of Illinois.

450. Pier Luca Lanzi and Stewart W. Wilson. Toward Optimal Performance in Classifier Systems. *Evolutionary Computation*, 8(4):393–418, 2000.

451. Larry Bull, David Wyatt and Ian Parmee. Initial modifications to XCS for use in interactive evolutionary design. In H.-P. Schwefel J.-J. Merelo Guervós, P. Adamidis, H.-G. Beyer, J.-L. Fernández-Villacañas, editor, *Parallel Problem Solving from Nature - PPSN VII, 7th International Conference, Granada, Spain, September 7-11, 2002. Proceedings*, number 2439 in Lecture Notes in Computer Science, LNCS, page 568 ff. Springer-Verlag, 2002.

452. Claude Lattaud. Non-Homogeneous Classifier Systems in a Macro-Evolution Process. In Wu [739], pages 266–271.

453. Claude Lattaud. Non-Homogeneous Classifier Systems in a Macro-Evolution Process. In Lanzi et al. [446], pages 161–174.

454. Blake Lebaron, W. Brian Arthur, and R. Palmer. The Time Series Properties of an Artificial Stock Market. *Journal of Economic Dynamics and Control*, 23:1487–1516, 1999.

455. Martin Lettau and Harald Uhlig. Rules of Thumb and Dynamic Programming. Technical report, Department of Economics, Princeton University, 1994.

456. Martin Lettau and Harald Uhlig. Rules of thumb versus dynamic programming. *American Economic Review*, 89:148–174, 1999.
457. Pen-Yang Liao and Jiah-Shing Chen. Dynamic trading strategey learning model using learning classifier systems. In *Proceedings of the 2001 Congress on Evolutionary Computation (CEC01)* [5], pages 783–789.
458. Gunar E. Liepins, M. R. Hillard, M. Palmer, and G. Rangarajan. Credit Assignment and Discovery in Classifier Systems. *International Journal of Intelligent Systems*, 6:55–69, 1991.
459. Gunar E. Liepins, Michael R. Hilliard, Mark Palmer, and Gita Rangarajan. Alternatives for Classifier System Credit Assignment. In *Proceedings of the Eleventh International Joint Conference on Artificial Intelligence (IJCAI-89)*, pages 756–761, 1989.
460. Gunar E. Liepins and Lori A. Wang. Classifier System Learning of Boolean Concepts. In Booker and Belew [72], pages 318–323.
461. Derek A. Linkens and H. Okola Nyongesah. Genetic Algorithms for fuzzy control - Part II: Off-line system development and application. Technical Report CTA/94/2387/1st MS, Department of Automatic Control and System Engineering, University of Sheffield, U.K., 1994.
462. Juliet Juan Liu and James Tin-Yau Kwok. An extended genetic rule induction algorithm. In *Proceedings of the 2000 Congress on Evolutionary Computation (CEC00)* [3], pages 458–463.
463. Xavier Llorà and Josep M. Garrell. Evolution of Decision Trees. In *Forth Catalan Conference on Artificial Intelligence (CCIA'2001)*, page to appear. ACIA Press, 2001.
464. Xavier Llorà and Josep M. Garrell. Evolving Partially-Defined Instances with Evolutionary Algorithms. In *Proceedings of the 18th International Conference on Machine Learning (ICML'2001)*, pages 337–344. Morgan Kaufmann Publishers, 2001.
465. Xavier Llorà and Josep M. Garrell. Knowledge-Independent Data Mining with Fine-Grained Parallel Evolutionary Algorithms. In Lee Spector, Erik D. Goodman, Annie Wu, W.B. Langdon, Hans-Michael Voigt, Mitsuo Gen, Sandip Sen, Marco Dorigo, Shahram Pezeshk, Max H. Garzon, and Edmund Burke, editors, *Proceedings of the Genetic and Evolutionary Computation Conference (GECCO'2001)*, pages 461–468, San Francisco, California, USA, 2001. Morgan Kaufmann Publishers.
466. Xavier Llorà and Josep M. Garrell. Coevolving different knowledge representations with fine-grained parallel learning classifier systems. In W. B. Langdon, E. Cantú-Paz, K. Mathias, R. Roy, D. Davis, R. Poli, K. Balakrishnan, V. Honavar, G. Rudolph, J. Wegener, L. Bull, M. A. Potter, A. C. Schultz, J. F. Miller, E. Burke, and N. Jonoska, editors, *GECCO 2002: Proceedings of the Genetic and Evolutionary Computation Conference*, pages 934–941. Morgan Kaufmann Publishers, 2002.
467. Xavier and Llorà. Automatic Classification and Artfificial Life Models. In *Proceedings of the International Worshop on Learning (Learning00)*, 2000.
468. Pattie Maes, Maja J. Mataric, Jean-Arcady Meyer, Jordan Pollack, and Stewart W. Wilson, editors. *From Animals to Animats 4. Proceedings of the Fourth International Conference on Simulation of Adaptive Behavior (SAB96)*. A Bradford Book. MIT Press, 1996.
469. Chikara Maezawa and Masayasu Atsumi. Collaborative Learning Agents with Structural Classifier Systems. In Banzhaf et al. [22], page 777. One page poster paper.
470. Bernard Manderick. Selectionist Categorization. In Schwefel and Männer [572], pages 326–330.
471. Ester Bernadó I Mansilla and Josep Maria Garrell i Guiu. MOLeCS: A MultiObjective Learning Classifier System. In Whitely et al. [699], page 390. One page poster paper.
472. Ramon Marimon, Ellen McGrattan, and Thomas J. Sargent. Money as a Medium of Exchange in an Economy with Artificially Intelligent Agents. *Journal of Economic Dynamics and Control*, 14:329–373, 1990. Also Technical Report 89-004, Santa Fe Institute, 1989.

473. Maja J. Mataric. A comparative analysis of reinforcement learning methods. A.I. Memo No. 1322, Massachusetts Institute of Technology, 1991.

474. Alaster D. McAulay and Jae Chan Oh. Image Learning Classifier System Using Genetic Algorithms. In *Proceedings IEEE NAECON '89*, 1989.

475. Chris Melhuish and Terence C. Fogarty. Applying A Restricted Mating Policy To Determine State Space Niches Using Immediate and Delayed Reinforcement. In Fogarty [246], pages 224–237.

476. J. A. Meyer and S. W. Wilson, editors. *From Animals to Animats 1. Proceedings of the First International Conference on Simulation of Adaptive Behavior (SAB90)*. A Bradford Book. MIT Press, 1990.

477. Zbigniew Michalewicz. *Genetic Algorithms + Data Structures = Evolution Programs*. Springer-Verlag, 1996. Contains introductory chapter on LCS.

478. John H. Miller and Stephanie Forrest. The dynamical behavior of classifier systems. In Schaffer [563], pages 304–310.

479. M. Mitchell and S. Forrest. Genetic Algorithms and Artificial Life. Technical Report 93-11-072, Santa Fe Institute, 1993. Contains a 2 page review of work on LCS.

480. Johann Mitlöhner. Classifier systems and economic modelling. In *APL '96. Proceedings of the APL 96 Conference on Designing the Future*, volume 26 (4), pages 77–86, 1996.

481. Chilukuri K. Mohan. *Expert Systems: A Modern Overview*. Kluwer, 2000. Contains an introductory survey chapter on LCS.

482. D. Montanari. Classifier systems with a constant-profile bucket brigade. In *Collected Abstracts for the First International Workshop on Learning Classifier System (IWLCS-92)* [2]. October 6–8, NASA Johnson Space Center, Houston, Texas.

483. David E. Moriarty, Alan C. Schultz, and John J. Grefenstette. Evolutionary Algorithms for Reinforcement Learning. *Journal of Artificial Intelligence Research*, 11:199–229, 1999. http://www.ib3.gmu.edu/gref/papers/moriarty-jair99.html.

484. Rémi Munos and Jocelyn Patinel. Reinforcement learning with dynamic covering of state-action space: Partitioning Q-learning. In Cliff et al. [145], pages 354–363.

485. Tadahiko Murata, Shuhei Kawakami, Hiroyuki Nozawa, Mitsuo Gen, and Hisao Ishibuchi. Three-objective genetic algorithms for designing compact fuzzy rule-based systems for pattern classification problems. In Lee Spector, Erik D. Goodman, Annie Wu, W.B. Langdon, Hans-Michael Voigt, Mitsuo Gen, Sandip Sen, Marco Dorigo, Shahram Pezeshk, Max H. Garzon, and Edmund Burke, editors, *Proceedings of the Genetic and Evolutionary Computation Conference (GECCO-2001)*, pages 485–492, San Francisco, California, USA, 7-11 July 2001. Morgan Kaufmann.

486. Jorge Muruzábal. Fuzzy and Probabilistic Reasoning in Simple Learning Classifier Systems. In *Proceedings of the 2nd IEEE International Conference on Evolutionary Computation*, volume 1, pages 262–266. IEEE Press, 1995.

487. Jorge Muruzábal. Mining the space of generality with uncertainty-concerned cooperative classifiers. In Banzhaf et al. [22], pages 449–457.

488. Jorge Muruzábal and A. Muñoz. Diffuse pattern learning with Fuzzy ARTMAP and PASS. In Davidor and Schwefel [169], pages 376–385.

489. Ichiro Nagasaka and Toshiharu Taura. 3D Geometric Representation for Shape Generation using Classifier System. In Koza et al. [424], pages 515–520.

490. Filippo Neri. *First Order Logic Concept Learning by means of a Distributed Genetic Algorithm*. PhD thesis, University of Milano, Italy, 1997.

491. Filippo Neri. Comparing local search with respect to genetic evolution to detect intrusions in computer networks. In *Proceedings of the 2000 Congress on Evolutionary Computation (CEC00)* [3], pages 238–243.

492. Filippo Neri. Relating two cooperative learning strategies to the features of the found concept description. In Lee Spector, Erik D. Goodman, Annie Wu, W.B. Langdon, Hans-Michael Voigt, Mitsuo Gen, Sandip Sen, Marco Dorigo, Shahram Pezeshk, Max H. Garzon, and Edmund Burke, editors, *Proceedings of the Genetic and Evolutionary Computation Conference (GECCO-2001)*, page 986, San Francisco, California, USA, 7-11 July 2001. Morgan Kaufmann.

493. Filippo Neri. Cooperative concept learning by means of A distributed GA. In W. B. Langdon, E. Cantú-Paz, K. Mathias, R. Roy, D. Davis, R. Poli, K. Balakrishnan, V. Honavar, G. Rudolph, J. Wegener, L. Bull, M. A. Potter, A. C. Schultz, J. F. Miller, E. Burke, and N. Jonoska, editors, *GECCO 2002: Proceedings of the Genetic and Evolutionary Computation Conference*, page 953. Morgan Kaufmann Publishers, 2002.

494. Filippo Neri and Attilio Giordana. A distributed genetic algorithm for concept learning. In Eshelman [227], pages 436–443.

495. Filippo Neri and L. Saitta. Exploring the power of genetic search in learning symbolic classifiers. *IEEE Trans. on Pattern Analysis and Machine Intelligence*, PAMI-18:1135–1142, 1996.

496. Volker Nissen and Jörg Biethahn. Determining a Good Inventory Policy with a Genetic Algorithm. In Jörg Biethahn and Volker Nissen, editors, *Evolutionary Algorithms in Management Applications*, pages 240–249. Springer Verlag, 1995.

497. M. O. Odetayo and D. R. McGregor. Genetic algorithm for inducing control rules for a dynamic system. In Schaffer [563], pages 177–182. It could be argued this is a GA as opposed to a classifier system approach.

498. Jae Chan Oh. Improved Classifier System Using Genetic Algorithms. Master's thesis, Wright State University, (year unknown – pre-2000).

499. Norihiko Ono and Adel T. Rahmani. Self-Organization of Communication in Distributed Learning Classifier Systems. In Albrecht et al. [9], pages 361–367.

500. G. Deon Oosthuizen. Machine Learning: A mathematical framework for neural network, symbolic and genetics-based learning. In Schaffer [563], pages 385–390.

501. F. Oppacher and D. Deugo. The Evolution of Hierarchical Representations. In *Proceedings of the 3rd European Conference on Artificial Life*. Springer-Verlag, 1995.

502. Ramon Alfonso Palacios-Durazo and Manuel Valenzuela-Rendon. Lessons learned from LCSs: An incremental non-generational coevolutionary algorithm. In Bart Rylander, editor, *Genetic and Evolutionary Computation Conference (GECCO) Late Breaking Papers*, pages 248–254, 2003.

503. Alexandre Parodi and P. Bonelli. The Animat and the Physician. In Meyer and Wilson [476], pages 50–57.

504. Alexandre Parodi and Pierre Bonelli. A New Approach to Fuzzy Classifier Systems. In Forrest [260], pages 223–230.

505. Mukesh J. Patel, Marco Colombetti, and Marco Dorigo. Evolutionary Learning for Intelligent Automation: A Case Study. *Intelligent Automation and Soft Computing*, 1(1):29–42, 1995.

506. Mukesh J. Patel and Marco Dorigo. Adaptive Learning of a Robot Arm. In Fogarty [246], pages 180–194.

507. Mukesh J. Patel and U. Schnepf. Concept Formation as Emergent Phenomena. In Francisco J. Varela and P. Bourgine, editors, *Proceedings First European Conference on Artificial Life*, pages 11–20. MIT Press, 1992.

508. Ray C. Paton. Designing Adaptable Systems through the Study and Application of Biological Sources. In Vic Rayward-Smith, editor, *Applications of Modern Heuristic Methods*, pages 39–54. Alfred Waller Ltd, 1995.

509. Nicolas Pech-Gourg and Jin-Kao Hao. A genetic algorithm for the classification of natural corks. In Lee Spector, Erik D. Goodman, Annie Wu, W.B. Langdon, Hans-Michael Voigt, Mitsuo Gen, Sandip Sen, Marco Dorigo, Shahram Pezeshk, Max H. Garzon, and Edmund Burke, editors, *Proceedings of the Genetic and Evolutionary Computation Conference (GECCO-2001)*, pages 1382–1388, San Francisco, California, USA, 7-11 July 2001. Morgan Kaufmann.

510. Rolf Pfeifer, Bruce Blumberg, Jean-Arcady Meyer, and Stewart W. Wilson, editors. *From Animals to Animats 5. Proceedings of the Fifth International Conference on Simulation of Adaptive Behavior (SAB98)*. A Bradford Book. MIT Press, 1998.

511. Steven E. Phelan. *Using Artificial Adaptive Agents to Explore Strategic Landscapes*. PhD thesis, School of Business, Faculty of Law and Management, La Trobe University, Australia, 1997.

512. A. G. Pipe and B. Carse. First results from experiments in fuzzy classifier system architectures for mobile robotics. In H.-P. Schwefel J.-J. Merelo Guervós, P. Adamidis, H.-G. Beyer, J.-L. Fernández-Villacañas, editor, *Parallel Problem Solving from Nature - PPSN VII, 7th International Conference, Granada, Spain, September 7-11, 2002. Proceedings*, number 2439 in Lecture Notes in Computer Science, LNCS, page 578 ff. Springer-Verlag, 2002.

513. A. G. Pipe and Brian Carse. A Comparison between two Architectures for Searching and Learning in Maze Problems. In Fogarty [246], pages 238–249.

514. A. G. Pipe and Brian Carse. Autonomous Acquisition of Fuzzy Rules for Mobile Robot Control: First Results from two Evolutionary Computation Approaches. In Whitely et al. [699], pages 849–856.

515. R. Piroddi and R. Rusconi. A Parallel Classifier System to Solve Learning Problems. Master's thesis, Dipartimento di Elettronica e Informazione, Politecnico di Milano, Milano, Italy., 1992.

516. Mitchell A. Potter, Kenneth A. De Jong, and John J. Grefenstette. A Coevolutionary Approach to Learning Sequential Decision Rules. In Eshelman [227], pages 366–372.

517. C. L. Ramsey and John J. Grefenstette. Case-based initialization of genetic algorithms. In Forrest [260], pages 84–91. http://www.ib3.gmu.edu/gref/.

518. C. L. Ramsey and John J. Grefenstette. Case-based anytime learning. In D. W. Aha, editor, *Case-Based Reasoning: Papers from the 1994 Workshop*. AAAI Press: Menlo Park, CA, 1994. Also Technical Report WS-94-07 http://www.ib3.gmu.edu/gref/.

519. Gregory J. E. Rawlins, editor. *Proceedings of the First Workshop on Foundations of Genetic Algorithms (FOGA91)*. Morgan Kaufmann: San Mateo, 1991.

520. Colin Reveley. A learning classifier system adapted for hold'em poker. Master's thesis, Birkbeck College, University of London, UK, 2002.

521. Robert A. Richards. *Zeroth-Order Shape Optimization Utilizing a Learning Classifier System*. PhD thesis, Stanford University, 1995. Online version available at: http://www-leland.stanford.edu/~buc/SPHINcsX/book.html.

522. Robert A. Richards. Classifier System Metrics: Graphical Depictions. In Koza et al. [423], pages 652–657.

523. Robert A. Richards and Sheri D. Sheppard. Classifier System Based Structural Component Shape Improvement Utilizing I-DEAS. In *Iccon User's Conference Proceeding*. Iccon, 1992.

524. Robert A. Richards and Sheri D. Sheppard. Learning Classifier Systems in Design Optimization. In *Design Theory and Methodology '92*. The American Society of Mechanical Engineers, 1992.

525. Robert A. Richards and Sheri D. Sheppard. Two-dimensional Component Shape Improvement via Classifier System. In *Artificial Intelligence in Design '92*. Kluwer Academic Publishers, 1992.

526. Robert A. Richards and Sheri D. Sheppard. A Learning Classifier System for Three-dimensional Shape Optimization. In H. M. Voigt, W. Ebeling, I. Rechenberg, and H.-P. Schwefel, editors, *Parallel Problem Solving from Nature – PPSN IV*, volume 1141 of *LNCS*, pages 1032–1042. Springer-Verlag, 1996.

527. Robert A. Richards and Sheri D. Sheppard. Three-Dimensional Shape Optimization Utilizing a Learning Classifier System. In Koza et al. [425], pages 539–546.

528. Rick L. Riolo. Bucket Brigade Performance: I. Long Sequences of Classifiers. In Grefenstette [307], pages 184–195.

529. Rick L. Riolo. Bucket Brigade Performance: II. Default Hierarchies. In Grefenstette [307], pages 196–201.

530. Rick L. Riolo. CFS-C: A Package of Domain-Independent Subroutines for Implementing Classifier Systems in Arbitrary User-Defined Environments. Technical report, University of Michigan, 1988.

531. Rick L. Riolo. *Empirical Studies of Default Hierarchies and Sequences of Rules in Learning Classifier Systems*. PhD thesis, University of Michigan, 1988.

532. Rick L. Riolo. The Emergence of Coupled Sequences of Classifiers. In Schaffer [563], pages 256–264.

533. Rick L. Riolo. The Emergence of Default Hierarchies in Learning Classifier Systems. In Schaffer [563], pages 322–327.

534. Rick L. Riolo. Lookahead Planning and Latent Learning in a Classifier System. In Meyer and Wilson [476], pages 316–326.

535. Rick L. Riolo. Modelling Simple Human Category Learning with a Classifier System. In Booker and Belew [72], pages 324–333.

536. Rick L. Riolo. The discovery and use of forward models for adaptive classifier systems. In *Collected Abstracts for the First International Workshop on Learning Classifier System (IWLCS-92)* [2]. October 6–8, NASA Johnson Space Center, Houston, Texas.

537. Joaquin Rivera and Roberto Santana. Improving the Discovery Component of Classifier Systems by the Application of Estimation of Distribution Algorithms. In *Proceedings of Student Sessions ACAI'99: Machine Learning and Applications*, pages 43–44, Chania, Greece, July 1999.

538. A. Robert, F. Chantemargue, and M. Courant. Grounding Agents in EMud Artificial Worlds. In *Proceedings of the First International Conference on Virtual Worlds, Paris (France), July 1-3*, 1998.

539. Gary Roberts. A Rational Reconstruction of Wilson's Animat and Holland's CS-1. In Schaffer [563], pages 317–321.

540. Gary Roberts. Dynamic Planning for Classifier Systems. In Forrest [260], pages 231–237.

541. George G. Robertson. Parallel Implementation of Genetic Algorithms in a Classifier System. In Grefenstette [307], pages 140–147. Also Technical Report TR-159 RL87-5 Thinking Machines Corporation.

542. George G. Robertson. Population Size in Classifier Systems. In *Proceedings of the Fifth International Conference on Machine Learning*, pages 142–152. Morgan Kaufmann, 1988.

543. George G. Robertson. Parallel Implementation of Genetic Algorithms in a Classifier System. In Davis [171], pages 129–140.

544. George G. Robertson and Rick L. Riolo. A Tale of Two Classifier Systems. *Machine Learning*, 3:139–159, 1988.

545. J. A. Meyer H. L. Roitblat and S. W. Wilson, editors. *From Animals to Animats 2. Proceedings of the Second International Conference on Simulation of Adaptive Behavior (SAB92)*. A Bradford Book. MIT Press, 1992.

546. Wesley Romão, Alex A. Freitas, and Roberto C. S. Pacheco. A genetic algorithm for discovering interesting fuzzy prediction rules: Applications to science and technology data. In W. B. Langdon, E. Cantú-Paz, K. Mathias, R. Roy, D. Davis, R. Poli, K. Balakrishnan, V. Honavar, G. Rudolph, J. Wegener, L. Bull, M. A. Potter, A. C. Schultz, J. F. Miller, E. Burke, and N. Jonoska, editors, *GECCO 2002: Proceedings of the Genetic and Evolutionary Computation Conference*, pages 1188–1195, New York, 9-13 July 2002. Morgan Kaufmann Publishers.

547. Peter Ross, Sonia Schulenburg, Javier Marín-Blázquez, and Emma Hart. Hyper-heuristics: Learning to combine simple heuristics in bin-packing problems. In W. B. Langdon, E. Cantú-Paz, K. Mathias, R. Roy, D. Davis, R. Poli, K. Balakrishnan, V. Honavar, G. Rudolph, J. Wegener, L. Bull, M. A. Potter, A. C. Schultz, J. F. Miller, E. Burke, and N. Jonoska, editors, *GECCO 2002: Proceedings of the Genetic and Evolutionary Computation Conference*, pages 942–948. Morgan Kaufmann Publishers, 2002.

548. S. Ross. Accurate Reaction or Reflective Action? Master's thesis, School of Cognitive and Computing Sciences, University of Sussex, 1994.

549. S. E. Rouwhorst and A. P. Engelbrecht. Searching the forest: Using decision trees as building blocks for evolutionary search in classification databases. In *Proceedings of the 2000 Congress on Evolutionary Computation (CEC00)* [3], pages 633–638.

550. A. Sanchis, J. M. Molina, P. Isasi, and J. Segovia. Knowledge acquisition including tags in a classifier system. In Angeline et al. [10], pages 137–144.

551. Adrian V. Sannier and Erik D. Goodman. Midgard: A Genetic Approach to Adaptive Load Balancing for Distributed Systems. In *Proc. Fifth Intern. Conf. Machine Learning*. Morgan Kaufmann, 1988.

552. Manuel Filipe Santos. *Learning Classifiers in Distributed Environments*. PhD thesis, Departamento de Sistemas de Informao, Universidade do Minho, Portugal, 2000.

553. Cédric Sanza, Christophe Destruel, and Yves Duthen. Agents autonomes pour l'interaction adaptative dans les mondes virtuels. In *5ème Journées de l'Association Francaise d'Informatique Graphique. Décembre 1997, Rennes, France*, 1997. In French.

554. Cédric Sanza, Christophe Destruel, and Yves Duthen. A learning method for adaptation and evolution in virtual environments. In *3rd International Conference on Computer Graphics and Artificial Intelligence, April 1998, Limoges, France*, 1998.

555. Cédric Sanza, Christophe Destruel, and Yves Duthen. Autonomous actors in an interactive real-time environment. In *ICVC'99 International Conference on Visual Computing Feb. 1999, Goa, India*, 1999.

556. Cédric Sanza, Christophe Destruel, and Yves Duthen. Learning in real-time environment based on classifiers system. In *7th International Conference in Central Europe on Computer Graphics, Visualization and Interactive Digital Media'99*, Plzen, Czech Republic, 1999.

557. Cédric Sanza, Cyril Panatier, Hervé Luga, and Yves Duthen. Adaptive Behavior for Cooperation: a Virtual Reality Application. In *8th IEEE International Workshop on Robot and Human Interaction September 1999, Pisa, Italy*, 1999.

558. Shaun Saxon and Alwyn Barry. XCS and the Monk's problem. In Wu [739], pages 272–281.

559. Shaun Saxon and Alwyn Barry. XCS and the Monk's Problems. In Lanzi et al. [446], pages 223–242.

560. Andreas Schachtner. A classifier system with integrated genetic operators. In H.-P. Schwefel and R. Mnner, editors, *Parallel Problem Solving from Nature*, volume 496 of *Lecture Notes in Computer Science*, pages 331–337, Berlin, 1990. Springer.

561. J. David Schaffer. *Some experiments in machine learning using vector evaluated genetic algorithms*. PhD thesis, Vanderbilt University, Nashville, 1984.

562. J. David Schaffer. Learning Multiclass Pattern Discrimination. In Grefenstette [305], pages 74–79.

563. J. David Schaffer, editor. *Proceedings of the 3rd International Conference on Genetic Algorithms (ICGA89)*, George Mason University, June 1989. Morgan Kaufmann.

564. Sonia Schulenburg and Peter Ross. An Adaptive Agent Based Economic Model. In Lanzi et al. [446], pages 263–282.

565. Sonia Schulenburg and Peter Ross. Strength and Money: An LCS Approach to Increasing Returns. In *Proceedings of the International Workshop on Learning Classifier Systems (IWLCS-2000), in the Joint Workshops of SAB 2000 and PPSN 2000* [4]. Extended abstract.

566. Sonia Schulenburg and Peter Ross. Strength and money: An LCS approach to increasing returns. In Lanzi et al. [447], pages 114–137.

567. Sonia Schulenburg and Peter Ross. Explorations in lcs models of stock trading. In Lanzi et al. [448], pages 151–180.

568. Alan C. Schultz and John J. Grefenstette. Evolving Robot Behaviors. Poster at the 1994 Artificial Life Conference. (NCARAI Report: AIC-94-017) http://www.ib3.gmu.edu/gref/.

569. Alan C. Schultz and John J. Grefenstette. Improving Tactical Plans with Genetic Algorithms. In *Proceedings of the Second International Conference on Tools for Artificial Intelligence*. IEEE, 1990.

570. Alan C. Schultz, Connie Logia Ramsey, and John J. Grefenstette. Simulation assisted learning by competition: Effects of noise differences between training model and target environment. In *Proceedings of Seventh International Conference on Machine Learning (ICML)*, pages 211–215. Morgan Kaufmann, 1990.

571. Dale Schuurmans and Jonathan Schaeffer. Representational Difficulties with Classifier Systems. In Schaffer [563], pages 328–333. http://www.cs.ualberta.ca/ jonathan/Papers/Papers/classifier.ps.

572. Hans-Paul Schwefel and Reinhard Männer, editors. *Parallel Problem Solving from Nature: Proceedings of the First International Workshop. Dortmund, FRG, 1–3 Oct 1990*, number 496 in Lecture Notes in Computer Science, Heidelberg, 1990. Springer.

573. Tod A. Sedbrook, Haviland Wright, and Richard Wright. Application of a Genetic Classifier for Patient Triage. In Booker and Belew [72], pages 334–338.

574. Sandip Sen. Classifier system learning of multiplexer function. Dept. of Electrical Engineering, University of Alabama, Tuscaloosa, Alabama. Class Project, 1988.

575. Sandip Sen. Sequential Boolean Function Learning by Classifier System. In *Proc. of 1st International Conference on Industrial and Engineering Applications of Artificial Intelligence and Expert Systems*, 1988.

576. Sandip Sen. Noise Sensitivity in a simple classifier system. In *Proc. 5th Conf. on Neural Networks & Parallel Distributed Processing*, 1992.

577. Sandip Sen. Improving classification accuracy through performance history. In Forrest [260], pages 652–652.

578. Sandip Sen. A Tale of two representations. In *Proc. 7th International Conference on Industrial and Engineering Applications of Artificial Intelligence and Expert Systems*, pages 245–254, 1994.

579. Sandip Sen. Modelling human categorization by a simple classifier system. In *WSC1: 1st Online Workshop on Soft Computing. Aug 19-30, 1996. http://www.bioele.nuee.nagoya-u.ac.jp/wsc1/papers/p020.html*, 1996.

580. Sandip Sen and Mahendra Sekaran. Multiagent Coordination with Learning Classifier Systems. In Gerhard Wei and Sandip Sen, editors, *Proceedings of the IJCAI Workshop on Adaption and Learning in Multi-Agent Systems*, volume 1042 of *LNAI*, pages 218–233. Springer Verlag, 1996.

581. Tiago Sepulveda and Mario Rui Gomes. A Study on the Evolution of Learning Classifier Systems. In *Proceedings of the International Workshop on Learning Classifier Systems (IWLCS-2000), in the Joint Workshops of SAB 2000 and PPSN 2000* [4]. Extended abstract.

582. F. Seredynski, Pawel Cichosz, and G. P. Klebus. Learning classifier systems in multi-agent environments. In *Proceedings of the First IEE/IEEE International Conference on Genetic Algorithms in Engineering Systems: Innovations and Applications (GALESIA'95)*, 1995.

583. F. Seredynski and C. Z. Janikow. Learning nash equilibria by coevolving distributed classifier systems. In Angeline et al. [10], pages 1619–1626.

584. Jiefu Shi. Genetic Algorithms for Game Playing. In C. Karr and L. M. Freeman, editors, *Industrial Applications of Genetic Algorithms*, pages 321–338. CRC Press, 1998.

585. Sotaro Shimada and Yuichiro Anzai. Component-Based Adaptive Architecture with Classifier Systems. In Pfeifer et al. [510].

586. Sotaro Shimada and Yuichiro Anzai. Fast and Robust Convergence of Chained Classifiers by Generating Operons through Niche Formation. In Banzhaf et al. [22], page 810. One page poster paper.

587. Sotaro Shimada and Yuichiro Anzai. On Niche Formation and Corporation in Classifier System. In Takadama [640].

588. Takayuki Shiose and Tetsuo Sawaragi. Extended learning classifier systems by dual referencing mechanism. In Takadama [640].

589. Lingyan Shu and Jonathan Schaeffer. VCS: Variable Classifier System. In Schaffer [563], pages 334–339. http://www.cs.ualberta.ca/~jonathan/Papers/Papers/vcs.ps.

590. Lingyan Shu and Jonathan Schaeffer. Improving the Performance of Genetic Algorithm Learning by Choosing a Good Initial Population. Technical Report TR-90-22, University of Alberta, CS DEPT, Edmonton, Alberta, Canada, 1990.

591. Lingyan Shu and Jonathan Schaeffer. HCS: Adding Hierarchies to Classifier Systems. In Booker and Belew [72], pages 339–345.

592. Olivier Sigaud. On the usefulness of a semi-automated Classifier System: the engineering perspective. In *Proceedings of the International Workshop on Learning Classifier Systems (IWLCS-2000), in the Joint Workshops of SAB 2000 and PPSN 2000* [4]. Extended abstract.

593. Olivier Sigaud and Pierre Gerard. Being reactive by exchanging roles: an empirical study. In *Balancing reactivity and Social Deliberation in Multiagent Systems*, volume 2103 of *LNAI*, pages 150–172. Springer–Verlag, 2001.

594. Olivier Sigaud and Pierre Gerard. Using classifier systems as adaptive expert systems for control. In *Advances in Classifier Systems*, number 1996 in LNAI, pages 138–157. Springer–Verlag, 2001.

595. Michael C. Simon. Using XCS to form hyper-heuristics for the set covering problem. In Alwyn M. Barry, editor, *GECCO 2003: Proceedings of the Bird of a Feather Workshops, Genetic and Evolutionary Computation Conference*, pages 246–249. AAAI, 2003.

596. George D. Smith. Economic Applications of Genetic Algorithms. In Vic Rayward-Smith, editor, *Applications of Modern Heuristic Methods*, pages 71–90. Alfred Waller Ltd, 1995. Contains 2 pages on LCS.

597. George D. Smith, Nigel C. Steele, and Rudolf F. Albrecht, editors. *Artificial Neural Networks and Genetic Algorithms*. Springer, 1997.

598. Robert E. Smith. *Default Hierarchy Formation and Memory Exploitation in Learning Classifier Systems*. PhD thesis, University of Alabama, 1991.

599. Robert E. Smith. A Report on The First International Workshop on Learning Classifier Systems (IWLCS-92). NASA Johnson Space Center, Houston, Texas, Oct. 6-9. ftp://lumpi.informatik.uni-dortmund.de/pub/LCS/papers/lcs92.ps.gz or from ENCORE, The Electronic Appendix to the Hitch-Hiker's Guide to Evolutionary Computation (ftp://ftp.krl.caltech.edu/pub/EC/Welcome.html) in the section on Classifier Systems, 1992.

600. Robert E. Smith. Is a classifier system a type of neural network? In *Collected Abstracts for the First International Workshop on Learning Classifier System (IWLCS-92)* [2]. October 6–8, NASA Johnson Space Center, Houston, Texas.

601. Robert E. Smith. Memory exploitation in learning classifier systems. In *Collected Abstracts for the First International Workshop on Learning Classifier System (IWLCS-92)* [2]. October 6–8, NASA Johnson Space Center, Houston, Texas.

602. Robert E. Smith. Genetic Learning in Rule-Based and Neural Systems. In *Proceedings of the Third International Workshop on Neural Networks and Fuzzy Logic*, volume 1, page 183. NASA. Johnson Space Center, January 1993.

603. Robert E. Smith. Memory Exploitation in Learning Classifier Systems. *Evolutionary Computation*, 2(3):199–220, 1994.

604. Robert E. Smith. Derivative Methods: Learning Classifier Systems. In Bäck et al. [15], pages B1.2:6–B1.5:11. http://www.iop.org/Books/Catalogue/.

605. Robert E. Smith and H. Brown Cribbs. Is a Learning Classifier System a Type of Neural Network? *Evolutionary Computation*, 2(1):19–36, 1994.

606. Robert E. Smith, B. A. Dike, R. K. Mehra, B. Ravichandran, and A. El-Fallah. Classifier Systems in Combat: Two-sided Learning of Maneuvers for Advanced Fighter Aircraft. In *Computer Methods in Applied Mechanics and Engineering*. Elsevier, 1999.

607. Robert E. Smith, B. A. Dike, B. Ravichandran, A. El-Fallah, and R. K. Mehra. The Fighter Aircraft LCS: A Case of Different LCS Goals and Techniques. In Wu [739], pages 282–289.

608. Robert E. Smith, B. A. Dike, B. Ravichandran, A. El-Fallah, and R. K. Mehra. The Fighter Aircraft LCS: A Case of Different LCS Goals and Techniques. In Lanzi et al. [446], pages 283–300.

609. Robert E. Smith, Stephanie Forrest, and A. S. Perelson. Searching for diverse, cooperative subpopulations with Genetic Algorithms. *Evolutionary Computation*, 1(2):127–149, 1993.

610. Robert E. Smith, Stephanie Forrest, and Alan S. Perelson. Population Diversity in an Immune System Model: Implications for Genetic Search. In L. Darrell Whitley, editor, *Foundations of Genetic Algorithms 2*, pages 153–165. Morgan Kaufmann, 1992.

611. Robert E. Smith and David E. Goldberg. Reinforcement Learning with Classifier Systems: Adaptive Default Hierarchy Formation. Technical Report 90002, TCGA, University of Alabama, 1990.

612. Robert E. Smith and David E. Goldberg. Variable Default Hierarchy Separation in a Classifier System. In Rawlins [519], pages 148–170.

613. Robert E. Smith and David E. Goldberg. Reinforcement learning with classifier systems: adaptative default hierarchy formation. *Applied Artificial Intelligence*, 6, 1992.

614. Robert E. Smith and H. B. Cribbs III. Cooperative Versus Competitive System Elements in Coevolutionary Systems. In Maes et al. [468], pages 497–505.

615. Robert E. Smith and H. B. Cribbs III. Combined biological paradigms. *Robotics and Autonomous Systems*, 22(1):65–74, 1997.

616. Robert E. Smith and Manuel Valenzuela-Rendón. A Study of Rule Set Development in a Learning Classifier System. In Schaffer [563], pages 340–346.

617. S. F. Smith. *A Learning System Based on Genetic Adaptive Algorithms*. PhD thesis, University of Pittsburgh, 1980.

618. S. F. Smith. Flexible Learning of Problem Solving Heuristics through Adaptive Search. In *Proceedings Eight International Joint Conference on Artificial Intelligence*, pages 422–425, 1983.

619. S. F. Smith. Adaptive learning systems. In R. Forsyth, editor, *Expert Systems: Principles and Case Studies*, pages 169–189. Chapman and Hall, 1984.

620. S. F. Smith and D. P. Greene. Cooperative Diversity using Coverage as a Constraint. In *Collected Abstracts for the First International Workshop on Learning Classifier System (IWLCS-92)* [2]. October 6–8, NASA Johnson Space Center, Houston, Texas.

621. Lee Spector, Erik D. Goodman, Annie Wu, W. B. Langdon, Hans-Michael Voigt, Mitsuo Gen, Sandip Sen, Marco Dorigo, Shahram Pezeshk, Max H. Garzon, and Edmund Burke, editors. *Proceedings of the Genetic and Evolutionary Computation Conference (GECCO-2001)*. Morgan Kaufmann, 2001.

622. Piet Spiessens. PCS: A Classifier System that Builds a Predictive Internal World Model. In *PROC of the 9th European Conference on Artificial Intelligence, Stockholm, Sweden, Aug. 6–10*, pages 622–627, 1990.

623. Bryan G. Spohn and Philip H. Crowley. Complexity of Strategies and the Evolution of Cooperation. In Koza et al. [424], pages 521–528.

624. Wolfgang Stolzmann. Learning Classifier Systems using the Cognitive Mechanism of Anticipatory Behavioral Control, detailed version. In *Proceedings of the First European Workshop on Cognitive Modelling*, pages 82–89. Berlin: TU, 1996. http://www.psychologie.uni-wuerzburg.de/stolzmann/.

625. Wolfgang Stolzmann. *Antizipative Classifier Systeme*. PhD thesis, Fachbereich Mathematik/Informatik, University of Osnabrück, 1997.

626. Wolfgang Stolzmann. Two Applications of Anticipatory Classifier Systems (ACSs). In *Proceedings of the 2nd European Conference on Cognitive Science*, pages 68–73. Manchester, U.K., 1997. http://www.psychologie.uni-wuerzburg.de/stolzmann/.

627. Wolfgang Stolzmann. Anticipatory classifier systems. In *Proceedings of the Third Annual Genetic Programming Conference*, pages 658–664. Morgan Kaufmann, 1998. http://www.psychologie.uni-wuerzburg.de/stolzmann/gp-98.ps.gz.

628. Wolfgang Stolzmann. Untersuchungen zur adquatheit des postulats einer antizipativen verhaltenssteuerung zur erklrung von verhalten mit ACSs. In W. Krause and U. Kotkamp, editors, *Intelligente Informationsverarbeitung*, pages 130–138. Deutscher Universitts Verlag, 1998.

629. Wolfgang Stolzmann. Latent Learning in Khepera Robots with Anticipatory Classifier Systems. In Wu [739], pages 290–297.

630. Wolfgang Stolzmann. An Introduction to Anticipatory Classifier Systems. In Lanzi et al. [446], pages 175–194.

631. Wolfgang Stolzmann and Martin Butz. Latent Learning and Action-Planning in Robots with Anticipatory Classifier Systems. In Lanzi et al. [446], pages 301–317.

632. Wolfgang Stolzmann, Martin Butz, J. Hoffmann, and D. E. Goldberg. First cognitive capabilities in the anticipatory classifier system. In et al. [228], pages 287–296. Also Technical Report 2000008 of the Illinois Genetic Algorithms Laboratory.

633. Christopher Stone and Larry Bull. Towards learning classifier systems for continuous-valued online environments. In E. Cantú-Paz, J. A. Foster, K. Deb, D. Davis, R. Roy, U.-M. O'Reilly, H.-G. Beyer, R. Standish, G. Kendall, S. Wilson, M. Harman, J. Wegener, D. Dasgupta, M. A. Potter, A. C. Schultz, K. Dowsland, N. Jonoska, and J. Miller, editors, *Genetic and Evolutionary Computation – GECCO-2003*, pages 1924–1925, Berlin, 2003. Springer-Verlag.

634. K. Takadama, H. Inoue, M. Okada, K. Shimohara, , and O. Katai. Agent architecture based on interactive self-reflection classifier system. *International Journal of Artificial Life and Robotics (AROB)*, 2001.

635. K. Takadama, H. Inoue, and K. Shimohara. How to autonomously decide boundary between self and others? In *The Third Asia-Pacific Conference on Simulated Evolution And Learning (SEAL'2000)*, 2000.

636. K. Takadama, S. Nakasuka, and K. Shimhara. Robustness in Organizational-learning Oriented Classifier System. *Journal of Soft Computing*, 6(3–4):229–239, 2002.

637. K. Takadama, S. Nakasuka, and T. Terano. Multiagent reinforcement learning with organizational-learning oriented classifier system. In *The IEEE 1998 International Conference On Evolutionary Computation (ICEC'98)*, pages 63–68, 1998.

638. K. Takadama and T. Terano. Good solutions will emerge without a global objective function: Applying organizational-learning oriented classifier system to printed circuit board design. In *The IEEE 1997 International Conference On Systems, Man and Cybernetics (SMC'97)*, pages 3355–3360, 1997.

639. K. Takadama, T. Terano, and K. Shimohara. Designing multiple agents using learning classifier systems. In *The 4th Japan-Australia Joint Workshop on Intelligent and Evolutionary Systems (JA'2000)*, 2000.

640. Keiki Takadama, editor. *Exploring New Potentials in Learning Classifier Systems. A Session of the 4th Japan-Australia Joint Workshop on Intelligent and Evolutionary Systems*. Ashikaga Institute of Technology, 2000.

641. Keiki Takadama. Organizational-learning oriented classifier system. Technical Report TR-H-290, ATR, 2000. In Japanese.

642. Keiki Takadama, S. Nakasuka, and Takao Terano. On the credit assignment algorithm for organizational-learning oriented classifier system. In *The 1997 System/information joint Symposium of SICE (The Society of Instrument and Control Engineers)*, pages 41–46, 1997. In Japanese.

643. Keiki Takadama, S. Nakasuka, and Takao Terano. Organizational-learning oriented classifier system. In *The 11th Annual Conference of JSAI (Japanese Society for Artificial Intelligence)*, pages 201–204, 1997. In Japanese.

644. Keiki Takadama, S. Nakasuka, and Takao Terano. Organizational-learning oriented classifier system for intelligent multiagent systems. In *The 6th Multi Agent and Cooperative Computation (MACC '97) of JSSST (Japan Society for Software Science and Technology)*, 1997. In Japanese.

645. Keiki Takadama, S. Nakasuka, and Takao Terano. Analyzing the roles of problem solving and learning in organizational-learning oriented classifier system. In H. Y. Lee and H. Motoda, editors, *Lecture Notes in Artificial Intelligence*, volume 1531, pages 71–82. Springer–Verlag, 1998.

646. Keiki Takadama, Shinichi Nakasuka, and Kasunori Shimohara. Designing multiple agents using learning classifier systems - suggestions from three levels analyses. In Takadama [640].

647. Keiki Takadama, Takao Terano, and Katsunori Shimohara. Agent-based model toward organizational computing: From organizational learning to genetics-based machine learning. In *The IEEE 1999 International Conference On Systems, Man and Cybernetics (SMC'99)*, volume 2, pages 604–609, 1999.

648. Keiki Takadama, Takao Terano, and Katsunori Shimohara. Can multiagents learn in organization? – analyzing organizational learning-oriented classifier system. In *IJCAI'99 Workshop on Agents Learning about, from and other Agents*, 1999.

649. Keiki Takadama, Takao Terano, and Katsunori Shimohara. Learning Classifier Systems meet Multiagent Environments. In *Proceedings of the International Workshop on Learning Classifier Systems (IWLCS-2000), in the Joint Workshops of SAB 2000 and PPSN 2000* [4]. Extended abstract.

650. Keiki Takadama, Takao Terano, Katsunori Shimohara, H. Hori, and S. Nakasuka. Making Organizational Learning Operational: Implications from Learning Classifier System. *Computational and Mathematical Organization Theory (CMOT)*, 5(3):229–252, 1999.

651. Keiki Takadama, Takao Terano, Katsunori Shimohara, H. Hori, and S. Nakasuka. Toward emergent problem solving by distributed classifier systems based on organizational learning. *Transactions of SICE (the Society of Instrument and Control Engineers)*, 35(11):1486–1495, 1999. In Japanese.

652. Takao Terano and Z. Muro. On-the-fly knowledge base refinement by a classifier system. *AI Communications*, 4(2), 1994.

653. Takao Terano and Keiki Takadama. An organizational learning model of multiagents with a learning classifier system. In *The 1997 Fall Conference of JASMIN (Japan Society for Management Information)*, pages 128–131, 1997. In Japanese.

654. Kurian K. Tharakunnel, Martin V. Butz, and David E. Goldberg. Towards building block propagation in XCS: A negative result and its implications. In E. Cantú-Paz, J. A. Foster, K. Deb, D. Davis, R. Roy, U.-M. O'Reilly, H.-G. Beyer, R. Standish, G. Kendall, S. Wilson, M. Harman, J. Wegener, D. Dasgupta, M. A. Potter, A. C. Schultz, K. Dowsland, N. Jonoska, and J. Miller, editors, *Genetic and Evolutionary Computation – GECCO-2003*, volume 2724 of *LNCS*, pages 1906–1917. Springer-Verlag, 2003.

655. S. Tokinaga and A. B. Whinston. Applying Adaptive Credit Assignment Algorithm for the Learning Classifier System Based upon the Genetic Algorithm. *IEICE Transactions on Fundamentals of Electronics Communications and Computer Sciences*, VE75A(5):568–577, May 1992.

656. Andy Tomlinson. *Corporate Classifier Systems*. PhD thesis, University of the West of England, 1999.

657. Andy Tomlinson and Larry Bull. A Corporate Classifier System. In A. E. Eiben, T. Bäck, M. Shoenauer, and H.-P. Schwefel, editors, *Proceedings of the Fifth International Conference on Parallel Problem Solving From Nature – PPSN V*, number 1498 in LNCS, pages 550–559. Springer Verlag, 1998.

658. Andy Tomlinson and Larry Bull. A Corporate XCS. In Wu [739], pages 298–305.

659. Andy Tomlinson and Larry Bull. On Corporate Classifier Systems: Increasing the Benefits of Rule Linkage. In Banzhaf et al. [22], pages 649–656.

660. Andy Tomlinson and Larry Bull. A zeroth level corporate classifier system. In Wu [739], pages 306–313.

661. Andy Tomlinson and Larry Bull. A Corporate XCS. In Lanzi et al. [446], pages 194–208.

662. Andy Tomlinson and Larry Bull. Cxcs: Improvements and corporate generalization. In Lee Spector, Erik D. Goodman, Annie Wu, W.B. Langdon, Hans-Michael Voigt, Mitsuo Gen, Sandip Sen, Marco Dorigo, Shahram Pezeshk, Max H. Garzon, and Edmund Burke, editors, *Proceedings of the Genetic and Evolutionary Computation Conference (GECCO-2001)*, pages 966–973, San Francisco, California, USA, 7-11 July 2001. Morgan Kaufmann.

663. Andy Tomlinson and Larry Bull. An accuracy-based corporate classifier system. *Journal of Soft Computing*, 6(3–4):200–215, 2002.

664. Kwok Ching Tsui and Mark Plumbley. A New Hillclimber for Classifier Systems. In *GALESI97*, 1997.

665. Patrick Tufts. Evolution of a Clustering Scheme for Classifier Systems: Beyond the Bucket Brigade. PhD Thesis proposal. http://www.cs.brandeis.edu/~zippy/papers.htm, 1994.

666. Patrick Tufts. Dynamic Classifiers: Genetic Programming and Classifier Systems. In E. V. Siegel and J. R. Koza, editors, *Working Notes for the AAAI Symposium on Genetic Programming*, pages 114–119, MIT, Cambridge, MA, USA, 1995. AAAI.

667. Kirk Twardowski. Implementation of a Genetic Algorithm based Associative Classifier System (ACS). In *Proceedings International Conference on Tools for Artificial Intelligence*, 1990.

668. Kirk Twardowski. Credit Assignment for Pole Balancing with Learning Classifier Systems. In Forrest [260], pages 238–245.

669. Kirk Twardowski. An Associative Architecture for Genetic Algorithm-Based Machine Learning. *Computer*, 27(11):27–38, November 1994.

670. J. Urzelai, Dario Floreano, Marco Dorigo, and Marco Colombetti. Incremental Robot Shaping. *Connection Science*, 10(3–4):341–360, 1998.

671. J. Urzelai, Dario Floreano, Marco Dorigo, and Marco Colombetti. Incremental Robot Shaping. In Koza et al. [423], pages 832–840.

672. Manuel Valenzuela-Rendón. Boolean Analysis of Classifier Sets. In Schaffer [563], pages 351–358.

673. Manuel Valenzuela-Rendón. *Two analysis tools to describe the operation of classifier systems*. PhD thesis, University of Alabama, 1989. Also TCGA technical report 89005.

674. Manuel Valenzuela-Rendón. The Fuzzy Classifier System: a Classifier System for Continuously Varying Variables. In Booker and Belew [72], pages 346–353.

675. Manuel Valenzuela-Rendón. The Fuzzy Classifier System: Motivations and First Results. In Hans-Paul Schwefel and Reinhard Männer, editors, *Parallel Problem Solving from Nature (PSSN-1)*, volume 496 of *Lecture Notes in Computer Science*, pages 338–342, 1991.

676. Manuel Valenzuela-Rendón. Reinforcement learning in the fuzzy classifier system. In *Collected Abstracts for the First International Workshop on Learning Classifier System (IWLCS-92)* [2]. October 6–8, NASA Johnson Space Center, Houston, Texas.

677. Manuel Valenzuela-Rendón and Eduardo Uresti-Charre. A Non-Genetic Algorithm for Multiobjective Optimization. In Bäck [14], pages 658–665.

678. Terry van Belle. A New Approach to Genetic-Based Automatic Feature Discovery. Master's thesis, University of Alberta, 1995. http://www.cs.ualberta.ca/~jonathan/.

679. Patricia Amancio Vargas, Christiano Lyra Filho, and Fernando J. Von Zuben. On-line approach for loss reduction in electric power distribution networks using learning classifier systems. In Lanzi et al. [448], pages 181–196.

680. Gilles Venturini. *Apprentissage Adaptatif et Apprentissage Supervisé par Algorithme Génétique*. PhD thesis, Université de Paris-Sud., 1994.

681. Nickolas Vriend. Self-Organization of Markets: An Example of a Computational Approach. *Computational Economics*, 8(3):205–231, 1995.

682. David Walter and Chilukuri K. Mohan. ClaDia: A Fuzzy Classifier System for Disease Diagnosis. In *Proceedings of the 2000 Congress on Evolutionary Computation (CEC00)* [3], pages 1429–1435.

683. L. A. Wang. Classifier System Learning of the Boolean Multiplexer Function. Master's thesis, Computer Science Department, University of Tennessee, Knoxville, TN, 1990.

684. Gerhard Weiss. Action-oriented learning in classifier systems. Technical Report FKI-158-91, Technical Univ. München (TUM), 1991.

685. Gerhard Weiss. The Action-Oriented Bucket Brigade. Technical Report FKI-156-91, Technical Univ. München (TUM), 1991.

686. Gerhard Weiss. Hierarchical chunking in classifier systems. In *Proceedings of the 12th National Conference on Artificial Intelligence*, pages 1335–1340. AAAI Press/MIT Press, 1994.

687. Gerhard Weiss. Learning by chunking in reactive classifier systems. Technical report, Technical Univ. München (TUM), 1994.

688. Gerhard Weiss. The locality/globality dilemma in classifier systems and an approach to its solution. Technical Report FKI-187-94, Technical Univ. München (TUM), 1994.

689. Gerhard Weiss. An action-oriented perspective of learning in classifier systems. *Journal of Experimental and Theoretical Artificial Intelligence*, 8:43–62, 1996.

690. Thomas H. Westerdale. The bucket brigade is not genetic. In Grefenstette [305], pages 45–59.

691. Thomas H. Westerdale. A Reward Scheme for Production Systems with Overlapping Conflict Sets. *IEEE Transactions on Systems, Man and Cybernetics*, SMC-16(3):369–383, 1986.

692. Thomas H. Westerdale. Altruism in the bucket brigade. In Grefenstette [307], pages 22–26.

693. Thomas H. Westerdale. A Defence of the Bucket Brigade. In Schaffer [563], pages 282–290.

694. Thomas H. Westerdale. Quasimorphisms or Queasymorphisms? Modelling Finite Automaton Environments. In Rawlins [519], pages 128–147.

695. Thomas H. Westerdale. Redundant Classifiers and Prokaryote Genomes. In Booker and Belew [72], pages 354–360.

696. Thomas H. Westerdale. Classifier Systems - No Wonder They Don't Work. In Koza et al. [424], pages 529–537.

697. Thomas H. Westerdale. An Approach to Credit Assignment in Classifier Systems. *Complexity*, 4(2), 1999.

698. Thomas H. Westerdale. Wilson's Error Measurement and the Markov Property – Identifying Detrimental Classifiers. In Wu [739], pages 314–321.

699. Darrell Whitely, David Goldberg, Erick Cantú-Paz, Lee Spector, Ian Parmee, and Hans-Georg Beyer, editors. *Proceedings of the Genetic and Evolutionary Computation Conference (GECCO-2000)*. Morgan Kaufmann, 2000.

700. Jason R. Wilcox. Organizational Learning within a Learning Classifier System. Master's thesis, University of Illinois, 1995. Also Technical Report No. 95003 IlliGAL.

701. Stewart W. Wilson. Aubert processing and intelligent vision. Technical report, Polaroid Corporation, 1981.

702. Stewart W. Wilson. On the retino-cortical mapping. *International Journal of Man-Machine Studies*, 18:361–389, 1983.

703. Stewart W. Wilson. Adaptive "cortical" pattern recognition. In Grefenstette [305], pages 188–196.

704. Stewart W. Wilson. Knowledge Growth in an Artificial Animal. In Grefenstette [305], pages 16–23. Also appeared in Proceedings of the 4th Yale.

705. Stewart W. Wilson. Knowledge Growth in an Artificial Animal. In *Proceedings of the 4th Yale Workshop on Applications of Adaptive Systems Theory*, pages 98–104, 1985.

706. Stewart W. Wilson. Classifier System Learning of a Boolean Function. Technical Report RIS 27r, The Rowland Institute for Science, 1986.

707. Stewart W. Wilson. Knowledge Growth in an Artificial Animal. In K. S. Narenda, editor, *Adaptive and learning systems: Theory and applications*, pages 255–264. Plenum Press: New York, 1986.

708. Stewart W. Wilson. Classifier Systems and the Animat Problem. *Machine Learning*, 2:199–228, 1987. Also Research Memo RIS-36r, the Rowland Institute for Science, Cambridge, MA, 1986.

709. Stewart W. Wilson. Hierarchical Credit Allocation in a Classifier System. In *Proceedings Tenth International Joint Conference on AI (IJCAI-87)*, pages 217–220. Morgan Kaufmann Publishers, 1987. Also Research Memo RIS-37r, the Rowland Institute for Science, Cambridge, MA, 1986.

710. Stewart W. Wilson. Quasi-Darwinian Learning in a Classifier System. In *Proceedings of the Fourth International Workshop on Machine Learning*, pages 59–65. Morgan Kaufmann, 1987.

711. Stewart W. Wilson. The genetic algorithm and biological development. In Grefenstette [307], pages 247–251.

712. Stewart W. Wilson. Bid Competition and Specificity Reconsidered. *Complex Systems*, 2(6):705–723, 1988.

713. Stewart W. Wilson. Hierarchical Credit Assignment in a Classifier System. In M. Elzas, T. Oren, and B. P. Zeigler, editors, *Modelling and Simulation Methodology: Knowledge Systems Paradigms*. North Holland, 1988.

714. Stewart W. Wilson. Hierarchical Credit Allocation in a Classifier System. In Davis [171], pages 104–115.

715. Stewart W. Wilson. Hierarchical credit allocation in a classifier system. In M. S. Elzas, T. I. Oren, and B. P. Zeigler, editors, *Modelling and simulation methodology*, pages 351–357. North-Holland: New York, 1989.

716. Stewart W. Wilson. The Genetic Algorithm and Simulated Evolution. In Chris Langton, editor, *Artificial Life: Proceedings of an Interdisciplinary Workshop on the Synthesis and Simulation of Living Systems*, volume VI of *Santa Fe Institute Studies in the Sciences of Complexity*. Addison-Wesley: Reading, MA, 1989.

717. Stewart W. Wilson. Perceptron redux: Emergence of structure. In *Special issue of Physica D (Vol. 42)* [1], pages 249–256. Republished in Emergent Computation, S. Forrest (ed.), MIT Press/Bradford Books.

718. Stewart W. Wilson. The Animat Path to AI. In Meyer and Wilson [476], pages 15–21. http://prediction-dynamics.com/.

719. Stewart W. Wilson. Classifier System mapping of real vectors. In *Collected Abstracts for the First International Workshop on Learning Classifier System (IWLCS-92)* [2]. October 6–8, NASA Johnson Space Center, Houston, Texas.

720. Stewart W. Wilson. Toward a GA solution of the discovery problem. In *Collected Abstracts for the First International Workshop on Learning Classifier System (IWLCS-92)* [2]. October 6–8, NASA Johnson Space Center, Houston, Texas.

721. Stewart W. Wilson. ZCS: A zeroth level classifier system. *Evolutionary Computation*, 2(1):1–18, 1994. http://prediction-dynamics.com/.

722. Stewart W. Wilson. Classifier Fitness Based on Accuracy. *Evolutionary Computation*, 3(2):149–175, 1995. http://prediction-dynamics.com/.

723. Stewart W. Wilson. Explore/exploit strategies in autonomy. In Maes et al. [468], pages 325–332.

724. Stewart W. Wilson. Generalization in XCS. Unpublished contribution to the ICML '96 Workshop on Evolutionary Computing and Machine Learning. http://prediction-dynamics.com/, 1996.

725. Stewart W. Wilson. Generalization in evolutionary learning. Presented at the Fourth European Conference on Artificial Life (ECAL97), Brighton, UK, July 27-31. http://prediction-dynamics.com/, 1997.

726. Stewart W. Wilson. Generalization in the XCS classifier system. In Koza et al. [423], pages 665–674. http://prediction-dynamics.com/.

727. Stewart W. Wilson. Get real! XCS with continuous-valued inputs. In L. Booker, Stephanie Forrest, M. Mitchell, and Rick L. Riolo, editors, *Festschrift in Honor of John H. Holland*, pages 111–121. Center for the Study of Complex Systems, 1999. http://prediction-dynamics.com/.

728. Stewart W. Wilson. State of XCS classifier system research. In Wu [739], pages 322–334. Also Technical Report 99.1.1, Prediction Dynamics, Concord MA. http://prediction-dynamics.com/.

729. Stewart W. Wilson. Get Real! XCS with Continuous-Valued Inputs. In Lanzi et al. [446], pages 209–219.

730. Stewart W. Wilson. Mining Oblique Data with XCS. In *Proceedings of the International Workshop on Learning Classifier Systems (IWLCS-2000), in the Joint Workshops of SAB 2000 and PPSN 2000* [4]. Extended abstract.

731. Stewart W. Wilson. Mining Oblique Data with XCS. Technical Report 2000028, University of Illinois at Urbana-Champaign, 2000.

732. Stewart W. Wilson. State of XCS Classifier System Research. In Lanzi et al. [446], pages 63–82.

733. Stewart W. Wilson. Function approximation with a classifier system. In Lee Spector, Erik D. Goodman, Annie Wu, W.B. Langdon, Hans-Michael Voigt, Mitsuo Gen, Sandip Sen, Marco Dorigo, Shahram Pezeshk, Max H. Garzon, and Edmund Burke, editors, *Proceedings of the Genetic and Evolutionary Computation Conference (GECCO-2001)*, pages 974–981, San Francisco, California, USA, 7-11 July 2001. Morgan Kaufmann.

734. Stewart W. Wilson. Advances in Learning Classifier Systems. In Lanzi et al. [448].
735. Stewart W. Wilson and David E. Goldberg. A Critical Review of Classifier Systems. In Schaffer [563], pages 244–255. http://prediction-dynamics.com/.
736. Mark S. Withall, Chris J. Hinde, and Roger G. Stone. Evolving readable Perl. In W. B. Langdon, E. Cantú-Paz, K. Mathias, R. Roy, D. Davis, R. Poli, K. Balakrishnan, V. Honavar, G. Rudolph, J. Wegener, L. Bull, M. A. Potter, A. C. Schultz, J. F. Miller, E. Burke, and N. Jonoska, editors, *GECCO 2002: Proceedings of the Genetic and Evolutionary Computation Conference*. Morgan Kaufmann Publishers, 2002.
737. Ian Wright. Reinforcement Learning and Animat Emotions. In Maes et al. [468], pages 272–281.
738. Ian Wright. Reinforcement learning and animat emotions. Technical Report CSRP-96-4, School of Computer Science. University of Birmingham, 1996. ftp://ftp.cs.bham.ac.uk/pub/tech-reports/1996/CSRP-96-04.ps.gz.
739. Annie S. Wu, editor. *Proceedings of the 1999 Genetic and Evolutionary Computation Conference Workshop Program*, 1999.
740. Derek F. Yates and Andrew Fairley. An Investigation into Possible Causes of, and Solutions to, Rule Strength Distortion Due to the Bucket Brigade Algorithm. In Forrest [260], pages 246–253.
741. Derek F. Yates and Andrew Fairley. Evolutionary Stability in Simple Classifier Systems. In Fogarty [246], pages 28–37.
742. Takahiro Yoshimi and Toshiharu Taura. Hierarchical Classifier System Based on the Concept of Viewpoint. In Koza et al. [423], pages 675–678.
743. Takahiro Yoshimi and Toshiharu Taura. A Computational Model of a Viewpoint-Forming Process in a Hierarchical Classifier System. In Banzhaf et al. [22], pages 758–766.
744. Zhaohua Zhang, Stan Franklin, and Dipankar Dasgupta. Metacognition in Software Agents Using Classifier Systems. In *AAAI-98. Proceedings of the Fifteenth National Conference on Artificial Intelligence*, pages 83–88, Madison (WI), 1998. AAAI-Press and MIT Press.
745. Hayong Harry Zhou. Classifier systems with long term memory. In Grefenstette [305], pages 178–182.
746. Hayong Harry Zhou. *CSM: A genetic classifier system with memory for learning by analogy*. PhD thesis, Department of Computer Science, Vanderbilt University, Nashville, TN, 1987.
747. Hayong Harry Zhou. CSM: A Computational Model of Cumulative Learning. *Machine Learning*, 5(4):383–406, 1990.
748. Hayong Harry Zhou and John J. Grefenstette. Learning by Analogy in Genetic Classifier Systems. In Schaffer [563], pages 291–297.
749. Raed Abu Zitar and Mohammad H. Hassoun. Regulator Control via Genetic Search Assisted Reinforcement. In Forrest [260], pages 254–263.

Author Index

Lecture Notes in Artificial Intelligence (LNAI)

Lecture Notes in Computer Science